THE BIGGEST
ROCK & POP
QUIZ BOOK

ISBN 1 84222 274 0

Project Editor: Vanessa Daubney
Design: Vaseem Bhatti
Production: Sarah Corteel

Questions set by The Puzzle House

Printed and bound in Great Britain

THE BIGGEST
ROCK & POP
QUIZ BOOK

CARLTON
BOOKS

Contents

INTRODUCTION

Here you have the perfect book for the pop music buff. It's a great gift for anyone who soaks up chart details or collects CDs, mini discs, even those funny old vinyl discs (remember them?), and who needs something to while away the hours when the music isn't available.

You may also be in need of questions for a competition or a quiz night and what better subject than music, something that almost everyone can enjoy. At the end of the book you'll find information on how to run a quiz evening and some sample templates which you can photocopy for entrants' use. So, all you really need to provide are some pens or pencils. However, a little liquid refreshment always goes a long way to adding to the atmosphere.

There are around 12,000 questions here, divided into sets of 20 questions and each set will either be based on a specialist subject, or it will be pot luck, which means you could be asked about absolutely anything.

There are three sections in the book – Easy, Medium and Hard – so that it caters for all levels of knowledge. Even if you're done no more than watch MTV before sneaking off to croon your favourite tunes to your hairbrush in the privacy of your bedroom (go on, admit it!), you will be able to answer many of the questions here. Those who take a more serious interest and try to keep abreast of the changes in pop will find the Medium section more to their taste. The Hard rounds are intended for the sort who not only sleeps with a copy of *NME* or *Billboard* on the bedside table but is able to quote from it at length. To give you more of an idea, you can read the descriptions of each section below:

Easy

The only qualification for entry at this level is to have a detectable pulse. It helps if you like pop music too. Regular listening to your local commercial radio channel will provide you with so much knowledge that you might almost be too well qualified for this section, so don't overdo it. You should know the difference between Cliff Richard and Keith Richards, but you needn't know whether Chuck Berry is related to Dave Berry.

Medium

OK, now it starts to get tougher. Some serious boning up is called for before you try this section. Do you know Bob Dylan's real name? What's the lead singer in Catatonia called, and is she Irish or Welsh? What's the first word of Cher's hit 'Believe'? If these sound to you like really tough questions you may be getting out of your depth here.

Hard

All right, you asked for it. Fancy your chances, eh? Listen pal, nobody loves a smart alec. Do you know Alice Cooper's real name? Who was Joe Cocker named after? What was Glen Campbell's autobiography called? Surviving so far? What about this: Which hit along with 'Share Your Love' did Lionel Richie produce for Kenny Rogers before embarking on a solo career? Hah! The drinks are on you.

Good luck!

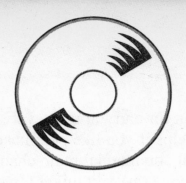

The Easy Questions

If you don't know the difference between Van Halen and Van Morrison, then you will no doubt struggle through the next few questions. For the rest of us though these are the EASY questions, so called because if the quizzee falters on these they are either drunk as a skunk or they're from another planet!

These questions are perfect when used in the first round of an open entry quiz as they lull everyone into a false sense of security – although you must beware that contestants don't shout answers out which creates a problematic precedent for later, harder questions. Another way of placing these questions is to dot them about throughout your quiz, thus making sure that on every team everyone should know the answer to at least one question despite their age.

If you are running a league quiz, then some of your team members may heap derision on such obvious questions, but don't worry, even the cleverest quiz team member can come a cropper.

1 How is Reg Dwight better known?
2 Which Bryan's first hit was "Run To You"?
3 What is the home country of Celine Dion?
4 What was Blondie's Heart made of in 1979?
5 In 1985 Talking Heads were taking the Road to where?
6 Who was lead singer with the Police?
7 Who joined Bennie on a 1976 hit by Elton John?
8 Which surname is shared by Carly and Paul?
9 How many members of the Carpenters were there?
10 What did Bill Haley sing after "See you later, alligator"?
11 Which musical instrument does Eric Clapton play?
12 Which David appeared on TV with the Partridge Family?
13 Which legendary dancer called Fred described Michael Jackson as "a wonderful mover"?
14 In which Queen No. 1 will you hear Beelzebub and Galileo?
15 Who led the Dreamers?
16 Who hit the top with "What Becomes of the Broken Hearted?" in 1996?
17 What was the Spice Girls' No. 1 album in late 1996?
18 What type of dance goes with Spandau in the charts?
19 Which Damon takes lead vocals with Blur?
20 Which London duo sang "You've got more rabbit than Sainsbury's"?

1   What is the first word sung in "Viva La Radio"?
2   Who did Celine Dion record "Immortality" with?
3   Who had an 80s No. 1 with "You Got It (The Right Stuff)"?
4   "Torn" was the first top ten hit for which vocalist?
5   Which word completes the song title "Because We ____ To"?
6   Who had an 80s No. 1 with "Land Of Make Believe"?
7   Lulu sent her son to which school where Princes William and Harry went?
8   Which legendary folk singer Joan shares a birthday with actress Susannah York?
9   Which group had a 70s No. 1 with "Another Brick In The Wall"?
10 Who released an album called Miss Bette Davis in 1976?
11 "Innuendo" was a 90s No. 1 for which band?
12 Which childlike middle name did veteran DJ David Jensen have?
13 "Mysterious Girl" was a top three hit for which singer?
14 Which Spice Girl had a hit with "I Want You Back"?
15 Who had an 80s No. 1 with "Oh Julie"?
16 Which band do Bjorn Again impersonate?
17 Which Rolling Stone said "Je Suis Un Rock Star" in 1981?
18 According to the 70s No. 1 what did Video kill?
19 Who had an 80s No. 1 with "The Lion Sleeps Tonight"?
20 Which Labour Party leader starred in Tracey Ullman's video "My Guy"?

1 What did Bill Haley and the Comets do after Shake and Rattle?
2 What rhymes with Cupid on the title of the Connie Francis No. 1?
3 Where did Fats Domino find his thrill in 1956?
4 Which Eddie had the Summertime Blues?
5 According to the Everly Brothers in 1959 All I Have to Do Is what?
6 What did Jerry Lee Lewis sing about Great Balls of in 1958?
7 What Gets in Your Eyes according to the Platters?
8 Which musical instrument did Russ Conway play?
9 What colour pink went with Apple Blossom White according to Perez Prado and Eddie Calvert in 1955?
10 Which Doris said "Whatever will be, will be" in 1956?
11 What were Guy Mitchell and Tommy Steele each singing for the first month of 1957 at the top of the charts?
12 Which Perry hit the top with "Don't Let the Stars Get in Your Eyes"?
13 How many Everly Brothers were there?
14 Which Adam hit the No. 1 spot with "What Do You Want"?
15 Which Craig was Only Sixteen in 1959?
16 Which Dickie's special day was possibly February 14?
17 Which British Frankie was behind the Green Door and in The Garden of Eden in the 50s?
18 What was the first name of the vocalist Mr Twitty?
19 In Eddie Cochran's "Three Steps to Heaven" at which step does she "fall in love with you"?
20 How was the Richard described who sang "Long Tall Sally" and "Lucille"?

1   What word describes the group, Kid Joe?
2   Which Bad professional was a 1996 hit for Terrorvision?
3   According to U2 what goes with "Hold Me Thrill Me Kiss Me"?
4   Who sang about Midnight in Chelsea in 1997?
5   In which country was the Rock and Roll Hall of Fame established?
6   Which liberated group had a hit with "All Right Now" first in the 70s but again in the 90s?
7   Which English city did the Animals come from?
8   Which Michael was lead singer with INXS?
9   What did Sheryl Crow think Would Do You Good in 1997?
10 Which part of the body was mentioned in the title of Reef's first top ten hit?
11 Who had a 70s hit with "Rebel Rebel"?
12 On which Side did Lou Reed Walk in 1973?
13 What did Dire Straits have Money For in 1985?
14 What did Garbage think they were in 1998?
15 "Running All Over The World" was based on a rock classic from which band?
16 How many members of Queen were there originally?
17 Chrissie Hynde led which band?
18 Which member of Simple Minds proposed buying Celtic Football Club with Kenny Dalglish?
19 What colour Heather was the title of a 1996 hit from Rod Stewart?
20 What instrument did Jools Holland of Squeeze play?

Quiz 5 Pot Luck 3

Answers – see page 11

1   Which Phil had an album called *No Jacket Required*?
2   Which musical instrument does Elton John play?
3   Who was Siouxsie's group?
4   What is the home country of A-Ha?
5   Which Buddy Holly group shares its name with insects?
6   Which Bob sang with the Wailers ?
7   Which part did David Essex play in the musical *Godspell*?
8   What goes with Shake and Rattle in the 50s song?
9   Who led the Pacemakers?
10   Which song title gave No. 1 hits to Jennifer Rush and Frankie Goes To Hollywood?
11   Which late zany DJ was born Maurice Cole?
12   For which sport was "Nessun Dorma" used as a theme in 1990?
13   What goes after Hillbilly Rock in the title of the Woolpackers' hit?
14   Which surname is shared by the singer Michael and bandleader Kenny?
15   What was A Boy Named according to Johnny Cash in 1969?
16   Which Heartbreak place did Elvis stay at in 1956?
17   Who was the original lead singer with the Supremes?
18   In 1978 Gerry Rafferty was in which London street?
19   How is Priscilla White better known?
20   Whose first hit was "Waterloo"?

1 "One For Sorrow" was a top ten hit for which group?
2 Who had a 90s No. 1 with "Sadness Part 1"?
3 Which David made the album Aladdin Sane?
4 In which decade was Tina Turner born?
5 What is the first word of "The Power Of Goodbye"?
6 In what language did Serge Gainsbourg and Jane Birkin sing their banned record from 1969?
7 Who charted in 1997 with "As Long As You Love Me"?
8 Who had a 70s No. 1 with "Walking On The Moon"?
9 "Dreams" was the first top ten hit for which group?
10 Which Mode were regular chart members in the 80s?
11 Who had an 80s No. 1 with "All Around The World"?
12 What according to Ben E. King should you do By Me?
13 Which surname is shared by Grace, Howard and Tom?
14 Who had a hit with "Not A Dry Eye In The House" in 1996?
15 Who had a 70s album called Liza With a Z?
16 Which word follows Say What You in the song by Texas?
17 Which group was Agnetha Faltskog a member of?
18 Who had an 80s No. 1 with "House Of Fun"?
19 What is the home country of Prince?
20 How many members were there in Dave Dee's 60s and 70s group?

1 Who was the drummer with the Dave Clark Five?
2 Which small Mod group were all under five foot six tall?
3 Who completed the line-up of Dave Dee, Dozy, Beaky and Mick?
4 In 1965 the Kinks sang about a Dedicated Follower of what?
5 What did Marvin Gaye Hear It Through in 1969?
6 What did the Beatles Want to Hold on their first US No. 1?
7 Which Corner had Andy Fairweather-Low as lead singer?
8 Which Little girl sang "The Locomotion" in 1962?
9 Which head of the Diddymen shed Tears in 1965?
10 What Is Over according to the Seekers in 1965?
11 Which Engelbert Humperdinck song's second line is "Let me go"?
12 Which 60s dance was popularized by Chubby Checker?
13 Which country were The Bachelors from?
14 What sort of Vibrations did the Beach Boys have in 1966?
15 Which Australian had the last No. 1 of the 60s with "Two Little Boys"?
16 What follows "Ob-La-Di" in the Marmalade No. 1?
17 Which lover of Romeo was a hit for the Four Pennies?
18 In 1960 what was the profession of Lonnie Donegan's dad?
19 Which Pretty pink bird was a No. 1 for Manfred Mann?
20 How old was the Sweet person Neil Sedaka wished Happy Birthday to in 1961?

1   Which fellow-songstress did Whitney record "When You Believe" with?
2   What relation is she to Dionne Warwick?
3   What was Whitney Houston "Saving For You" in her first No. 1?
4   Which Bobby sang with Whitney on "Something In Common"?
5   Which Kevin starred opposite her in *The Bodyguard*?
6   What was the title of her first album?
7   Who did she Want to Dance with on her 1987 hit?
8   In which country is the home of the Whitney Houston fan club?
9   Which colour is Whitney's married name?
10 What follows "I Want To Dance" on the title of her second No. 1?
11 Which 1988 sporting event did "One Moment In Time" tie in with?
12 Which blonde country singer wrote "I Will Always Love You"?
13 In 1992 who was the only woman to have had more No. 1s than Whitney Houston?
14 Which Des interviewed Whitney on UK TV to promote *The Bodyguard*?
15 Which Queen of Soul is Whitney's godmother?
16 What was the single word title of her second album?
17 Whose 70th birthday concert did Whitney sing at in Wembley in 1988?
18 In 1991 she raised funds for which war with a recording of "The Star-Spangled Banner"?
19 Which famous Tamla Motown lady was earmarked for the Whitney Houston role in *The Bodyguard* many years earlier?
20 What is the name of Whitney's daughter, named after the baby's father?

Quiz 9 Pot Luck 5

LEVEL 1

Answers – see page 23

1 What is the home country of Bryan Adams?
2 Who did Dexy's Midnight Runners tell to Come On in 1982?
3 Which surname is shared by the musical star Darren and the 50s singer Doris?
4 Which Supply's first hit was "All Out of Love"?
5 Which Sheena was a Modern Girl in 1980?
6 What was the first name of the rock star Zappa?
7 In which US state are music towns Memphis and Nashville?
8 Were the Isley Brothers really brothers?
9 Who had a 1994 No. 1 with "Doop"?
10 Who are Vic Reeves's backing band?
11 What do the letters HMV stand for?
12 Which trio of record producers are credited on the 1989 "Ferry 'Cross the Mersey"?
13 What was the Bangles' Flame like in 1989?
14 How is Mark Feld better known?
15 Which "Doctor Who" machine were the Timelords Doctorin' in 1988?
16 Right Said Fred were Deeply what in 1992?
17 How many members of Abba were there?
18 Who is lead singer with Simply Red?
19 In 1967 the Beatles were in which Lane?
20 Which Hearts did Elton John sing about in 1985?

Answers

Pot Luck 7 (Quiz 13)
1 Cilla Black. 2 Debbie Harry. 3 Mae. 4 Roxy Music. 5 Shapiro.
6 Paul Anka. 7 Cockney Rebel. 8 Neil Diamond. 9 Australia.
10 Guitar. 11 Joseph. 12 k.d. 13 Greece. 14 Turner. 15 Yates.
16 Philadelphia. 17 Softly. 18 Starr. 19 Miss Molly. 20 Abbey Road.

1 Who had a 70s No. 1 with "When You're In Love With A Beautiful Woman"?
2 Which Ian famous for his Rhythm Stick shares a birthday with actress Susan Hampshire?
3 Which soloist had a 90s No. 1 with "Any Dream Will Do"?
4 Which media figure is responsible for Ginger Productions?
5 Under which name did Isaiah Turner become famous?
6 Which lads made No. 2 in 1998 with "Only A Woman"?
7 Which instrument did the late Cozy Powell play?
8 What is the first word in the song, "Bring It All Back"?
9 Which son of John Lennon has had 80s and 90s chart success?
10 Which punk performer recorded the 1979 album *Sid Sings*?
11 What follows Everything I Do in a 90s No. 1 title?
12 Jimi Hendrix charted with Purple what?
13 What type of crossing are The Beatles crossing on the front of *Abbey Road*?
14 What word completes the song title, "Spice Up Your..."?
15 Who had an 80s No. 1 with "Sealed With A Kiss"?
16 In a country classic Roger Miller was King of the what?
17 How did Charles Aznavour refer to the lady who gave him his only UK No. 1?
18 Jim Morrison was lead singer with which group?
19 Who had a No. 1 album with *Diva*?
20 Who had a 70s No. 1 with "Down Down"?

1 Which People were with the "YMCA" in 1979?
2 Who was the lead singer with Wings?
3 Which seasonal Nights did John Travolta and Olivia Newton-John sing about?
4 Which country did the Eurovision winner Dana come from?
5 Who had a single called "Killer Queen"?
6 Who were Stayin' Alive?
7 Which birds of prey stayed at the Hotel California?
8 Which glam group had an album called *Sweet Fanny Adams*?
9 Who had hits with "Close to You" and "We've Only Just Begun"?
10 What colour ribbons did Dawn tie round the Old Oak Tree?
11 Which Ms Knight was backed by the Pips?
12 Which Roberta was "Killing Me Softly With His Song"?
13 Which Gary was "Leader of the Gang"?
14 Whose single and album *Bridge Over Troubled Water* went to No. 1?
15 Which former Supreme was Still Waiting in 1971?
16 What did the New Seekers say They'd Like to Teach the World to do in 1972?
17 What did Tyrannosaurus Rex change their name to?
18 Which Tubular sounds were a hit for Mike Oldfield?
19 What type of Loaf had a Bat Out of Hell?
20 Which Zeppelin had a string of No. 1 albums during the 70s?

LEVEL 1

1   In which decade did Elton John have his first solo hit single?
2   What was included with Tiaras in the title of the documentary about Elton John?
3   What did Elton John have fitted in July 1999 after a health scare?
4   Which part of London did Reg Dwight come from?
5   Elton John was Chairman of which 80s FA Cup finalists?
6   Who did he originally duet with on "Don't Go Breaking My Heart"?
7   Who is Elton John's long-term writing partner?
8   Which eating disorder did Elton John have in common with Diana, Princess of Wales?
9   What was the name of the record label Elton John started?
10 In what month of 1997 did "Candle In The Wind 1997" reach No. 1?
11 What Say So Much according to the 1984 hit?
12 Which opera star sang on "Live Like Horses"?
13 What's the first word of "Your Song"?
14 What colour eyes were in the title of a 1982 hit?
15 "Circle Of Life" came from which film?
16 Elton John's charity foundation raises funds for what?
17 Who was the bride at a 1999 wedding Elton John had to miss through ill health?
18 What flower is named in the first line of "Candle In The Wind 1997"?
19 Which Billy did Elton John tour with in 1994?
20 Which Paul duetted with Elton John on "Don't Go Breaking My Heart" in 1994?

Quiz 13 Pot Luck 7

Answers – see page 19

LEVEL 1

1 Which Liverpool lady had a No. 1 with "Anyone Who Had a Heart" in 1963?
2 Who was lead singer with Blondie?
3 Which Vanessa's album was called *The Violin Player*?
4 Which Music group was Bryan Ferry lead singer with?
5 Which Helen was Walking Back to Happiness in 1961?
6 Whose first hit was "Diana" in 1957?
7 Who were Steve Harley's backing group?
8 How is Noah Kaminsky better known?
9 What is the home country of Kylie Minogue?
10 Which musical instrument does Queen's Brian May play?
11 Which character with a Technicolour Dreamcoat did Jason Donovan play on the London stage?
12 What are the initials of the Canadian Ms lang?
13 Which country is Nana Mouskouri from?
14 Which Tina's life story was in the film *What's Love Got to Do With It?*?
15 Which Paula was Mrs Bob Geldof?
16 Which US city is mentioned with Freedom in a hit from 1975?
17 How were the Fugees Killing Me in 1996?
18 Which surname is shared by Edwin and Ringo?
19 Who did Little Richard say Good Golly to back in 1958?
20 Which Road famous for its recording studios is the title of a Beatles album?

Answers

Pot Luck 5 (Quiz 9)
1 Canada. 2 Eileen. 3 Day. 4 Air Supply. 5 Easton. 6 Frank. 7 Tennessee. 8 Yes. 9 Doop. 10 The Wonder Stuff. 11 His Master's Voice. 12 Stock, Aitken and Waterman. 13 Eternal. 14 Marc Bolan. 15 The TARDIS. 16 Dippy. 17 Four. 18 Mick Hucknall. 19 Penny. 20 Breaking.

1 Who had a 90s No. 1 with "I Wanna Sex You Up"?
2 What is the first name of Julian Lennon's stepmother?
3 "Lovefool" was a 90s top three hit for which group?
4 "I Am I Feel" was the first hit for which group?
5 Who had a 90s No. 1 with "No Limit"?
6 Who made the album *A Twist Of Lemmon*?
7 In which decade did Kim Carnes have her first chart success?
8 Which first name did singer/songwriter Gerald Hugh Sayer use?
9 What is the first word of "Perfect Moment"?
10 Who had an 80s No. 1 with "Eternal Flame"?
11 "Ray Of Light" was a 90s hit for which singer?
12 Which cuddly toy is the title of an early Elvis Presley hit?
13 How is Declan McManus better known?
14 Not a lot of people know that, but which Michael Caine film theme song was a big Cilla Black hit?
15 Who had an 80s No. 1 with "Billie Jean"?
16 What is the first name of songwriter Bacharach?
17 What kind of Guy gave Roxy Music a big 80s hit?
18 Who had a 70s No. 1 with "Lonely This Christmas"?
19 What word completes the song title, "I Love The Way You ___ Me".
20 Which band had a 90s No. 1 with "The Fly"?

Quiz 15 The 80s

Answers – see page 21

LEVEL 1

1 Which Olivia got "Physical" in 1981?
2 How many Tribes were a big hit for Frankie Goes to Hollywood?
3 Which Boy was a "Karma Chameleon"?
4 Which ex-Supreme joined Lionel Richie on "Endless Love"?
5 Which Careless sound was a hit for George Michael?
6 Which Kenny and Dolly recorded "Islands in the Stream"?
7 Who had a Celebration with Kool?
8 What were the USA for on "We Are the World"?
9 Noddy Holder was the lead singer with which band?
10 What did Wham! say to do Before You Go Go?
11 Which Sultans of Swing took the Walk of Life?
12 Which Irish group's name is made up of one letter and a number?
13 Which Boys had a No. 1 with "West End Girls"?
14 Which Simon sang with Duran Duran?
15 Which highwayman demand did Adam and the Ants give in 1981?
16 Which House provided Madness with their first No. 1?
17 Who had huge album success with *Thriller*?
18 Which Bruce was "Born in the USA"?
19 What was Whitney Houston's first album called?
20 Which Purple weather was a film soundtrack album for Prince?

1   Who was the leading lady on the chart-topping "Five Live" EP?
2   Who had a 90s No. 1 with "(I Can't Help) Falling In Love With You"?
3   What is the first word of "Don't Cry For Me Argentina"?
4   Who had an 80s No. 1 with "Woman"?
5   What was the first No. 1 for Kate Bush?
6   Which group had a 90s No. 1 with "Breathe"?
7   Which Abba song mentions Napoleon?
8   "Sleeping Satellite" was the first No. 1 for which artist?
9   Who had an early 70s smash with "In The Summertime"?
10   "A Little Time" became the first time that which group made No. 1?
11   Which Lady featured in the title of a No. 1 for The Beatles?
12   Which Spice Girl No. 1 contains the line, "Everlasting like the sun"?
13   Who had an 80s No. 1 with "Red Red Wine"?
14   What was the name of Robbie Williams' first No. 1?
15   "You Are Not Alone" was a 90s No. 1 for which singer?
16   "The Power Of Love" was the third 80s No. 1 in a row for which group?
17   What is the first word on the 1997 version of "Candle In The Wind"?
18   Which singer and piano man had a No. 1 with "Uptown Girl"?
19   Which Pickets made it to No. 1?
20   "C'est La Vie" was the first No. 1 for which group?

1   Which song was a No. 1 for the Equals and Pato Banton?
2   Who formed a duo with Lyle?
3   How many c.c. were in the group which sang "I'm Not in Love"?
4   Which Yorkshire town's Fair was the subject of a Simon and Garfunkel song?
5   What Killed the Radio Star according to the Buggles?
6   What is the home country of Björk?
7   Which Elvis song has the line "I gave a letter to the postman, He put it in his sack"?
8   Where did the Police find a Message in 1979?
9   Which Orchestra joined Olivia Newton-John on "Xanadu"?
10 Which Bob wrote "Knockin' On Heaven's Door"?
11 Which instrument does Acker Bilk play?
12 Who took "Sloop John B" into the 60s charts?
13 Who was Alone Again (Naturally) in 1972?
14 How many members of the Thompson Twins were there?
15 Which surname is shared by Cat and Shakin'?
16 Which country star pleaded for Jolene not to take her man in 1976?
17 Whose first hit was "Love and Affection"?
18 How is Robert Zimmerman better known?
19 Who was lead singer with the Mechanics?
20 Which thoroughfare did Elton John say Goodbye to in 1973?

1   What is the first word of "Albatross" by Fleetwood Mac?
2   Who had a 90s No. 1 with "Oh Carolina"?
3   Which Cheryl, once of Bucks Fizz, is the mother of twins?
4   *Spice* was the debut album from which group?
5   "Don't Worry" was the first solo hit for which Kim?
6   What is the first word of "No Regrets" by Robbie Williams?
7   Who had an 80s No. 1 with "Hand On Your Heart"?
8   Who sang with Jennifer Warnes on "Up Where We Belong"?
9   Where did Supertramp have Breakfast in 1979?
10 What's the last word in the name of the Urban Cookie group?
11 What was the first 90s No. 1 for Vic Reeves?
12 What was the name of the Honeyz' first single?
13 Which soccer side does Jasper Carrott support?
14 Who were "Staring At The Sun" in 1997?
15 Who had a 70s No. 1 with "If"?
16 "Ain't That Just The Way" was a hit in 1997 for which singer?
17 Which country did New Kids On The Block come from?
18 Who had an 80s No. 1 with "Let's Dance"?
19 Who were Kool's backing group?
20 Famine in which country led to the worldwide Live Aid concert?

Answers

Pot Luck 12 (Quiz 22)
1 No.   2 Another Level.   3 Bonnie Tyler.   4 Watts.   5 Michael Jackson.
6 Prince.   7 Galway.   8 Marc Almond.   9 Scotland.   10 Radiohead.
11 Four.   12 Art Garfunkel.   13 Mavericks.   14 Two.   15 Duran Duran.
16 Rush.   17 The Vandellas.   18 Charles and Eddie.
19 "He Ain't Heavy, He's My Brother".   20 Irene Cara.

1 Which Melody took Robson and Jerome to No. 1?
2 How long were Take That Back For in 1995?
3 Which Paradise was a hit for Coolio Featuring LV?
4 Which Night was special for Whigfield?
5 What is the nationality of chart-topper Alanis Morissette?
6 Whose *Immaculate Collection* was a 1991 bestseller?
7 What was Oasis's first album called?
8 Which opera singer had a hit with "Nessun Dorma" in 1990?
9 Which Ms O'Connor had a No. 1 with "Nothing Compares 2 U"?
10 How many Spice Girls are there?
11 Which superstar's first solo No. 1 was "Sacrifice" in 1990 after more than 50 hit singles?
12 Which Jimmy was famous for his Crocodile Shoes?
13 Which Tasmin reached No. 1 with her first single "Sleeping Satellite" in 1992?
14 Which group named themselves after the hit record "Boys to Men"?
15 Which Mariah had a hit with "Without You" in 1994?
16 What Is All Around according to Wet Wet Wet in 1994?
17 Where was Celine Dion Falling Into in 1996?
18 Which country do Boyzone come from?
19 Which former Wham! member released an album called *Older*?
20 Which Peter chose the right Flava to get to No. 1?

1 Who was the oldest woman in the charts in 1998 with "Believe"?
2 Which Brothers went to No. 1 in 1990 with "Unchained Melody" 25 years after first hitting No. 1 with the same song?
3 What did Aretha Franklin sing at a 1998 Grammy awards ceremony, deputising for Luciano Pavarotti?
4 Which glamorous Granny Shirley had her first hit in the 50s and enjoyed a 90s revival?
5 Which Club had a *Greatest Moments* album after a Reunion Tour in the late 90s?
6 Which French singer's 70s hit "She" was recorded by Elvis Costello for the film *Notting Hill* in 1999?
7 Which Queen single was a Christmas No. 1 in 1975 and again in 1991?
8 Which Lou had his song "Perfect Day" released as a charity single in 1997 over 20 years after it was first heard?
9 Which band led by Suggs made a comeback single in 1999?
10 With which Boys did Dusty Springfield have a comeback hit, "What Have I Done to Deserve This"?
11 How is Cherilyn La Pierre better known?
12 Whose first live album for 25 years was *Natural Wonder* in 1995?
13 Which Young comic outfit did Cliff Richard re-release "Living Doll" with, nearly 30 years after the original?
14 Which Debbie had a comeback with "Maria" and Blondie?
15 Which Australian reappeared in the charts with "Stairway To Heaven" after a 24-year chart absence?
16 Which band headed by Simon Le Bon hosted a sell-out concert at Wembley in 1998?
17 Which 80s Style band released a Best Of album in 1998?
18 Which late great pop icon had a comeback virtual concert at Wembley Arena in 1998?
19 Which Jason got back into the limelight in 1999 with *The Rocky Horror Show* after 80s chart success?
20 Spandau Ballet's Martin Kemp resurfaced in the 90s in which soap?

1   What is the home country of Michael Bolton?
2   Who is lead singer with the Rolling Stones?
3   Which Peggy was a classic 50s hit for Buddy Holly?
4   Which surname is shared by Neil and Paul?
5   Which continent is famous for its pan pipes?
6   Which brass instrument did Louis Armstrong play?
7   Which Lesley had the original hit with "It's My Party"?
8   Which Welsh city was Shirley Bassey born in?
9   Which Osmond had a hit with "Young Love"?
10   Which trio was made up of Sheila Ferguson, Valerie Thompson and Fayette Pickney?
11   What was Otis Redding Sittin' On in 1968?
12   Which record producer was known as the Fifth Beatle?
13   Which group was formed when the Small Faces disbanded?
14   What name is shared by Dolly and Stella?
15   Which politician did the Spice Girls say was an original Spice Girl?
16   Whose first hit was "Love Changes Everything"?
17   Which People was Heather Small lead singer of?
18   Who were Martha Reeves's backing group?
19   Which ex-Police man sang "Fields of Gold" in 1993?
20   Which Dionne was a Heartbreaker in 1982?

1 What is the first word of "Goodbye" by the Spice Girls?
2 "Be Alone No More" was the first hit for which group?
3 Who had an 80s No. 1 with "Total Eclipse Of The Heart"?
4 Which Stone Charlie shares a birthday with actor Stacy Keach?
5 Who had a No. 1 with "Black And White"?
6 Who in 1993 asked to be known by a symbol rather than a name?
7 Which Irish flute player James is the father of twins?
8 Who had an 80s No. 1 with "Something's Gotten Hold Of My Heart" with Gene Pitney?
9 The instrumental version of "Amazing Grace" featured a band from which country?
10 "No Surprises" was a 1998 top five hit for which group?
11 How many members were there in The Four Tops?
12 Who had a 70s No. 1 with "I Only Have Eyes For You"?
13 "Dance The Night Away" was a 1998 hit for which group?
14 How many members of Wham! were there?
15 Who had an 80s No. 1 with "Is There Something I Should Know"?
16 What followed After The Gold in the album title by Neil Young?
17 Who backed Tamla Motown's Martha?
18 Who had a 90s No. 1 with "Would I Lie To You"?
19 Which song begins, "The road is long, with many a winding turn"?
20 Who had an 80s No. 1 with "Fame"?

1 How many members made up the Rolling Stones when they first charted?
2 Which musical instrument does Charlie Watts play?
3 Which former Rolling Stone's real name is William Perks?
4 Which words go in brackets before the 1965 No. 1 "Satisfaction"?
5 Which two words describe the Rooster in the Stones' No. 1 in November 1964?
6 Which Merseysiders, later seen as the Stones' rivals, wrote the Stones' first top 20 hit "I Wanna Be Your Man"?
7 The Stones' first album was called *The Rolling Stones*. What was the second one called?
8 Which Nervous Breakdown features in the title of the 1966 hit?
9 In which part of his home was Brian Jones found dead in July 1969?
10 Which controversial song was on the B-side of "Ruby Tuesday"?
11 Who did Bianca Rose Perez Moreno de Macias marry in 1970?
12 Complete the title of the 70s album *Goat's Head____*.
13 Which record label signed the Stones in the early 1990s?
14 Who was Jagger Dancin' In The Street with at the Live Aid concert?
15 Who quit the Stones in 1992?
16 Which Stones guitarist sang with the X-pensive Winos?
17 What colour did the Rolling Stones Paint It in 1966?
18 What was Tumbling for the Stones in their top five hit in 1972?
19 Which record label did the Stones record on throughout the Sixties?
20 What was the Stones' own record label called?

1 Who was the lead vocalist Carpenter who died in 1983?
2 What was Jimi Hendrix's band called?
3 Who was the first rock'n'roll star when he decided to "Rock Around The Clock"?
4 What follows No Woman on the Bob Marley classic?
5 Which late great was backed by The Crickets before his death aged 22?
6 In which country did American Eddie Cochran die?
7 What was Nilsson's first name?
8 What shape was the Box in the track by Nirvana made the year before Kurt Cobain's death?
9 Which Big letter described Roy Orbison?
10 Which country singer was born John Deutschendorf and hit the top spot with "Annie's Song"?
11 Which member of his own family killed Marvin Gaye?
12 Who led the band who released the album *Morrison Hotel*?
13 What did Faroukh Bulsara change his surname to when he founded Queen?
14 Otis Redding was doing what on "The Dock Of The Bay" in his classic hit?
15 Which song did Frank Sinatra re-enter the charts with in 1994 when he was 78 years old?
16 Which First Lady of Country's autobiography was called *Stand By Your Man*?
17 Which multi-hit-making Boys from California did the late Carl Wilson belong to?
18 Which star of the classic Road films teamed up with David Bowie in 1982 for "Peace On Earth'/'Little Drummer Boy"?
19 Ex-boxer Sonny Wilson changed his first name to what before having a posthumous No. 1 with "Reet Petite"?
20 Which instrument did The Who's crazy Keith Moon play?

1 Which surname is shared by Chuck, Dave and Nick?
2 How many members of the Bee Gees are there?
3 Which Livin' object was Cliff Richard's first No. 1?
4 Which Andrew wrote the music for *Jesus Christ Superstar*?
5 Which Miss Clark had a 60s hit with "Downtown"?
6 Procul Harum sang about a Whiter Shade of what?
7 Which Mungo sang "In The Summertime" in 1970?
8 Which part of East London had the 1994 Christmas No. 1 "Stay Another Day"?
9 Which 90s band sounds like a fertile part of a desert?
10 Whose first hit was "Surfin' USA"?
11 Which initials went with Duncan on "Let's Get Ready to Rhumble" in 1994?
12 What sort of Rampage did Sweet go on in 1974?
13 Which Alvin originally charted as Shane Fenton?
14 Which relative was seen to Swing Out with "Breakout" and "Surrender" in the 80s?
15 "Mandy" gave which Barry his first UK hit?
16 Who was lead singer with Genesis in the 80s?
17 Martha Reeves, David Bowie and Mick Jagger have all been Dancing where?
18 Which Stewart sang "You're In My Heart" in 1977?
19 Who makes up the trio with Emerson and Lake?
20 What is the home country of Tom Jones?

1 "Children" was a top ten hit in 1996 for who?
2 "Perfect 10" was perfect as a top ten hit for which group?
3 Who had an 80s No. 1 with "Every Breath You Take"?
4 What did Harry Connick put after his name?
5 Which two months gave Barbara Dickson a hit?
6 What is the name of Sam Brown's famous dad?
7 What is the first word of "Ray Of Light"?
8 What was the name of No Doubt's first No. 1?
9 "You're Still The One" was the debut hit for which singer?
10 Who had an 80s No. 1 with "Orinoco Flow"?
11 Which comedy duo were backed by The Stonkers?
12 What went with Ebony on the Paul McCartney/Stevie Wonder hit?
13 "Wherever I Lay My Hat (That's My Home)" gave which male singer a No. 1?
14 Which 80s singer was known as Shaky?
15 What Diana sang about a Chain Reaction?
16 Who had an 80s No. 1 with "Baby Jane"?
17 What is the home country of Mariah Carey?
18 Whose first hit was "Hangin' Tough"?
19 Who had a 70s No. 1 with the dance favourite "Dancing Queen"?
20 Which Sister had a hit with Frankie?

Quiz 27 Michael Jackson

Answers – see page 41

1   With which group did Michael Jackson have chart success?
2   Whose superstar's daughter did he marry in 1994?
3   Which Jackson album broke all records in 1982?
4   What type of dance "walking" did Jackson introduce in 1983?
5   On which soul label did Jackson record his early hits?
6   Which animal was the single "Ben" about?
7   *The Wiz*, in which he starred, was a remake of which film?
8   Which Beatle did Jackson duet with in "The Girl is Mine"?
9   Jackson was the narrator on the soundtrack of which "extra-terrestrial" film?
10 Jackson co-wrote "We Are the World" to raise money for the USA's campaign
    against what?
11 Which US TV talk-show hostess conducted a famous interview with the star in 1993?
12 Which much-married famous film star was married at Michael Jackson's ranch in 1991?
13 What type of animal is Jackson's pet Bubbles?
14 Which Billie took Jackson to No. 1 in 1983?
15 Which album was the follow-up to his 1982 massive success, which had a video
    showing Jackson in belts, buckles and straps?
16 Who was Rockin' on Jackson's 1972 hit?
17 Which anthem-like song went straight to No. 1 at Christmas 1995?
18 Which member of Pulp interrupted Jackson's receiving a BRIT Award in 1996?
19 Who did Jackson say Farewell to on his 1984 summer album?
20 Which ex-Supreme was credited with discovering the Jacksons?

Quiz 28 Ads

Answers – see page 42

LEVEL 1

1   Who sang "Like A Prayer" to advertise Pepsi?
2   I'd Like To Teach The World to do what in the classic Coca-Cola ad?
3   Which King sang "Stand By Me" to advertise Coca-Cola?
4   What type of product did Wiseguys hit "Ooh La La" advertise?
5   Who was dropped from a Coca-Cola campaign after adverse publicity about his private life?
6   Which German cars were advertised to the sound of "Young At Heart" by The Bluebells?
7   Bob Geldof has advertised which drink?
8   Which brand of jeans used The Clash's "Should I Stay Or Should I Go"?
9   What follows He Ain't Heavy in the title of the Hollies hit to advertise Miller Lite?
10 Which phone company used Elvis's "You Were Always On My Mind"?
11 Which ice cream was advertised to a version of "O Sole Mio"/"It's Now Or Never"?
12 Which face cream was advertised to the accompaniment of "Blue Velvet"?
13 Which product from Buxton had Elgar's Cello Concerto as an advertising theme?
14 The theme from *Raging Bull*, Mascagni's "Cavalleria Rusticana', was used to promote what type of drink?
15 Bach's "Air On A G String" advertised a brand of what that is no longer advertised on television?
16 Which Tina advertised Pepsi?
17 The Marriage of who was an operatic theme used to advertise Citroen cars?
18 Perez Prado's "Guaglione" advertised which drink?
19 Which Goon who made the charts with Sophia Loren was the voice of all the chimps on the first Brooke Bond ad?
20 Roger Daltrey of which band promoted American Express?

1 Who is Zak Starkey's famous dad?
2 What part of her did Kylie Minogue put on her Heart in 1989?
3 The Colour of what was Celine Dion's top-selling album of 1995?
4 Which instrument did Suzi Quatro play?
5 Which singer called David played Che in the original stage production of *Evita*?
6 What did the painter paint along with Matchstalk Men?
7 Who were Gerry's backing group?
8 Which quartet's only UK No. 1 was "Reach Out I'll Be There"?
9 Which country does Demis Roussos come from?
10 Whose first hit was "Love Me Do"?
11 What is the home country of Lulu?
12 Who was Cher's husband when she recorded her first singles?
13 In 1985 Tears For Fears said Everyone Wants to Rule what?
14 Which record label shares its name with an ocean?
15 Which country were the Three Degrees from?
16 Which Bonnie had a 1984 hit with Shakin' Stevens?
17 Which surname is shared by Rod and Dave, formerly of the Eurythmics?
18 Which temptress provided Tom Jones with a 60s hit?
19 Who was lead singer with the Boomtown Rats?
20 Which fruity Fields were the Beatles in in 1967, 1976 and 1987?

1 "Let Me Entertain You" was a top ten hit for which singer in 1998?
2 Which David who appeared in *That'll Be The Day* is the father of twins?
3 "Barbie Girl" was the first No. 1 single for which group?
4 Who had an 80s No. 1 with "Pass The Dutchie"?
5 Jocelyn Brown sang Don't Talk Just do what?
6 Who had a 70s No. 1 with "Under The Moon Of Love"?
7 Frankie Valli was lead singer of which Four?
8 Who had a 90s No. 1 with "All That She Wants"?
9 What is the first word of "Last Thing On My Mind" by Steps?
10 Who asked "When Will I Be Famous"?
11 In which decade did Richard Marx first make the charts?
12 "The Rockafeller Skank" was the first top ten hit hit for which act?
13 Who had an 80s No. 1 with "Call Me"?
14 Which Images had hits with "Happy Birthday" and "I Could Be Happy"?
15 Who had a 70s No. 1 with "Don't Give Up On Us"?
16 What was coupled with "Bohemian Rhapsody" when it made No. 1 in the 90s?
17 Who had an 80s No. 1 with "Do They Know It's Christmas"?
18 Who had an 80s No. 1 with "Happy Talk"?
19 James Brown was Living In which country according to a big 80s hit?
20 Which word follows Walk Like A in the song by the All Seeing I?

Quiz 31 Groups

Answers – see page 37

1 Which group includes the two Gallagher brothers?
2 Which group did Robbie Williams leave in 1995?
3 Frankie Goes To where in the name of the 80s group?
4 Which Boys were famous for their surfing sound in the 60s and 70s?
5 Which City Rollers were teen idols in the 70s?
6 Which Club was fronted by Boy George?
7 What was the ELO's full name?
8 Which group shares its name with the first book of the Bible?
9 Who were the other half of the Mamas?
10 Which band's three-word name describes the British weather?
11 Which group is made up of the Gibb brothers?
12 Which ex-Beatle formed Wings?
13 Which group had albums called *The Wall* and *Dark Side of the Moon*?
14 Which group were 5 until they lost Michael?
15 What follows Earth and Wind in the group of the 70s?
16 Which point of the compass is Beautiful?
17 Which group was Sweden's biggest export?
18 Which group did Diana Ross leave to go solo?
19 Which 90s group shares its name with a district of London?
20 Which band with Mark Knopfler had the album *Brothers in Arms*?

Answers

Michael Jackson (Quiz 27)
1 Jackson 5. 2 Elvis Presley's. 3 *Thriller*. 4 Moonwalking. 5 Tamla Motown.
6 Rat. 7 *The Wizard of Oz*. 8 Paul McCartney. 9 *E.T.* 10 Famine in Africa.
11 Oprah Winfrey. 12 Elizabeth Taylor. 13 Chimpanzee. 14 Jean. 15 *Bad*.
16 Robin. 17 "Earth". 18 Jarvis Cocker. 19 Summer Love. 20 Diana Ross.

1 Catatonia's second hit was the name of a 90s crime; what was it?
2 Which compass point had the album Quench?
3 Which London band with a London link had a hit called "Walthamstow"?
4 Which Backstreet Boys album sounded like it belonged to the end of the 20th century?
5 How many girls are there out of four Vengaboys?
6 Which Courtney, Mrs Kurt Cobain, fronted the band Hole?
7 Which Scandinavian country did Cartoons hail from?
8 Who were Michael, Jackie, Marlon, Tito and Jermaine?
9 Which food made an appearance on the 1999 No. 1 by Shanks & Bigfoot?
10 Which sticky group did Paul Weller lead?
11 What was Private in 911's 1999 hit?
12 Where in the UK do Stereophonics hail from?
13 Which soul label did Boyz II Men record on?
14 Which BBC series did S Club 7 appear in?
15 Which Dutch town was the title of a Beautiful South smash hit?
16 Your Kisses Are what according to Culture Club in 1999?
17 The Cardigans were the First Band where according to their 1996 album?
18 How are Russell and Jason, singers of Turn Around, better known?
19 Which debut release by Catatonia included their name?
20 How many members make up Semisonic?

1   Which surname is shared by Elkie and Garth?
2   According to Kirsty MacColl, "There's A Guy Works Down The Chipshop Swears he's who?
3   What Can't Barry Manilow do Without You according to his 1978 hit?
4   How many members of the Beach Boys were there?
5   What is the home country of Clannad?
6   Which Belinda sang "Heaven is a Place on Earth" in 1987?
7   Which Captain took "Happy Talk" to No. 1 in 1982?
8   What was In the Window when the 50s star Lita Roza asked How Much it was?
9   In which musical, revived in the West End in the 90s, does Fagin appear?
10 Which Moody group sang "Nights In White Satin"?
11 Which Dina pleaded "Don't Be A Stranger" in 1993?
12 What did Chaka Demus and Pliers do as well as Twist at No. 1 in 1993?
13 What was the middle name of Natalie Cole's father Nat?
14 In which decade did Hot Chocolate first make the charts?
15 Roger Daltrey was lead singer of which 60s wild group?
16 Which Cyndi proved Girls Just Want to Have Fun in 1984?
17 Which Sweet girl was a 1971 hit for Neil Diamond?
18 Who was lead singer with Duran Duran?
19 In which London thoroughfares was Ralph McTell in 1974?
20 What's Gotten Hold Of My Heart according to Gene Pitney in 1967?

1   Chart topper Telly Savalas was the godfather of which star of Friends?
2   Which singer had a 90s No. 1 with "Flava"?
3   Who charted in 94 with "Shine"?
4   What was the title of Dana International's first single?
5   Who had an 80s No. 1 with "I Don't Wanna Dance"?
6   "Design For Life" was a hit for which group in 1996?
7   Which song has ben a No. 1 for Harry Belafonte and Boney M?
8   Who had a 70s No. 1 with "When I Need You"?
9   "Outside" was a No. 2 hit in 1998 for which vocalist?
10 What did Aqua wish they could Turn Back in 1998?
1   Which song from the movie *Waiting To Exhale* entered the UK charts in 1995?
12 Which Nigel took Vivaldi's "The Four Seasons" into the album charts?
13 Who had an 80s No. 1 with "I Know Him So Well" with Elaine Paige?
14 Which female singer had an early 90s hit with "If You Were With Me Now"?
15 Who did Elvis's daughter marry in 1994?
16 What did Madonna get Into according to her first UK No. 1?
17 What sort of Rear View was a top-selling debut album for Hootie & The Blowfish?
18 Which word follows Better Best in the song by Steps?
19 Who had an 80s No. 1 with "Do You Really Want To Hurt Me"?
20 Which DJ recorded "The Floral Dance"?

Quiz 35 Space Oddity

Answers – see page 49

1 Which 90s group had a hit with "Female of the Species"?
2 Which Alvin had a No. 1 with "Jealous Mind"?
3 Which Way were OMD Walking on in 1996?
4 Which Man did Elton John sing about in 1972?
5 Which star was in the title of the hit Elton John had with George Michael?
6 Which space puppets Are Go in the FAB hit of 1990?
7 Which David sang "Space Oddity" back in 1969?
8 What was "In The Sky" according to Doctor and the Medics in 1986?
9 What Always Shines On TV according to A-Ha in 1985?
10 The Dark Side of which celestial body was a classic album for Pink Floyd?
11 Which all-girl group sang "Venus" in 1986?
12 Which Song was a 1995 No. 1 for Michael Jackson?
13 What was the Satellite doing on Tasmin Archer's No. 1?
14 What did M/A/R/R/S Pump Up in 1987?
15 Who did Sarah Brightman Lose Her Heart To in 1978?
16 What was David Essex Gonna Make You in 1974?
17 What sort of Craft were the Carpenters Calling All Occupants of in 1977?
18 Where were the Police Walking on in 1979?
19 What sort of Star did gravel-voiced Lee Marvin sing about in 1970?
20 Which intergalactic Wars theme got into the top ten in 1977?

1 Who left a soap and found a Perfect Moment in 1999?
2 Which singer's real name is Michael Bolotin?
3 Whose Army provided Elvis Costello with an early hit?
4 Whose most famous hit was "Lady In Red"?
5 Which soap did Adam Rickitt leave to start on a singing career?
6 How is Fatboy Slim also known?
7 What does the R stand for in R Kelly's name?
8 Who was - initially - Miss Chatelaine in 1993 ?
9 Which solo singer with Cleopatra contributed to Thank Abba For The Music?
10 Which artist with canine connections was originally named Calvin Broadus?
11 Where was Peter Andre brought up?
12 According to Baz Luhrmann, Everybody's Free To Wear what?
13 Which Robinson went solo after singing with The Miracles?
14 How was Sealhenry Samuel better known?
15 Who won a Brit Award for best dance act after announcing his engagement to Zoe Ball?
16 Which Neil had his first hit back in 1959 but had a successful album in the 90s?
17 Which soap did Michelle Gayle leave to pursue a solo pop career?
18 Who is Eagle-Eye Cherry's singing sibling?
19 Who did Morrissey leave behind when he went solo?
20 Which religious leader's picture did Sinead O'Connor tear up on a US show?

1 Who was lead singer with Queen?
2 Which Little girl did the Everly Brothers tell to Wake Up in 1957?
3 Which Hank was part of the Shadows and has had solo success?
4 Which surname is shared by the singer/drummer Phil and singer Judy?
5 Which military duo were the top-selling album artists of 1995?
6 What is the home country of Men At Work, who had a No. 1 with "Down Under"?
7 In which band does Francis Rossi play guitar and take lead vocals?
8 Which Bette is known as "The Divine Miss M"?
9 How is Ultravox's James Ure better known?
10 Which Irish group had a hit with the Osmonds' "Love Me For A Reason" in 1994?
11 What goes before Order and Model Army in the names of groups of the 80s and 90s?
12 Which Gary took "Cars" to the top in 1979?
13 Which 90s Disney film was Peter Andre's "Kiss The Girl" taken from?
14 Which animal links the performer Roland and the subject of the song "Ben"?
15 How many Tops were in the group that sang "Reach Out I'll Be There"?
16 How is Thomas Woodward better known?
17 Which sporting event shot the Lightning Seeds to fame?
18 Elvis sang about what kind of Heart in 1961?
19 What is the home country of Mariah Carey?
20 Which Hollies hit begins "The road is long, with many a winding turn"?

1 "I Know Where It's At", was the first top ten hit for which group?
2 Who had a 90s hit with "Julia Says"?
3 Who had a 1996 hit with "Always Breaking My Heart"?
4 Which band was named after a shop where everything was for sale apart from the person who worked there?
5 Who had an 80s No. 1 with "You Can't Hurry Love"?
6 Who had a US No. 1 with "4 Seasons Of Loneliness"?
7 Which word follows Sweetest in the song by U2?
8 Who had a 90s No. 1 with "Tears On My Pillow"?
9 "Stand By Me" was a hit for which group in 1997?
10 At Christmas 1980, St Winifred's School choir said "There's No One Quite Like" which member of their family?
11 Which duo made the album *Bookends*?
12 Who had an 80s No. 1 with "Private Eyes"?
13 Which Matt sang "Get Out Of Your Lazy Bed"?
14 Who had a 70s No. 1 with "Angelo"?
15 Who declared "I'll Be There" in an early 90s hit?
16 Who had a late 80s hit with "I Want It All"?
17 What is the first word of "Look At Me"?
18 Who had an 80s No. 1 with "Swing The Mood"?
19 Which member of Oasis has Patsy tattooed on his arm?
20 Whose first No. 1 was "It Doesn't Matter Any More" in the 50s?

Answers

Pot Luck 18 (Quiz 34)
1 Jennifer Aniston. 2 Peter Andre. 3 Aswad. 4 "Diva". 5 Eddy Grant.
6 Manic Street Preachers. 7 "Mary's Boy Child". 8 Leo Sayer.
9 George Michael. 10 Time. 11 "Exhale". 12 Kennedy.
13 Barbara Dickson. 14 Kylie Minogue. 15 Michael Jackson.
16 The Groove. 17 Cracked. 18 Forgotten. 19 Culture Club.
20 Terry Wogan.

1 Who managed the rare double of Christmas No. 1 single and album in 1996?
2 Which Gina sang "Ooh Aah Just a Little Bit" in May 1996?
3 Who had three consecutive No. 1s with "Knowing Me, Knowing You", "The Name of the Game" and "Take A Chance on Me"?
4 Which American solo singer has had the most No. 1 hits?
5 Who did Kylie Minogue share the top spot with in 1988?
6 How many Lions topped the charts in June 1996?
7 What did Billy Ocean say happened When the Going Gets Tough?
8 Which football side were the first to have a No. 1 in 1994 with "Come On You Reds"?
9 Which Liverpool group has had a record-breaking 17 No. 1 hits?
10 Which No. 1 artist was pink with yellow spots?
11 Which Scottish female singer had her first hit "Shout" in 1964, before any of Take That were born, but topped the charts with them in 1993?
12 Which star of *The Bodyguard* took "I Will Always Love You" to the No. 1 spot making it the best selling CD single at that time?
13 Which cartoon group did "The Bartman" in 1991?
14 Whose first solo No. 1 was in 1990, 14 years after hitting the top spot with Kiki Dee and "Don't Go Breaking My Heart"?
15 Which New Kids had their first No. 1 in 1989?
16 Which Canadian Bryan was at No. 1 for 16 weeks in 1991?
17 Where were David Bowie and Mick Jagger Dancing in 1985?
18 According to Robson and Jerome, who have had love that's now departed?
19 In 1984 Stevie Wonder Just Called to Say what?
20 Whose Midnight Runners sang "Come On Eileen" in 1982?

Quiz 40   Oldies But Goldies

Answers – see page 46

LEVEL 1

1   Which grandfather became a father again for the seventh time in 1999 and has led a pop group for more than 30 years?
2   Which Brown was dubbed Soul Brother Number One?
3   Which Bryan embarked on a solo career while still with Roxy Music?
4   Which band was headed by Mick Fleetwood?
5   Which ex-Beatle joined the oldie rock supergroup The Travelling Wilburys?
6   Johnny Cash is famous for performing in what colour?
7   Which Welshman duetted with Robbie Williams at the 1998 BRIT Awards?
8   Which lead singer of The Faces still makes headlines 30 years after their debut?
9   What middle name did rocker Jerry Lewis have?
10   Other than as a vocalist, Phil Collins is famous as what type of instrumentalist?
11   Who later joined Crosby, Stills & Nash?
12   Which lead singer with The Kinks released the solo album *The Storyteller* in 1998?
13   Which musical instrument does Ray Charles play?
14   In which decade did King of Skiffle Lonnie Donegan shoot to fame?
15   Which soccer star recorded "Fog On The Tyne" with the veterans Lindisfarne?
16   Whose many albums and singles included *Slowhand*?
17   What did L stand for in ELO?
18   Which brothers were Don and Phil?
19   Simon and Garfunkel's "Mrs Robinson" came from which classic 60s film?
20   How is the size conscious Richard Penniman better known ?

Answers

Soloists   (Quiz 36)
1   Martine McCutcheon.   2   Michael Bolton.   3   Oliver's.   4   Chris de Burgh.
5   Coronation Street.   6   Norman Cook.   7   Robert.   8   k.d. lang.
9   Billie.   10   Snoop Doggy Dogg.   11   Australia.   12   Sunscreen.
13   Smokey.   14   Seal.   15   Fatboy Slim.   16   Sedaka.   17   EastEnders.
18   Neneh Cherry.   19   The Smiths.   20   The Pope.

1 Who was lead singer with the Sex Pistols?
2 Which Olivia had a 70s hit with "Sam"?
3 Which Christie featured on a 90s "Walk Like A Panther"?
4 How many members of Bucks Fizz were there?
5 What is the home country of Chris de Burgh?
6 What Seemed to be the Hardest Word in 1976?
7 Which country does Bonnie Tyler come from?
8 Which birthday did Shirley Bassey celebrate in January 1997?
9 Which US state had a hit with "White On Blonde"?
10 Which hostel did the Village People stay at?
11 How does the country singer Whitman describe his physique?
12 How many times did Dawn say to knock on the ceiling in their 1971 hit?
13 Who was the shortest Beatle?
14 Which Roy was lead singer with Wizzard?
15 Which record label shares its name with a fruit?
16 Which Deep colour is the name of a band who first found fame in the 70s?
17 What goes with Parsley and Sage in the Simon and Garfunkel song?
18 What do the letters R and B stand for?
19 Who is Tom Jones singing about when he sings "My, my, my" then "Why why why"?
20 Which soul singer Heard It Through The Grapevine?

1 What is the first word of "Let Me Entertain You"?
2 Who first made the top ten in the 90s with "Sweet Harmony"?
3 Who had a No. 1 with "Nothing Compares 2 U"?
4 Which Birkin/Gainsbourg song with a French title was banned by the BBC?
5 Whose first top ten single was "Cornflake Girl"?
6 "From This Moment On" was a top ten hit for which singer?
7 Which Night did The Drifters enjoy At The Movies?
8 Who had an 80s No. 1 with "I Think We're Alone Now"?
9 Which US president in 1984 said the album "Born In The USA" was a celebration of America?
10 In which decade was Mariah Carey born?
11 Who had an 80s No. 1 with "My Camera Never Lies"?
12 In which decade did Depeche Mode first make the charts?
13 What type of Stories were the title of a 90s Madonna album?
14 Which group had a 70s No. 1 with "Tie A Yellow Ribbon Round The Old Oak Tree"?
15 Which Attraction were Perfect in 1988?
16 Which word goes after Life Is A in the song by Ace Of Base?
17 Who had a hit with 5.6.7.8?
18 Who was lead singer with The Sex Pistols?
19 The Supremes' first UK No. 1 mentioned what kind of Love?
20 Which Julian made an 80s record as The Joan Collins Fan Club?

Answers

Pot Luck 24 (Quiz 46)
1 Abba. 2 Kylie Minogue. 3 Björk. 4 Backstreet Boys. 5 Donna Summer.
6 U2. 7 She's. 8 Iron Maiden. 9 Peter Andre. 10 Annie Lennox.
11 Three. 12 Spitting Image. 13 The Doors. 14 Twilight. 15 White.
16 Simon & Garfunkel. 17 Two. 18 Hot Chocolate. 19 90s. 20 Alright.

Quiz 43 Instrumentals

Answers – see page 57

1 What instrument did Nigel Kennedy play on his album-charting version of *The Four Seasons*?
2 Which country does the bandleader James Last come from?
3 Which film about the Olympics won a music Oscar for the composer Vangelis?
4 Which musical instrument does Vanessa-Mae play?
5 What relation is the cellist Julian Lloyd-Webber to the composer Andrew?
6 Which Herb had a Tijuana Brass?
7 Which Perez had chart success in 1994 with "Guaglione"?
8 In '96 Hank Marvin released an album of which late 50s star's songs?
9 Which song from *Evita* did the Shadows release in 1978?
10 The *Riverdance* album has music from which country?
11 Which musical instrument features most strongly on the Royals Scots Dragoon Guards' recording of "Amazing Grace"?
12 Who played lead guitar on *Tubular Bells*?
13 On which Richard Branson label was it first released?
14 Who left the Shadows with Jet Harris and took "Diamonds" to No. 1?
15 What is the nationality of Jean-Michel Jarre?
16 Which classical guitarist John was a member of Sky?
17 Who joined the Good on the orchestral No. 1 film theme for Ennio Morricone?
18 Which TV cop show gave Jan Hammer chart success with "Crockett's Theme"?
19 What instrument does trad jazz man Acker Bilk play?
20 Which anthem did Queen play as an instrumental?

1 Who were getting "Good Vibrations" back in the 60s?
2 Which words were used in the 1997 Labour election campaign from the D:Ream No. 1?
3 What went after Boom Boom on the title of the Vengaboys 1999 hit?
4 Who put the words to Elton John's "Candle In The Wind 1997"?
5 Where were the Three Lions in the hit released in 1996?
6 Who was with The Bartender on the hit from Stereophonics?
7 What was the word following "Feed the" in Band Aid's best-selling single?
8 Which Christmas song begins, "Long time ago in Bethlehem, so the Holy Bible say"?
9 Which hit, re-released in the 90s due to a film, is the UK's best seller with "sexy" in the title?
10 Which coastal town was in the title of a big hit for Robson and Jerome?
11 What goes before the line "Let the reason be love", in the single by Boyzone?
12 What did R Kelly believe he could do in 1997?
13 In "Love Is All Around" where did Wet Wet Wet feel it after they felt it in their fingers?
14 Which charity single had the line "I'm glad I spent it with you"?
15 What did Spacedust have with Tonic in 1998?
16 What follows "When you walk through a storm" in "You'll Never Walk Alone?
17 In "Money For Nothing" what sort of ovens do they sing about?
18 Which 90s Madonna hit begins, "It won't be easy, you'll think it strange"?
19 Which Lennon & McCartney classic begins, "Picture yourself in a boat on a river, with tangerine trees and marmalade skies"?
20 Which game follows, "That deaf dumb and blind kid sure plays a mean..."?

1 Who were Desmond Dekker's backing group?
2 Which surname is shared by the brothers Barry, Maurice and Robin?
3 Who had an album called *Seven Deadly Cyns ... And Then Some*?
4 Which record label did the Four Tops record their 60s hits on?
5 Which Brotherhood won the Eurovision Song Contest for the UK in 1976?
6 Which Abba single is a distress signal?
7 Who was Culture Club's singer?
8 What is the first name of the US vocalist Ms Benatar?
9 Which country do R.E.M. come from?
10 Which late country singer recorded "I Love You Because"?
11 What type of institution is Johnny Cash performing in on *Johnny Cash at San Quentin*?
12 Whose albums have been Simply called *Stars* and *Life*?
13 Which Carole had a best-selling 70s album called *Tapestry*?
14 How did Frankie Goes To Hollywood tell us to unwind in 1984?
15 Which animal-sounding US group had a British vocalist, Davy Jones?
16 What is the home country of Jason Donovan?
17 Which 90s Madonna hit shares its name with a glossy magazine?
18 Robson and Jerome were Up On what part of the house in 1995?
19 Which Jumpin' character was a hit for the Rolling Stones and Aretha Franklin?
20 Who is U2's lead singer ?

1 Benny Andersson of which supergroup shares a birth date with The Bill actor Christopher Ellison?
2 Who had an 80s No. 1 with "I Should Be So Lucky"?
3 Which controversial singer has an Icelandic rune tattooed on one shoulder?
4 Who charted in 1997 with "Quit Playing Games"?
5 Who had a 70s No. 1 with "I Feel Love"?
6 Which band do The Joshua Trio impersonate?
7 What is the first word of "Perfect 10"?
8 Who had a 90s No. 1 with "Bring Your Daughter ... To The Slaughter"?
9 Who was Lonely in 1997?
10 In 1995 who said there would be "No More I Love You's"?
11 How many made up the Fun Boy band of the 80s?
12 Who had an 80s No. 1 with "The Chicken Song"?
13 Who first recorded "Riders On The Storm"?
14 2 Unlimited were in what sort of Zone in an early 90s hit?
15 What did the W stand for in the group often known as AWB?
16 Which duo made the album *Bridge Over Troubled Water*?
17 According to Rod Stewart and Tina Turner, It Takes how many?
18 Who had a 70s No. 1 with "So You Win Again"?
19 In which decade did Gabrielle have her first chart success?
20 Which word completes the song title by Sweetbox, "Everything's Gonna Be _____"?

1 Which Barry sang about the Copacabana?
2 Which David's hits include "I'm Gonna Make You a Star" and "Hold Me Close"?
3 Which Billy sang about his Uptown Girl in 1983?
4 Which ex-Police man Spread A Little Happiness in 1982?
5 Which Genesis drummer went solo to No. 1 with "You Can't Hurry Love"?
6 Which Ms Franklin commanded Respect in 1967 and had A Deeper Love in 1994?
7 Which Icelandic singer's first Top 20 hit was "Play Dead" in 1993?
8 Who starred opposite Kevin Costner in *The Bodyguard*?
9 Which Chris was Driving Home for Christmas in 1988?
10 Which Elvis was supported by the Attractions?
11 Which Barbra sang "As If We Never Said Goodbye" in 1994?
12 What did Gabrielle say to give her a Little More of in 1996?
13 What did Gina G sing immediately after "Ooh aah"?
14 In 1986 George Michael sang about a Different what?
15 Which regal-sounding soloist had his first No. 1 with "The Most Beautiful Girl In The World"?
16 Eric Clapton sang I Shot who back in 1974?
17 Which glamorous granny had a No. 1 with "What's Love Got To Do With It"?
18 Who changed his name from Robert Zimmerman and found fame?
19 Which Mr Astley was Never Gonna Give You Up in 1987?
20 Which Ocean produced "When the Going Gets Tough, the Tough Get Going"?

1 Whose debut album on leaving a girl band was Schizophonic?
2 What is teen sensation Billie's surname?
3 Björk hails from which country?
4 Which original Spice Girl had a hit with Bryan Adams?
5 Which Miss Bobb lost one name and took on an eyepatch?
6 Lolly said to Viva to what in 1999?
7 Which Ms Reddy declared "I Am Woman"?
8 Who or what was Prodigal on Beverley Knight's award-winning album?
9 What is the first name of Ms Lennox, once of the Eurythmics?
10 Where were Kylie Minogue's Tears in one of her early hits?
11 Who sang "Say It Again" in the Eurovision Song Contest?
12 Which classic book title by a Bronte sister was a debut hit for Kate Bush?
13 Enya originally belonged to which Irish band?
14 Honeyz' first single was Finally what?
15 Sheryl Crow's first break was singing a jingle for which world-famous fast food chain?
16 Who went solo with "Word Up"?
17 Whose real name is Susan Kay Quatrocchio?
18 What is Marianne Faithfull's real surname?
19 Which Tina teamed up with other girls for Thank Abba for the Music?
20 Which Caribbean island is Gloria Estefan from?

1 How many members were there in Dave Clark's group altogether?
2 Which David celebrated his 50th birthday on January 8, 1997?
3 What are the surnames of Robson and Jerome?
4 Which Life was a 1994 album for Blur?
5 What did Seal call his first two albums?
6 Which Prince were Adam and the Ants in 1981?
7 Which Alison's nickname is Alf?
8 In which part of the day did Starland Vocal Band experience Delight in 1976?
9 Which musical instrument does Richard Clayderman play?
10 Which Elvis Presley home gave Paul Simon an album title?
11 Who had albums in 1988 called *Mistletoe and Wine* and *Private Collection*?
12 What was the first name of the record producer called Most?
13 What was the surname of the Bros twins, Matt and Luke?
14 Which 90s group was made up of Howard, Gary, Jason, Robbie and Mark?
15 What is the home country of Julio Iglesias?
16 Marti Pellow is lead vocalist with which group?
17 Which musical instrument does the veteran musician Bert Weedon play?
18 Which surname is shared by Rolf and Emmylou?
19 Which Barbara was a 60s hit for the Beach Boys?
20 Who was lead singer with T. Rex?

1 "No Regrets" was a hit in 1998 for which singer?
2 In which building was Elvis Crying in 1965?
3 What is the first word of "Torn"?
4 Who had an 80s No. 1 with "La Isla Bonita"?
5 Who sang about the End Of A Century in the middle of the 90s?
6 Who named themselves after Pink Anderson and Floyd Council?
7 What is Marty Wilde's singing daughter called?
8 What sort of Life was a hit album for Sade?
9 Who had a 70s No. 1 with "Angel Fingers"?
10 Which actress was chosen to be Liam Gallagher's first child's godmother?
11 In which decade did Genesis first make the charts?
12 Which word completes the song by Shania Twain, "You're ____ The One"?
13 Who had a 90s No. 1 with "Your Woman"?
14 What Kept Falling on Sacha Distel's Head?
15 What did Sammy Davis put after his name?
16 Who's album *Arrival* featured "Dancing Queen" and "Money, Money, Money"?
17 Which word goes before Of Mine in the song by Eternal?
18 Which Motown star was shot dead by his own father?
19 Which Postman gave Ken Barrie an early 1980s hit?
20 Who had an 80s No. 1 with "I Feel For You"?

Pot Luck 28 (Quiz 54)
1 Pet Shop Boys. 2 Donny Osmond. 3 Mariah Carey. 4 Football.
5 Oleta Adams. 6 Queen. 7 Backstreet Boys. 8 Police. 9 Ladies.
10 Berlin. 11 Billie Myers. 12 George Harrison. 13 Ace Of Base.
14 Kangaroo. 15 Flatley. 16 U2. 17 John Lennon. 18 You.
19 80s. 20 2 Unlimited.

Answers

1 Which city do Oasis come from?
2 Which Gallagher brother was lead vocalist in the mid 90s?
3 With which band was there a media feud to decide on the top BritPop act?
4 What is Paul McGuigan's nickname?
5 How many people were in Oasis when they had their first No. 1 single?
6 What was the band's debut album?
7 What goes in brackets before *Morning Glory* on the album title?
8 Who is the elder of the two Gallagher brothers?
9 Which actress Patsy married Liam in the 90s?
10 Which drug was Liam charged with possession of in 1996?
11 Which football team do the Gallaghers support?
12 What is the nationality of Noel and Liam's parents?
13 What is their mother called?
14 Which musical instrument does Noel play?
15 In which country was a tour cancelled in 1996 when Liam returned home?
16 After which TV pop show did Oasis sack their drummer in 1995?
17 Which Wonder record was a 1995 hit for the band?
18 In 1996, how did Oasis say Don't Look Back?
19 At which Somerset Festival did Oasis perform in front of 30,000 fans in 1994?
20 What goes With It on the record title in 1995?

1 Which Beatles classic was a 1997 hit for Wet Wet Wet?
2 What word described the Ono Band which featured on John's early solo recordings?
3 Give My Regards to which Street was a work by McCartney?
4 What was the name of John's first wife?
5 Which seasonal wish preceded War Is Over on a John and Yoko single?
6 Which Joe shot to fame with "A Little Help From My Friends" in 1968?
7 Free As what was the title of a 1993 "new" recording?
8 In which Japanese city was Paul McCartney convicted of cannabis possession in 1980?
9 Which Motown star did Paul sing "Ebony and Ivory" with?
10 Which line follows the word "Imagine" at the start of the John Lennon classic?
11 Which superstar Michael bought the catalogue of much of Lennon and McCartney's music?
12 Which city gave its name to a McCartney-penned Oratorio?
13 Which Cold Lennon single was about the agonies of drug withdrawal?
14 Which profession did Linda Eastman follow before her marriage to Paul?
15 Which middle name of John Lennon's was taken after a wartime leader?
16 How many sons does Paul have?
17 Which nursery rhyme did McCartney release as a single?
18 How many female performers were there in Wings?
19 What did Lennon say to Give A Chance in his debut single?
20 For which city did McCartney pledge funds to open an Institute for the Performing Arts?

1   Which surname is shared by sisters Janet and LaToya?
2   What was the name of the duet which the soloist who compiled the 1992 album *Diva* left and rejoined at the start and finish of the 90s?
3   Which word goes before "In the Black Forest" and "On the Wild Side" in song titles?
4   What did Eddy Grant Not Wanna do in 1982?
5   Which singer took "Begin The Beguine" into the charts?
6   "Free" was a top ten hit in 1997 for which singer?
7   What is the home country of New Kids on the Block?
8   Which Joe and Jennifer were Up Where We Belong in 1983?
9   What is the singing daughter of Nat King Cole called?
10 Who makes up the trio with Peter and Paul?
11 Who was Adam's backing group?
12 Which Judy Collins record entered the charts an Amazing eight times in the 70s?
13 Which ex-Supreme had a hit every year for 33 years?
14 Which Chameleon hit the top for Culture Club in 1983?
15 Which Nik was a Wide Boy in 1985?
16 What was the home country of Kraftwerk, who had a 1981 No. 1 with "Computer Love"?
17 Which surname is shared by the jazz singer Cleo and the 50s vocalist Frankie?
18 Which son Lennon recorded the album *Valotte*?
19 Who were the Sutherland Brothers in the Arms of in 1976?
20 Who was lead singer with the Doors?

Answers

Pot Luck 25 (Quiz 49)
1 Five. 2 Bowie. 3 Green and Flynn. 4 *Parklife*. 5 They were both called *Seal*.
6 Charming. 7 Moyet. 8 Afternoon. 9 Piano. 10 Graceland.
11 Cliff Richard. 12 Mickie. 13 Goss. 14 Take That. 15 Spain.
16 Wet Wet Wet. 17 Guitar. 18 Harris. 19 Barbara Ann. 20 Marc Bolan.

LEVEL 1

1 In which Boys' video of Heart did Ian McKellen appear?
2 Who had a 70s hit with "Twelfth Of Never"?
3 "My All" was a top three hit for which singer?
4 Spanish star Julio Iglesias used to play which sport?
5 Whose first top ten hit was "Get Here"?
6 Whose first hit was "Seven Seas Of Rhye" in 1974?
7 Who charted in 1998 with "All I Have To Give"?
8 Who made the album *Regatta de Blanc*?
9 What is the first word of "Everybody's Free (To Wear Sunscreen)"?
10 Who had an 80s No. 1 with "Take My Breath Away"?
11 Who had a top five hit in 1998 with "Kiss The Rain"?
12 Which Beatle made *All Things Must Pass* which included "My Sweet Lord"?
13 Who had a 1994 hit with "Don't Turn Around"?
14 Which animal was the subject of Rolf Harris's first ever hit?
15 Which Michael choreographed *Riverdance*?
16 Which group had a 90s No. 1 with "Discotheque"?
17 Who brought the Plastic Ono Band together?
18 Which word completes the song by Boyzone, "Picture Of _____"?
19 In which decade did Everything But The Girl first make the charts?
20 Who had an early 90s hit with "Workaholic"?

Quiz 55 Kids' Stuff

Answers – see page 61

LEVEL 1

1 Which Little Jimmy wanted to be A Long Haired Lover from Liverpool at the age of nine?
2 Which Roses did his 14-year-old sister Marie sing about in 1973?
3 Which 10-year-old Lena took "Ma, He's Making Eyes at Me" to No. 10?
4 Where was the choirboy Aled Jones Walking in 1985?
5 Which Brenda was known as "Little Miss Dynamite"?
6 Which Helen said "Don't Treat Me Like a Child" aged 14 in 1961?
7 Which 15-year-old girl from Glasgow was heard to "Shout" in 1964?
8 Which Stevie was called Little in his early showbiz years?
9 Which late-80s teen group were revamped as NKOTB in 1993?
10 Which Michael first sang with his four brothers at the age of six?
11 Which Mary hit the No. 1 spot with "Those Were the Days" after winning *Opportunity Knocks*?
12 Which Australian teenager had a No. 1 with "I Should Be So Lucky"?
13 To two years either way, how old was Cliff Richard when he had his first hit "Move It" in 1958?
14 Which dancer/singer called Bonnie won *Opportunity Knocks* aged six?
15 Which Donny sang professionally with his brothers from the age of six and had chart success with "Puppy Love" and "Too Young"?
16 Which 17-year-old Sandie had a 60s hit with "Always Something There To Remind Me"?
17 Which Neil wrote "Oh Carol" for Carole Klein, later Carole King, whom he met at high school?
18 Which Genesis drummer called Phil was a former child actor?
19 The kids from which TV dance show had chart success in the 80s?
20 Which girl, later the name of a famous princess, gave 16-year-old Paul Anka chart success in 1957?

1 Madonna hit the charts in 1996 with songs from which movie in which she starred?
2 Which ex-James Bond and Saint appeared in *Spice World The Movie*?
3 Ewan McGregor's opening dialogue from which 1996 movie was included on "Choose Life" with PF Project?
4 Who starred in and sang the theme from *The Bodyguard* – "I Will Always Love You"?
5 Which romantic film with Claire Danes and Leonardo DiCaprio was directed by chart artist Baz Luhrmann?
6 Which Top film did Berlin's "Take My Breath Away" come from?
7 Which colourful film was Prince's first film soundtrack?
8 Which Swedish supergroup's music was used in *Muriel's Wedding*?
9 "Up Where We Belong" was a hit from which movie with Richard Gere?
10 Which singer/actor/drummer played the title role in *Buster*?
11 Which Doors were the subject of a film which Aqua's "Turn Back Time" featured in?
12 Bryan Adams' record-breaking "Everything I Do" was from the movie about which *Prince of Thieves*?
13 Which film featured a north Dublin soul band?
14 In which movie did 911's "More Than A Woman", penned by The Bee Gees, originally appear?
15 Which Busters took Ray Parker Jr into the charts in the 80s?
16 Which hugely successful film used Hot Chocolate's "You Sexy Thing"?
17 Which Perfect song, used later as a charity single was on the soundtrack of *Trainspotting*?
18 1998 was which anniversary of *Grease* and saw a string of re-releases?
19 Which 1997 Bond film provided a chart hit for Sheryl Crow?
20 Which Jim did Val Kilmer play in *The Doors*?

Lennon and McCartney (Quiz 56)
1 "Yesterday". 2 Plastic. 3 Broad Street. 4 Cynthia. 5 Happy Xmas.
6 Cocker. 7 A Bird. 8 Tokyo. 9 Stevie Wonder. 10 There's no heaven.
11 Jackson. 12 Liverpool. 13 Turkey. 14 Photographer. 15 Winston.
16 One. 17 Mary Had A Little Lamb. 18 One. 19 Peace. 20 Liverpool.

1 How many members of Bros were there?
2 Which Family group sang with Limmie in the 70s?
3 What is the home country of Daniel O'Donnell?
4 Which word describes the vocalists Eva and Richard?
5 What type of Love did Love Affair have in 1968?
6 Which People were "Moving On Up" in 1993?
7 Which country does Craig McLachlan come from?
8 Which blonde US singer appeared in the film *Who's That Girl*?
9 Which Street Preachers had a hit with the "Theme from M*A*S*H" in 1992?
10 Which song was a No. 1 for Elvis Presley and UB40?
11 Which Donna and Barbra had chart success in 1979 with "No More Tears (Enough is Enough)"?
12 How many people made up the 80s group Tears For Fears?
13 Why was the No. 1 album called *Walthamstow* very appropriately named for East 17?
14 Which punk group had the soloist who recorded *Sid Sings* left?
15 How many Seasons were in the group that sang "Rag Doll"?
16 Which group takes its name from an Unemployment Benefit card?
17 How is the Irishman Raymond Edward O'Sullivan better known?
18 Which surname is shared by Tom and Aled?
19 Who was Clyde's co-gangster on Georgie Fame's 60s Ballad?
20 Which Johnson was lead singer with Frankie Goes to Hollywood?

Quiz 58 Pot Luck 30

Answers – see page 72

LEVEL 1

1   "Sweetest Thing" was a 90s top three hit for which group?
2   Simply Red and The Cardigans both made albums called what?
3   Boney M sang about which Russian character?
4   Who had a 90s No. 1 with "Words"?
5   What is the first word of "Turn Back Time"?
6   What was Sugar Coated in the title of the 1997 hit from The Lightning Seeds?
7   Who had a US No. 1 with "I'll Make Love To You"?
8   Who had a 70s No. 1 with "Space Oddity"?
9   Which Billy, famous for his politics and his music, made Back To Basics?
10 Which two words describe Little Richard's Sally?
11 Which David co-wrote the football anthem "Three Lions"?
12 According to the football anthem, what will you Never Alone?
13 Whose first film was A Hard Day's Night?
14 Who first sang the perennial favourite White Christmas?
15 Whose best-selling 70s album *Tapestry* was out again in the 90s?
16 What went with Diamonds on the title of Prince's 1991 album?
17 Which decade was Cliff Richard born in?
18 What sort of Dancing became a top film soundtrack?
19 Which word follows You Get What You in the song by the New Radicals?
20 How many members of Police were there?

Answers

Pot Luck 32 (Quiz 62)
1 Dina Carroll.   2 "Bat Out Of Hell II".   3 Thin.   4 I've.   5 Paper Lace.
6 Rules.   7 Shirley Bassey.   8 Val Kilmer.   9 Prodigy.   10 *The Lion King*.
11 Lifetime.   12 The White Album.   13 Father.   14 Plane crash.   15 80s.
16 Cline.   17 "We Are The World".   18 Australia.   19 Lancashire.
20 Cliff Richard.

1   Which musical instrument does Ray Charles play?
2   Which Motown star's real name is Steveland Judkins?
3   Which Dionne had a hit with "Walk on By" in 1964 and "Heartbreaker" 18 years later?
4   Who completed the Holland, Dozier trio who wrote many of the Motown hits of the 60s and 70s?
5   Which major all-male Tamla Motown group recorded "I'm Gonna Make You Love Me" with Diana Ross and the Supremes?
6   Which Baby gave the Supremes their first No. 1?
7   Who sang "Endless Love" with Diana Ross in 1981?
8   Which letters took the Jackson Five into the Top Ten in 1970?
9   What did Michael Jackson say to his Summer Love in 1984?
10 Which Marvin was Too Busy Thinking 'Bout his Baby in 1969?
11 Which Queen is Aretha Franklin known as?
12 Which Four were Standing In The Shadows Of Love in 1967?
13 Which Brothers charted with "This Old Heart Of Mine" in 1966 and 1968?
14 Which James was "Living in America" in 1986?
15 How were Martha Reeves and the Vandellas billed on their first Motown hits?
16 Who was Smokey Robinson's backing group?
17 How were Gladys Knight's brother Merald and cousins Edward and William known as collectively?
18 At the start of which decade did Berry Gordy set up the Tamla label?
19 Which Jackie recorded "Reet Petite" in 1957?
20 In which US city did Motown begin?

Answers

Novelty Songs (Quiz 63)
1 "Mr Blobby".   2 The Goodies.   3 John Kettley.   4 Abbott.   5 Keith Harris.
6 Terry Wogan.   7 Harry Enfield.   8 19.   9 Julian Clary.   10 Ernie.
11 Rolf Harris.   12 Woolpackers.   13 Billy Connolly.   14 Dudley Moore.
15 Elephant.   16 Snooker players.   17 Combine Harvester.   18 Roland Rat.
19 The Smurfs.   20 Dave Lee Travis.

LEVEL 1

1 Which line follows, "I'm dreaming of a white Christmas" at the start of the song?
2 Who spent Christmas in Blobbyland in 1995?
3 According to the Jackson Five in 1975 who was coming to town?
4 Who's Day was an Christmas No. 1 for Cliff Richard in 1990?
5 Which 90s knight sang "Step Into Christmas" in 1973?
6 Which Tale did David Essex take into the charts in the 80s?
7 Which Welshman first sang "Merry Christmas Everyone" in 1985?
8 Which animated film had "Walking In The Air" as its theme?
9 In the Christmas classic, what nuts are roasting on an open fire when Jack Frost is nipping at your nose?
10 What was on the other side of Queen's "These Are The Days Of Our Lives" in 1991?
11 In 1988, how was Chris Rea travelling Home for Christmas?
12 What did 2 Become in the Spice Girls Christmas hit?
13 What was Band Aid's Christmas No. 1 in 1984 and 1989?
14 Which Song took Michael Jackson up the Christmas charts in 1995?
15 What colour was Elvis Presley's Christmas in 1964?
16 "Knockin On Heaven's Door"/"Throw These Guns Away" was a success over Christmas in the wake of which tragedy?
17 Which Little animal first entered the charts in 1959?
18 What went with Wine on Cliff Richard's 1988 Xmas No. 1?
19 Which incoherent quartet said "Eh Oh" in 1997?
20 Which duo sang about "Last Christmas" in the mid-80s?

1 Which surname is shared by Carole, Ben E. and B.B.?
2 Who has albums called *Bad* and *Dangerous*?
3 Which Caribbean island was Bob Marley from?
4 Which Neil added his name to Crosby, Stills and Nash in 1970?
5 Which Rita was married for six years to Kris Kristofferson?
6 Where were there Tears on Eric Clapton's 1990s single?
7 How are the duo Charles Hodges and Dave Peacock better known?
8 Which 70s group's name was abbreviated to AWB?
9 Which Marc once described himself as "The Acid House Aznavour"?
10 Which clothes were Swinging on the Hippy Hippy Shake in 1963?
11 Who sang with Ant on "When I Fall In Love"?
12 Which Luther duetted with Mariah Carey on "Endless Love"?
13 Which band took its name from the acronym for Rapid Eye Movement?
14 How did the soul singer Otis Redding meet his early death?
15 Who had a hit with "Strangers In the Night" in 1966?
16 How many Pet Shop Boys were there?
17 How did Madonna describe Jessie on her 1989 hit?
18 Who was lead singer with the Commodores?
19 What is the home country of Gilbert O'Sullivan?
20 How is Elaine Bikerstaff better known?

1   Who had a top three hit with "Escaping" in 1996?
2   What was the follow-up to Meat Loaf's "Bat Out Of Hell"?
3   What would be the most obvious charateristic of the group Lizzy which charted with "Whiskey In The Jar"?
4   What is the first word of "That Don't Impress Me Much"?
5   Who had a 70s No. 1 with "Billy Don't Be A Hero"?
6   Livin' Joy sang Follow The what in 96?
7   Who sang the Bond theme song for *Moonraker*?
8   Who played Jim Morrison in the rock movie *The Doors*?
9   In 1997, who wanted to "Smack My Bitch Up"?
10   Which King did Messrs John and Rice write songs about?
11   Which word follows In Our in the song by Texas?
12   Which Beatles album is known by the colour of its cover?
13   Which relative did LL Cool J take into the 1998 charts?
14   How did Buddy Holly meet his death?
15   In which decade did Frankie Goes To Hollywood first make the charts?
16   Which Patsy was the first female soloist to be inducted into the Country Music Hall of Fame?
17   What was the title of the USA For Africa's charity record?
18   Gina G represented the UK at Eurovision but which country is she from?
19   What is Lisa Stanstfield's home county?
20   Who had a 70s No. 1 with "We Don't Talk Anymore"?

1   What was Mr Blobby's first No. 1 hit called?
2   Dr Graeme Garden was part of which comedy trio which had hits in the 1970s?
3   Which Weatherman was immortalized in song by Tribe of Toffs in '88?
4   Which Russ spread some Atmosphere in 1984?
5   Who helped Orville to sing "Orville's Song"?
6   Which Irish DJ performed a Floral Dance on disc?
7   Who had Loadsamoney in 1988?
8   Which number was important for Paul Hardcastle in 1985?
9   Who or what was the Joan Collins Fan Club, a 1988 chart entrant?
10 What was the name of Benny Hill's "Fastest Milkman in the West"?
11 Which Australian has charted with a didgeridoo?
12 Which Packers danced a Hillbilly Rock in 1996?
13 Which Scots comedian filed for D.I.V.O.R.C.E. in 1975?
14 Who said "Goodbye-ee" with Peter Cook in 1965?
15 What type of animal was Nellie, who took the Toy Dolls to No. 4 in the charts in 1984?
16 Which type of sportsmen made up the Matchroom Mob with Chas and Dave in 1986?
17 Which piece of farm equipment gave the Wurzels a No. 1 to "Brand New Key" in 1976?
18 Which Superstar was Rat Rapping in 1983?
19 Which cartoon characters lost Father Abraham from the 70s and refound chart success in 1996?
20 Which bearded DJ joined Paul Burnett to become Laurie Lingo and the Dipsticks?

Quiz 64 All Time Greats

Answers – see page 70

LEVEL 1

1 What was Whitney Houston's first UK No. 1?

2 Who had a 90s No. 1 with "Think Twice"?

3 In which decade was "You Sexy Thing" first released?

4 What is the first word of the classic Beatles song "Yesterday"?

5 Which painter gave Don McLean a huge hit?

6 Who wrote and sang the original version of "She"?

7 Who had an 80s No. 1 with "Hello"?

8 According to Cher, "If you want to know if he loves you so, It's in his…" what?

9 Who cut the soulful track "When A Man Loves A Woman"?

10 Which pop classic contains, "Any way the wind blows, Nothing Really Matters"?

11 Who took "Earth Song" to No. 1?

12 What were Elvis's shoes made out of in his 50s hit?

13 Which Soft Cell hit of 81 was back in the charts in 91?

14 Which Jackie Wilson song gave him a posthumous No. 1 in the 80s?

15 Who sang "You're So Vain"?

16 Which much-recorded song gave Sybil and Gabrielle hits in the 90s?

17 Which hit begins, "I feel it in my fingers, I feel it in my toes"?

18 "Albatross" was the big-selling instrumental from which band?

19 Who had a 90s No. 1 with "How Deep Is Your Love"?

20 In which song does Sinatra go "Do Be Doo Be Doo, Doo Be Doo Doo Be…"?

1 How many members were there in Dave Dee's group altogether?
2 Which *Cabaret* star had a 70s album called *Liza With a "Z"*?
3 What is the home country of Prince?
4 Where did Ben E. King say to Stand in 1961 and again in 1987?
5 Which Charles Aznavour hit contained just three letters?
6 What was Blondie's Heart made of on their 70s single?
7 Which Irish group includes the vocalist Ronan Keating?
8 Which musical instrument is the jazzman Buddy Rich famous for?
9 Which Reddy Australian is best remembered for "I Am Woman"?
10 Which former Radio 1 DJ is nicknamed Ginger?
11 How did Neil Sedaka describe Breaking Up in 1962 and 1976?
12 Which zodiac sign first name did Gerald Hugh Sayer adopt?
13 Which Four had Frankie Valli as their lead singer?
14 Which Images sang "Happy Birthday" and "I Could Be Happy"?
15 Which 60s musical creatures included Eric Burdon and Alan Price?
16 Which Midlands city does Jasper Carrott come from?
17 How did the 6' 7" tall singer John Baldry describe himself?
18 Which group did Bob Geldof and Midge Ure found to raise money to combat famine in Africa?
19 Which Tori was a "Cornflake Girl" in 1994?
20 Which surname is shared by the rocker Jerry Lee and Huey?

1 What is the first word of "Dr Jones"?
2 Which actor Robert was waiting in the song by Bananarama?
3 Who made the album Alf, taken from her nickname?
4 Who had a 70s No. 1 with "D.I.V.O.R.C.E".?
5 Which word completes the song by Ocean Colour Scene, "The _____ Song"?
6 Which Mr Fuller was sacked by the Spice Girls at the height of their fame?
7 Space thought it was Me And You Versus The what?
8 What was Rod Stewart Crossing on the title of his 70s album?
9 Which Sarah was Andrew Lloyd-Webber's second wife?
10 Who had a 90s No. 1 with "Killing Me Softly"?
11 Which word goes after End Of The in the song by the Honeyz?
12 Which part of the UK do Wet Wet Wet come from?
13 Whose "(Sittin' On) The Dock Of the Bay" charted after his death?
14 Which word goes before Really Matters in the song by Madonna?
15 Who had an 80s No. 1 with "Caravan Of Love"?
16 Which first name did singer and guitarist Charles Edward Anderson Berry take?
17 Who had a 70s No. 1 with "Can't Give You Anything (But My Love)"?
18 "Crush On You" was a debut hit for which singer?
19 Which solo star made the album *Delilah*?
20 Semisonic sang about a Secret what?

LEVEL 1

1   Which city did the Beatles come from?
2   Which Beatle's real name was Richard Starkey?
3   Which guitarist was left-handed?
4   What did the Beatles Want to Hold in their third No. 1 of 1963?
5   Which Brian was the Beatles' manager until his death in 1967?
6   What type of Writer was the subject of a song in 1966?
7   Which club in the Beatles' home town is linked with their success?
8   What kind of Band did Sgt Pepper have?
9   Which is the most-recorded Beatles song of all time?
10 Which Beatles LP title was the name of a gun?
11 Which fruit was the Beatles' own record label?
12 What was the Beatles' second film?
13 Which Japanese artist did John Lennon marry?
14 In which city was John Lennon murdered?
15 Which Yellow craft was the subject of a single and album?
16 Which song has "Yeah, yeah, yeah" at the end of each chorus line?
17 Which Tripper could be found on the other side of "We Can Work it Out"?
18 In which European country did the Beatles work before finding fame in the UK?
19 According to their 1964 No. 1 Money Can't Buy Me what?
20 Which Beatle played lead guitar?

1　What's the first word in the title of Billie's first No. 1?
2　What was left On The Dance Floor according to Michael Jackson?
3　Who featured on Melanie B's first No. 1?
4　Who was the subject of "Candle In The Wind", 1997?
5　What was the first No. 1 for Cornershop?
6　"All That She Wants" made No. 1 for which band?
7　What type of Love was George Michael into in 1996?
8　What was Mr Blobby's first No. 1 called?
9　Which song took Right Said Fred to the top of the charts?
10　The 1996 anthem told you there were how many lions on an England shirt?
11　What was East 17's first No. 1 called?
12　Which song originally recorded by The Troggs made it big in 1994?
13　What took Andrew Davis, the BBC Symphony Orchestra – and a few others – to No. 1?
14　Who had a 90s No. 1 with Abba in the title?
15　What was the Spice Girls 1998 Christmas No. 1?
16　Which song starts, "As I walk this land of broken dreams…"?
17　Who did Faith Evans team up with to reach No. 1?
18　Which doctor did Aqua sing about?
19　What was the TV ad-linked No. 1 of The Steve Miller Band?
20　"Girlfriend" was the second solo No. 1 for who?

Quiz 69 Pot Luck 35

Answers – see page 75

 LEVEL 1

1 How is David Solberg better known?
2 Which surname is shared by Martha of the Vandellas and the late country star Jim?
3 Whose 1993 album was called *Bat Out Of Hell II*?
4 Which Midlands city does Joan Armatrading come from?
5 Which Boys included three members of the Wilson family?
6 Which musical instrument does Jeff Beck play?
7 Who had a No. 1 with "Under The Moon Of Love"?
8 Who was Gloria Estefan's backing group?
9 What is the home country of Sheena Easton?
10 Who is Bon Jovi's lead vocalist?
11 Which zany TV Timmy joined Bombalurina on "Seven Little Girls Sitting in the Backseat" in 1990?
12 Which Boy's autobiography was called *Take It Like A Man*?
13 Which Emily Brontë novel inspired Kate Bush's 1978 No. 1?
14 What colour did Stevie Wonder's Woman wear in 1984?
15 What went with Powder and Paint on Shakin' Stevens's 1985 hit?
16 Pete Townshend and Keith Moon were members of which group?
17 Which 80s duo was Andrew Ridgeley part of?
18 Which part of the UK do Wet Wet Wet come from?
19 Which brothers wrote Dionne Warwick's 1982 hit "Heartbreaker"?
20 Which first name did the singer/guitarist Charles Edward Anderson Berry take?

LEVEL 1

1 Mulder and Scully was a hit for which group?
2 With whom did Tina Turner first chart with the classic "River Deep Mountain High"?
3 Who had a number two hit with Tubthumping?
4 Stevie Wonder's 1976 album was Songs In The Key of what?
5 Who released the single "Killer Queen"?
6 Who had a 70s No. 1 with "Ms Grace"?
7 Which song took Rolf Harris back into the charts in the 90s?
8 Whose *Unplugged* album in 1993 led the trend for acoustic recordings of old favourites?
9 What goes before Clearwater Revival in a group name?
10 New Order bass guitarist Peter Hook was married which comedian Caroline famous for her Mrs Merton alter ego?
11 Who had a 90s No. 1 with "Spaceman"?
12 Who first sang "Ba-Ba-Ba-Ba-Barbara Ann"?
13 In which decade did Guns 'N' Roses first make the charts?
14 What was the first word of Jimi Hendrix's "Purple Haze"?
15 "If I Never See You Again" was a top ten hit in 1997 for which group?
16 In the Gene Vincent classic what goes before A-Lula?
17 Which actor Steve was the title of an album from Prefab Sprout?
18 Who had a 70s No. 1 with "Fernando"?
19 How many members of The Eurythmics were there?
20 What is the name of Elvis's daughter?

1 Which group was Marc Bolan associated with?
2 Which Janis died in Hollywood in 1970?
3 Who won an award for his classic hit "Pretty Woman" after his death?
4 Whose death triggered "Bohemian Rhapsody"/"These Are the Days of Our Lives" entering the charts at No. 1?
5 How did Buddy Holly meet his death?
6 Which Big star died at the same time as Buddy Holly?
7 Which live recording of a Frank Sinatra classic went into the top ten for Elvis Presley in January 1978?
8 Kurt Cobain was a member of which band?
9 Which famous Liverpudlian was murdered outside his New York flat?
10 Which musical instrument did Jimi Hendrix play?
11 Which Patsy became the first female solo performer to be inducted into the Country Music Hall of Fame?
12 Whose first Top Ten hit, "(Sittin' On) The Dock of the Bay" charted after his death?
13 Who was without his first name Harry when he sang "Without You"?
14 Which was the most famous group Mama Cass was a member of?
15 Which Rolling Stone died in 1969?
16 Whose pioneering rock 'n' roll career came to an end in 1981 after selling more than 60 million discs Round the Clock?
17 Which soul singer Marvin was shot by his own father?
18 Which highly successful female Motown group was the late Florence Ballard a member of?
19 Which band did Sid Vicious belong to?
20 Which Small group were fronted by the late Steve Marriott?

1 Which lady sang "I Wanna Dance With Somebody (Who Loves Me)"?
2 The movie that helped give Bryan Adams his biggest hit was about which character?
3 Who wrote the classic, "Imagine"?
4 Who sang lead vocals on "Bohemian Rhapsody"?
5 Under what name did a group of artists perform a charity version of "You'll Never Walk Alone"?
6 Who had an 80s No. 1 with "Dancing In The Street" with Mick Jagger?
7 Which Wings hit mentions "Mist Rolling In From The Sea"?
8 In which decade did Bill Haley first "Rock Around The Clock"?
9 Who had a big 80s No. 1 with "It's A Sin"?
10 Who appeared with Cliff Richard the second time that "Living Doll" was No. 1?
11 Who checked into "Heartbreak Hotel"?
12 Who had an 80s smash with "Who's That Girl"?
13 Which Don McLean song talks about "the day the music died"?
14 Who had an 80s No. 1 with "La Bamba"?
15 Which song based on biblical quotes was a 2 million seller for Boney M?
16 Who wrote "Let It Be"?
17 Who recorded "Two Tribes"?
18 Who had an 80s No. 1 with "Careless Whisper"?
19 Who sang "I Just Called To Say I Love You"?
20 In the 80s who was playing the "Pipes Of Peace"?

1 What is the home country of Rolf Harris?
2 How many members of the Eurythmics were there?
3 Who was lead singer with the Boomtown Rats?
4 Which Toni was heard to Breathe Again in 1994?
5 What goes before "A-Lula" on the Gene Vincent classic?
6 In which branch of the armed services were the Village People in 1979?
7 How did Bobby Velline reduce his surname when he had chart success in the 50s?
8 Which American band was inspired by the all-UK Band Aid?
9 What sort of Dancer is Tina Turner on her first solo album?
10 How many members made up Tyrannosaurus Rex?
11 Which 70s star recorded the classic album *Sweet Baby James*?
12 Which Glen was a Rhinestone Cowboy?
13 Which Tracy made a memorable appearance at the Nelson Mandela 70th Birthday Tribute Concert at Wembley in 1988?
14 How was Salvatore Bono better known?
15 Which country are the Chieftains from?
16 For which war children did Luciano Pavarotti perform benefit concerts in the mid-1990s ?
17 Which musical instrument does James Galway play?
18 What did Connie Francis see On Your Collar in 1959?
19 Which surname is shared by sisters Kylie and Dannii?
20 Which Eric has been part of Cream and Derek and the Dominoes?

Quiz 74 Pot Luck 38

Answers – see page 88

1 Who had an 80s No. 1 with "Respectable"?
2 Anita Dobson had a chart hit after starring in which soap?
3 "Try Me Out" was a 90s hit for which female singer?
4 Which Johnny is known as The Man In Black?
5 Who had a 70s No. 1 with "The Streak"?
6 Which member of Cilla Black's family was her long-time manager?
7 Which Enya hit is subtitled "Sail Away"?
8 Which comic Ken topped the charts for six weeks in the middle of the Swinging 60s?
9 What is the first word of "Tubthumping" by Chumbawamba?
10 Which film about the Great Train Robbery starred Phil Collins?
11 Simply Red took their name from which soccer side?
12 Who had a mega dance hit in the 70s with "Rivers Of Babylon"?
13 Which word completes the song by Oasis, "Stand ___ Me"?
14 Which singer had a 90s No. 1 with "I Feel You"?
15 Which relatives were Kissin' in an Elvis hit of the 60s?
16 "Up And Down" was a hit for which act in 1998?
17 Which word goes before Days in the song by Robbie Williams?
18 Who were Bill Haley's backing group?
19 Who had a 70s hit with "I Have A Dream"?
20 Which singer's surname is Ciccone?

1 Who sang "The Shoop Shoop Song" in 1990?
2 Which group wrote the music for *Saturday Night Fever*?
3 Which hero was the subject of the film for which Bryan Adams sang "(Everything I Do) I Do It For You"?
4 Who sang "Ben" from the film about a rat?
5 Which Meg Ryan/Billy Crystal film's songs were sung by Harry Connick Jr?
6 Who appeared in and had hits with songs from *Grease* and *Xanadu*?
7 Which Dire Straits guitarist played "Going Home" from *Local Hero*?
8 What was or were Falling On My Head in the theme music from *Butch Cassidy And The Sundance Kid*?
9 In which Lloyd Webber film did Madonna play the title role?
10 Which 1981 film starring Dudley Moore, Liza Minnelli and John Gielgud had a Theme sung by Christopher Cross?
11 Who sang "Love Is All Around" from *Four Weddings And A Funeral*?
12 Whose first film was *A Hard Day's Night*?
13 Which Welsh-born female vocalist had a hit with "Goldfinger"?
14 Which film about the 1924 Paris Olympics won an Oscar for the composer Vangelis?
15 Which classic film with Humphrey Bogart and Ingrid Bergman includes the song "As Time Goes By"?
16 Which duo sang "Mrs Robinson" from *The Graduate* in 1968?
17 Who Does It Better according to Carly Simon from *The Spy Who Loved Me*?
18 Which creatures were the subject of the film *Born Free*?
19 Which Disney film does "Circle of Life" come from?
20 Who was Forever in the film to which Seal sang the theme song?

Answers

Cliff Richard (Quiz 79)
1 Harry Webb. 2 India. 3 The Shadows. 4 *Summer Holiday*. 5 Wimbledon.
6 "Congratulations". 7 Knighthood. 8 *Heathcliff*. 9 Livin'.
10 "Bachelor Boy". 11 Mistletoe. 12 Sue Barker. 13 Twelfth. 14 Hello.
15 Sarah Brightman. 16 Newton-John. 17 Saviour's. 18 "Move It".
19 Lips. 20 Phil.

1 Which numerical group had the album There It Is?
2 Which *Carry On Up* title was a Best Of album from The Beautiful South?
3 Whose *Cream Of* album included "Layla" and "I Shot The Sheriff"?
4 Which 1999 album by James suggests their earlier albums made them very rich?
5 Whose best of album was called The Nail File?
6 Which Tree was the title of an epic album by U2?
7 Whose *Gold* album included "Mamma Mia" and "Knowing Me Knowing You"?
8 Charlotte Church had the voice of what according to the title of her debut album?
9 Which George Michael album is a Best Of compilation for both sexes?
10 Which initial was Kula Shaker's initial album?
11 What were Status Quo Under in the title of their 1999 album?
12 What did Steps call their first album?
13 Which superstar recorded *The Big Picture* which included "Something About The Way You Look Tonight"?
14 Whose album *Woman In Me* featured her successful "Arms Around The World"?
15 Which sweet substance is in the title of Billie's debut album?
16 Which Peter released the album *Time* in the 90s?
17 What sort of Waters were an album title for The Bee Gees?
18 What sort of dance was the subject of an album by Bill Whelan?
19 Which Scandinavian group had the album *Aquarium*?
20 Which Michelle from EastEnders had the album *Sensational*?

LEVEL 1

1 Which surname is shared by Rick, Sandy and Willie?
2 What is the home country of Sinead O'Connor?
3 Which Eric was *Unplugged* in 1993?
4 Which instrument did Dave Clark play?
5 How are Reginald Smith and his daughter Kim better known?
6 Who was Diana Ross's backing group?
7 Which city are the Hollies from?
8 How many Degrees were in the group which sang "When Will I See You Again?"?
9 Which fruity band's first album was *Everybody Else is Doing It, So Why Can't We?*?
10 Which showbiz veteran recorded the Singalonga series of albums?
11 Who has won Grammy awards for "I Left My Heart in San Francisco" 32 years apart?
12 What sort of Moon was Rising for Creedence Clearwater Revival in 1969?
13 Which Phil was record producer for the Crystals?
14 Which record labels were founded by Richard Branson?
15 Which Cat's debut single was "I Love My Dog"?
16 What sort of Life was a debut album for Sade?
17 Whose real name is Sealhenry Samuel?
18 Which musical instrument does Neil Sedaka play?
19 Which group's members have included Hank Marvin and Brian Bennett?
20 Which nautical chief joined Tennille on disc?

1   Whose real name is Eric Clapp?
2   Who had a 70s No. 1 with "Sugar Baby Love"?
3   Who recorded his *Graceland* album?
4   Who had a No. 1 with "The Power'
5   Which colour Roses feature in Jimmy Nail's 1997 single?
6   Which Dani presented The Word?
7   What is the first word of "Frozen" by Madonna?
8   Which word goes before "I Fall In Love" and "A Child Is Born" to complete song titles?
9   What's the weight description word used in the name of Twister Mr Checker?
10 Who had an 80s No. 1 with "Every Loser Wins"?
11 What follows "Cooley High" on the debut album of Boyz II Men?
12 In which decade did U2 first make the charts?
13 Back in the 50s which solo superstar made the classic "Songs For Swingin' Lovers"?
14 What was the name of Billie's first No. 1?
15 Who were doing a "Tribal Dance" in 1993?
16 Which football side had a No. 1 in 1994 with "Come On You Reds"?
17 Which musical instrument does Vanessa-Mae play?
18 What is the home country of Jason Donovan?
19 Which group did Dusty Springfield leave to go solo?
20 Which No. 1 artist was very tall, pink and covered in yellow spots?

1   What is Cliff Richard's real name?
2   In which country was he born?
3   What was the name of his backing group, which included Bruce Welch?
4   In which film did Cliff head for the continent on a London Transport bus?
5   In 1996 where did Cliff give a concert with Martina Navratilova and Virginia Wade in his backing group?
6   Cliff came second with which song in the 1968 Eurovision Song Contest?
7   Which award did Cliff receive from the Queen in 1995?
8   In which musical based on a novel by Emily Brontë did Cliff play the title role?
9   With what type of Doll did Cliff chart accompanied by The Shadows and then the Young Ones?
10 Which 60s hit began with "When I was young my father said ..."?
11 What features in the title with Wine on Cliff's Christmas No. 1 in 1988?
12 Which blonde tennis star had her name linked with Cliff in the 80s?
13 What date of Never was a hit for Cliff in 1964?
14 What did Cliff say to Samantha when he said Goodbye to Sam?
15 Which wife of Andrew Lloyd-Webber did Cliff duet with in "All I Ask Of You" from *Phantom of the Opera*?
16 Which Olivia sang with Cliff on "Suddenly" and "Had To Be"?
17 Whose Day was the Christmas No. 1 in 1990?
18 What was Cliff's first hit single?
19 Which part of Cliff was Lucky in the title of his 1964 hit?
20 Which Everly did Cliff duet with in "She Means Nothing to Me"?

Quiz 80 Cher

Answers – see page 86

LEVEL 1

1 In which country was Cher born?
2 Which song is subtitled "It's In His Kiss"?
3 Who were with the Tramps and Thieves on Cher's solo hit from 1971?
4 Which Eric featured on "Love Can Build A Bridge"?
5 Who sang with Cher on "I Got You Babe"?
6 Which film about sea creatures gave her a No. 1 hit with "The Shoop Shoop Song"?
7 A 1990 hit was Just Like which outlaw?
8 Which Cher song was the top-selling single of 1998?
9 What does Love do in the title of her 90s single and album?
10 What was the Heart made from in the album title from 1989?
11 In what type of accident did ex-husband Sonny die?
12 Which number features in a hit single title from 1995?
13 Which cartoon characters sang "I Got You Babe" with Cher in 1994?
14 What were there Many To Cross in 1993?
15 How was her double act with her first husband known?
16 Which film that Cher appeared in is also the name of her daughter?
17 What went before "My Baby Shot Me Down" in the title of her first solo million seller?
18 What was the name of the album "Believe" came from?
19 Which Chrissie sang on "Love Can Build A Bridge"?
20 Which member of The Allman Brothers band was Cher's second husband?

Answers

Novelty Songs (Quiz 76)
1 911. **2** The Charts. **3** Eric Clapton. **4** Millionaires. **5** Jimmy Nail. **6** *The Joshua Tree.* **7** Abba. **8** Angel. **9** *Ladies & Gentlemen.* **10** K. **11** The Influence. **12** *Step One.* **13** Elton John. **14** Louise. **15** Honey. **16** Andre. **17** Still. **18** *Riverdance.* **19** Aqua. **20** Gayle.

Answers – see page 95

LEVEL 1

1   Which surname is shared by Elvis and Reg?
2   How many Seasons were there?
3   Which Helen held the record for making more than 12 radio and TV appearances before the age of 15 in 1961?
4   Which barefoot pop star's autobiography was called *The World At My Feet*?
5   What was Tina Turner's first husband called?
6   What is the home country of Daniel O'Donnell?
7   Whose second solo album was called *There Goes Rhymin' Simon*?
8   Which music paper is often abbreviated to *NME*?
9   Which football team does Simply Red's Mick Hucknall support?
10 Which Midlands town do Slade originate from?
11 Which Family group backed Sly?
12 Who makes up the trio with Stock and Aitken?
13 What is the home country of Shirley Bassey?
14 Which East End gangsters did Spandau Ballet's Kemp twins portray on film?
15 Which band were Rockin' All Over the World in 1977?
16 What was Sting's profession before he entered show business?
17 What do the letters CD stand for?
18 Who started out as the Guildford Stranglers?
19 Which Paul links the Style Council and the Jam?
20 What is Art short for in Art Garfunkel's name?

LEVEL 1

1   Who had an 80s No. 1 with "The Sun Always Shines On TV"?
2   Who was Noel Gallagher talking about in saying he hoped two of its members would die of AIDS?
3   Whose first UK hit was "(They Long to Be) Close To You"?
4   Which word completes the song by James, "I Know What I'm _____ For"?
5   Which song was a No. 1 for both Rosemary Clooney and Shakin' Stevens?
6   Which Gary was dubbed the King of Glam Rock?
7   Which Fern sang "Together We Are Beautiful"?
8   Who had a 90s No. 1 with "Dub Be Good To Me"?
9   What is the first word of "Witchdoctor" by The Cartoons?
10 Nancy Spungen was the girlfriend of a member of which group?
11 Which TV star Michael starred in the musical *Barnum*?
12 Who had an 80s No. 1 with "West End Girls"?
13 Whose *Bridge Over Troubled Water* album became one of the all time best-sellers?
14 In 1996 Technohead declared I Wanna Be A what?
15 Who were Eric Clapton's backing group when he recorded under the name Derek?
16 What separated The Good from The Ugly in the movie title and chart-topping theme music?
17 Whose Midnight Runners were popular in the 1980s?
18 Who was Jumpin' in a hit for both The Rolling Stones and Aretha Franklin?
19 Who had a 90s No. 1 with "Should I Stay Or Should I Go"?
20 Which record label did The Four Tops record their 60s hits on?

1   The TV series *Heartbeat* features music from which decade?
2   In which TV series did Robson and Jerome find fame?
3   Which TV soap do the Woolpackers come from?
4   Which long-running pop show began on January 1, 1964?
5   For which TV programme did Dennis Waterman sing "I Could Be So Good For You"?
6   Which environmentalists sang their songs on Wimbledon Common?
7   Which company used Marvin Gaye's "I Heard It Through The Grapevine" to advertise their jeans?
8   Which Irish band provided the "Theme from Harry's Game" and "Robin (The Hooded Man)"?
9   Which TV series starring Don Johnson as Crockett gave Jan Hammer his first UK chart success with its theme tune?
10 Whose Crocodile Shoes entered the charts in 1994?
11 Which "EastEnders" landlady was played by Anita Dobson, who charted with "Anyone Can Fall In Love" in 1986?
12 Which TV show was introduced by Jools Holland and Paula Yates?
13 How was Charlene Mitchell better known in the pop charts?
14 Which singer Maguire played Aidan in *EastEnders*?
15 Which medical series theme was bracket-titled "Suicide Is Painless"?
16 Which two TV series have taken Nick Berry into the charts?
17 Which show asked a panel of four to judge a record a hit or a miss?
18 Which theme music from a series about a boatyard did Marti Webb record as "Always There"?
19 On which TV channel is the Eurovision Song Contest broadcast?
20 Which puppets hit the top of the charts with "The Chicken Song"?

Answers

All-Girl Groups (Quiz 87)
1 Spice.   2 Nolans.   3 Eternal.   4 The Bangles.   5 Three.   6 Shakespear's.
7 Three.   8 Ronettes.   9 The Supremes.   10 2 Wilsons, 1 Phillips.
11 "Da Doo".   12 Love.   13 Reeves.   14 Yes.   15 Salt.   16 Of The Pack.
17 Sledge.   18 The Judds.   19 Spice Girls.   20 The Ronettes.

1 Which solo singer sold more records than Elvis throughout the 20th century?
2 What type of Dog was a 1956 UK top ten hit?
3 Where was Elvis Crying in 1965?
4 What was the first name of Colonel Parker, Elvis's manager?
5 Which colour featured on two early Elvis hits, one referring to a planet, the other to footwear?
6 What was his Heart not made of in 1961?
7 Which Hotel gave Elvis his first UK hit?
8 *GI Blues* and *King Creole* were albums linked to what?
9 Which US state was Blue in the title of a 60s album?
10 Which cuddly toy was the title of an Elvis hit from 1957?
11 Elvis wore what type of uniform on the album *King Creole*?
12 What was the name of Elvis's mansion where he died?
13 Where did Elvis Rock behind bars in 1958?
14 Which song's second line was "address unknown"?
15 Who was In Disguise in 1963?
16 Which town followed Viva in the 1964 movie?
17 Which Royal title was Elvis nicknamed?
18 "Wooden Heart" was partly sung in which language, reflecting where Elvis was stationed in the army?
19 Which Trilogy included the US national anthem?
20 In which soap did Elvis's ex-wife star?

1 Who has had albums called *Complete Madness* and *Divine Madness*?
2 Which John's album chart debut was *Rocky Mountain High*?
3 In which language other than English did Celine Dion record in the 80s?
4 Which showbiz first name did Anthony James Donegan adopt?
5 Who was backed by the Blockheads?
6 Which TV pop show sounded like the start of a race?
7 How is Annie-Mae Bullock better known?
8 Which instrument does Bob Dylan play other than guitar?
9 Which group did Tony Orlando lead?
10 What is the home country of Van Morrison?
11 Which song has been a No. 1 for Tommy Roe and Vic Reeves?
12 What were Dolly Parton's working hours in 1981?
13 Which Rose shares her surname with part of the name of a car?
14 Which British group had to change its name from the Drifters because of the existence of the US group?
15 Who left Clannad and had her first solo single in 1988?
16 Which actor/singer was born David Cook in Plaistow?
17 Which Caribbean island is Gloria Estefan originally from?
18 Who was the female singer of the Eurythmics?
19 Which Neil made a Beautiful Noise in the 70s?
20 Which surname is shared by Smokey and Tom?

1 "Around The World" was a 1997 hit for which act?
2 Who had a 70s No. 1 with "Wuthering Heights"?
3 What completes the title from U2's The Joshua Tree, "Where the ____ Have No Name"?
4 What went after Scritti in the name of the 80s band?
5 "If It Makes You Happy" was a top ten hit for which singer?
6 "Babe" was a 90s No. 1 for which group?
7 Which number follows Cloud Number in the song by Bryan Adams?
8 In which decade did The Wombles first make the charts?
9 Model Yasmin Le Bon's husband was in which pop band?
10 Malandra Burrows had a chart hit after starring in which soap?
11 Who had an 80s No. 1 with "There Must Be An Angel (Playing With My Heart)"?
12 Which group had a 90s top ten hit with "Forever"?
13 Which Elvis film title contained the same word three times?
14 I Was Born A what according to Babybird's 1995 release?
15 Which group with No in their name charted with "Just A Girl"?
16 What is Geri Halliwell's full first name?
17 Who had an 80s No. 1 with "Super Trouper"?
18 What were Adam And The Ants Kings of in 1980?
19 Designer and Clothes Show presenter Jeff Banks married which 60s pop star?
20 Who had a 70s No. 1 with "She"?

LEVEL 1

1 Which Girls' debut single was "Wannabe"?
2 Which Irish sisters were In the Mood for Dancin' in the 70s?
3 Which groups's debut album was *Always and Forever* – like their name?
4 Which group were once called the Bangs?
5 How many people made up Bananarama?
6 Which Sister did Bananarama's Siobhan Fahey co-found after she left the group?
7 How many Degrees said Take Good Care of Yourself in 1975?
8 Which Phil Spector group had Ronnie Bennett on lead vocals?
9 Which Motown group consisted of Diana Ross, Mary Wilson and Florence Ballard?
10 In Wilson Phillips, do the Wilsons outnumber the Phillipses or vice versa?
11 What goes before "Ron Ron" on the title of the Crystals' first major hit?
12 The Chapel of what became a million-seller for the Dixie Cups?
13 What was the surname of Martha who was often backed by the Vandellas?
14 Were the Pointer Sisters really sisters?
15 Who was Pepa's partner in the 80s rap group?
16 Which Leader provided a once-banned hit for the Shangri-Las?
17 Which Sister group had a No. 1 with "Frankie"?
18 Which mother-and-daughter country group consisted of Wynonna and Naomi?
19 Who switched on the London Christmas lights in December 1996?
20 Whose first hit was "Be My Baby" in 1963?

1   Which solo singer with a single name accompanied Rod and Bryan Adams on "All For Love"?
2   Which Swedish blonde hit the headlines with Rod Stewart during the 70s?
3   Which Jeff featured with Rod on "I've Been Drinking"?
4   Which group did Rod Stewart front until 1975?
5   What sort of Heart was an album hit of 1991?
6   To which charity did he donate the proceeds of Scorland's 1996 World Cup anthem?
7   Which international soccer side recorded with Rod Stewart in 1996?
8   Which day of the week went with Ruby in 1993?
9   Which Rachel was Rod's second wife, though the couple split in 1998?
10 Which huge hit with a nautical feel was on the album *Atlantic Crossing*?
11 Who Have More Fun according to the album title?
12 Which Alley was the title of the album from 1970?
13 "Sailing" was originally used as the theme for a documentary about what?
14 Every what Tells A Story according to the 1971 album?
15 Which soft drinks company did he sign a deal with in 1994?
16 Rod Stewart had a sports trial to be a professional in which sport?
17 Which girl's name featured on Rod's first solo No. 1?
18 Which job did Rod Stewart famously have before success in the music business?
19 What sort of Wedding featured in the title of a minor 1993 hit?
20 Who was his other half on "It Takes Two"?

1 Which Brothers were known as Little Donnie and Baby Boy Phil?
2 Which Linda, Dolly and Emmylou recorded the album *Trio*?
3 What did Suzi Quatrocchio change her surname to?
4 Which Robert was Addicted to Love in 1986?
5 Which Boys had a hit with "Always On My Mind" in 1988?
6 On which soul record label was Jimmy Ruffin's version of "What Becomes of the Broken Hearted?"?
7 Who sang about a Smooth Operator in 1984?
8 Which Del was a Runaway in 1961?
9 Which Great Train Robber featured on the Sex Pistols' "No One Is Innocent"/ "My Way"?
10 Which Percy released "When A Man Loves a Woman" in '66 and '87?
11 Who had a minor hit with "Doggy Dogg World"?
12 Which Billie Jo put her Blanket On The Ground in 1975?
13 Which *The Tube* presenter was a member of Squeeze?
14 How did Status Quo alter the title of "Rockin' All Over The World" to promote the Race Against Time in 1988?
15 How were Shakin' Stevens and Bonnie Tyler billed on "A Rockin' Good Way"?
16 In 1975 10.c.c., said Life was like which kind of soup?
17 What is the home country of k.d. lang?
18 Which group backed Brian Poole?
19 How many Pennies sang "Juliet"?
20 Which surname is shared by Hank and former Take That star Robbie?

Quiz 90 Pot Luck 46

Answers – see page 104

LEVEL 1

1. "It's All Coming Back To Me Now" was a hit for which female singer?
2. Which word goes before Wants You in a Billie title?
3. What is the first word of "National Express" by The Divine Comedy?
4. Who had a 90s No. 1 with "Boombastic"?
5. Love Over what was the fourth album by Dire Straits?
6. Which two words followed Chirpy Chirpy on Middle Of The Road's 70s No. 1?
7. "How Do You Want Me To Love You" was a hit for which group in 1998?
8. Which word completes the title of the David Bowie film, _The Man Who ____ To Earth_?
9. Who controversially said that The Beatles were more popular than Jesus?
10. Which Super group released "I Should Coco" in 1995?
11. Which word completes the song by Eternal, "I Wanna Be The Only ____"?
12. Whose farewell UK concert was called Sid Sods Off?
13. In 1989 Jason Donovan spent 36 weeks in the charts with which other singer?
14. Who had an 80s No. 1 with "Ride On Time"?
15. Which word completes the song title by Police, "Don't ____ So Close To Me"?
16. Who was the first artist to have two hits with just numerical titles – 7 and 1999?
17. Which family of brothers wrote and co-produced Barbra Streisand's "Woman In Love"?
18. Which solo singer released "I Do Not Want What I Haven't Got" in 1990?
19. Who had a 70s No. 1 with "I'm Not In Love"?
20. Who had a 90s hit with "Father And Son"?

Pot Luck 48 (Quiz 94)
1 Simply Red. 2 Johnny. 3 No Mercy. 4 kd lang. 5 Put.
6 Jason Donovan. 7 Here. 8 Faithfull. 9 Mariah Carey. 10 Terry Jacks.
11 80s. 12 I. 13 George Best. 14 Michael. 15 Alexei Sayle. 16 Speak.
17 New Seekers. 18 Waddle. 19 Desire. 20 1977.

Quiz 91 Queen

Answers – see page 105

1 Who was Queen's lead vocalist?
2 How many people made up Queen?
3 Which 1974 hit had the band's name in the title?
4 Which Rhapsody was at No. 1 for two months when first released?
5 Which Queen song has become a football anthem?
6 Which group of US comedy brothers made films whose titles gave Queen the names of two albums?
7 Which 1977 Queen album shares its name with a Sunday tabloid newspaper?
8 Which musical instrument is Brian May most famous for?
9 In 1980 Queen became the first rock band to appear in which annual publication as some of Britain's highest-paid executives?
10 Where did Bob Geldof say Queen's lead singer could "ponce about in front of the whole world"?
11 In which London park did Queen give a free concert in 1976?
12 Which soap star's name was linked with Brian May's from the mid-80s?
13 Which Heart Attack gave Queen a No. 2 album in 1974?
14 Which Queen EP shares its name with a BBC radio network?
15 Which George joined Queen on a version of "These Are The Days Of Our Lives"?
16 What is the surname of the Queen drummer Roger?
17 According to its title, where was their 1995 No. 1 Made?
18 Which Olympic Games gave their lead singer a hit in 1992?
19 Which Radio gave Queen a hit in 1984?
20 Which David had a No. 1 with Queen in 1981?

1 In which decade was Madonna born?
2 Which cosmetics company did Madonna become the face of in 1999?
3 In 1996 Madonna had two hit records from which film?
4 Maverick is Madonna's own what?
5 "This Used to Be My" what according to a 1992 hit?
6 Who was Madonna's first husband?
7 "Like A Prayer" advertised which soft drink?
8 What was Madonna's first album called?
9 Which girl's name was in the title of Madonna's first major film?
10 What followed Blonde in the name of Madonna's 1990 world tour?
11 Who was Madonna's co-star in Dick Tracy with whom she had a brief affair?
12 How was Madonna's greatest hits Collection named?
13 On which Irish presenter's chat show did Madonna guest in 1992?
14 What crime was Robert Hoskins convicted of against Madonna in 1996?
15 What role as a member of her staff did the father of Madonna's first child have?
16 Which hit was publicised by Madonna reading to an audience dressed in pyjamas?
17 In which country was Madonna born?
18 Images of which blonde film actress appear in many of Madonna's videos?
19 Where was the Surprise in the film Madonna made with Sean Penn?
20 How was her character Mahoney described in Dick Tracy?

1 Which Tina's album was *Simply the Best* in 1991?
2 Which Austrian city was a No. 1 for Ultravox in 1981?
3 Which country is Mary Hopkin from?
4 Which Suzanne was in "Tom's Diner" in 1990?
5 How did Barry White complete the song title "You're My First My Last"?
6 Which dance did Wizzard See My Baby do in 1973?
7 Who is Vic Reeves's backing group?
8 What was Venus wearing according to Mark Wynter in 1962?
9 Abba are credited with being from Sweden and which other Scandinavian country?
10 How is Terry Nelhams better known?
11 Who was K.C.'s backing band?
12 What is the home country of Whitney Houston?
13 Whose debut album was called *Boomania*?
14 Which musical instrument does Harry Connick Jr play?
15 Curiosity Killed what according to the name of the 80s band?
16 Chrissie Hynde was lead singer with which group?
17 Who had the classic "Whiter Shade of Pale" in the 60s?
18 Which Jarvis sings with Pulp?
19 What qualification do Hook and Feelgood have?
20 Which surname is shared by the late Jackie and the beehive hair-do queen Mari?

1   Who had a 90s No. 1 with "Fairground"?
2   What is the name of Rosanne Cash's father?
3   Who had a 1997 hit with "Where Do You Go"?
4   Which Canadian solo singer's 1992 album was Ingenue?
5   Which word goes before Your Arms Around Me in the song by Texas?
6   Who had an 80s No. 1 with "Too Many Broken Hearts"?
7   What is the first word of "Heartbeat" by Steps?
8   Which Marianne was Mick Jagger's 60s girlfriend?
9   Who joined Boyz II Men for the 1995 hit "One Sweet Day"?
10 Who had a 70s No. 1 with "Seasons In The Sun"?
11 In which decade did Yazz first make the charts?
12 Which word is missing from The Corrs 1998 hit, "What Can __ Do"?
13 The song "Belfast Boy" was a tribute to which Irish soccer genius?
14 Which member of the Jackson family was the first to chart with Diana Ross?
15 In 1984 who asked, "Ullo John Got a New Motor?"?
16 Which word follows Don't in the song by No Doubt?
17 Who had a 70s No. 1 with "You Won't Find Another Fool Like Me"?
18 In the soccer hit by Glenn and Chris, who was Chris?
19 Which word goes after Freed From in the song by Gala?
20 Which Ash album paid credit to the year Star Wars was first released?

1 What was the surname of Richard and Karen?
2 Who are Barbra and Neil who had a hit with "You Don't Send Me Flowers" in 1978?
3 Which Sarah duetted with Steve Harley on "Phantom of the Opera" 1986?
4 Which cockney duo had an album *Street Party* in 1995?
5 How were the comedy recording duo Pete and Dud better known?
6 Who was Dave Stewart's 'other half' in the Eurythmics?
7 Which Spanish star duetted with Willie Nelson on "All the Girls I Loved Before"?
8 Which two relatives were in the title of a Boyzone hit in 1995?
9 Which Neighbours hit No. 1 with "Especially For You" in 1988?
10 Which blonde did Cliff duet with on disc in 1980 and again in 1995?
11 What is the surname of the brother and sister Donny and Marie?
12 Who duetted with Elaine Paige on the No. 1 "I Know Him So Well"?
13 Who was Up Town Top Ranking with Althia?
14 Who duetted on "Barcelona" with Montserrat Caballe?
15 Whose Greatest Hits album was called *Tears Roll Down*?
16 Whose only album was *River Deep, Mountain High*?
17 Whose film soundtrack album *The Graduate* charted in 1968?
18 Which father and daughter sang "Somethin' Stupid" in 1967?
19 Who are Linda and James on the 1987 hit "Somewhere Out There"?
20 Who duetted with Womack on the hit "Teardrops"?

LEVEL 1

1 How many people made up Wham!?
2 Which record company was Michael in conflict with at the beginning of the 90s?
3 How was the Whisper described in his last major hit with Wham!?
4 In which British city was George Michael born?
5 With which Queen of Soul did he sing "I Knew You Were Waiting"?
6 What was the name of Wham!'s 1984 Christmas single?
7 Which band did he record the *Five Live* EP with?
8 On which charity single did he sing in December 1984?
9 On which show did George Michael first talk about his arrest in the USA in 1998?
10 From which more mature album was the single "Jesus To A Child" taken?
11 Who were with Cowboys on his 1991 minor hit?
12 What was he Spinning in 1996?
13 Who wrote "Don't Let The Sun Go Down On Me" which he recorded with its writer?
14 What nationality of restaurant did George Michael's father own?
15 Which George Michael title was banned by the BBC in 1987?
16 Which animal was the title of a hit from the *Faith* album?
17 What was Michael's jacket made from on the cover of *Faith*?
18 He appeared in a 1988 tribute concert to whom?
19 What was his Best Of album called?
20 How many solo No. 1 albums did he have in the 80s?

1 Who was lead singer with the Faces?
2 Which pop star wrote a financial advice column "Faith in the City" for the *Mail on Sunday*?
3 What other word describes the Young Cannibals?
4 Which group took "Mamma Mia" to No. 1?
5 Which Convention had Sandy Denny on vocals?
6 Which group's only No. 1 in 25 years was "Down Down"?
7 Which Jose had a hit with "Light My Fire"?
8 Which flowers did Tiny Tim Tiptoe Through in the 60s?
9 Which model Jerry appeared on the cover of Roxy Music's *Siren* album?
10 Which country star's songs have taken him to Galveston, Phoenix and Wichita?
11 Which soap did Peter Noone of Herman's Hermits appear in the 60s?
12 In which city were Frankie Goes To Hollywood first based?
13 In which group did Axl Rose take lead vocals?
14 Who was the youngest of the Gibb brothers, who died in 1988?
15 How many Steps To Heaven did Eddie Cochran sing about?
16 Which Georgie's backing group were called the Blue Flames?
17 Which Billy, who died in 1983, was a former schoolmate of Ringo Starr?
18 Which group included brothers Ray and Dave Davies?
19 Who was Billy J. Kramer's backing group?
20 How many Tops sang "Reach Out"?

1 What is the first word of "Say What You Want"?
2 Who had an 80s No. 1 with "A Groovy Kind Of Love"?
3 Nick Berry had a chart hit after starring in which soap?
4 What was the imaginative title of Green and Flynn's debut album?
5 "Belissima" was a hit for who?
6 Which female singer had an early 90s hit with "Give Me Just A Little More Time"?
7 Who had a 70s No. 1 with "Welcome Home"?
8 Which year was the title of a 1983 album from Prince?
9 "The Day We Caught The Train" was a 1996 hit for which group?
10 Which actor Sean's first job was in the chorus of *South Pacific* in London's West End?
11 Who had a 90s No. 1 with "Boom Boom Boom"?
12 Which Marvin was "Too Busy Thinking 'Bout My Baby" in the 60s?
13 "When The Lights Go Out' was a top five hit for which group?
14 Which Spice Girl featured on Bryan Adams' album *On A Day Like Today*?
15 "I Heard It Through The Grapevine" was used as a TV ad for which product?
16 Which Jimmy had the original hit with "What Becomes of the Broken Hearted"?
17 What were R.E.M. Out Of in 1991?
18 Which word follows Big, Big in the song by Emilia?
19 In which decade did Seal first make the charts?
20 Which Keith was responsible for Orville the duck singing?

1   What is the name of Dannii Minogue's older sister?
2   What was the name of Paul McCartney's late wife?
3   What relation was Richard Carpenter to Karen?
4   Which group is made up of the Gibb brothers?
5   Which Brothers included Alan, Merrill, Jay and Donny?
6   What is their singing sister called?
7   How many Jacksons are credited on "I Want You Back"?
8   What is the name of John Lennon's elder son?
9   Which surf sound group included Brian, Dennis and Carl Wilson?
10   What relation are Whitney Houston and Dionne Warwick?
11   What is the first name of Marty Wilde's singing daughter?
12   What is the surname of the brothers whose hits included "Wake Up Little Susie"?
13   Which Brothers had hits with "You've Lost That Lovin' Feelin" and "Unchained Melody"?
14   Which singer, who died in 2000, had daughters Fifi Trixibelle, Peaches and Little Pixie?
15   In the Sinatra duo what relation is Nancy to Frank?
16   What is Nat King Cole's vocalist daughter called?
17   Who is Sam Brown's dad who used to sing with The Bruvvers?
18   Which relative did Clive Dunn sing about in 1970?
19   Which trio included the twins Matt and Luke Goss?
20   Who had her first No. 1 hit when she was Mrs Sonny Bono?

1   In which country was Celine Dion born?
2   In which language did Celine Dion sing her early songs?
3   Her song "My Heart Will Go On" came from which movie?
4   Which superstar duetted with her on "Tell Him"?
5   Which Disney theme gave her her first UK top ten hit?
6   How did Celine Dion Think on her first UK No. 1?
7   Who did Celine Dion represent when she won the Eurovision Song Contest?
8   "When I Fall In Love" was originally a hit for which King?
9   Which member of her staff did Celine Dion marry in 1994?
10   Which name of a trade union was Celine Dion's first English-speaking album?
11   Which opera superstar featured on "Let's Talk About Love"?
12   Which brotherly band teamed up with Celine Dion on Immortality?
13   Who duetted with Celine Dion on Beauty & The Beast?
14   Which Celine Dion hit had been a mega hit for Jennifer Rush?
15   In 1998 Celine said I'm Your what?
16   What is the main colour of the cover of Falling Into You?
17   How many roads were in a 1995 song title?
18   How many times did Celine Think in 1994?
19   What comes after River Deep in the title of the classic on *Falling Into You*?
20   In which French city did Celine record a live album in 1996?

1 Which musical instrument does Bobby Crush play?
2 Which singer once played football for Real Madrid?
3 How is George Ivan Morrison better known?
4 What were we on the Eve of according to Barry McGuire in the 60s?
5 What did the Fugees call Roberta Flack's "Killing Me Softly With His Song"?
6 Who were Pretenders To The Throne in 1995?
7 Which Great was a hit for The Platters and Freddie Mercury?
8 Who had a US No. 1 album with "Please Hammer Don't Hurt 'Em"?
9 How was Linda Eastman better known?
10 Which Debbie played Sandy in the London revival of *Grease*?
11 Who was Huey Lewis's backing group?
12 Which Midlands city were the Move from?
13 Which 60s TV group included Mickey Dolenz and Mike Nesmith?
14 Which singer gave birth to baby Lourdes in 1996?
15 Suggs was lead singer with which crazy-sounding group?
16 Which Scots pop star married the hairdresser John Frieda?
17 How is George O'Dowd better known?
18 How many Lions feature on the Lightning Seeds' Euro '96 football anthem?
19 Which country were Japan from?
20 Which Eddy was lead singer with the Equals?

1   "Guaglione" was a hit for which act in 1995?
2   Which word completes the song by the Vengaboys, "We Like To _____"?
3   "The Real Thing" was a 90s No. 1 for which singer?
4   What is the first word of "Bootie Call" by All Saints?
5   Queen's 1995 album was Made In where?
6   Which first name was shared by two of the original members of Oasis?
7   Which 60s star Billy's "Wondrous Place" is used on the 90s Toyota TV ad?
8   Who had an 80s No. 1 with "The Edge Of Heaven"?
9   Style Council's first No. 1 album was Our Favourite what?
10 Who left husband Ike for a solo career?
11 In her Euro song what did Gina G sing immediately after "Ooh"?
12 Who had an early 90s hit with "Get Ready For This"?
13 The 80s album Reilly: Ace Of Themes celebrated which TV series?
14 Which country do R.E.M. come from?
15 How is singer Elaine Bickerstaff better known?
16 Who made the classic "My Generation" in 1965?
17 An Oasis tour in which country was cancelled in 1996 when Liam returned home?
18 Which 60s singer was nicknamed Little Miss Dynamite?
19 It's A Shame About who on The Lemonheads' 1992 album?
20 Who had an 80s No. 1 with "Papa Don't Preach"?

1 Which Hotel gave Elvis his first UK hit?
2 Which 'rank' was Elvis's manager Tom Parker known by?
3 What was the first name of Elvis's wife?
4 What were Elvis's shoes made out of in his 1956 hit?
5 Elvis's gyrations on stage gave him which nickname?
6 In which European country was G.I. Elvis stationed?
7 What is the name of Elvis's mansion in Memphis?
8 What was the instruction with the letter Elvis sang about in 1962?
9 Although known as The King, which King was he in the 1958 film?
10 Which Elvis film title contained the same word three times?
11 Which relatives are Kissin' in the 1964 top ten hit?
12 What is the name of Elvis's daughter?
13 Which country of the UK is the only one Elvis visited?
14 Which Rock was a film and a No. 1 hit in 1958?
15 Where was Elvis Crying in 1965?
16 What was special about the camera work on Elvis's up-tempo songs on the USA's *Ed Sullivan Show*?
17 Which "canine" hit did Elvis have in 1956?
18 Which commemoration to Elvis was issued by the US Post Office in 1993?
19 The name of which toy was the title of an Elvis hit in 1957?
20 Who did Elvis's daughter marry in 1994?

Quiz 104 Stadium Fillers

Answers – see page 110

 **LEVEL 1**

1 Which country do the Manic Street Preachers come from?
2 Which Michael fronts R.E.M.?
3 Who were the Sultans of Swing?
4 Which Australian singer inspired INXS's "Suicide Blonde"?
5 How does the title of the album This Is My Truth end?
6 Who named Queen, Queen?
7 Which nickname did The Verve's Richard Ashcroft have?
8 R.E.M. played live at which U.S. President's inauguration in 1992?
9 Whose memory was celebrated at the 1992 Concert For Life?
10 Which Lancashire town do The Verve hail from?
11 What was the most famous song on Queen's A Night At The Opera?
12 Richey Edwards' car was found abandoned near which bridge in 1995?
13 What Don't Work according to the Verve's 1997 chart topper?
14 With which music legend did U2's Bono sing "I've Got You Under My Skin"?
15 Who recorded "Walk Of Life"?
16 At which charity show did Bob Geldof say of Queen, "Freddie could ponce about in front of the world"?
17 How many members did the Manic Street Preachers originally have?
18 Which Mick wrote the official anthem for Euro 96?
19 Which Queen song was sung by the people in the stadium after the 1998 World Cup Final?
20 What sort of Soul was the title of The Verve's 1995 album?

1 Which Marianne's first hit was written by the Rolling Stones?
2 Which Eurovision winning group was the TV presenter Cheryl Baker formerly a member of?
3 Which Dog was a big hit for Elvis Presley?
4 Which Busters gave Ray Parker Jr chart success?
5 Which Lace had a hit with "Agadoo"?
6 What were the Carpenters Calling Occupants of in 1977?
7 Where were there Orchestral Manoeuvres in the 80s and 90s?
8 Who have had No. 1 hits with "Pray" and "Everything Changes"?
9 Whose second album was called *Gentleman Jim*?
10 Which Chubby star was dubbed The King of Twist?
11 Which girl did Buddy Holly love with a heart so rare and true?
12 Who had a hit with "Rat Trap"?
13 Which Ruby gave Melanie a 70s hit?
14 Which singer/songwriters were nicknamed Mr and Mrs Music?
15 Which Johnny joined Deniece Williams on "Too Much Too Little Too Late"?
16 Which male vocalist shared his name with late-actress Miss Monroe?
17 Who had an album called *Everything Comes Up Dusty*?
18 Which US state were the Mamas and Papas Dreamin' of in 1966?
19 Which punk band was Malcolm McLaren manager of in the 70s?
20 How many members of the Hollies were there?

LEVEL 1

1 Who had an 80s No. 1 with "You Win Again"?
2 After a 1995 appearance on which TV show did Oasis sack their drummer?
3 The death of which member of his family led Eric Clapton to write "Tears In Heaven"?
4 Which word follows Unbreak My in the song by Toni Braxton?
5 Which Johnson was lead singer with Frankie Goes To Hollywood?
6 Who had a 70s No. 1 with "Knowing Me Knowing You"?
7 What were All Saints having a War Of?
8 What was written on Elvis' letter after Return To?
9 Which country does kd.lang come from?
10 Who had a 90s No. 1 with "Let Me Be Your Fantasy"?
11 What relation is Andrew Lloyd Webber to cellist Julian?
12 Which word follows Call The in the song by Celine Dion?
13 Georgie Fame sang a song about gangsters Bonnie and who?
14 Who had an 80s No. 1 with "Stand By Me"?
15 What type of Steps did the Boo Radleys make with their 1993 album?
16 Which instrument did Keith Moon of The Who play?
17 Who had a 70s No. 1 with "Chanson D'Amour"?
18 Which surname links Carole and BB?
19 Which Sunset by the Kinks did Cathy Dennis revive in 1997?
20 Which Caribbean island did Bob Marley come from?

1   Which all-male band had a hit with the Bee Gees' "Words" in 1996?
2   Which song was a hit for Roberta Flack and the Fugees?
3   Which date marked a special night for the Four Seasons and Clock?
4   Which duet have had most of their 90s chart successes with covers of 60s classics?
5   Bryan Hyland and Jason Donovan had letters sealed with what?
6   Which football anthem took Gerry and the Pacemakers, and then the Crowd to the top of the charts?
7   Who joined Cliff Richard on the second version of "Livin' Doll"?
8   What was No. 1 for Joe Cocker and Wet Wet Wet?
9   Which Osmond covered Tab Hunter's No. 1 "Too Young"?
10 Who backed Doctor on "Spirit in the Sky" a No. 1 for Norman Greenbaum in 1970?
11 Who did the 80s version of Rosemary Clooney's "This Ole House"?
12 Which Boy followed Ken Boothe's No. 1 of "Everything I Own"?
13 Who had the original No. 1 with "Take A Chance on Me" which featured on Erasure's No. 1 EP?
14 Which Mariah recorded a cover version of Nilsson's "Without You"?
15 Whose Boy Child gave hits for Boney M and Harry Belafonte?
16 Which Jimmy Ruffin hit did Robson and Jerome take to the top of the charts in autumn 1996?
17 What did Cher call Betty Everett's and Linda Lewis's "It's In His Kiss"?
18 Which revealing outfit did Bombalurina sing about 30 years after Bryan Hyland's original?
19 Who had the original hit with "You're the One That I Want"?
20 Where did first the Equals, then Pato Banton, tell their Baby to come?

1   Which Liverpool Club was associated with the early days of The Beatles?
2   What was the first Beatles film?
3   Who was the last member to join the band?
4   Which country was John's second wife Yoko Ono from?
5   What sort of Writer was the subject of a 1966 song?
6   Who wrote "Yesterday"?
7   What is the name of Paul's designer daughter?
8   Which early album shared its name with a firearm?
9   Which fruit was the name of their own record label?
10   Which song introduced "yeah, yeah, yeah"?
11   Which Brian was their first manager?
12   A 1994 compilation was released of The Beatles live at which broadcasting station?
13   Which band did Paul McCartney form after The Beatles?
14   Who "picks up the rice in the church where a wedding had been"?
15   Who was the only Beatle to change his surname?
16   Which Scottish location was the title of a hit for Paul McCartney?
17   In which city was John Lennon murdered?
18   Which George produced the early Beatles hits?
19   Which Lane was on the other side of Strawberry Fields Forever?
20   Who sang the solo on "Yellow Submarine"?

1 Which record label shares its name with the inventor of the telephone?
2 Who was Ian Dury's backing group?
3 Which Bunny had a string of party hits in the 80s?
4 Which former manager of Newcastle United had a 70s hit with "Head Over Heels In Love"?
5 Which Beatle had a solo No. 1 with "My Sweet Lord"?
6 Brian Bennett replaced Tony Meehan as drummer in which group?
7 Which surname is shared by the US star Crystal and the UK's Michelle?
8 How many Star members enjoyed great success in the 80s?
9 Who took the *Abba-esque EP* to No. 1 in 1992?
10 Which composer is told to Roll Over on the classic rock song?
11 Which country does Val Doonican come from?
12 Which 70s/80s duo shared its name with American money?
13 Who made up the trio with Crosby and Stills?
14 Which Canadian sang "Miss Chatelaine" in 1993?
15 Which Level had "Lessons in Love" in 1986?
16 What was Harold Melvin's backing group?
17 Where did Phyllis Nelson invite us to Move in the 80s and 90s?
18 Which Spanish insect was a hit for Herb Alpert?
19 Which Des had Careless Hands in 1967?
20 Which Daniel pondered "Whatever Happened to Old-Fashioned Love" in 1993?

1   "If You Ever" was a top ten hit for Gabrielle and which group?
2   Which Nirvana vocalist took his own life?
3   Who had a 70s No. 1 with "Combine Harvester (Brand New Key)"?
4   Which group had a 90s hit with "Come Back To What You Know"?
5   Who duetted "Endless Love" with Diana Ross in 1981?
6   What is the first word of the song "Always Have, Always Will"?
7   Who had an 80s No. 1 with "Heart"?
8   In the 80s 16-year-old Mandy Smith revealed a two-year affair with which rocker?
9   How many members of Take That were there in the early 90s?
10 Who had a "Like A Prayer" video banned by the Vatican?
11 Which Streets was Bruce Springsteen in in 1994?
12 Who had "People Hold On (The Bootleg Mixes)" back in the top five in 1997?
13 Which Alice had a stage act involving a guillotine and live snakes?
14 Who had a 1997 hit with "Baby Can I Hold You"?
15 Who made the album "Please Hammer Don't Hurt 'Em"?
16 Which word comes before Up in the song by Melanie G?
17 Which Elton John duettist had a solo hit with "Amoureuse"?
18 Who had an 80s No. 1 with "Perfect"?
19 Who had a 60s hit with "Strangers In the Night"?
20 What sort of Terrorists were the Manic Street Preachers with their 1992 album?

1   Which group were voted Best Newcomer at the 1995 Brit Awards?
2   Whose performance of "Earth Song" did Jarvis Cocker interrupt at the 1996 Brit Awards?
3   In which band does Damon Albarn sing lead vocals?
4   Which film about drug addiction released in 1996 features a Pulp song on the soundtrack?
5   Which Class was Pulp's first album?
6   Which two BritPop bands were the subject of a media-led feud?
7   Which film about prisoners of war shares its name with a Blur album?
8   Which Yorkshire city do Pulp hail from?
9   Which House entered the charts at No. 1 for Blur in 1995?
10 Which Life was a top selling single and album for Blur in 1994?
11 Which edible sounding record label do Blur record on?
12 To two years either way, in which year did Blur have their first Top Ten single?
13 Which musical instrument does Damon Albarn play?
14 Which Labour MP Ken appeared on a Blur No. 1 in 1995?
15 Why did Jarvis Cocker have to spend time in a wheelchair in 1986?
16 What was Blur's 1995 book called?
17 How many members of Blur are there?
18 Which instrument does Dave Rowntree play?
19 In May 1996 why did Noel Gallagher turn down an Ivor Novello Songwriter of the Year award?
20 The singing of which song at Manchester City's football ground made Noel Gallagher cry?

1   What two words go in front of Rolling Stone in the group's hit of '95?
2   What's the name of the real-life Charlie?
3   Who did Mick Jagger team up with for "Dancin' In The Street" at the Live Aid concert?
4   The Stones own record label was called Sticky what?
5   What colour was the Stones' Little Rooster?
6   Which two names are credited as writing most of the group's material?
7   Which long-time member of the group was born William Perks?
8   What word comes after "I Can't Get No" in a 60s smash?
9   Which Ron joined the band in the 70s?
10 What's the missing colour in the song title, "Paint It _____"?
11 What was the name of the 1994 album and the world tour to promote it?
12 In 1992 who decided to quit the Stones?
13 How many members were in the Stones when they first hit the charts?
14 What instrument does Jagger blow on stage?
15 ·Who hosted a 99 TV special with exclusive backstage interviews from the Stones?
16 Where did Brian Jones die?
17 Which 60s girlfriend of Mick Jagger recorded their song, "As Tears Go By"?
18 Which Stone was described by Joan Rivers as having "child-bearing lips"?
19 The Rolling Stones were named after what?
20 Which letter in Keith Richards' name did he keep adding and taking away from it?

1   Which Kenny and Sheena duetted on "We've Got Tonight"?
2   Which first name links the Muffins and the Vandellas?
3   Which US state did Ray Charles have on his mind in 1960?
4   Paul Shane and the Yellowcoats sang the "Holiday Rock" from which TV show?
5   Who rhymed with Telegram on the title of the T. Rex single?
6   Which zany DJ recorded a "Snot Rap" in 1983?
7   Which country is Craig McLachlan from?
8   Which TV presenter Shane played the lead role in *Grease* in the West End?
9   Which Doctor had "Sexy Eyes" in 1980?
10 Who was Blondie's female singer?
11 In 1982 It Started With what for Hot Chocolate?
12 Who was backing Katrina when she was "Walking on Sunshine"?
13 What colour Box did Simply Red Open Up in 1986?
14 Matt Monro is famous for singing "Born Free", a film about which animals?
15 What is the surname of the country stars Johnny and Roseanne?
16 Which singer is nicknamed The Boss?
17 Which record label was founded in Detroit?
18 Whose first hit was "Space Oddity" in 1969?
19 Whose first solo hit was "Orinoco Flow" in 1988?
20 How is the jazz singer Clementine Campbell better known?

Quiz 114 Pot Luck 58

LEVEL 1

1 Which word comes after Viva La in the hit song by Lolly?
2 Who became the first chart-topper to be named Ocean?
3 Who had a No. 1 with "Killer"?
4 Who managed the rare double of Xmas single and album in 1996?
5 Which Dionne made the 60s version of "Walk On By"?
6 What followed Free Peace in the title of Dodgy's 1996 album?
7 Who had a No. 4 hit in 1998 with "Life Ain't Easy"?
8 For which soap did Tony Hatch write the theme?
9 Who said "Everybody Get Up" in 1998?
10 Elvis's gyrations on stage earned him which nickname?
11 Who had a 90s No. 1 with "Ain't No Doubt"?
12 Pink Floyd looked at The Dark Side of what?
13 Which band had a 1994 smash with "Always"?
14 Which Boys released the classic Pet Sounds?
15 What is Jewel's real first name?
16 Who had a 70s No. 1 with "Gonna Make You A Star"?
17 Which US solo male singer has had the most No. 1 hits in the UK?
18 What accessory does Gabrielle place on her face?
19 Where did the Village People think it was fun to stay?
20 Perez Prado was back in the charts in the 90s after his music backed a TV ad for what?

1 In which US west-coast city had you to be sure to "wear some flowers in your hair" in 1967?
2 Which Dutch city gave a hit to the Beautiful South?
3 Which group shares its name with Germany's capital city?
4 What did the Ferry cross in the hit by Gerry and the Pacemakers?
5 Which Scottish location gave Paul McCartney a No. 1 in 1977?
6 Which US gangster town gave its name to the group who had a No. 1 with "If You Leave Me Now"?
7 Where was the 1972 Long-Haired Lover from?
8 Where did Madonna implore them not to cry for her in 1996?
9 Which Triangle provided Barry Manilow with a Top Twenty hit?
10 Which Northern Irish city is in the title of Simple Minds' 1989 No. 1?
11 Which home of Sherlock Holmes was a hit for Gerry Rafferty?
12 Which 1992 Olympic venue was a hit for Montserrat Caballe and Freddie Mercury?
13 Where were Typically Tropical heading for on Coconut Airways in 1975?
14 Which West Coast state gave its name to the Eagles' Hotel in 1977?
15 What did Tony Bennett Leave in San Francisco?
16 The Streets of which city featured on a Ralph McTell classic song?
17 Where did Bruce Springsteen say he was born, in 1985?
18 Where did Supertramp have Breakfast in 1979?
19 Which features of Babylon did Boney M sing about in 1978?
20 Which city's name appears twice in the title of Frank Sinatra's 80s hit?

Quiz 116 Blondie

Answers – see page 130

1 Which hit contains the line, "Go insane and out of your mind"?
2 In which decade did the group have their first UK No. 1?
3 What completes the title that starts "I'm Always Touched By Your..."?
4 What's the first name of guitar man Stein?
5 Eat To The what was an album from 1979?
6 What was the group's first UK top ten hit?
7 Without getting personal, in which decade was Deborah Harry born?
8 How many people appeared on the cover of the album No Exit?
9 What was the last UK No. 1 before "Maria"?
10 What were Blondie "Hanging On" in a 78 hit?
11 In which city were the group formed?
12 What was the first colour to feature in a Blondie single title?
13 Which female helped Blondie to No. 1 in 1999?
14 In which movie – that is almost, but not quite, the name of a Blondie hit – did Deborah Harry made her acting debut?
15 What was the group's first UK No. 1?
16 Deborah Harry first put solo singles out using what name?
17 Which re-mix saw Blondie back in the top 20 for the first time in the 90s?
18 What was the best run of successive UK No. 1s for the band?
19 In "Denis', what colour are Denis's eyes?
20 In which country was French Kissing going on according to a song title?

1　Whose 80s best-selling album was *Born In The USA*?
2　Whose first hit was "Wuthering Heights"?
3　What completes the Paul Young song title "Wherever I Lay My Hat ..."?
4　What is the vocalist Ms Cherry's first name?
5　Which musical instrument does Barry Manilow play?
6　Which country do the Nolans come from?
7　Which country did Gina G represent in the Eurovision Song Contest in 1996?
8　Which band did No Way Sis try to imitate?
9　How is Declan McManus better known?
10　Who had a 1979 No. 1 album called *Reggatta De Blanc*?
11　Which record label did the Commodores first record on?
12　Which US vocalist is the daughter of the founder of the publishers Simon & Schuster?
13　Which Beatle's younger son is called Sean?
14　Who is not one of the Jackson sisters – Janet, LaToya, Jackie?
15　Which northern city is Sonia from?
16　Which first name is shared by Estefan and Gaynor?
17　What follows UB in the name of the band?
18　Who was Kid Creole's backing group?
19　Which part of the UK is Barbara Dickson from?
20　How many times did Celine Dion Think on her best-selling 1995 single?

1   Who went "To The Moon And Back" in 1998?
2   Who had a 90s No. 1 with "World In Motion"?
3   Which 90s group had a hit with "Female Of The Species"?
4   In which city is Jim Morrison buried?
5   Which word comes before It Again in the 1999 Eurovision song by Precious?
6   Who had a 70s No. 1 with "Merry Xmas Everybody"?
7   Whose 1994 album was Enter The Wu-Tang?
8   Which female singer's first hit was "If Not For You"?
9   Who recorded "Song 2" in 1997?
10 According to A-Ha the sun always shines where?
11 "Goodnight Girl" was which group's first 90s No. 1?
12 Which Biblical lady provided Tom Jones with a 60s hit?
13 Which group had a thing about Fat Bottomed Girls?
14 What was Not Required on the title of a Phil Collins album?
15 Who was Bobbie Gentry's Ode to?
16 Which Five were Glad All Over in 1963?
17 In 1996 Alanis Morissette was Head Over what?
18 Mayfair hairdresser John Frieda married which 60s pop star?
19 How is David Robert Jones better known?
20 Who had a 70s No. 1 with "Always Yours"?

1 Which Maggie gave Rod Stewart his first No. 1 in 1971?
2 Which group, no longer Small, did Rod join in 1969?
3 What Tells a Story on Rod's first No. 1 album?
4 Which No. 1 was used for a BBC series about HMS *Ark Royal*?
5 Which Swedish actress did Rod begin an affair with in 1975?
6 What do blondes have more of according to the 70s single and album?
7 Which album cover showed a boot in the USA and one in the UK?
8 Which country's World Cup Squad did Rod record with in 1978?
9 Which Motown hit did Rod record in 1975 and again in 1989, the latter with Ronald Isley?
10 Which glamorous granny did Rod duet with in "It Takes Two"?
11 Rod asked Do You Think I'm what in 1978?
12 To which disaster fund did Rod donate the proceeds of a concert on his American tour in 1994?
13 Which New Zealand model did Rod marry in 1990?
14 What had Rod Reason to do with his first hit in 1971?
15 Which two solo singers joined Rod on the 1994 hit "All For Love"?
16 The second line of which Rod song is "You're in my soul"?
17 Which Alley was the title of Rod's first album?
18 In which decade did Rod first have a No. 1 solo album?
19 Which line followed "Have I Told You Lately" in 1993?
20 Rod was Foot Loose and what in 1977?

1   What is the surname of the members of The Bee Gees?
2   Which female solo star did they record "Immortality" with?
3   What sort of Love was a 1991 hit?
4   In which country were The Bee Gees brought up?
5   Which female sang on the Barry Gibb-produced country best-seller, "Islands In The Stream"?
6   In which decade did "You Win Again" top the UK charts?
7   Which New England state was the title of an early Bee Gees hit?
8   Spirits Having what was a No. 1 album from 1979?
9   How many brothers are there in The Bee Gees?
10 "Saturday Night Fever" was a world best-seller until which blockbuster from Michael Jackson?
11 Which song later became No. 1 for Boyzone?
12 Which member of The Bee Gees, if any, actually appeared in *Saturday Night Fever*?
13 What sort of Reaction did the Bee Gees write for Diana Ross?
14 Which city was the subject of a Mining Disaster in their first hit?
15 What was the verdict of Barbra Streisand's hit with Barry Gibb?
16 On which Isle were the Bee Gees born?
17 They featured on the album *Nobody's Child* to raise money for which country's orphans?
18 In which 80s sitcom with David Jason did Barry Gibb make a cameo appearance?
19 What sort of Breaker was a hit they penned for Dionne Warwick?
20 What followed "Still Waters" in the 1997 hit title?

1 Which 70s band's first No. 1 was "Coz I Love You"?
2 What sort of Bullets did 10c.c. take up the charts in 1973?
3 Was it Sonny or Cher who wrote their single "I Got You Babe"?
4 Which singer was nicknamed Ol' Blues Eyes?
5 Who had a 1997 hit with "Picture Of You"?
6 Which Army asked Are 'Friends' Electric in 1979?
7 What is the first name of Sharkey, who had a No. 1 with "A Good Heart" in 1985?
8 Which Spinners sang "Working My Way Back to You" in 1980?
9 Whose first hit was "Peggy Sue"?
10 Which comedians sang with the Lightning Seeds on "Three Lions"?
11 Who had the 1988 No. 1 "Theme From S Express"?
12 Which Alice sang "School's Out"?
13 Which country singer's autobiography is called *Stand By Your Man*?
14 Who was once backed by the Revolution?
15 Whose Ding-A-Ling took him to No. 1 in 1972?
16 What do the letters r.p.m. stand for?
17 Which family had a hit with "Love Me For A Reason" in 1974?
18 Which Simon and Garfunkel classic has the lines "When tears are in your eyes, I will dry them all"?
19 Which painter is Don McLean's hit "Vincent" about?
20 How many members of The Mamas And The Papas were there?

1 What does E stand for in the medical abbreviation R.E.M.?
2 Who were doing a Tribal Dance in 1993?
3 Which word comes after Private in the song by 911?
4 Who were Smokey Robinson's backing group?
5 Which single word was the title of George Michael's first solo album?
6 In 1997 which group was in the media spotlight after its lead singer said Ecstasy was completely safe?
7 In the 1990 hit which puppets "Are Go"?
8 Who had a 90s No. 1 with "Please Don't Go"/"Game Boy"?
9 Who released The Fat Of The Land in 1997?
10 Who was the guest vocalist with KLF on "Justified And Ancient"?
11 Which solo star made the album *Falling Into You* in 1996?
12 Who had a 70s No. 1 with "Sunday Girl"?
13 "The Ballad Of Tom Jones" was a hit for Cerys of Catatonia and which indie group?
14 In which decade did The Rolling Stones first make the charts?
15 Which Tina made the album *Private Dancer*?
16 Rapper Turbo B left Snap after the release of which monster hit?
17 Which famous US record label did Berry Gordy found?
18 Who made the classic Purple Rain in 1984?
19 The album *Pan Pipe Moods* featured traditional music from which continent?
20 Who had a 70s No. 1 with "Ring My Bell"?

1 What gave Band Aid a Christmas No. 1 in 1984 and 1989?
2 Which Brenda was Rockin' Around the Christmas Tree in 1962?
3 What went with Mistletoe on Cliff Richard's 1988 Christmas No. 1?
4 Who recorded the evergreen "Merry Xmas Everybody"?
5 Who went from Crinkley Bottom to the Christmas top spot in 1993?
6 At Christmas 1980 St Winifred's School Choir said "There's No One Quite Like" who?
7 Whose Day gave Cliff Richard a Christmas No. 1 in 1990?
8 Who had two little toys in Rolf Harris's 1969 hit?
9 Which 80s duo sang about Last Christmas in 1984, 1985 and 1986?
10 What colour Christmas did Elvis Presley have in 1964?
11 How was Chris Rea getting Home for Christmas in 1988?
12 Who did Greg Lake say he believed in in 1975?
13 Which Christmas cartoon film had "Walking in the Air" as its theme?
14 Which line follows "I'm dreaming of a White Christmas"?
15 In 1975 where is Santa Claus Coming, according to the Jackson Five?
16 Which Christmas song begins "Long time ago in Bethlehem, so the Holy Bible say"?
17 Which Little animal first entered the charts in 1959?
18 Which singer/piano player invited us to Step into Christmas in 1973?
19 Which Tale did David Essex take to No. 2 in 1982?
20 What are "roasting on an open fire" with "Jack Frost nipping at your nose"?

1 Which toy did Aqua sing about?
2 Which band were an emergency call?
3 What followed "Quit Playing Games" in the title of the Backstreet Boys 1997 hit?
4 Where do Ace Of Base hail from?
5 Which band led by Christian Mills had the No. 1 album, K?
6 Which People were led by Heather Small?
7 Which band took their name from The Verve's "Man Called Sun"?
8 Which Liam fronted Prodigy?
9 Space and Cerys of Catatonia sang whose Ballad in 1998?
10 Which Catatonia hit had a taste of The X Files about it?
11 Which 90s newcomers had the album *Word Gets Around*?
12 The Cardigans debut single was dedicated to which British soap?
13 What was The Stone Roses' debut album?
14 What sort of Summer did Ace Of Base have in 1998?
15 Who brought "Trash" to the 1996 charts?
16 Which fruity group did Dolores O'Riordan join in 1990?
17 Which band's name was a London postcode?
18 Which numbers did Steps take in their first chart success?
19 Where do Ash hail from?
20 What type of storm did Cast take into the charts?

1 Which Scandinavians were a Super Trouper in 1980?
2 Who was Scaffold's Mike McGear's famous brother?
3 Whose first of many hits was "Your Song" in 1971?
4 Which Flying group had a No. 1 with "Only You" in 1983?
5 In which SE Asian capital did Murray Head spend One Night in 1984?
6 Which song has been recorded by Elvis Presley, the Sex Pistols and Frank Sinatra?
7 Which Beach were Martha and the Muffins on in 1980?
8 Where was Sylvia going on holiday in "Y Viva España"?
9 Who was Herman's backing group?
10 Was Donovan the singer's first name or surname?
11 Which record label shares its name with a feeling of dizziness?
12 Who sang with Derek on "Layla"?
13 Which surname is shared by Karen and Mary-Chapin?
14 Who were Fame and Price Together?
15 What was the first name of the Blues guitarist Korner?
16 Which UK jazz singer is married to John Dankworth ?
17 Whose first names are Kathryn Dawn although she does not use them in full as a stage name?
18 What was odd about the two members of Milli Vanilli's performances on their hit records?
19 Which country is Vangelis from?
20 What happened to Bobby Goldsboro's Honey in 1968?

1   "Insomnia" was a hit for which act in 1996?
2   Which Four Forty were Lost In Space?
3   Who had a 1994 hit with "The Sign"?
4   Which album did "Wannabe" first appear on?
5   Who had a top ten hit in 1997 with "Drop Dead Gorgeous"?
6   Which single-named pop star founded the Rainforest Foundation in 1988?
7   Who charted in 1990 with the Space Jungle?
8   Who had an 80s No. 1 with "Desire"?
9   Robbie Williams had No what in the title of his 1998 song?
10 Which word comes before At Me in the song by Geri Halliwell?
11 How many members of Bucks Fizz were there?
12 Which word completes the song by The Mavericks, "Dance The ____ Away"?
13 Which singer had a 90s No. 1 with "I Believe I Can Fly"?
14 Whose album *She's So Unusual* featured "Girls Just Want To Have Fun"?
15 10 Years Of Hits was released in 1987 to celebrate the 20th anniversary of which radio station?
16 What type of Divas were En Vogue in 1992?
17 What did Adam Rickitt do again in his debut single?
18 Which word goes before Rage in the song by Catatonia?
19 Who had an 80s No. 1 with "First Time"?
20 Who was in Chains in 1995?

Quiz 127 Country Style

Answers – see page 133

1   Which Johnny had a hit with "A Boy Named Sue"?
2   Which country singer owns a theme park called Dollywood?
3   Which Spanish singer duetted with Willie Nelson on "To All The Girls I've Loved Before"?
4   Who did Tammy Wynette Stand By in her 70s No. 1?
5   Kenny Rogers was the Coward of where in 1980?
6   Which late country star had an album called Country Gentleman?
7   Which Olivia had a hit with "Take Me Home, Country Roads"?
8   Whose Song was a No. 1 for John Denver in 1974?
9   From which dale do the Woolpackers originate?
10   Which Patsy was the subject of a biopic called *Sweet Dreams*?
11   What real crime was committed against Tammy Wynette in 1979?
12   Who was Bobbie Gentry's Ode to?
13   Which Loretta was the subject of a film called *Coal Miner's Daughter*?
14   Which fictional village does the country "star" Eddie Grundy hail from?
15   Who had a hit with "Don't It Make My Brown Eyes Blue"?
16   Which opera tenor recorded "Perhaps Love" with John Denver?
17   Carl Perkins' early recordings were in country style on which musical instrument?
18   How is the country star Hiram Williams better known?
19   What was the relationship between the Judds, who enjoyed considerable success in the 80s?
20   Which Ms Carpenter had a debut chart album *Stones in the Road*?

1 In which city were Eternal based?
2 Which song with a French title was one of 1998's top-selling singles, by B*witched?
3 Which girl band were cast to star in Dave Stewart's film, *Honest*?
4 Before The what was an album success for Eternal?
5 How many girls were originally in Bananarama?
6 What was the surname of the sisters in All Saints?
7 Which member of Boyzone married Eternal's Easther?
8 How many members did Salt 'n' Pepa have?
9 Shakespear's Sister Siobhan Fahey had previously been in which successful girl group?
10 In which decade did The Supremes have their final live show?
11 Which footballer did ex Eternal star Louise marry?
12 Which band started out as The Bangs?
13 On which unclothed album did Louise sing "Undivided Love"?
14 Whose 1998 Xmas No. 1 was "Goodbye" shortly after one of their number left?
15 Two members of B*witched were sisters of a member of which boy band?
16 Which ex-member of Milan starred in EastEnders and had a 1999 No. 1?
17 What was Louise's surname when she was in Eternal?
18 How did the Spice Girl style herself on her solo venture "Word Up"?
19 How many Eternal hits did Louise sing on her first solo tour?
20 Which valuable group sang "Say It Again" in the 1999 Eurovision Song Contest?

1 Which Mac had a top-selling album with *Rumours*?
2 What do the initials R & B stand for?
3 Which song was a No. 1 for Nilsson and Mariah Carey?
4 Who had the original hit with "Cracklin' Rosie"?
5 Which football team recorded the "Anfield Rap"?
6 Which country is Sacha Distel from?
7 What is the TV actor Terence Donovan's son called?
8 Which famous US record label did Berry Gordy found?
9 Which royal couple attended the Live Aid Concert?
10 How was the jazzman Edward Kennedy Ellington better known ?
11 In which decade did Frankie Goes to Hollywood find success?
12 Which Gary's first hit was "Rock and Roll (Parts 1 & 2)" in 1972?
13 Which part of the UK is Aled Jones from?
14 Who was Zag's puppet partner on "Them Girls Them Girls" in 1994?
15 Which word goes before Affair and Unlimited in the names of groups?
16 Which band was originally called Curiosity Killed the Cat?
17 Which singer was nicknamed The King?
18 Which glam group went on a "Teenage Rampage"?
19 How is David Robert Jones better known?
20 How many members of Meat Loaf are there?

1 "Heaven's What I Feel" was a top ten hit for which singer?
2 Dannii Minogue had a chart hit after starring in which soap?
3 "Say What You Want" was a top ten hit for which group in 1997?
4 Who had an 80s No. 1 with "One Moment In Time"?
5 Which actor did Madonna marry in 1985?
6 In which decade did Queen first make the charts?
7 Which Stevie released the album *Innervisions* in 1973?
8 "Cotton Eyed Joe" was a 90s No. 1 for which group?
9 Which word describes where The Lighthouse Family were lost in?
10 Who did Tennille sing with?
11 Which Madonna album beginning with Like A, followed "Like A Virgin"?
12 Who had a 70s No. 1 with "Figaro"?
13 What was Dina Carroll without in her 1999 song?
14 Who was backed by The Blockheads?
15 What connects Gloria Estefan and Fidel Castro?
16 Who had a 90s No. 1 with "Saturday Night"?
17 What is Tina Turner's original surname?
18 Who were in Angel Street in 1998?
19 Elton John sang about what colour of eyes?
20 Who had an 80s No. 1 with "He Ain't Heavy, He's My Brother"?

Answers

Pot Luck 68 (Quiz 134)
1 LeAnn Rimes. 2 East 17. 3 60s. 4 Aerosmith. 5 That. 6 Gary Numan.
7 Life. 8 Genesis. 9 James Taylor. 10 Take That. 11 Down. 12 Clannad.
13 Tuesday. 14 60s. 15 Barry. 16 Africa. 17 Earth. 18 Annie Lennoz.
19 Doctor. 20 Supremes.

Quiz 131 Stage Shows

Answers – see page 145

1 Which Swedish group had members who co-wrote "Chess"?
2 Who joined Elaine Paige on the hit single "I Know Him So Well"?
3 Which 60s musical was controversial for its nudity and language?
4 Which musical gave Elaine Paige her first Top Ten hit "Memory"?
5 Which Michael got to No. 2 with "Love Changes Everything" from *Aspects of Love*?
6 Which show is Michael Crawford's "The Music of the Night" from?
7 Which musical about US high school kids in the 50s gave Craig McLachlan chart success?
8 Which rock opera by the Who is about a "deaf, dumb and blind kid"?
9 Which children's TV presenter had a hit with "Close Every Door" from *Joseph and the Amazing Technicolor Dreamcoat*?
10 Who had a No. 1 with "Any Dream Will Do" from the same show?
11 Which Boulevard provided Barbra Streisand with 90s hit singles?
12 Which Cliff Richard film did Darren Day take to the stage in 1996?
13 In which city did Cliff Richard's musical *Heathcliff* have its 1996 premiere?
14 On which day did Marti Webb say to Tell Me in 1980?
15 Which Superstar opened in the West End in 1971 and again in 1996?
16 Which musical includes the No. 1 "Don't Cry For Me Argentina"?
17 Which show based on a Dickens novel includes "As Long As He Needs Me"?
18 What do the performers in *Starlight Express* wear on their feet?
19 Which pop veteran did Sarah Brightman duet with in "All I Ask of You"?
20 The stage show that includes the hit song "On My Own" is based on which Victor Hugo novel?

1 Which city are all the original members of Boyzone from?
2 Which charity benefited from the single "When The Going Gets Tough"?
3 How many members of Boyzone were there originally?
4 On which show did the group sing requests when fans phoned in their favourites?
5 What is Keith's surname?
6 Shane attracted publicity in 1999 by racing what?
7 Which chocolate company did Boyzone advertise?
8 Ronan recorded a song from the soundtrack of which major 1999 movie?
9 Who had the original hit with "Words"?
10 Which redhead apologised to Ronan on TFI Friday for previous rude remarks about the band?
11 In which country is Boyzone's official fan club?
12 "No Matter What" came from which musical?
13 Which soap cast featured on the charity single "When The Going Gets Tough"?
14 In which country did Boyzone have their first major hit?
15 "Picture Of You" came from which Rowan Atkinson movie?
16 Which member of the band hosted the Eurovision Song Contest?
17 Shane's sisters are members of which girl band?
18 Which member of the band hosted *Get Your Act Together*?
19 Which Spice Girl did Ronan duet with at the "99 Wicked Women charity concert?
20 Which songwriter appeared with Boyzone on *Top of the Pops*?

1   How many members of the Monkees were there?
2   Who were Joe Brown's backing group?
3   Whose first solo hit was "Careless Whisper" in 1984?
4   Which famous Manchester prison features on the title of an album by The Smiths?
5   Which country does Bob Geldof come from?
6   How did Michael Bolotin slightly change his name for show business?
7   Which group sold in excess of 8 million records with "I'm A Believer"?
8   What sort of Band were the Brighouse and Rastrick?
9   Which country is Belinda Carlisle from?
10   Which singer/drummer appeared in the UK and US performances of Live Aid?
11   Which blonde 60s and 70s star sang with the Pet Shop Boys in 1987?
12   Which word goes before Believe and Feel Fine in a song title?
13   Which film star's eyes were a hit for Kim Carnes?
14   What was Bruce Springsteen Born to do in 1987?
15   Which wine was Elkie Brooks singing about in 1978?
16   What went with Gypsys and Tramps on Cher's 1971 single?
17   Which Crisis had an 80s hit with "Arizona Sky"?
18   The Bangles were heard to Walk Like who in 1986?
19   Which Lynn had an international hit with "Rose Garden"?
20   Whose remix of "Downtown" re-entered the charts in 1988?

LEVEL 1

1 "How Do I Live" was a hit for which female vocalist in 1998?
2 Which chart-topping group had 17 in its name?
3 In which decade did David Bowie record Space Oddity?
4 Whose first top ten hit was "I Don't Want To Miss A Thing"?
5 Which Way did the Backstreet Boys want it in their 1999 hit?
6 Who had a 70s No. 1 with "Cars"?
7 What did Iggy Pop have a Lust for on his 1977 album?
8 Which group confessed "We Can't Dance" in the 90s?
9 Who recorded the album *Sweet Baby James*?
10 Who had a 90s No. 1 with "Back For Good"?
11 Which word completes the song by 5ive, "If Ya Gettin'_____"?
12 Which group did Enya leave in the late 80s?
13 Which Night Music Club was a 1993 album for Sheryl Crow?
14 In which decade was *Top Of The Pops* first shown on BBC?
15 Which Gibb – the oldest – was not a twin?
16 Paul Simon's Graceland particularly featured music from which continent?
17 What goes with Wind and Fire in the group of the 70s?
18 Who took "Whiter Shade Of Pale" into the charts in the 90s?
19 Which word goes before Jones in the song by Aqua?
20 Which group did Diana Ross leave to go solo?

1 In which decade was the Stock, Aitken and Waterman "hit factory" established?
2 Which member of the trio's first name is Mike?
3 Which female *Neighbours* star was an early SAW signing?
4 Which Page 3 model's record "Nothing Gonna Stop Me Now" was an SAW production?
5 Which Rick from the SAW stable had Europe's best selling single of 1987, "Never Gonna Give You Up"?
6 Which Band's 1989 Christmas charity remake did SAW produce?
7 Who was Mel's singing partner on SAW's production of "F.L.M."?
8 On which charity No. 1 did they feature with the Christians, Holly Johnson, Paul McCartney and Gerry Marsden?
9 What were there Too Many of in the song sung by Jason Donovan?
10 What completes the SAW slogan "the sound of a bright young…"?
11 With which Donna did SAW produce "This Time I Know It's For Real"?
12 Which pop veteran had a hit with "I Just Don't Have The Heart"?
13 Which female trio had a hit with "I Heard a Rumour" in 1987?
14 Which charity band had a SAW-produced No. 1 with "Let It Be" after the *Herald of Free Enterprise* tragedy?
15 Which of the trio introduced "The Hitman and Her" on TV?
16 Which single-named performer had a No. 1 with the SAW written and produced "You'll Never Stop Me Loving You"?
17 Where were the Tears on Kylie Minogue's 1990 No. 1?
18 Which traffic hazard was a hit for SAW as performers in 1987?
19 How many Good Reasons were on the title of Jason Donovan's first No. 1 album?
20 How many charity No. 1's did SAW have?

1 How many were in the original Take That line-up?
2 Which member of the group's first solo single was "Forever Love"?
3 Which letter came after "Do What" in the title of their first single?
4 What did they add to their name to make the title of their first album?
5 Which 60s star sang with them on "Relight My Fire"?
6 What did Robbie see Life Thru in his album title?
7 Which Fab Four were the artists to precede Take That with four consecutive No. 1s?
8 Which 1993 No. 1 shared its name with a film about a pig?
9 Who was the first member of Take That to announce he was leaving?
10 Which member of the band shared his surname with a famous Liverpool soccer player called Michael?
11 What sort of Days were a summer hit for Robbie in 1997?
12 Who made the classic "Let Me Entertain You" after going solo?
13 What sort of Road was Gary Barlow's debut album?
14 In 1998/99 Robbie Williams had a much-publicised on/off relationship with Nicole of which group ?
15 Robbie won the 99 Brit Award for Best Video for which historical sounding song?
16 Which city is Gary Barlow from?
17 Robbie had No what on his second release from *I've Been Expecting You*?
18 Which George had a hit with Robbie's first solo hit, "Freedom"?
19 Which eating style does Jason Orange share with the late Linda McCartney?
20 Which children's charity reportedly had many calls from youngsters distraught at Take That disbanding?

Quiz 137 Pot Luck 69

Answers – see page 151

1. Whose first hit was "Heaven is a Place on Earth" in 1987?
2. Which word goes before Way and Pretty One in the song titles?
3. Where is the Fog on the best-selling album by Lindisfarne?
4. Which Leppard were the most successful heavy-metal band of the 80s?
5. Which Club sang "Do You Really Want to Hurt Me?" in 1982?
6. Which heavy rock band shares its name with a village in the Bible?
7. Which 50s vocal Girls were the name of a football pools company?
8. Which number follows Haircut in the name of the 80s band?
9. Which 60s band's first album was called *Are You Experienced*?
10. Which country did INXS come from?
11. Which record label shares its name with a substance in a thermometer?
12. Which number follows U in the name of the band?
13. Which singer was nicknamed "The Big O"?
14. Which Motown Brothers sang "Behind A Painted Smile" in 1969?
15. Which girl is the youngest of the singing Jackson family?
16. Which part of the UK is Annie Lennox from?
17. Which actress Julia was Lyle Lovett married to?
18. Which area of New York was transferred to the name of a vocal quartet?
19. Which actor/singer had an album called *Just Good Friends* after the sitcom in which he starred?
20. Which Monkee had the same name as David Bowie's real name?

1 What did Chaka Demus and Pliers do as well as Shout in 1993?
2 Who had a 70s No. 1 with "Daydreamer"/"The Puppy Song"?
3 "Until The Time Is Through" was a hit for which group?
4 Which word follows If You Had My in the song by Jennifer Lopez?
5 In which decade did Prefab Sprout first make the charts?
6 Who had a 90s No. 1 with Rhythm Is A Dancer?
7 Which ex-Beatle recorded "Band On The Run"?
8 Who or what was Sleeping in the title of a Tasmin Archer's No. 1?
9 Which superstar's real name is Steveland Judkins?
10 In which film based on a cartoon did Madonna co-star with Warren Beatty?
11 Who usually duetted with Womack?
12 What's the name of Nat King Cole's singing daughter?
13 What colour are the Smurfs?
14 Which word completes the song by Toni Braxton, "I Don't ____ To"?
15 The long-running TV show where a panel judged a record a hit or a miss was called Juke Box what?
16 What is the home country of Sinead O'Connor?
17 Which word describes vocalists Eva and Richard?
18 Who was lead singer with Duran Duran?
19 Who had a 90s No. 1 with "Ebeneezer Goode"?
20 Which band put out the album *Brothers in Arms*?

1   What goes before "(Who Have Nothing)" in the title of the Shirley Bassey hit?
2   Who joined Elton John to take his composition "Don't Let The Sun Go Down On Me" to the top of the charts?
3   Who went to the top of the charts with "One Moment in Time" in 1988?
4   Whose dream of The Green, Green Grass of Home went to No. 1?
5   Which Last dance gave Englebert Humperdinck a No. 1 in 1967?
6   Which Frank Sinatra classic entered the charts 10 times in 15 years?
7   Which Elaine Paige hit begins "Midnight, not a sound from the pavement"?
8   Which Canadian-born lady was All By herself at the start of 1997?
9   According to the Hollies, He Ain't Heavy He's what?
10 Which Boys had someone Always On their Mind in 1988?
11 What colour did Chris De Burgh's Lady wear in 1986 ?
12 The Power of what gave Jennifer Rush a No. 1 hit in 1985?
13 Which hit has the lines "Walk on, walk on, with hope in your heart"?
14 Which show did the hit "I Know Him So Well" come from?
15 How many times was someone a lady on the Commodores hit?
16 Which Barbra had a No. 1 hit with "Woman in Love"?
17 Love Changes what according to the Michael Ball ballad?
18 Which Beatles' ballad has been recorded more than any other?
19 What were Simply Red Holding Back in in 1986?
20 Which ballad had a record-breaking run at No. 1 with Bryan Adams?

1 What's the first word of "Wannabe"?
2 What did Mel B call herself after her marriage?
3 What was Mel B's daughter's first name?
4 Which record label did the Spice Girls first record on?
5 Which pop magazine gave the Spice Girls their famous nicknames?
6 Which slogan was the title of the Spice Girls' book about themselves?
7 Which single was the first, ironically, not to go straight to No. 1?
8 What Night Divas were the Spice Girls on *Spiceworld*?
9 In which country did Posh Spice marry David Beckham?
10 Which Girl had a solo hit with "Missy Misdemeanour Elliott"?
11 Geri became an Ambassador for which international organisation?
12 What is Mel C's surname?
13 Which early song did they release to coincide with Mother's Day?
14 What did the Girls suggest you Spice Up in 1997?
15 Where were the Spice Girls on tour when Geri left the band?
16 Which Girl was nicknamed Sporty?
17 Which Richard played their manager in *Spiceworld: The Movie*?
18 Which Spice Girl came from Leeds?
19 What colour outfits did Victoria and David Beckham wear for their wedding reception?
20 What is the Adams/Beckham son called?

1 Which Maiden took "Bring Your Daughter to the Slaughter" to No. 1?
2 Which dirty-sounding group had a hit with "Tiger Feet"?
3 Who were Freddie's backing group?
4 How was Rick Nelson known in his early career?
5 Which word goes before Still Waiting and Alive in the song titles?
6 Which first name is shared by Messrs Newman and Travis?
7 What is Mike Oldfield's musical sister called?
8 Which colour goes before Angel and Bayou on Roy Orbison's singles?
9 Which TV/pop family included Shirley Jones and David Cassidy?
10 Which country does Luciano Pavarotti originate from?
11 Who was Pepsi's singing partner?
12 What did Pink Floyd See Emily do on their 1967 single?
13 What Gets In Your Eyes according to The Platters?
14 Which former DJ Peter was Anthea Turner married to?
15 Who had an Amazing Dancing Bear according to Alan Price?
16 Which Suzi's first No. 1 was "Can The Can"?
17 Which Fred said "I'm Too Sexy" in 1991?
18 Which Great book by Charles Dickens is the title of the debut album by Tasmin Archer?
19 Whose first hit was "I Should Be So Lucky" in 1988?
20 How many members of New Kids on the Block were there?

1 In the 90s the classic "No Woman, No Cry" was a hit for which group?
2 Which Family sang with Limmie in the 70s?
3 Who sang about Stereotypes in 1996?
4 Which female singer had an early 90s hit with "Confide In Me"?
5 Which musical instrument does Ray Charles play?
6 *The Times They Are A-Changin'* was a best-selling album from which influential artist?
7 Who charted in 1998 with the "The Incidentals"?
8 According to Cyndi Lauper "Girls Just Want to Have..." what?
9 *Tears Roll Down* was a greatest hits album by which group?
10 What was Cliff Richard's 90s Bronte-based musical called?
11 Which lady made the *Watermark* album in 1988?
12 Which Jean-Michel keeps returning with a bit more Oxygene?
13 Which word follows My Favourite in the song by The Cardigans?
14 Who had a 90s No. 1 with "Things Can Only Get Better"?
15 Who did Roger Daltrey sing with?
16 What was Cleopatra's first top ten hit?
17 What colour was the title of R.E.M.'s 1988 album release?
18 Which country did the group featuring Bay City in its name come from?
19 Which female singer had an early 90s hit with "Hero"?
20 Which group did Morrissey sing with?

Quiz 143 Food for Thought

Answers – see page 149

LEVEL 1

1 Which Girls had the Christmas No. 1 single and album in 1996?
2 Which Jasper is known for comedy but has enjoyed chart success?
3 Which bubbly drink gave the UK Eurovision success in 1981?
4 Which drink went with Mistletoe on Cliff Richard's 1988 Christmas hit?
5 Which 70s glam-rock band were obviously not sour?
6 Who recorded "Bat Out Of Hell"?
7 Which meal did Deep Blue Something have at Tiffany's in 1996?
8 Which flavour Ice had a No. 1 with "Ice Ice Baby" in 1990?
9 Which Marc had a 1989 hit with Gene Pitney?
10 Which Song was an 80s No. 1 for Spitting Image?
11 Which group's name would go with scones or even tarts?
12 Which 60s band would make a good topping for strawberries?
13 Which David Gates group would be good if you wanted a sandwich?
14 Which 60s group would go well with toast?
15 According to Millie what was My Boy called?
16 Which Hot drink sang "You Sexy Thing"?
17 Which Jason was a member of Take That?
18 Which fruit was at the core of Beatles' singles on their own label?
19 Which type of Sugar was a hit for the Rolling Stones?
20 What American food was a hit for Don McLean?

Answers

Big Ballads (Quiz 139)
1 I. 2 George Michael. 3 Whitney Houston. 4 Tom Jones. 5 Waltz.
6 "My Way". 7 "Memory". 8 Celine Dion. 9 My Brother. 10 Pet Shop Boys.
11 Red. 12 Love. 13 "You'll Never Walk Alone". 14 *Chess*. 15 Three.
16 Streisand. 17 Everything. 18 "Yesterday". 19 The Years.
20 "(Everything I Do) I Do It For You".

1 Which member of Blur has used the anagram of his name Dan Abnormal and written a song of the same name?
2 What means of transport features on the cover of *The Great Escape*?
3 What was the first name of the band's Rowntree?
4 What is Blur's fanzine called?
5 Which nourishing record label did Blur record on on their early albums?
6 Which band were seen as Blur's major rivals in the Britpop war?
7 What sort of Man took them into the charts in 1996?
8 What sort of house was a hit single for Blur?
9 Which instrument did Graham Coxon play in addition to saxophone?
10 Which Blur album was dubbed the Sgt Pepper of the 90s?
11 What sort of World reached the top 30 in 1993?
12 Which Beetle song was a follow-up to "Country House"?
13 How many performers were originally in Blur?
14 In which county was Damon Albarn brought up?
15 Which eating style does Damon Albarn share with the late Linda McCartney?
16 What was the first name of their bass player James?
17 Damien Hirst has directed Blur videos but what is his "day job"?
18 Which debut album by Blur has a non-working title?
19 Albarn duetted with Ray Davies of which 60s band on the song "Waterloo Sunset"?
20 In 1995 the band performed on the roof of the HMV store in which London street?

LEVEL 1

1   Whose *Bridge Over Troubled Water* album is one of the best sellers of all time?
2   Which singer was nicknamed Little Miss Dynamite?
3   Which record label shares its name with a London Circus?
4   Which American female has had more than 40 Top 40 hits?
5   Which Jimmy had the original hit with "What Becomes of the Broken Hearted?"?
6   Which Alexei asked "'Ullo John, Got a New Motor?" in 1984?
7   Which group's name sounds like a structure for execution?
8   What went after Scritti in the name of the 80s band?
9   Which haven't entered the UK charts – Singing Dogs, Singing Pigs or Singing Sheep?
10 Which Soft band had Tainted Love in 1981?
11 Which Bobby had a 50s No. 1 with "Mack The Knife"?
12 Which one-time Elton John duettist had a hit with "Amoureuse"?
13 What did the Drifters say to Save on their best-selling hit?
14 Which Boris sang "I Want To Wake Up With You" in 1986?
15 Which number was important for Paul Hardcastle in 1985?
16 Which country did 60s vocalist Françoise Hardy come from?
17 Which Frankie said "WelcomeTo The Pleasure Dome"in 1985?
18 Which two words followed Chirpy Chirpy on Middle of the Road's 70s No. 1?
19 Who recorded the album with his own name and "Schmilsson" in the title?
20 Whose first hit was "Move It" in 1958?

LEVEL 1

1 "Stupid Girl" was a hit for which group?
2 In 1993 Billy Joel was going to The River Of what?
3 What did the E stand for in ELO?
4 Who had an 80s No. 1 with "Living Doll"?
5 Which word goes before Trippin" in the track by Fatboy Slim?
6 Who had a 70s No. 1 with "When A Child Is Born"?
7 In the group name what goes in front of Mary Chain?
8 Which Brothers charted with "This Old Heart Of Mine"?
9 Suggs sang with which nutty-sounding group?
10 Which Club was led by Boy George?
11 Who had an 80s No. 1 with "Green Door"?
12 In which decade did the Pet Shop Boys first make the charts?
13 Which Queen was Aretha Franklin known as?
14 Which singer had a baby named Lourdes in 1996?
15 Who sang with the Papas?
16 "End Of The Line" was a hit for which group?
17 How many Seasons were in the group which sang "Rag Doll"?
18 Which word goes after Beautiful in the Madonna hit title?
19 Who had an 80s No. 1 with "Rock Me Amadeus"?
20 Under what name did Raymond Edward O'Sullivan become better known?

1 Whose video for "Like A Prayer" was banned by the Vatican?
2 Which 60s group was famous for breaking up guitars on stage?
3 Which Nirvana vocalist shot himself in 1994?
4 Which group's records were suspended on some radio networks in January 1997 after its former singer said Ecstasy was completely safe?
5 Which Doors member was buried in Paris after his family disowned him?
6 Which Alice appeared on stage with a guillotine and live snakes?
7 Which band was Noel Gallagher referring to when he said he hoped two of its members would die of AIDS?
8 Which member of the Sex Pistols was charged with the murder of his girlfriend Nancy Spungen?
9 Which singer Marianne was arrested with Mick Jagger in 1969?
10 Who was performing in New York when semi-nude female cyclists appeared as the band sang "Fat Bottomed Girls"?
11 Who was arrested at the 1996 Brit Awards for his behaviour when Michael Jackson was on stage?
12 Which Rolling Stone drowned "while under the influence of alcohol and drugs"?
13 Which Jane Birkin/Serge Gainsbourg song was banned by the BBC?
14 Which Jimi ended his act by playing guitar with his teeth then burning it?
15 Which Motown star Marvin was shot dead by his own father?
16 Which Jerry married his 13-year-old third wife when he was 22?
17 Who was shown on TV from the waist up only in 1957 as his gyrations were said to be too provocative?
18 Who caused a storm by saying the Beatles were more popular than Jesus?
19 In 1986 16-year-old Mandy Smith revealed a two-year affair with whom?
20 Which Eric played with Cream before going solo?

1 How many people were there in the group where Michael Jackson found fame?
2 What regal name does Michael Jackson's eldest son have?
3 Which record label did Michael first record on?
4 What type of Walk was Jackson's trademark?
5 What was the name of Jackson's famous chimpanzee companion?
6 Who did he marry in May 1994?
7 Which 80s hit written by Paul McCartney was the same word three times?
8 Which ex-member of The Commodores did he write "We Are The World" with?
9 Where was Blood in the title of a 1997 hit?
10 Which bird featured in the title of a 70s top ten hit?
11 Which ex-Beatle recorded "The Girl Is Mine" with Jackson?
12 Which Song was a Christmas No. 1 in 1995?
13 What was Jackson's album follow-up to *Thriller*?
14 Which season featured in the title of an 80s hit which began Farewell?
15 Which co-founder of Comic Relief and star of *Chef!* and *Hope and Glory* was born the same day as Jackson?
16 Which female Motown star is credited on the early minor hit "Ease On Down The Road"?
17 Which other member of the family was credited on the single "Scream"?
18 What relation if any to Jackson were 3T?
19 Which Quincy produced *Bad*?
20 In which decade was the album *Dangerous* released?

1   How many members of Take That were there in the early 90s?
2   Which word goes before I Fall In Love and A Child Is Born in two song titles?
3   Which colour Roses feature in Jimmy Nail's 1997 single?
4   Who were Lulu's backing group?
5   Which country were A-Ha from?
6   Whose real name is Eric Clapp?
7   Which Twist artist was named after Fats Domino?
8   Whose first UK hit was "(They Long to Be) Close To You"?
9   Whose first No. 1 was "It Doesn't Matter Any More" in 1959?
10 What was Living in a Box's first single in 1987?
11 What was Little Richard's Sally like?
12 Which Matt sang "Get Out of Your Lazy Bed"?
13 Which musical instrument does Herb Alpert play?
14 Which Thin group sang "Whiskey in the Jar" in 1973?
15 Which Diddyman's first hit was "Love is Like a Violin"?
16 Which Roger was Leavin' Durham Town in 1969?
17 Which Five were Glad All Over in 1963?
18 Whose first hit was "Apache" in 1960?
19 Which TV holiday programme is also the title of an album by Pink Floyd?
20 Which group was a Wannabe in 1996?

1 How many girls did Bombalurina have Sitting In The Backseat?
2 "Smoke" was a top five hit for which singer?
3 Who had an 80s No. 1 with "One Day In Your Life"?
4 In "My Way" what do you face "now the end is near"?
5 Which lady fronted The Miami Sound Machine?
6 Which song became a No. 1 for Elvis Presley and UB40?
7 Which record label has the same name as an ocean?
8 Who had an 80s No. 1 with "A Different Corner"?
9 Which word follows You Might Need in the song by Shola Ama?
10 Sixties singer Marianne Faithfull had a four-year relationship with which Rolling Stone?
11 Which TV show was introduced by Jools Holland and Paula Yates?
12 Which country does Alanis Morissette come from?
13 Who had an 80s No. 1 with "If I Was"?
14 Who wrote the autobiography called Take It Like A Man?
15 Who called himself the Doggfather in 1998?
16 Which word is missing from the title of a Barry White No. 1, "You're My First, My Last, My _____"?
17 Which medical series did "Suicide Is Painless" come from?
18 Who had an 80s No. 1 with "Chain Reaction"?
19 Which instrument did Suzi Quatro play?
20 In an 80s hit what did Michael Jackson say to his Summer Love?

1 What is Madonna's real first name?
2 Which Madonna film was premiered in December 1996?
3 Who was Madonna Desperately Seeking in her first major film role?
4 Madonna was Like a what on her second album?
5 What was Madonna Into on her first UK No. 1?
6 Who did Madonna tell not to Preach on her 1986 single?
7 Which actor did Madonna marry in 1985?
8 What type of Ambition describes her world tour in 1990?
9 In which film based on a cartoon character did she co-star with Warren Beatty?
10 Which Collection album was made up of greatest hits?
11 What name was given to her 1992 album and accompanying book?
12 What type of Girl is Madonna on her 1985 hit?
13 What were Madonna fans wearing on her video "Bedtime Story"?
14 Which pop show did Madonna appear on in November 1995 after an 11-year gap?
15 Which True colour was Madonna in 1986?
16 Which magazine shares its name with a 1990 No. 1?
17 Robert Hoskins was convicted of which crime against Madonna in January 1996?
18 Did Madonna give birth to a son or a daughter in autumn 1996?
19 What type of Girl is Madonna on her 1993 hit?
20 "Like A Prayer" was used to advertise which drink?

Quiz 152 Mariah Carey

Answers – see page 158

LEVEL 1

1 In which country was Mariah Carey born?
2 With which US female vocalist did she have a hit in 1998?
3 What type of singer was Mariah Carey's mother?
4 Which Nilsson classic was Mariah Carey's first UK No. 1?
5 What was her first album called?
6 Who did she sing with on "Endless Love"?
7 What did Mariah Carey "Want For Christmas" in 1994?
8 What did she have a Vision of in 1990?
9 What was the first Mariah Carey single which was also the title of an album?
10 What type of Lover did she have in 1993?
11 Which insect was the title of a 1997 hit?
12 What preceded Unplugged in the title of her 1992 EP?
13 What are the predominant colours on the cover of *Ones*?
14 Which group did she record "One Sweet Day" with?
15 Mariah was named after a name in what?
16 Mariah Carey married the president of which record company which was once in dispute with George Michael ?
17 Which US male singer is the only solo artist to have spent longer at the top of the US charts than Mariah Carey?
18 Which Box was a 1993 success?
19 Who was the female duettist on "Endless Love" before Mariah Carey's version?
20 Anytime You Need a what became her second top ten hit of 1994?

1 Which daughter of a famous singer had hits with Lee Hazelwood?
2 Which Tony and Jackie wrote the theme music for *Neighbours*?
3 Which musical instrument is Buddy Greco famous for?
4 What type of guitar did Jimi Hendrix play – electric or acoustic?
5 Which Caribbean island does reggae originate from?
6 Which Sabbath are a heavy-metal band?
7 Which singer is nicknamed the Spanish Sinatra?
8 Which song was a No. 1 for Rosemary Clooney and Shakin' Stevens?
9 Which half of a 70s duo recorded his *Graceland* album?
10 What was Messrs Green and Flynn's No. 1 debut album?
11 What extra accessory does Gabrielle wear on her face?
12 Which 90s reptiles gave Partners in Kryme a No. 1 hit?
13 Whose first hit was "If Not For You" in 1971?
14 Which Fern sang "Together We Are Beautiful"?
15 How were the Motown Spinners later known?
16 For which country did Johnny Logan win the Eurovision Song Contest?
17 Who sang about Major Tom stranded in space?
18 Who had a triple platinum album with *Zenyatta Mondatta* in the 80s?
19 Which family of brothers wrote and co-produced Barbra Streisand's No. 1 "Woman in Love"?
20 Whose first album was called *Blue Gene* in 1964?

Quiz 154 Pot Luck 78

Answers – see page 168

1   "Baby Come Back" was a 90s No. 1 for which singer?
2   "Sit Down" was the first top ten hit for which group?
3   How many people made up Tears For Fears?
4   What is the first word of "Too Much" by The Spice Girls?
5   Who had an 80s No. 1 with "Jealous Guy"?
6   Which word follows Professional in the song by Tori Amos?
7   What was the first name of Elvis's wife?
8   Which pop veteran duetted with Sarah Brightman on "All I Ask Of You"?
9   Who is credited on Tamperer's 1998 No. 1 "Feel It"?
10 Which word completes the song by Oasis, "D'You Know What I ____"?
11 Who was doing a Bat Dance at the end of the 90s?
12 Who did Harry meet in the film that featured the siinging of Harry Connick Jr?
13 Who had an 80s No. 1 with "Stand And Deliver"?
14 Whose Best Of album was called *Twelve Deadly Cyns... And Then Some*?
15 How is George Ivan Morrison better known?
16 Which animal-sounding US group had Davy Jones as frontman?
17 Who had a 70s No. 1 with "Tragedy"?
18 Which word follows You're in the song by Babybird?
19 What is the home country of Sheena Easton?
20 In which decade did Dolly Parton first make the charts?

1 Who was the 50s' top-selling male artist?
2 Who had one of the best-selling US hits ever with "The Chipmunk Song"?
3 Which British singer was a top-selling artist in the USA in the 80s particularly when she got Physical?
4 What is the surname of Pat and Debby, US chart-toppers in the 50s and 70s respectively?
5 Who were Stayin' Alive at the top of the US charts in 1978?
6 Which (originally Tamla) duo had Endless Love in the 80s?
7 Which Star film theme was a best-seller for Meco in 1977?
8 Which new dance made Chubby Checker and his song a 60s hit?
9 Which Garth is a US top-selling artist?
10 Which band, whose name is shared with a city famous for its tea party, had a best-selling album of the same name?
11 Which Boyz are among the top-selling bands of the 90s in the US?
12 Which Mariah joined them on a single in 1995?
13 Whose Boy Child provided a hit for Harry Belafonte?
14 What was the title of USA For Africa's charity record?
15 Who sang "White Christmas", the best-seller of all time in the US?
16 Which veteran US singer has had around 70 chart albums in his career?
17 Which female singer shares her surname with the most populous city in Texas?
18 Which King gave two British writers a top-selling US album?
19 Who backed Prince on the 80s album *Purple Rain*?
20 What sort of Dancing was a top film soundtrack?

1 Which Spice Girl had a hit with "I Want You Back"?
2 Which Dutch place gave the Beautiful South a hit?
3 "MmmBop" was a hit for which group?
4 Who were "Free As A Bird" in 1995?
5 Who sang the theme from *GoldenEye*?
6 Which song brought Louis Armstrong back to the charts in the 90s?
7 "Mysterious Girl" was a top three hit for which singer?
8 Which Street linked to Sherlock Holmes charted in the 90s?
9 Who duetted with Luther Vandross in "The Best Things In Life Are Free"?
10 Which comedian teamed up with Smokie?
11 Which female singer recorded "Anywhere Is"?
12 What was East 17's weather-linked hit?
13 Who was up to "Hanky Panky" in 1990?
14 What name is shared by hitmakers Melanie, Robbie and Vanessa?
15 "No Surprises" was a 1998 top five hit for which group?
16 Which Common is the place to go Wombling free?
17 Who did DNA team up with at Tom's Diner?
18 What kind of Ground did UB40 sing about?
19 Who was "In Too Deep"?
20 Which drink provided a mixer with Mase and Monica?

1   How many members of the Police were there?
2   Which decade was Cliff Richard born in?
3   Which Kid is also known as August Darnell?
4   Who had a No. 1 with "Super Trouper"?
5   Which country does Jimmy Nail come from?
6   Which daughter of Cissy Houston duetted with her on "I Know Him So Well" on the daughter's album?
7   Which Brenda had a hit with "Speak To Me Pretty"?
8   Which Matt and Luke were in a trio with Craig Logan?
9   Which Enya hit is subtitled "Sail Away"?
10 "1988 Summer Olympics"/"One Moment In Time" was made for the Games hosted by which country?
11 Which singer's surname is Ciccone?
12 Which Continental artist had a No. 1 with "Begin the Beguine" in 1981?
13 Which Johnny is nicknamed the Man in Black?
14 Which member of Cilla Black's family is her manager?
15 What do the letters LP stand for?
16 Who were Bill Haley's backing group?
17 Is Vangelis the artist's first name or surname?
18 Whose first hit was "Only The Lonely" in 1960?
19 Which number follows East in the name of the band?
20 Which game of reptiles and climbing apparatus is the title of an album by Gerry Rafferty?

1 Who had an 80s No. 1 with "The Reflex"?
2 Which word goes before Of Light in the song by Madonna?
3 Who had a 90s No. 1 with "Inside"?
4 What is the home country of Clannad?
5 In 1987 what did M/A/R/R/S Pump Up?
6 "Virtual Insanity" was a 1996 hit for which group?
7 Who had an 80s No. 1 with "This Ole House"?
8 Which US TV series gave Jan Hammer his first UK chart success with its theme tune?
9 Who had a big 70s hit with "Money Money Money"?
10 Which word goes after Love Won't in the song by Gary Barlow?
11 "Pray" was a 90s No. 1 for which group?
12 How many Degrees sang "When Will I See You Again"?
13 Which creature featured in a hit from the Spitting Image team?
14 What was the name of Billie's first No. 1?
15 Which country are The Chieftains from?
16 Who had a 70s No. 1 with "I Don't Want To Talk About It"?
17 Which word completes the song by Celine Dion, "Because You ____ Me"?
18 In the 50s favourite Connie Francis discovered Lipstick On Your what?
19 Who had an 80s No. 1 with "Wake Me Up Before You Go Go"?
20 Wendy Richard had a chart hit before starring in which soap?

LEVEL 1

1 Which gravel-voiced jazz trumpeter was nearly 68 when he had a No. 1 with "What a Wonderful World"?
2 Which duo's combined ages were over 100 when they hit the top spot with the reissued "Unchained Melody" in 1990?
3 Who was 78 when he re-entered the charts with "My Way" in 1994?
4 Which grandmother had a No. 1 album *What's Love Got to Do With It?*?
5 Who was the Leader of the Gang in the 70s but kept rockin' into the 90s?
6 Which Welsh grandad, once described as "sweat personified" topped the bill at the 1996 Royal Variety Show and sang his 80s hit "Kiss"?
7 Which singer teamed up with David Bowie for the 1982 hit "Peace on Earth–Little Drummer Boy"?
8 Which 90s Radio 2 man had two consecutive No. 1s in the 50s?
9 Which French singer, most famous for "She", released a CD of songs in English in 1996?
10 Which two-letter song title did Telly (Kojak) Savalas take to No. 1?
11 Who had a No. 1 with "Saviour's Day" shortly after his 50th birthday?
12 Which Neil, famous for "Oh Carol", started in the 50s and was still touring in the 90s?
13 Which Italian over-60 joined Elton John on a 1996 single?
14 Which elderly relative did Clive Dunn portray when he was only 49?
15 Which TV presenter took "A Stairway to Heaven" to No. 7 in 1993?
16 Which Shirley had her first hit in 1957 and enjoyed a 90s revival?
17 Which TV presenter Des was in the Top Ten in the 80s at the age of 54?
18 Which Rod is enjoying chart success in his 50s as he did in his 20s?
19 Which US singer Perry was enjoying chart success when he was over 60?
20 Which Dartford-born grandfather has been lead singer in one of the country's most controversial pop groups for more than 30 years?

1 Which group recorded "Brass In Pocket"?
2 What happens "When The Going Gets Tough"?
3 Who had an 80s No. 1 with "The Coward Of The County"?
4 "Atomic" topped the charts for which group?
5 Which solo female singer made No. 1 with "Together We Are Beautiful"?
6 What went with Sir Cliff's "Mistletoe"?
7 Who had an 80s No. 1 with "Especially For You"?
8 Which group were "Going Underground"?
9 How many No. 1s did The Osmonds have in the 80s?
10 Who was named in the title of Sister Sledge's only 80s No. 1?
11 Who sang with UB40 on "I Got You Babe"?
12 Which No. 1 contained the word Belfast in the title?
13 Which male singer was "Crying" at No. 1?
14 Who was in "Xanadu" with the Electric Light Orchestra?
15 Which song first took Jennifer Rush to No. 1?
16 Which group sang "The Winner Takes It All"?
17 Who had an 80s No. 1 with "Ashes To Ashes"?
18 "Start" made the top for which group?
19 "Relax" was the first No. 1 for who?
20 Who highlighted classroom perils in "Don't Stand So Close To Me"?

Quiz 161 Pot Luck 81

Answers – see page 175

1 Which part did Elvis Presley play in the film *Frankie and Johnny*?
2 Which Brothers in Arms had Money For Nothing in album terms?
3 Which Brothers were Scott, John and Gary?
4 In which decade was Celine Dion born?
5 Is Toyah the artist's first name or surname?
6 Which Scots singer's first husband was the Bee Gee Maurice Gibb?
7 In which country was Elton John born?
8 Which singer is nicknamed the Queen of Soul?
9 Which DJ/pop pundit called Jonathan had a hit record with "Everyone's Gone to the Moon"?
10 Which Tommy was considered to be Britain's first rock 'n' roll star?
11 How many guitarists made up the Shadows?
12 Which 80s rock band possessed England's most common surname?
13 Which Park gave hit records for Donna Summer and Richard Harris?
14 Who has hosted the Eurovision Song Contest on BBC1 in the 90s?
15 Which country does Gina G come from?
16 Which Gilbert appeared on stage in short trousers, cropped hair and cloth cap?
17 Which Australian appeared in "The Sullivans" and "The Hendersons" before enjoying chart success?
18 Whose first hit was "Love Me For a Reason" in 1994?
19 What is George's surname and Mr Bolton's first?
20 Whose first album was called *Otis Blue* in 1966?

Answers

Pot Luck 83 (Quiz 165)
1 1960s. 2 Mama Cass. 3 The Partridge Family. 4 Paula Yates. 5 Simon.
6 England. 7 Marvin. 8 Leather. 9 Puckett. 10 His trousers.
11 The Rubettes. 12 Keyboards. 13 Hynde. 14 The 50s. 15 Pink Floyd.
16 Pickett. 17 Bing Crosby. 18 Telly Savalas. 19 10c.c. 20 Four.

1 "Tattva" was a top three hit for which group?
2 Who had a 70s No. 1 with "Bright Eyes"?
3 Who makes up the trio with Lake and Palmer?
4 Who had an 80s No. 1 with "Working My Way Back To You"?
5 George O'Dowd is better known as who?
6 Which movie tough guy had a surprise 70s hit with "Wand'rin' Star"?
7 Which word follows The Drugs Don't in the song by the Verve?
8 Who was the singer with Lone Justice?
9 Who are the only group to have had Procul as part of their name?
10 In which decade did New Order first make the charts?
11 "Truly Madly Deeply" was a 90s top ten for which group?
12 Who had an 80s No. 1 with the "Theme From M*A*S*H"?
13 Which Brotherhood won the Eurovision Song Contest in 1976?
14 Which word completes the song by Ocean Colour Scene, "The Day We _____ The Train"?
15 What sort of Cowboy did Glen Campbell sing about?
16 Dennis Waterman's hit "I Could Be So Good For You" was a theme for which TV series?
17 Who had a 70s No. 1 with "Lucille"?
18 Which surname is shared by singers Phyllis, Ricky, Shara and Willie?
19 Which ex-Take That member made the album I've Been Expecting You?
20 Clannad provided the TV theme music for whose Game?

LEVEL 1

1 Which karaoke classic begins "First I was afraid, I was petrified"?
2 Which song starts "And now the end is near"?
3 What are the first three words of "Unchained Melody"?
4 Which Rhapsody begins "Is this the real life? Is this just fantasy?"?
5 Which Boyzone hit begins "Smile an everlasting smile"?
6 How many times is "Yeah" sung in the chorus of the Beatles' "She Loves You"?
7 Which soccer anthem begins "When you walk through a storm"?
8 Which words follow "Wake up Maggie" in Rod Stewart's "Maggie May"?
9 Which words from the Abba hit go before "It's a rich man's world"?
10 What five words does Stevie Wonder sing after "I just called..."?
11 How many times are the words "We are the champions" sung in the chorus of the song?
12 Which line follows "If I said you had a beautiful body"?
13 Which Cliff Richard classic begins, "When I was young my father said"?
14 Which Slade Christmas hit includes the line "Does your grandma always tell ya, That the old songs are the best?"?
15 What did Carly Simon sing before "I bet you think this song is about you"?
16 Which Robson and Jerome hit included the lines "for every drop of rain that falls, A flower grows"?
17 Which Wet Wet Wet hit begins "I feel it in my fingers, I feel it in my toes"?
18 Which Cher No. 1 includes the lines "If you want to know if he loves you so, It's in his kiss"?
19 Which Don McLean song asks "Do you believe in rock 'n' roll?"?
20 Which song begins "Never seen you looking so gorgeous as you did tonight"?

1 Which girl group had a US No. 1 with "Venus"?
2 Which major 80s band came "Through The Barricades"?
3 Which soloist sang about "The Love Of The Common People"?
4 Which "Baby" gave Rod Stewart his first 80s No. 1?
5 "Like A Prayer" was a 1989 hit for which singer?
6 What colour were the group Lace who had a huge hit with "Agadoo"?
7 Who recorded "Walk Like An Egyptian"?
8 Who was "Upside Down"?
9 Whose death in 1980 led to a string of posthumous hits and No. 1s?
10 Which not-so-big country did frequent chart visitors Big Country come from?
11 Who had "Breakfast In Bed" with Chrissie Hynde?
12 Who was producing hits with Aitken and Waterman?
13 What were Simply Red "Holding Back"?
14 Which TV sitcom actress made No. 2 with "Starting Together"?
15 Which female singer sang with the Pet Shop Boys on "What Have I Done To Deserve This"?
16 Which Bunny kept hopping to No. 1?
17 In the late 80s who put the "Cat Among The Pigeons"?
18 Whose many hits include "Wild Boys" and "Notorious"?
19 Which 60s star returned to the charts with "Heartbreaker"?
20 Which group took the traditional song "The Irish Rover" into the charts?

1 In which decade was Whitney Houston born?
2 How was Cass Elliott better known?
3 Who was David Cassidy's backing group?
4 Who was Mrs Bob Geldof at the start of the 90s?
5 What is Paul's surname and Mr Le Bon's first?
6 Which part of the UK does Lisa Stansfield come from?
7 Which first name is shared by Messrs Gaye and Rainwater?
8 What were Suzi Quatro's stage outfits usually made from?
9 Which Gary sang with the Union Gap?
10 What was P.J. Proby's most famous split on stage?
11 Whose first hit was "Sugar Baby Love" in 1974?
12 Which instrument does Alan Price play?
13 Which Chrissie sang with the Pretenders?
14 In which decade did the Platters enjoy their greatest success?
15 Which 70s supergroup included Roger Waters and David Gilmour?
16 Which Wilson was "In the Midnight Hour" in the 60s and in the 80s?
17 Which late US crooner is nicknamed the Old Groaner?
18 Which TV detective star's only album was called *Telly*?
19 Who had a hit with "I'm Not In Love" in 1975?
20 How many members of Queen were there?

1 Who had a 70s No. 1 with "I'm The Leader Of The Gang (I Am)"?
2 "Freed From Desire" was a 90s hit for which singer?
3 What other body part featured with Heart in a Kylie Minogue No. 1?
4 What is the first word of the song "Because We Want To"?
5 Whose 1993 album was "Everybody Is Doing It So Why Can't We"?
6 Who had an 80s No. 1 with "Dreams Of Children"?
7 Celine Dion's mid-90s album was titled the Colour Of what?
8 Producer Phil Spector created the famous Wall Of what?
9 Who had a 1994 hit with "No Good (Start The Dance)"?
10 Chris Evans' first radio job was on Piccadilly Radio in which city?
11 "Living On My Own" was a 90s No. 1 for which singer?
12 Seal sang the movie theme song about which hero who was Forever?
13 Who charted in the 90s with "The Days Of Pearly Spencer"?
14 Which band made the album Everything Must Go?
15 How was Salvatore Bono better known?
16 Who sang the Bond theme song for Diamonds Are Forever?
17 Which word goes after Black Eyed in a Texas song title?
18 The music for Chariots Of Fire was in a film about which sporting event?
19 Who had a 70s No. 1 with "Young Love"?
20 Tears For Fears said that Everybody Wants To Rule what?

Quiz 167　Colour Coded

Answers – see page 173

1　What colour of Brick Road did Elton John say Goodbye to in 1973?
2　What colour is Simply Mick Hucknall?
3　What colour Rain did Prince sing about in 1984?
4　Which Shade of Pale featured on the Procul Harum classic?
5　What were Elvis Presley's Blue Shoes made from?
6　What is the Colour on the Beautiful South's 1996 album?
7　Which colour surname did Priscilla White change her name to?
8　What Christmas was a hit for Bing Crosby?
9　Which Jason had a colourful surname in Take That?
10　What was the base colour of the Polka Dot Bikini?
11　Which Joe played with the Bruvvers?
12　What colour was Lily in the Scaffold song?
13　Which Finger provided Shirley Bassey with a hit record?
14　Which Door was Shakin' Stevens behind in 1981?
15　What colour Jeans were Swinging in the 60s group?
16　What colour was Tom Jones's Grass of Home?
17　According to Crystal Gayle, Don't It Make which Eyes Blue?
18　What colour was the Beatles' Submarine?
19　Which colour Wine gave Elkie Brooks chart success?
20　Which colour Wine gave UB40 chart success?

1   Who topped the charts with "Can The Can"?
2   "See My Baby Jive" took which group to No. 1?
3   What colour was the ribbon tied "Round The Old Oak Tree"?
4   What instrument did Gilbert O'Sullivan play on "Get Down"?
5   Oasis made a 90s version of "Cum On Feel The Noize" but who made the original?
6   Which glam band recorded "Blockbuster"?
7   Who had a 70s No. 1 with "Oh Boy"?
8   Which T-Rex hit contains the line, "Bang A Gong"?
9   Which group said "Bye Bye Baby"?
10 "We Don't Talk Anymore" was the only 70s No. 1 for which singer?
11 Who wrote and sang "Annie's Song"?
12 What type of fighting was Carl Douglas doing?
13 Who recorded the 70s version of "Love Me For A Reason"?
14 Which group sang "When Will I See You Again"?
15 Which George said "Rock Your Baby"?
16 Which novelty song celebrated the craze for running round without any clothes on?
17 Who had a giant No. 1 with "Sailing"?
18 Which People sang about the YMCA?
19 Who had a 70s hit with "Mary's Boy Child"/"Oh My Lord"?
20 Who asked "Do Ya Think I'm Sexy"?

1 Which decade was Phil Collins born in?
2 What is Jackie's surname and Mr Pickett's first?
3 What name was given to the group made up of four Osmond sons?
4 Which Roy's vocal sound was once described as "the slow fall of teardrops"?
5 What was the nationality of John Lennon's second wife?
6 Which singer was nicknamed the First Lady of Jazz?
7 Who is the country singer Margo O'Donnell's famous brother?
8 Which Irish band has the Edge?
9 How did Sinead O'Connor's hair add to her striking appearance?
10 Which record label shares its name with a long book or film?
11 In 1983 Gary Numan gave public support to whose re-election campaign?
12 Which surname is shared by the country star Willie and Prince?
13 Which Alison sang with Yazoo?
14 Is Morrissey the performer's first name or surname?
15 Which corporation did George Michael begin his lawsuit against in the 1990s?
16 Which Jamaican singer was given a state funeral in 1980?
17 Whose first hit was "My Coo-Ca-Choo" in 1973?
18 Which four herbs were the title of an album by Simon and Garfunkel?
19 On which comedy duo's show did Shirley Bassey sing wearing a hobnail boot?
20 Who had a 70s No. 1 album with *Slayed*?

1 What is the first word of the Spice Girls" hit "Stop"?
2 Which band were originally called Sweetshop?
3 Who had an 80s No. 1 with "True Blue"?
4 Which name links singer/drummer Phil and singer Judy?
5 Whho had "A Million Love Songs" in 1992?
6 What have Martha Reeves, David Bowie and Mick Jagger all been doing in the Street?
7 Which country does Tom Jones come from?
8 Which singer had a 90s No. 1 with "Return Of The Mack"?
9 USA For Africa was the US equivalent of which charity?
10 "Little Bit Of Lovin'" was a 90s top ten hit for which singer?
11 Who had an 80s No. 1 with "Prince Charming"?
12 Which Queen single made No. 1 before and after Freddie Mercury's death?
13 In which decade did Barry Manilow first make the charts?
14 What hat first name did James Ure take?
15 Who had a 70s No. 1 with "Devil Gate Drive"?
16 *Brothers In Arms* was the first album to sell a million in what format?
17 In which decade did the UK albums chart begin?
18 Nigel Kennedy spent a record number of weeks in the charts with *The Four Seasons* playing which instrument?
19 What goes with Parsley, Sage and Rosemary in the folk song?
20 Who had an 80s No. 1 with "Tainted Love"?

1 Which song contest shot Abba to fame?
2 Which song won it for them?
3 Why is the group called Abba?
4 Which Abba song includes the line, "It's a rich man's world"?
5 The name of which Abba hit is also a distress signal?
6 Which musical did two group members write with Tim Rice?
7 Abba's income was said to exceed which Swedish motor company's?
8 Which Abba hit had an Italian title?
9 In which Abba song is the line "Since many years I haven't seen a rifle in your hand"?
10 Which album did the single "Super Trouper" come from?
11 Which Abba song title repeats the same two words five times?
12 What are the first names of the two Abba members who wrote most of their songs?
13 What did Abba Thank You For in 1983?
14 Which two female singers had a No. 1 in 1985 with "I Know Him So Well" written by two of the group?
15 What did The Winner take in the title of the 1980 No. 1?
16 Which Abba hit has a French title?
17 What did Abba ask you to Take A Chance on in 1978?
18 Which monarch was Dancing in 1976?
19 What follows Gimme, Gimme, Gimme in the 1979 hit title?
20 Which song title is the same as a famous quote by Martin Luther King?

1 Who had a huge hit with "Shang A Lang"?
2 Which Hotel did The Eagles check in to?
3 Who claimed to have "Shot The Sheriff"?
4 What was Barry Blue doing on a "Saturday Night"?
5 "You Make Me Feel Brand New" came from which US group?
6 Who sang "Love To Love You Baby"?
7 Which John had a big hit with "Sandy"?
8 Which group paraded their "Little Willy" in the charts?
9 "Nathan Jones" was a big hit for which group?
10 Which group became the first ever to use the word Minestrone in a hit title?
11 Who asked "Metal Guru, Is it You?"?
12 "Bright Eyes" was about which creatures?
13 Jools Holland was in the charts with which band?
14 Which female singer said that "Nobody Does It Better"?
15 Which Abba hit gave its name to a 90s TV comedy?
16 "Virginia Plain" was the first top ten hit for which band?
17 Who declared "Hooray Hooray It's A Holi-Holiday"?
18 Who was the youngest Osmond to have a solo hit?
19 Who was being followed by a "Moon Shadow"?
20 What type of "Mind" did Alvin Stardust have?

1   In which decade was Elton John born?
2   Which name is guitar legend Les's second and Mr Anka's first?
3   What did folk singer Ralph May change his surname to?
4   Which Barry had a hit with the 60s protest song "Eve of Destruction"?
5   Which Lulu song has been a hit for her twice?
6   How is the rock 'n' roller Richard Penniman better known?
7   Which part of the UK do Lindisfarne come from?
8   Which musical instrument did Liberace play?
9   Which Janis was the subject of the Bette Midler film *The Rose*?
10 Which singer Grace is famous for hitting Russell Harty during his chat show?
11 Which Girl was an 80s hit for Billy Joel?
12 What is the surname of father and son composers Maurice and Jean-Michel?
13 David Sylvian was lead singer of which oriental-sounding group?
14 In which country was Engelbert Humperdinck brought up?
15 Which record label did Holland-Dozier-Holland leave in 1968?
16 Which hero of *Cinderella* gave his name to an album by Adam Ant?
17 Whose first solo hit was "Give Peace A Chance" in 1969?
18 How many members of the Righteous Brothers are there?
19 Who was Bob Marley's backing group?
20 What do, or did, the letters MW stand for on your radio?

1 Which 90s No. 1 hit begins, "Smile an everlasting smile"?
2 Which US singer appeared in the movie *Who's That Girl*?
3 Who had an 80s No. 1 with "Begin The Beguine (Volver A Empezar)"?
4 Will Mellor had a chart hit after starring in which soap?
5 What is the first word sung in "Under The Bridg'e?
6 Which star of *The Mask Of Zorro* sang "True Love Ways" with David Essex?
7 Whose first hit was "Love Me Do"?
8 Which member of The Goons duetted with Sophia Loren on "Goodness Gracious Me"?
9 Who had an 80s No. 1 with "Don't Leave Me This Way"?
10 Who was Bon Jovi's lead vocalist?
11 "Sure" was a 90s No. 1 for which group?
12 Men At Work had a hit with "Down Under," but where did they come from?
13 Who wrote "Do They Know It's Christmas?" with Midge Ure?
14 Who had a 70s No. 1 with "Tiger Feet"?
15 Who was backed by The Pacemakers?
16 Jagged Little Pill was a bestselling debut album by which singer?
17 Which soap did Mel B's sister appear in?
18 Who had an 80s No. 1 with "The Lady In Red"?
19 Which Boys included three members of the Wilson family?
20 Which group revived "Love Me For A Reason" in 1994?

1 Which animals were in the title of an Elton John/Pavarotti hit?
2 What was the 1990 Pavarotti hit used for the 1990 World Cup Finals?
3 How are Pavarotti, Domingo and Carreras known collectively?
4 What is Domingo's first name?
5 What is the nationality of Carreras?
6 Who composed the work *Four Seasons* which appeared in the charts in the 80s?
7 Which BBC radio network broadcasts 24-hour classical music?
8 Which Sarah sang "Amigos Para Siempre (Friends For Life)" with Carreras?
9 Which '96 sports event sent Beethoven's "Ode to Joy" into the charts?
10 Which TV theme is made up of classical-sounding music with dots and dashes?
11 Which opera singer Lesley recorded "Ave Maria" with the young Amanda Thompson?
12 Which flute-player had a 70s hit with "Annie's Song"?
13 Which Jennifer had chart success with Domingo in 1989?
14 Which former Motown star joined Carreras and Domingo on the album *Christmas In Vienna*?
15 What is the home country of the "World In Union" singer Kiri Te Kanawa?
16 "World in Union" was recorded for a championship in which sport?
17 What is the nationality of Montserrat Caballe, who joined Freddie Mercury on "Barcelona"?
18 Which fellow Welshman did the opera baritone Bryn Terfel join on a 1996 TV Christmas special?
19 In which rainy London Park did Pavarotti give a concert in 1992?
20 Which opera star did John Denver make an album with in 1981?

1 At what time of year did Eddie Cochran get the blues?
2 Which group backed Buddy Holly?
3 Which creature comes next after "See you later, alligator"?
4 Which glitter rocker gave a 70s version of "Rock And Roll"?
5 Which Hill did Fats Domino sing about?
6 Which Elvis song has the line, "You ain't never caught a rabbit"?
7 Who was "Half Way To Paradise" in 1961?
8 In the 50s who was the British King Of Skiffle?
9 Which Big named vocalist died with Buddy Holly?
10 Who were Duane Eddy's backing group?
11 What was Cliff Richard's first top ten hit?
12 In which US state was Elvis born?
13 Which instrument did Little Richard play on stage?
14 Which Carl penned and performed "Blue Suede Shoes"?
15 In which country did Eddie Cochran die?
16 What completes the lines, "Cruising and playing the radio, With no particular place..."?
17 What was the colour of retro rocker Shakin' Stevens' Door in the 80s?
18 "Great Balls Of Fire" was the first UK No. 1 for which artist?
19 Which British rock'n'roll singer called Marty is the father of 80s hit-maker Kim?
20 In the rock'n'roll song, what is said before Miss Molly?

Quiz 177 Pot Luck 89

Answers – see page 191

LEVEL 1

1 Whose first hit was "Mandy" in 1975?
2 Who had a No. 1 album with *Bolan Boogie*?
3 Which singer/comedian is nicknamed the Big Yin?
4 In which decade was Michael Jackson born?
5 What did Charles Hardin Holley change his name to?
6 Which 60s group had Allan Clarke on lead vocals?
7 Which jazz vocalist called Billie was portrayed by Diana Ross on film?
8 Which Happy gospel hit was sung by the Edwin Hawkins Singers?
9 Which North London suburb was the birthplace of Elton John and Tony Hatch?
10 Emmylou Harris was born in Birmingham. True or false?
11 Which song begins "One, Two, Three o'clock"?
12 Which soft drink did "I'd Like To Teach The World To Sing" advertise?
13 Which song's second line is "And I'll cry if I want to"?
14 Who had a 70s No. 1 with "Jealous Mind"?
15 What did Seal sing about a Kiss From in 1994?
16 Which Gary was famous for his platform soles and silver outfits?
17 Which Bob formed the company that first produced Channel 4's "The Big Breakfast"?
18 Which Gloria sang "Never Can Say Goodbye" in 1974?
19 Which battle provided Abba with the title of their first album?
20 Who played bass guitar in Suzi Quatro's group?

Answers

Pot Luck 91 (Quiz 181)
1 1940s. 2 Marvin. 3 Elkie Brooks. 4 England. 5 Genesis.
6 Frankie Goes To Hollywood. 7 Four Tops. 8 Fleetwood Mac. 9 Feliciano.
10 Gloria Estefan. 11 *Shepherd Moons*. 12 Guitar. 13 California.
14 Massachusetts. 15 Andrew Lloyd-Webber. 16 Four. 17 Essex, Faith.
18 Piano. 19 *Thriller*. 20 Don McLean.

(side label) **Answers**

1   What is the first word of the song "My Heart Will Go On"?
2   Which word goes before Flip and Girls in the names of 90s chart acts?
3   In the song, "When You Walk Through A Storm" what do you hold up high?
4   Who had an 80s No. 1 with "Freedom"?
5   Which new record label did Richard Branson set up?
6   "Mandy" was the first UK chart hit for which Barry?
7   Which Bonnie teamed up with Shakin' Stevens in the 80s?
8   Don Johnson starred in which US cop series before duetting with Barbra Streisand on "Til I Loved You"?
9   Who had a 70s No. 1 with "You're The One That I Want"?
10   Which Andrew wrote the music for *Jesus Christ Superstar*?
11   Which group had a 90s No. 1 with "Ready Or Not"?
12   Dame Barbara Cartland released an album in 1978 of what type of songs?
13   "I Love You Always Forever" was a hit for which female?
14   Who had an 80s No. 1 with "Don't You Want Me"?
15   Where did Bob Geldof's Rats come from?
16   What goes with Powder and Paint in Shakin' Stevens' 1985 hit?
17   Which surname links rock'n'roller Chuck and actor/singer Nick?
18   The Three Degrees came from which country?
19   According to Kirsty MacColl where does the guy work who swears he's Elvis?
20   Who had an 80s No. 1 with "Every Little Thing She Does Is Magic"?

1 What did soccer fan Rod Stewart throw to the audience on tour?
2 Who had a tour called "Blonde Ambition"?
3 In which city is the NEC?
4 In which country might an artist play at Sun City?
5 At which London venue did Cliff Richard end his 1990 "From A Distance" tour?
6 How many times did Elvis Presley tour Britain?
7 Which Fab Four were a support act for Helen Shapiro on her 1963 tour?
8 In which country is the famous Shea Stadium?
9 In which country did Tina Turner play at the "Rock In Rio" festival?
10 Who used to return from tour between gigs to watch Watford play?
11 In which city is the Hammersmith Odeon?
12 What do the initials NEC stand for?
13 On a tour of which continent was Michael Jackson crowned King of the Sanwis in 1992?
14 In which country are the Maple Leaf Gardens a tour venue?
15 In which US city is Carnegie Hall?
16 Who introduced his character Ziggy Stardust on a 70s UK tour?
17 In which country did the Beatles play their last live show?
18 Which area of Los Angeles has a famous venue called The Bowl?
19 Which London Park is a popular open-air tour venue?
20 Buddy Holly perished in a plane crash during a tour of which country?

1 Who said "My Weakness Is None Of Your Business"?
2 Every day was like which day for Morrissey?
3 Who charted with "Reverend Black Grape"?
4 "There's No Other Way" was the first top ten hit for which group?
5 Which word goes before Return in the title of The Bluetones' 1996 single?
6 In 1995 who sang "Wake Up Boo!"?
7 "Good Enough" was the first top ten hit for who?
8 Which label do Oasis record on?
9 What was the colour of New Order's Monday?
10 What sort of people concerned Pulp in their 1995 hit?
11 In August '99 who announced he was leaving Oasis?
12 Who charted in 1990 with "All Together Now"?
13 Which group recorded "Lovefool" in 1997?
14 In what sort of state was Radiohead's Android?
15 On which day of the week do Cure say I'm In Love?
16 What goes before Little Indian in the record label?
17 Which Sisters were in a Temple Of Love in 92?
18 Which city did The Smiths come from?
19 Who charted with "Avenging Angels" in 1998?
20 "True Faith" and a remix made the top ten for which band?

1 In which decade was Olivia Newton-John born?
2 What is Lee's surname and Mr Gaye's first?
3 How is Elaine Bookbinder better known?
4 Which country is Joe Cocker from?
5 Which band included Phil Collins and Peter Gabriel?
6 Which band's name was sometimes abbreviated to FGTH?
7 Which top Motown group did not change their line-up for 30 years?
8 Which band was led by Mick Fleetwood?
9 Which Jose recorded the Doors' "Light My Fire"?
10 Which singer's maiden name was Gloria Maria Fajardo?
11 Which Moons were a best selling album for Enya?
12 What was Duane Eddy's musical instrument?
13 Which West Coast US state were the Eagles from?
14 Which East Coast state provided a hit for the Bee Gees?
15 Who wrote the music for *Evita*?
16 How many members of the Shadows were there?
17 Which David and Adam co-starred in the film *Stardust*?
18 Which musical instrument does Georgie Fame play?
19 Which word for an exciting book or film is the name of an album by Michael Jackson?
20 Whose first hit was "American Pie" in 1972?

1 "Undivided Love" was a 90s top ten hit for which singer?
2 In which decade did Kirsty MacColl first make the charts?
3 Pete Townshend and Keith Moon were members of which group?
4 What was Oasis's top-selling album of the 90s?
5 Where was Elton John's first public performance of "Candle In The Wind "97"?
6 What followed Dog Man on the title of Suede's 1994 album?
7 In which decade was Jewel born?
8 Which word goes before Drive in the hit by The Lighthouse Family?
9 Which Elvis Presley album was the first album in history to sell a million?
10 Which country did Kraftwerk come from?
11 Who was backed by The Attractions?
12 Who made up the folk trio with Peter and Paul?
13 Who sang the Bond theme "The Spy Who Loved Me"?
14 Who had an 80s No. 1 with "When The Going Gets Tough, The Tough Get Going"?
15 What sort of Dancer is Tina Turner on her first solo album?
16 Which original Radio 1 DJ announced in 1999 he was leaving the BBC because it was too boring?
17 Which Nik was a Wide Boy and asked Wouldn't It Be Good in the 80s?
18 "Circle Of Life" features in which Disney film?
19 Who had a 1997 hit with "Coming Home Now"?
20 What is the last name of rapper Missy Misdemeanour?

1 Which outrageous optical accessories was Elton John famous for?
2 Who is Elton singing about with the song which begins "Goodbye Norma Jean"?
3 Which Disney movie provided Elton with an Oscar in 1995?
4 What Captain is named on a 1975 album title?
5 Which instrument did Elton John study at the Royal Academy?
6 In which rock opera film by the Who did Elton John sing "Pinball Wizard"?
7 Who did Elton duet with on "Don't Go Breaking My Heart" in 1976?
8 What seemed to be the Hardest Word in 1975?
9 To combat which illness is the Elton John Foundation providing funds?
10 According to the 1973 hit, what is Saturday Night Alright for?
11 Which Football Club did Elton become chairman of in 1977?
12 Where did Elton John sing "Don't Let the Sun Go Down on Me" with George Michael in July 1985?
13 Which reptile Rock was a hit in 1972?
14 Who is linked with the Jets on the 1976 single?
15 In 1992 Elton John matched which American singer's run of 22 consecutive years of Top 40 hits in the Top 100 in the USA?
16 Which lyricist collaborated with Elton John on his early hits?
17 Which hit began "It's a little bit funny, This feeling inside"?
18 Which Man gave Elton his second hit in 1972?
19 Who was "travellin' tonight on a plane" in 1973?
20 Which festival did Elton Step Into in 1973?

1   Who were "Livin' On The Edge" in the 1993 charts?
2   Which country do AC/DC come from?
3   Which classic band were "Paranoid"?
4   Slash is in which group?
5   Who were producing "Holy Smoke" in 1990?
6   Which 80s and 90s group has the name of a cattle and sheep disease?
7   Which sentimental head bangers asked "Is This Love" in 1987?
8   Who had the Hindenburg airship on the cover of their first album?
9   Metallica were in the 96 charts with Until It what?
10 Def Leppard were formed in which country?
11 Deep Purple took a Black what into the singles charts?
12 Hysteria was a No. 1 album for which band?
13 What instrument does veteran John Lord play?
14 What word goes before Fudge in the band name of the early heavies?
15 Who produced albums A Real Live One and A Real Dead One in 93?
16 Which part of the guitar named a 70s No. 1 album from Deep Purple?
17 What did Van Halen take their name from?
18 Who was Led Zeppelin's main vocals man?
19 Who were in the charts with "Wind Of Change" in the early 90s?
20 Which 60s group of super guitarists-to-be made the hit, "Evil Hearted You"?

Quiz 185 Pot Luck 93

Answers – see page 199

LEVEL 1

1 Which Scottish city is Sheena Easton from?
2 In which decade was Roy Orbison born?
3 Which type of Singer was Neil Diamond in his 1980 film?
4 Which time of day is associated with Dexy's Runners?
5 Which singer is nicknamed the Rhinestone Cowboy?
6 Desmond Dekker was one of the first artists in which brand of Jamaican music?
7 Which Chris had a hit on both sides of the Atlantic with "Who Pays the Ferryman?"?
8 Which illness did Ian Dury suffer from in childhood?
9 Which jazz singer called Cleo duetted with the guitarist John Williams?
10 Which record producer called Phil was famous for his "wall of sound"?
11 Which national football side recorded "Back Home" in 1970?
12 Which Harry is famous for his songs on the soundtrack of *When Harry Met Sally*?
13 Which part of house gave its name to an album by Pink Floyd?
14 Which veteran Perry enjoyed chart success in the 70s with "And I Love You So"?
15 Who had a top-selling album with *The Rise and Fall of Ziggy Stardust And The Spiders From Mars*?
16 Which Judy had a best-seller with "Amazing Grace"?
17 Which Eddie had a hit with "Summertime Blues" in 1958?
18 Which country star Patsy was an inspiration to k.d. lang?
19 What is the home country of Richard Clayderman?
20 Whose first hit was "Holiday" in 1984?

Answers

Pot Luck 95 (Quiz 189)
1 England. 2 Wings. 3 1940s. 4 It was the surname of three of them.
5 Chicago. 6 London. 7 Piano. 8 Of the Board.
9 Cassidy. 10 The Medics. 11 Yesterday. 12 Take That.
13 Wizzard. 14 The Roof. 15 Bob Marley and the Wailers.
16 Two. 17 Stevens. 18 Dee. 19 Jamaica. 20 Caribou.

1 "I'm Your Angel" was a top three single for Celine Dion and which other artist?
2 Which charity group did Bob Geldof and Midge Ure put together?
3 Where was the Emergency on Jamiroquai's 1993 album?
4 Which female singer had an early 90s hit with "Sleeping Satellite"?
5 Who sang in and starred in the movies Grease and Xanadu?
6 Which 80s duo was Andrew Ridgeley part of?
7 Who had a 70s No. 1 with "Make Me Smile (Come Up And See Me)"?
8 Who sang about a Charmless Man in 1996?
9 Under which colour was a 1993 album for Tori Amos?
10 Which word describes singer John Baldry?
11 In which decade did M People first make the charts?
12 Which No. 1 was on the other side of Elton John's "Healing Hands"?
13 Who first charted with "Only The Lonely" back in 1960?
14 Which monarch did Supergrass take into the 1997 charts?
15 Who was a member of a group called Hollycaust?
16 How many members made up Tyrannosaurus Rex?
17 Which Spice Girl advertised Milky Bar as a small child?
18 Which 60s vocalist famous for her lack of shoes wrote "The World At My Feet"?
19 "Do They Know It's Christmas?" was originally released to aid famine relief in which country?
20 Who had a 70s No. 1 with "Give A Little Love"?

1   Which Joan had a hit with "There But For Fortune"?
2   In which language was the banned Serge Gainsbourg/Jane Birkin song recorded in?
3   What were These Boots Made For according to Nancy Sinatra in 1966?
4   Which former member of the Springfields took "You Don't Have To Say You Love Me" to No. 1?
5   Which word described Manfred Mann's Flamingo?
6   Which Ray sang "I Can't Stop Loving You" in 1962?
7   In which country did Frank Ifield begin his singing career?
8   Which Miss Clark had a hit with "Sailor"?
9   Which precious jewels took Jet Harris and Tony Meehan to No. 1?
10   Who were Sweets for in the Searchers' No. 1 hit?
11   Which Brian had a backing group called the Tremeloes?
12   Which former cloakroom attendant from Liverpool's Cavern Club had a No. 1 with "Anyone Who Had a Heart"?
13   Whose real name was Clive and found Fame in the 60s?
14   Who had a No. 1 with "It's Not Unusual" in 1965?
15   What were the initials of the outrageous Mr Proby?
16   What was innovative about the Beatles jackets?
17   Which Adam sang "Poor Me" in 1960?
18   What was on a String on Sandie Shaw's third No. 1 hit?
19   What went with Pins on the Searchers' 1964 hit?
20   Which Lily was a hit for Scaffold?

Quiz 188 Easy Listening

Answers – see page 202

1   Who had a first top ten hit with "Love Changes Everything"?
2   Who hit the charts with the Bond film song, "All The Time In The World"?
3   Which country does Shirley Bassey come from?
4   What is the first word of the 70s world wide hit, "Feelings"?
5   Which musician took the vocals on "This Guy's In Love With You"?
6   Which veteran crooner appeared at Glastonbury in the late 90s?
7   What type of hat does Acker Bilk wear?
8   What was History doing on the 1997 comeback hit for Shirley Bassey?
9   What was Ramblin' in a Nat King Cole song title?
10 Eurovision singer Dana ran for president of which country in 1998?
11 What was the first name of 50s piano queen Atwell?
12 Which duo recorded "Yesterday Once More"?
13 How is Noah Kaminsky better known?
14 Which big band leader shared his name with a prime minister?
15 Who is the famous actress daughter of 50s star Eddie Fisher?
16 From which musical is the classic Edelweiss from?
17 In which language does Charles Aznavour sing most of his European hits?
18 Singer Jane McDonald found fame in a docu soap about what?
19 Which triple No. 1 singer had a Radio 2 weekday show throughout the 90s?
20 John Williams made the charts with the theme from The Deer Hunter playing which instrument?

1 Which country is Petula Clark from?
2 Who was Paul McCartney's backing group?
3 In which decade was Eric Clapton born?
4 Why were the Christians so-called?
5 Which band was originally called Chicago Transit Authority?
6 Which city are Chas and Dave from?
7 Which musical instrument does Ray Charles play?
8 Which Chairmen asked: Give Me Just a Little More Time?
9 Which David played the role of Keith Partridge on TV?
10 Who was Doctor's backing group?
11 What follows "Yester-me, Yester-you" on Stevie Wonder's hit?
12 Who had No. 1 hits with "Babe" and "Sure" before disbanding in '96?
13 Which Roy Wood group sounds like a magician?
14 Where did the Supremes Go Up the Ladder to in 1970?
15 Whose first hit was "No Woman No Cry" in 1975?
16 How many members of the Style Council were there?
17 Which Cat had a 70s hit with "Morning Has Broken"?
18 Which surname is shared by the 60s group leader Dave and Kiki?
19 Which Caribbean island do Chaka Demus and Pliers come from?
20 Which type of deer gave its name to an album by Elton John?

1 What kind of Talkin' came from Saturday Night Fever?
2 Which disco legend was back in the charts in the 90s with "I Feel Love"?
3 Baccara said "Yes Sir I Can Do What"?
4 Still staying together today who were "Staying Alive" in the 70s?
5 What was U2's 90s record about disco called?
6 Boney M's "Brown Girl" was to be found in what?
7 Which Van did The Hustle?
8 Which two letters go in front of And The Sunshine Band?
9 "You're The First The Last My Everything" was the first and last UK No. 1 of the century for who?
10 What words comes after, "Woman, Take Me In Your Arms, Rock Your..."?
11 What's the number in the title of Pulp's "Disco"?
12 Which Tina sang "I Love To Love"?
13 Which group declared they were "In The Navy"?
14 Who charted with "We Are Family" in the 70s and with a remix in 93?
15 What kind of Shack did the B 52s sing about?
16 Who had the disco hit "When You're In Love With A Beautiful Woman"?
17 Which Daddy gave Boney M their first UK top ten hit?
18 Who decided that Love's Unkind?
19 What was N Trance's 1997 cover of an 80s favourite called?
20 Which disco track gave Blondie their first UK No. 1?

LEVEL 1

1 Which Beatle had a No. 1 with "My Sweet Lord"?
2 What was the name of the Fastest Milkman in the West?
3 Which Amazing record was by the Scots Dragoon Guards and played on the bagpipes?
4 Which type of Guru did T. Rex sing about?
5 Which Donny had a No. 1 with "Puppy Love"?
6 Which TV family was David Cassidy a member of?
7 Which electric instrument did Suzi Quatro play?
8 What type of bullets did 10 c.c. fire in 1973?
9 Which Alvin had a Jealous Mind?
10 What is the nationality of Charles Aznavour?
11 Which band were the final chart-toppers of the 70s with "Another Brick in the Wall"?
12 Which relative of Sylvia was Dr Hook a hit with?
13 Where did the Police put their Message?
14 Which day of the week did the Boomtown Rats not like?
15 Which Rivers were a hit for Boney M?
16 Which Kate scaled Wuthering Heights in 1978?
17 On which New TV talent show did Showaddywaddy get their big break?
18 Which Queen was a 1976 hit for Abba?
19 Which country were the Bay City Rollers from?
20 Where in the Caribbean were Typically Tropical heading in 1975?

Answers

60s Revisited (Quiz 187)
1 Baez. 2 French. 3 Walkin'. 4 Dusty. 5 Pretty. 6 Charles. 7 Australia.
8 Petula. 9 Diamonds. 10 My Sweet. 11 Poole. 12 Cilla Black.
13 Georgie Fame. 14 Tom Jones. 15 P.J.
16 Collarless. 17 Faith. 18 Puppet. 19 Needles. 20 The Pink.

1 In which country did the Three Tenors come together for their first World Cup concert?
2 What was the moniker of the violinist known as Kennedy when he had a first name?
3 "Rock Me Amadeus" was about which classical composer?
4 Who did Sarah Brightman duet with on "Time To Say Goodbye"?
5 What is Pavarotti's first name?
6 Who did Chuck Berry tell to Roll Over?
7 Charting as the USA World Cup theme, which musical does "America" come from?
8 "O Sole Mio" was the basis of which Elvis Presley hit?
9 Whose song – minus the lyrics – gave flautist James Galway a hit?
10 Who had a big 80s hit with the Can Can?
11 Which country is the tenor Jose Carreras from?
12 On TV who was the Oxford detective who loved opera?
13 Which sporting event led to Beethoven's "Ode To Joy" making the charts?
14 What has become Pavarotti's theme tune?
15 A Bach-inspired tune produced the 60s smash A Whiter what?
16 Which Rush duetted with Domingo in 89?
17 Kiri Te Kanawa sang an anthem for a world event in which sport?
18 Who sang with Monsterrat Caballe about Barcelona?
19 Music by Fauree was in the 90s charts after being used as a TV theme for what?
20 Which Light Orchestra took "Rockaria" into the 70s charts?

Quiz 193 Pot Luck 96

Answers – see page 207

LEVEL 1

1 Which Mode were regular chart members in the 80s?
2 In which decade was Tina Turner born?
3 Which two months were an 80s hit for Barbara Dickson?
4 What is Sacha Distel's only UK chart success?
5 Whose "Riders on the Storm" entered the chart at least four times?
6 Which Night did the Drifters enjoy at the Movies?
7 Which Attraction were Perfect in 1988?
8 How many made up the Fun Boy band of the 80s?
9 In which decade did Gabrielle have her first chart success?
10 Who joined Guys on the 1975 song "There's a Whole Lot of Loving"?
11 Which record label sounds like a sweet or savoury pastry dish?
12 Which comedy duo were backed by the Stonkers?
13 Which number follows in East and Heaven in band names?
14 What colour Haze was a hit for Jimi Hendrix?
15 Which flower was a hit for Vince Hill in 1967?
16 Whose first hit was "Hangin' Tough" in 1989?
17 How is the punk star John Lydon better known?
18 Which word to describe a workout is used by Olivia Newton-John on her 1981 album?
19 Which particular style of alpine singing was Frank Ifield famous for?
20 Which Irish band had a top-selling album with *The Joshua Tree*?

1   What kind of Year did Dina Carroll have in 1993?
2   Which single letter starts a string of a cappella hits?
3   "Straight Up" was the first top ten hit for which vocalist?
4   Who had a smash hit in 1998 with "Bamboogie"?
5   Who had an 80s No. 1 with "Let's Party"?
6   Who Found A Cure in 1998?
7   Which colour of Box took a "Ride On Time"?
8   "Rock Da House" was a hit for which Masters?
9   Which word goes before Ocean and Starr in group names?
10 What is Whigfield's country?
11 Which group did Heather Small front in the mid 90s?
12 Which Baby was So Pure in 1996?
13 In 1993 Usura told you to Open Your what?
14 Which Party sang "Don't Give Me Your Life"?
15 Which comic duo featured on EMF's "I'm A Believer"?
16 What number goes after Heaven in the group name?
17 In 1998 Enigma had a return to what?
18 Who many members were originally in Five Star?
19 Which DJ had a huge 97 hit with "Belissimo"?
20 In a 1991 hit what did Cathy Dennis invite you to do All Night Long?

1   What kind of Guy gave Roxy Music a No. 1 hit in 1980?
2   Which Beatle was murdered in December 1980?
3   Which Fizz were telling you to Make Your Mind Up in 1981?
4   Which Spanish singer took "Begin the Beguine" into the charts in 1981?
5   Which 80s singer was known as Shaky?
6   What went with Ivory on the Paul McCartney/Stevie Wonder hit?
7   What did Eddy Grant Not Wanna do in '82?
8   Which Ballet had a No. 1 with "True"?
9   What follows "Wherever I Lay My Hat" on the Paul Young single?
10 "Every Breath You Take" was a final No. 1 for which band, who were a great force in the 80s?
11 Which Pickets took "Only You" to the top?
12 Which pop concert was organized for famine in Africa in July 1985?
13 Which Sister had a hit with "Frankie"?
14 Which Annie was one half of the Eurythmics?
15 Which Chrissie sang guest vocals on UB40's "I Got You Babe"?
16 What Reaction did Diana Ross have in 1986?
17 Which Jackie hit the top with "Reet Petite" nearly 30 years after the record was released?
18 Who was Respectable with Mel?
19 Where were the Firm Trekkin' in 1987?
20 What was the Only Way, according to Yazz in 1988?

1   What was the 90s No. 1 of Vanilla Ice?
2   "I'll Be Missing You" was based on which song by Sting?
3   Who had a 1998 hit with "Intergalactic"?
4   In which country did rap originate?
5   Who Shot The Sheriff in the 97 hit?
6   Who was vs Jason Nevins on the monster No. 1 "It's Like That"?
7   How many Booms make up the title of the Outhere Brothers 1995 No. 1?
8   Which initials did Hammer lose?
9   Which sports star was responsible for "Geordie Boys"?
10 What's the first name of hip hop originator Bambaataa?
11 Who released "Mr Wendal" in 1993?
12 Gangsta's Paradise" was a No. 1 for who?
13 What colour did Will Smith's men wear?
14 Which Boys rapped the Yo Twist with Chubby Checker?
15 Who appeared with the Furious Five?
16 Who had Mo Money Mo Problems in 1997?
17 Who partnered Salt?
18 What goes after Milli in the rap duo name?
19 Who did Jazzy Jeff rap with?
20 Double what found some Street Turf in 1989?

1 How many members of Wham! were there?
2 Whose albums include *Regatta de Blanc* and *Every Breath You Take – The Singles*?
3 In which decade was Mariah Carey born?
4 Which song was a No. 1 for Harry Belafonte and Boney M?
5 Which former Lebanese hostage made a 90s single with Carol Kidd?
6 Which singer/jazz trumpeter was nicknamed Satchmo?
7 Which surname is shared by Brenda and Peggy?
8 Who founded the Plastic Ono Band?
9 What was Phil Everly's first solo album called?
10 Which Annie had a No. 1 album with *Diva*?
11 Which New group had a 70s No. 1 with "You Won't Find Another Fool Like Me"?
12 How are Orchestral Manoeuvres in the Dark sometimes known?
13 Which porky pair recorded "Reet Petite" in 1993?
14 What relation are the individual members of the Nolans to each other?
15 What did Isaiah Turner change his first name to?
16 Which supergroup was Agnetha Faltskog a member of?
17 Which summer month gave its name to an album by Eric Clapton?
18 Whose first hit was "Seven Seas of Rhye" in 1974?
19 Which Roger was King of the Road in 1965?
20 What completes the trio with Earth and Wind?

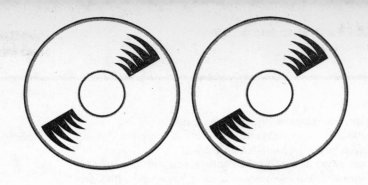

The Medium Questions

This next selection of questions is getting a little more like it. For an open entry quiz you should have a high percentage of medium level questions – don't try to break people's spirits with the hard ones, just make sure that people play to their ability.

Like all questions, this level of question can be classed as either easy or impossible depending on whether you know the answer or not and although common knowledge is used as the basis for these questions there is a sting in the tail of quite a few. Also, if you have a serious drinking squad playing, then they can more or less say goodbye to the winners' medals, but that isn't to say they will feel any worse about it.

Specialists are the people to watch out for, as those with a good knowledge of a particular subject will doubtless do well in these rounds so a liberal sprinkling of pot-luck questions is needed to flummox them.

1　In which decade was Bruce Springsteen born?
2　Which Baby girl did Helen Reddy sing about in 1975?
3　Who had a No. 1 with "Angel Fingers"?
4　Whose first hit was "Shout"?
5　Who had a 70s album called *Arrival*?
6　Which film star's Eyes did Kim Carnes sing about?
7　Which band was King of the Road in 1990?
8　How is Terence Nelhams better known?
9　Which surname is shared by Michael and Randy?
10　Which city did The Smiths hail from?
11　Who sang about Love and Affection in 1976?
12　Which Barry Manilow hit song became a stage show?
13　Which record label showed a dog listening to a gramophone?
14　Which university town do Supergrass come from?
15　Who had a 1953 hit with "She Wears Red Feathers"?
16　Whose backing group were the Rebel Rousers?
17　What is Whigfield's home country?
18　Who is the female half of The Eurythmics?
19　Who had a 1992 hit with "You're All That Matters to Me"?
20　In which decade did Roxy Music have their first hit?

Answers

Pot Luck 3 (Quiz 5)
1 Michael Ball.　2 Baby Jane.　3 MacArthur.　4 Wayne Fontana.　5 Guitar.
6 Blondie.　7 Stevie Wonder (his name backwards!).　8 Linda McCartney.
9 "One Fine Day".　10 Brian Epstein.　11 His car hit a tree.
12 Mick Jagger, David Bowie.　13 Hatch and Trent.　14 Bryan Adams.
15 1950s.　16 1980s.　17 The Housemartins.　18 Shakin' Stevens.
19 "Summer In The City".　20 Perry Como.

1 What was the follow up to "Stay" by Shakespear's Sister?
2 Who released the 80s album *Hounds Of Love*?
3 Who was lead vocalist with The Crowd on their fund-raising charity hit?
4 Who had a 70s No. 1 with "One Day At A Time"?
5 Who recorded the 1992 album *Good Stuff*?
6 Who was Up On The Roof in the 60s UK charts long before Robson and Jerome got there?
7 Which word follows Golden in the song title by The Stranglers?
8 What was Joan Armatrading singing about in her 1976 UK No. 10?
9 Supergrass hail from which university town?
10 What was "She" wearing in the 1953 hit by Guy Mitchell?
11 What was the name of Cliff Bennett's backing group?
12 In which decade did Adam Ant first have a top ten single?
13 Which country is home to "Saturday Night" star Whigfield?
14 Which was the first Beatles song that Elton John had a chart success with?
15 Who sang in a trio with brother Tom and Mike Hurst before going solo?
16 Which word goes before By You in the song title by Brian May ?
17 Who is the uncredited vocalist on Heaven 17's "Temptation"?
18 Who were the first girl group to top the UK charts?
19 On the original version, what was on the other side of Boney M's "Rivers Of Babylon"?
20 Who had a big hit in 1989 with the album "Don't Be Cruel"?

1 Who sang with the Checkmates?
2 Which film did "The Harry Lime Theme" come from?
3 Which girl was on the other side of "All I Have To Do Is Dream" for the Everly Brothers?
4 Which first No. 1 for Adam Faith was a question?
5 What was the 50s' best-selling single?
6 Who took "Mary's Boy Child" in to the charts in the 50s?
7 Which 50s classic begins "I'm so young and you're so old"?
8 Which singer was married to Debbie Reynolds and Elizabeth Taylor?
9 Who had a Secret Love in 1954?
10 Who sang "Yes Tonight Josephine"?
11 Which singer with which group had a hit with "Livin' Doll"?
12 Whose girl was Only Sixteen at No. 1 in 1959?
13 Which instrumentalist hit the top with "Let's Have Another Party"?
14 Which Buddy Holly hit was the first after his death and went to No. 1?
15 Who told The Story of His Life in 1958?
16 Who went from the Green Door to the Garden of Eden?
17 Who had a 1955 No. 1 with "Unchained Melody"?
18 Who had a "Dreamboat" in 1955?
19 Which 50s musical provided Vic Damone with a 1958 No. 1?
20 What does Anne Shelton finally sing after "Lay Down Your Arms" in her 1956 No. 1?

1 Who featured on the Soul II Soul No. 1 "Back To Life"?
2 Heavenli left which girl band whose first hit was "Finally Found"?
3 Levi Stubbs was lead singer with which band who performed together for 44 years?
4 Which band hadn't Found What I'm Looking For in 1990?
5 How do the Fugees also style themselves?
6 Who sang "Get Here" in 1991?
7 Tamla star Marvin Gaye had a trial with which town's football team after the death of singing partner Tammi Terrell?
8 What went after Don't Let Go on En Vogue's 1997 single?
9 Which US president presented Ray Charles with a National Medal of Arts Award in 1994?
10 In addition to George Michael, which George has duetted with Queen of Soul Aretha Franklin?
11 Which "Mr Whitney Houston" charted with "On Our Own" from *Ghostbusters*?
12 Which Burt Bacharach song, once a hit for Dionne Warwick, helped Gabrielle win Brit's Best female singer in 1997?
13 Which James duetted with Linda Ronstadt on "Somewhere Out There" in 1987?
14 What followed "Back To Life" on Soul II Soul's No. 1?
15 Which legendary Motown star sang with Babyface on "How Come, How Long" in 1997?
16 How many Supremes were there originally?
17 Whose "My Girl" reached No. 2 in the UK in 1992, 27 years after topping the US charts?
18 Which soul singer charted with the Bond theme "Licence To Kill" in 1989?
19 Whose "Breathe Again" came from her album of her own name?
20 Which Brothers' hits over five decades includes the classic "This Old Heart Of Mine"?

1 Who had an 1989 hit with "Love Changes Everything"?
2 Which Baby girl did Rod Stewart sing about in 1983?
3 Which Park was Donna Summer in in 1978?
4 Whose backing group was the Mindbenders?
5 Which musical instrument does Johnny Marr play?
6 Whose first hit was "Denis"?
7 Who has recorded under the name of Eivets Rednow?
8 Who was the female member of Wings?
9 Which Goffin and King song by the Chiffons shares its name with an aria from Puccini's *Madame Butterfly*?
10 Who was Cilla Black's first manager?
11 How did T. Rex's Marc Bolan meet his death?
12 Which duo with combined ages of over 80 topped the charts in September 1985 for four weeks?
13 Who were the first husband-and-wife team to top the charts?
14 Who had a 90s album called *Waking Up The Neighbours*?
15 In which decade was Karen Carpenter born?
16 In which decade did The Beautiful South have their first hit?
17 Who had a No. 1 with "Caravan of Love"?
18 How is Michael Barratt better known?
19 Which Summer song did Lovin' Spoonful sing in 1966?
20 Who had a 1953 hit with "Don't Let The Stars Get In Your Eyes"?

1. Who made the late 80s albums *Eponymous* and *Green*?
2. In which decade did A-Ha first have a top ten single?
3. Which word follows Letter From in the song title by Proclaimers?
4. Which film had the theme 'Take My Breath Away'?
5. What was UB40's follow up to 'Don't Break My Heart'?\
6. In which decade did Paul Anka first have a top ten single?
7. What was Soul II Soul's follow up to 'Get A Life'?
8. Which Celine Dion hit begins, "When I was young, I never needed anyone"?
9. Who had a 90s album called Brother Sister?
10. Which word goes before Again in the song title by Toni Braxton?
11. Who had a 70s No. 1 with "Way Down"?
12. Which words appear in brackets in Madonna's 1998 hit "Drowned World"?
13. Hank Marvin released a 90s album of material by which early rock star?
14. Lulu won the Eurovision Song Contest with which song?
15. What is the surname of Katrina of Katrina and the Waves fame?
16. Which word completes the song title by Status Quo, "In The _____ Now"?
17. Who is the A in A&M records?
18. What kind of woman gave Crystal Waters a big 1991 chart hit?
19. Who made up Cream with Eric Clapton and Ginger Baker?
20. Who had an 80s album called *Push*?

1   What was Elvis's job before he shot to fame?
2   What was Elvis's middle name?
3   Which Elvis hit was based on the Italian song "O Sole Mio" also used to advertise Cornetto ice cream?
4   What follows "I'm Left, You're Right" in the song title?
5   Which No. 1 is Elvis singing at a live show when he dissolves into giggles in a section that is spoken?
6   In which movie does he sing "Wooden Heart"?
7   Which Nashville quartet backed Elvis on many records starting with "Don't Be Cruel" in 1956?
8   Which Beatle, critical of Elvis's post-*G.I.* music, said that Elvis died the day he joined the Army?
9   Which two US states are named on album titles in the Sixties?
10 Which part of Elvis was removed in an operation in 1960?
11 Which Tom Jones No. 1 was a top thirty hit for Elvis in 1975?
12 What follows "Don't Cry" in the 1970 hit?
13 What Official Elvis organization was launched in 1957?
14 In which film does Elvis play Vince Everett, a man accused of manslaughter, who becomes a rock star?
15 What were the first names of Elvis's parents?
16 Which up-tempo song went to No. 1 on Elvis's death?
17 Who was In Disguise in the 1963 No. 1?
18 Why did saying he went to L.C. Humes High School convince sceptical listeners that Elvis was white, not black?
19 What was Priscilla Presley's surname before her marriage?
20 Who did Elvis say Lawdy to in 1957?

Quiz 8   Cliff Richard

Answers – see page 212

LEVEL 2

1   In which country was Cliff born?
2   On which type of transport did Cliff travel in Summer Holiday?
3   How many times did Cliff represent the UK in the Eurovision Song Contest in the 20th century?
4   Which hit starts, "Imagine a still summer's day when nothing is moving...'?
5   Which musical based on a Brontë novel did Cliff appear in in the 90s?
6   Which two-word title song was his first top ten hit?
7   Which female vocalist appeared regularly with Cliff in his 70s TV shows?
8   Cliff plays and support youngsters training in which sport?
9   Which theatrical great appeared with Cliff in the musical *Time*?
10   What were his long-time backing group called before they became The Shadows?
11   Which Phil duetted with Cliff on "She Means Nothing To Me"?
12   Which 50s hit was re-released in the 80s with "The Young Ones"?
13   Which song, which became a Cliff classic, was his last No. 1 of the 60s?
14   Which girl's name gave Cliff his first top ten hit of the 80s?
15   Which drink features in a 1988 Christmas hit?
16   Which tennis player was romantically linked with Cliff in the 1980s?
17   Who did Cliff duet with in "All I Ask Of You" from *Phantom Of The Opera*?
18   Which composer of the musical *Oliver!* wrote "Livin' Doll"?
19   What was Cliff's first film where he had a major starring role?
20   "Slow Rivers" was a hit for Cliff with which star?

1 Who was the female member of the Pretenders?
2 In which decade did Jeff Beck have his first solo hit?
3 Whose backing group was the MG's?
4 Who had a No. 1 with "Clair"?
5 Whose first No. 1 under his name alone was "Pipes Of Peace" in 1984?
6 What did Tina Charles say "I Love" to do in 1976 and 1986?
7 How is Steven Demetri Georgiou better known in the charts?
8 Which surname is shared by Cleo and Frankie?
9 Who sang "Heart and Soul" in 1987?
10 When was Barry Blue Dancing in 1973?
11 Which song title links Jennifer Rush and Frankie Goes to Hollywood?
12 Which group was once called the Anni-Frid Four?
13 Which David Bowie song hero was "floating in my tin can"?
14 In which film did Madonna play the part of Breathless Mahoney?
15 Whose first hit was "Make It With You"?
16 Which colour provided a hit for Los Bravos and La Belle Epoque?
17 What was Johnny Logan's original home country?
18 In which decade was Adam Faith born?
19 Which girl who "doesn't live here any more" did Cliff Richard sing about in 1980?
20 Who had a 90s album called *Said And Done*?

1. Who had a 90s No. 2 album called *VS*?
2. What was Cliff Richard's follow-up to "My Pretty One"?
3. Which word follows Just An in the song title by Imagination?
4. Which film about the Olympics earned a music Oscar for composer Vangelis?
5. Which singer founded the clothing line Groove Girl?
6. Who was the subject of the 80s biopic *La Bamba*?
7. Which song features the line, "Look at those cavemen go"?
8. Who was featured on the Source hit You Got The Love?
9. Which country does master album-seller James Last come from?
10. Which word completes the song title by Inner City, "Ain't ___ Better"?
11. What was the name of Booker T's backing group?
12. Who had a 70s No. 1 with "Float On"?
13. Who was Dancing On A Saturday Night in 1973?
14. Which band featured John Foxx and Chris Cross?
15. The album *Johnny Cash At San Quentin* was recorded in what type of building?
16. What was Diana Ross's follow-up to "When You Tell Me That You Love Me"?
17. Who wrote Jimi Hendrix hit "All Along The Watchtower"?
18. "To Cut A Long Story Short" was the first top ten hit for which group?
19. In which decade did Amazulu first have a top ten single?
20. What is Shakin' Steven's real name?

1 Who had a best-selling album called *Rumours*?
2 Whose first No. 1 was "Tiger Feet"?
3 Who had Tony Orlando as their lead singer?
4 Who had a "Year of Decision" in 1974?
5 Whose first hit was "Get Down And Get With It"?
6 Which instrument did Marc Bolan play on "Ride A White Swan"?
7 Which pop sensation included Derek and Alan Longmuir?
8 Which record label were Wings' early records on?
9 Which Sweet No. 1 began with police sirens wailing?
10 Who was the original drummer with the ELO?
11 Who sang about Pretty Little Angel Eyes in 1978?
12 How many founder members of the Eagles were there?
13 Which musical instrument did Karen Carpenter play?
14 Whose debut album was *New Boots And Panties!*?
15 Which 1978 Bee Gees album was the bestseller of all time at that time?
16 Which Brotherhood of Man No. 1 shares its name with an opera?
17 Which group had Errol Brown as lead singer?
18 Which rock legend died in August 1977?
19 Which US state did Pussycat sing about?
20 Who was the chart-topper Detective Ken Hutchinson better known?

1   Queen Latifah duetted with which male rapper on "Mama Gave Birth To The Soul Children"?
2   Which Dr went Zoom with LL Cool J in 1998?
3   How is rapper Andre Levins of Enjoy Yourself fame better known?
4   House Of what took Jump Around into the top ten?
5   Which No. 1 for 10c.c. became a chart hit in 1997 for Fun Lovin' Criminals?
6   Sean Combs topped the charts on both sides of the Atlantic with "I'll Be Missing You" but how is he better known?
7   Which word follows We Call It in the song title by D Mob?
8   Which US resort took Will Smith into the charts in 1998?
9   Which numbers went before Sumpin' New in Coolio's 96 top 20 hit?
10   Whose rap version of Prince's "Pray" charted in 1990?
11   Which band joined Afrika Bambaataa on "Reckless" in 1988?
12   Which US star performed with Melle Mel And The Furious Five?
13   Which Marky Mark and the Funky Bunch hit had the same title as a Beach Boys classic but was a different song?
14   Which duo had a hit with "Whatta Man" in 1994?
15   There was No Sleep Till where on the Beastie Boys 1987 single?
16   Which 1996 hit for Warren G had charted for Tina Turner from the biopic about her life?
17   Who backed Morris Minor on "Stutter Rap"?
18   Whose anthem was LL Cool J's "Hit 'Em High"?
19   Wyclef Jean featured with which rock group on "Another One Bites The Dust"?
20   What was the title of Jay-Z's Ghetto Anthem?

Quiz 13 Pot Luck 7

Answers – see page 217

1   In which decade did the Bee Gees have their first hit?
2   Whose backing group was the Blue Flames?
3   Who sang "Heart Of Gold" in 1972?
4   Which colour Monday was a hit for New Order in 1983 and 1988?
5   How is Mary O'Brien better known?
6   Which Park were the Small Faces in in 1967?
7   Who had a No. 1 with "Down Under"?
8   Which greeting linked Stevie Wonder and Altered Images in 1981?
9   Who was the first member to leave Take That in 1995?
10 Who was the female member of Blondie?
11 In which decade was Neil Sedaka born?
12 Who had a No. 1 with "I Can't Give You Anything (But My Love)"?
13 What was Sting's first solo single?
14 Who had a backing group called The Steelmen?
15 Whose man was So Macho in 1986?
16 Which Summer song did Abba sing in 1978?
17 What did Shanice say "I Love" in 1991 and 1992?
18 Whose first hit was "School's Out"?
19 Who had a 90s album called *Auberge*?
20 Whose Clown were the Everly Brothers in 1960?

1 What appears on the cover of *Parklife*?
2 Which word follows Got To in the song title by Leila K?
3 What was Queen's follow up to "Don't Stop Me Now"?
4 Who had a 90s album called *Boomania*?
5 Under which name did Robert Velline make the charts in the 50s and 60s?
6 Singer songwriter Lynsey de Paul wrote the TV theme for Hearts of what?
7 Which song features the line, "Blowing through the jasmine in my mind"?
8 Who had 90s hits with versions of songs by George McCrae and KC And The Sunshine Band?
9 Which daughter of a famous singing father had hits with Lee Hazelwood?
10 Who had an 80s No. 1 album called *Once Upon A Time*?
11 Where was the football stadium fire which prompted the charity song by The Crowd?
12 Which word completes the song title by Junior, "Another ___ (Closer To You)'?
13 When did Curtis Stigers have a No. 6 with "You're All That Matters To Me"?
14 Who is the lead singer of the Cranberries?
15 Who had a No. 5 UK hit in 1978 with "MacArthur Park"?
16 Who were Wayne Fontana's backing group?
17 Which word follows Big in the song title by Kajagoogoo?
18 "Freedom" was the first top ten hit for which solo singer?
19 Karen Carpenter was born in which decade?
20 In which decade did ABC first have a top ten single?

1   Who had Paul Weller as their lead singer at the beginning of the 80s?
2   Who was Roxy Music's "Jealous Guy" recorded in honour of?
3   What was the nationality of Aneka who performed "Japanese Boy" on *Top of the Pops* dressed in a kimono?
4   How was Julio Iglesias's single "Volver A Empezar" better known?
5   Who took "The Lion Sleeps Tonight" to the top of the charts?
6   Who played Coco Hernandez in *Fame* and charted with the single?
7   Who had an album called *Business As Usual*?
8   Which group took its name from the Jane Fonda film *Barbarella*?
9   Which girlfriend/supermodel did Billy Joel dedicate "Uptown Girl" to?
10 Which Radio 1 DJ refused to play Frankie Goes to Hollywood's "Relax" on his breakfast show?
11 How many Red Balloons did Nena release in 1984?
12 Who sang "All Night Long" at the closing ceremony of the Los Angeles Olympics?
13 Who was the elder of the two Wham! members?
14 Which trio produced Dead or Alive's "You Spin Me Round (Like a Record)"?
15 Which band was named after Mr Spock's Vulcan friend in *Star Trek*?
16 Which twins did Craig Logan leave when he left their band?
17 Which band was Morten Harket part of?
18 Who wrote the Ferry Aid No. 1 which charted in 1987?
19 Whose first No. 1 was "You Got It (The Right Stuff)" in 1989?
20 Who had an album called *Rattle And Hum*?

1   Which group charted with Fun Boy Three in 1982?

2   Courtney Love, Mrs Kurt Cobain, was lead singer with which band?

3   Miss Nurding left which girl group in the 90s?

4   Which Pointer Sisters hit suggests an Eric Clapton pseudonym?

5   Which 90s group were the daughters of Brian Poole who charted in the 60s with The Tremeloes?

6   Which family group sang "We Are Family" back in 1979?

7   Whose album *Always And Forever* was at the top of the charts for over a year?

8   The biography of which girl group was called *Where Did Our Love Go*?

9   What was on the other side of All Saints' "Under The Bridge"?

10   Who were at the End Of The Line with their second single in 1998?

11   Which US group made the classic biker anthem "Leader Of The Pack"?

12   What is the first name of All Saints' Ms Lewis?

13   *Before The Rain* was a follow-up album for which group?

14   Siobhan Fahey left Bananarama to form which band?

15   Where in the Commonwealth outside the UK were two of All Saints born?

16   Which member of Bananarama married Dave Stewart of Eurythmics fame?

17   How many members of Salt N Pepa were there?

18   What is the surname of the two girls from B*witched who are the sisters of a member of Boyzone?

19   How many members of En Vogue were there before Dawn Robinson left to join The Firm?

20   Which No. 1 from Shakespear's Sister was on the album *Hormonally Yours*?

1   What did T. Rex say "I Love" to do in 1976?
2   Which surname is shared by Iris and Deniece?
3   What was Abba's Anni-Frid Lyngstad's home country?
4   In which decade did Blondie have their first hit?
5   Who sang "Heart on My Sleeve" in 1976?
6   How is Christopher John Davidson better known?
7   Who had a No. 1 with "Eternal Flame"?
8   Which colour Lady provided a hit for David Soul in 1977?
9   In which decade was Lisa Stansfield born?
10 What time did Smokie say to Meet You in 1976?
11 Which song title linked Demis Roussos and Slik in 1976?
12 Which planet was a hit for Shocking Blue?
13 Whose first No. 1 was "Runaway" in 1961?
14 Who took "Ebeneezer Goode" to the top in 1992?
15 Which girl did Tyrannosaurus Rex sing about in 1968?
16 Who was the female member of the Seekers?
17 Who had a 90s album called *Our Town – Greatest Hits*?
18 Whose first hit was "Sylvia's Mother"?
19 Who had a 70s album called *Voulez-vous*?
20 Whose backing group was the Crickets?

1 Which female's first top ten hit was "Straight Up"?
2 Who had a 1993 hit album called *Conscience*?
3 Father Abraham had once been part of which group back in the 90s charts?
4 What was Spandau Ballet's follow-up to "Instinction"?
5 Which word follows Never Too in the song title by Kylie Minogue?
6 Who had a big 80s No. 1 album called *The Lexicon Of Love*?
7 Which band has included Tony Banks and Michael Rutherford?
8 What was Alice Cooper's first top ten hit?
9 Which Abba reissue first saw them back in the top 20 in the 90s?
10 Who had a 70s No. 1 with "Everything I Own"?
11 Who was *Wired For Sound* in an 80s album?
12 Which 80s No. 1 was a song from the musical *South Pacific*?
13 What was The Specials' follow up to "Gangsters"?
14 Which word completes the song title by Modern Romance, "Best ____ Of Our Lives"?
15 Which country singer had a first UK hit with "I Love You Because"?
16 Which band had "Chrissie Boy" Foreman and Lee "Kix" Thompson in its line-up?
17 Which comic had a 70s No. 1 album, *We All Had Doctors' Papers*?
18 Which member of Abba was not Swedish?
19 Which Take That hit contains the line, "Cos we're livin' in a world of fools"?
20 What was loved by Shanice in 1992?

1   Who sang about "Saturday Night" in 1994?
2   What was on the other side of Robson and Jerome's "I Believe"?
3   What goes after Meat Loaf's "I Would Do Anything For Love"?
4   Which soundtrack was a top-selling 1992 album in the UK and the US?
5   Which '91 chart toppers share a name with an instrument of torture?
6   Which band included Siobhan Fahey and Marcella Detroit?
7   Which 1994 chart topper was written by the Troggs' Reg Presley?
8   Who were Baby, Posh, Scary, Ginger and Sporty?
9   Who had the album *Automatic For The People*?
10   Who was Take That's usual lead vocalist?
11   Which No. 1 artist was the creation of the TV producer Mike Leggo?
12   Whose first No. 1 was "End of the Road"?
13   What was Boyzone's first chart hit?
14   Which superstar did Bobby Brown marry in 1992?
15   Who had the best-selling album *Blue is the Colour*?
16   What was the Dunblane single called?
17   Which veteran band released *Voodoo Lounge* in 1994?
18   Whose 1994 Greatest Hits album was called *End of Part One*?
19   Which band included the bass player Paul McGuigan?
20   What was reported in the press as "Cliffstock"?

1 Which chocolate bar used "(I Can't Get No) Satisfaction" in a 1991 TV ad?
2 What number Nervous Breakdown brought them 60s chart success?
3 Why did the Stones cancel their 1998 UK tour?
4 Which Stone wrote the book *Stone Alone*?
5 Which original member of the Stones owns the restaurant chain Sticky Fingers?
6 Who wrote "The Last Time"?
7 Where did Mick Jagger go to make the film *Ned Kelly* in 1969?
8 Which 1997 album was also the name of their late 90s tour?
9 Who was the oldest of the original Stones?
10 Which technological product used "Start Me Up" in an advertising campaign?
11 Which record label did they leave in 1970?
12 A 60s UK & US hit said Get Off My what?
13 Which London School did Mick Jagger attend which also had President Kennedy as a former student?
14 Brian Jones died at the former house of the creator of which much-loved children's character?
15 What was the first name of Jagger's first wife?
16 Which member of the band performed with the X-Pensive Winos?
17 Darryl Jones replaced which member of the band?
18 Who shared vocals with Mick Jagger on "State Of Shock", not recorded with the rest of the band?
19 Their 60s track "Dandelion" is named after what or whom?
20 Which member of the band founded his own orchestra which played at Ronnie Scott's?

1   Zager and Evans sang about which year – among others – in 1969?
2   Which girl did Slade say Gudbuy T' in 1972?
3   What did Cat Stevens say "I Love" to in 1966?
4   Which duo sang "Heartache" in 1987?
5   Who was the female member of Steeleye Span?
6   Which Summer song did Hylda Baker and Arthur Mullard sing in the 80s?
7   Which colour Velvet provided a hit for Alannah Myles in 1990?
8   Who had a No. 1 with "I Want to Know What Love Is"?
9   How is Sean Sherrard better known?
10 Which song title links Johnny Nash in 1975 and Kylie Minogue in 1990?
11 Whose first No. 1 was "Sweets for My Sweet"?
12 Which TV presenter had a hit with "Close Every Door"?
13 Which national soccer side had a hit with "Ole Ola (Mulher Brasileira)"?
14 Which 70s chart-topper often performed dressed as a circus clown?
15 In which decade were the Everly Brothers born?
16 Who had a 90s album called *One Woman – The Ultimate Collection*?
17 Whose first hit was "Modern Girl"?
18 Who were in Creeque Alley in 1967?
19 In which decade did the Carpenters have their first hit?
20 Whose backing group were The Pirates?

1 What was The Charlatans' first No. 1 album called?
2 "Take On Me" was the first top ten hit for which group?
3 Which colour gave Los Bravos a 1966 hit?
4 Who had an 80s No. 1 with "The Final Countdown"?
5 Whose first top ten hit was "Daydreamin'"?
6 Where was David Bowie's Major Tom floating in "Space Oddity"?
7 What was Bread's first UK top ten hit?
8 Which country was the original home of Johnny Logan?
9 What was Tears For Fears' follow up to "Change"?
10 Which word completes the song title by Pointer Sisters, '___ (For My Love)'?
11 Who had a 90s No. 1 album called *Love Hurts*?
12 How are Paul Tucker and Tunde Baiyewu known?
13 Who had a 70s No. 1 with "Sad Sweet Dreamer"?
14 In the group name which French word goes in front of Belle Epoque?
15 In which decade was Adam Faith born?
16 Who used to "room on the second floor" in Cliff Richard's 1980 hit?
17 Who recorded the late 70s album *Night Flight To Venus*?
18 Which word follows I Go To in the song title by The Pretenders?
19 Which Hollies hit featured in a 1997 ad campaign by Boots?
20 Which legal procedure gave Billy Connolly a huge hit?

1 Which three instruments could Stevie play by the age of seven?
2 How was Stevie known in his early days on stage?
3 What was the first record label he recorded on?
4 Which single had the subtitle "Everything's Alright"?
5 On whose *Duets II* album did he sing in 1994?
6 Which 1984 album was from a film soundtrack?
7 In which decade was Stevie Wonder born?
8 Who did he duet with on "My Love" in 1988?
9 To which monument did he sing "Happy Birthday" in Paris in 1989?
10 Who was his song "Sir Duke" dedicated to?
11 Which Miss Wright did Stevie Wonder marry in 1970?
12 Who sang with Stevie on his first No. 1?
13 To which black leader did he dedicate his Oscar?
14 Who were the other named Friends on Dionne Warwick's "That's What Friends Are For"?
15 In which Key were the Songs on his 1976 album?
16 Who are Aisha Zakia and Kita Swan Di?
17 Who did he sing "Get It" with?
18 What was his first Top Five hit?
19 In 1984 Stevie was given the keys to which city, where he enjoyed much success?
20 For which song did he win an Oscar in 1985?

1 Who is Blur's main keyboard player?
2 Who left Suede to join Elastica?
3 What were Shed Seven Chasing in 1996?
4 How High was the City on Ocean Colour Scene's 1997 hit?
5 Which Oasis hit did Phil Tufnell choose to accompany him on the field during a cricket tour?
6 What were Suede billed as on a US tour to distinguish them from a US alternative?
7 Who were Flying in 1996?
8 Who had a Smart album in 1995?
9 Wibbling Rivalry was an argument between Liam Gallagher and whom?
10 According to Shed Seven She Left Me on what day?
11 In 1995 Oasis contributed "Fade Away" for the benefit album Help to help victims of which conflict?
12 "Travellers' Tune" was a hit for which Britpop band?
13 Cast hailed from which city?
14 Why was a Rolls-Royce an unsuitable gift from his manager for Noel Gallagher in 1995?
15 Which famous stately home did Oasis play in 1996?
16 Which minor Blur hit had a day of the week in the title?
17 Who released the album *Changegiver* in 1994?
18 Which radio elder statesman gave Pulp a spot on his show in 1981?
19 What was on the other side of Pulp's "Sorted For E's And Whizz"?
20 Who appeared on Top Of The Pops in 1991 with "There's No Other Way"?

1 Whose backing group was the Dakotas?
2 What did Nick Lowe Love The Sound Of in 1978?
3 Which surname is shared by Dinah and Geno?
4 Where was Billy Ocean born?
5 Who sang "Black Betty" in 1977 and 1990?
6 How is Marvin Lee Aday better known?
7 Which month was a No. 1 for Pilot in 1975?
8 Who sang "Heartbreaker" in 1982?
9 Which song title links Frankie Laine in 1956 and Barbra Streisand in 1980?
10 Who was Happy to Be on an Island in the Sun in 1975?
11 Who accompanied First Edition on "Ruby Don't Take Your Love to Town"?
12 In which decade was Annie Lennox born?
13 Which association was a hit for Jeannie C. Riley in 1968?
14 Which girl took The Overlanders to No. 1 in January 1966?
15 Whose first hit was "Rock On"?
16 Which girl did The Damned sing about in 1986?
17 In which decade did the Jacksons have their first hit?
18 Who had a No. 1 with "I'm Into Something Good"?
19 Who had a 90s album called *In Utero*?
20 Who was the female member of Fairport Convention?

1 Which female won four Grammy Awards in February 1999?
2 Who had a 80s album called *London 0 Hull 4*?
3 What was ABC's follow up to "The Look Of Love"?
4 Which word goes before "Yeah" in the song title by Yello?
5 Which all-boy group released an album called *Said And Done* in the 90s?
6 What was the name of Georgie Fame's backing group?
7 In which decade did Herb Alpert first have a top ten single?
8 Whose first album was The Kick Inside?
9 "Don't Worry" was the first top ten hit for which singer?
10 Who had a 70s No. 1 with "Are 'Friends' Electric"?
11 What was Dusty Springfield's real name?
12 Who had a UK No. 3 hit with the original version of "Itchycoo Park"?
13 Which word goes before Train in the song title by Farm?
14 In which US city did Motown begin?
15 Whose real name is Elaine Bookbinder?
16 What gave the Brighouse and Rastrick Brass Band a surprise 70s hit?
17 Phil Oakley and Susanne Sully were in which band?
18 Paula Jones and Mike D'Abo both sang with which 60s band?
19 Which word follows Find My in the song title by Fairground Attraction?
20 Who had an 80s No. 1 with "Let It Be"?

Quiz 27 Karaoke

LEVEL 2

1 Which song has the words "Scaramouche, will you do the fandango?"?
2 Which No. 1 had the line "Ya I'll tell you what I want, what I really, really want"?
3 Which title line follows "Our thoughts to them are winging, when friends by shame are undefiled" in the Enya song?
4 Which Dire Straits hit starts "Here comes Johnny singing oldies, goldies"?
5 Which song begins "When I was young, I never needed anyone"?
6 In which song would you find the lines "Daylight. I must wait for the sunrise, I must wait for a new life. And I mustn't give in"?
7 Which Christmas classic has the lines "Man will live for evermore, because of Christmas Day"?
8 Which film song begins "From the day we arrive on the planet and, blinking, step into the sun"?
9 In the 60s who sang "We skipped the light fandango…"?
10 What is the first line of Kiki Dee's "Amoureuse"?
11 Which song has the line "Do the fairies keep him sober for a day"?
12 Which excuse for a massacre gave the Boomtown Rats a hit song?
13 What follows "The truth is I never left you" in the song from *Evita*?
14 In which song did Phil Collins sing "Wouldn't you agree, baby you and me"?
15 What follows "When I find myself in times of trouble, Mother Mary comes to me"?
16 What is the first line of The Supremes' "You Keep Me Hangin' On"?
17 Which Bee Gees hit has the line "Cause we're livin' in a world of fools"?
18 Who sang "Isn't she precious, less than one minute old?"?
19 Which song has the line "And just like the guy whose feet were too big for his bed"?
20 Which classic begins "She packed my bags last night, pre-flight"?

Quiz 28 Gone & Forgotten?
Answers – see page 240

LEVEL 2

1 Which band had a 70s hit about a Russian mystic?
2 What was the surname of the brothers in The Beach Boys?
3 Which Eurovision Song Contest winner came third in an election for President of Ireland?
4 Which former political party leader had a band called The Raving Savages?
5 Which member of Bucks Fizz went on to present *Record Breakers* on TV?
6 Which folk singer received critical acclaim as a serious actress in *Band Of Gold*?
7 Julie Driscoll's vocals were heard over the opening credits of which 90s sitcom?
8 The Bay City Rollers were named after a town in which country?
9 The Dubliners re-recorded "The Irish Rover" with which band in 1987?
10 Which trio of sisters, Joy, Babs and Teddy, reappeared in a cameo role in Girls On Top in the 80s?
11 *Ferry 'Cross The Mersey* was a 90s musical based on which 60s singer?
12 Gary Glitter's hits were used in which late 90s successful movie?
13 Who had great success duetting with Elton John and released the album *Almost Naked* in 1996 with nudity on the cover?
14 Who backed Booker T?
15 How many original members of The Pretenders – subject of the 1995 documentary No Turn Left Unstoned – were there?
16 Which punk band had Joe Strummer on vocals?
17 Which Brothers, 60s chart-toppers, topped the chart again in 1990 after the single was used in Demi Moore's *Ghost*?
18 Which David performed with The Partridge Family?
19 Frankie Goes To Hollywood were named after a newspaper headline about which singer?
20 Which raunchy dance troupe did Sarah Brightman belong to?

1   What was a Lazy day for the Small Faces in 1968?
2   Who had a 90s album called *Very*?
3   How is Reginald Smith better known?
4   Who had a No. 1 with "Keep On Running"?
5   What did Gary Glitter follow "I Love You" with in 1973?
6   Whose first hit was "Saving All My Love For You"?
7   Which surname is shared by Scott and Junior?
8   In which decade was Gilbert O'Sullivan born?
9   Who sang "Heart" in 1988?
10 Which colour provided a hit for Spandau Ballet in 1983?
11 Which song title links Sandie Shaw and Olivia Newton-John?
12 Which Crash was a hit for Suzi Quatro?
13 Which year was a hit for Prince in 1983?
14 What was Queen's second hit?
15 Who was the female member of Vinegar Joe?
16 Which Summertime song did Eddie Cochran sing in 1958 and 1968?
17 Who were in a Dead End Street in 1966?
18 Which girl did the Four Pennies sing about in 1964?
19 In which decade did Kool and the Gang have their first hit?
20 Whose backing group were the Raiders?

1 How did Robert Van Winkle become better-known?
2 What was Kim Wilde's follow-up to "You Came"?
3 Which Diana Ross hit contains the line, "Inside out and round and round"?
4 Which big ballad singer once played Malcolm Nuttall on TV in *Coronation Street*?
5 Which veteran comic's first hit was "Love Is Like A Violin"?
6 Who had a 90s album called *Full Moon, Dirty Hearts*?
7 Which word follows Save Our in the song title by Eternal?
8 Which major 60s group had Carl Wayne as vocalist?
9 Which singer was part of the grand opening of Euro Disney in Paris in 1992?
10 Elton John was born and brought up in which north London suburb?
11 Which word completes the song title by Prefab Sprout, "The ____ Of Rock 'n' Roll"?
12 Who had a 70s No. 1 with "Up Town Top Ranking"?
13 Robbie Williams was the first member to leave which group in 1995?
14 Which group had a hit with "Hanging On The Telephone"?
15 Which decade saw the birth of writer/singer Neil Sedaka?
16 Whose first solo single was "Spread A Little Happiness"?
17 What was the name of Tommy Steele's backing group?
18 What was Sinitta's man in her UK No. 2 in 1986?
19 Who took "Summer Night City" to a UK No. 5 in the 70s?
20 In which decade did Beat first have a top ten single?

1 Which group included Agnetha and Anni-Frid?
2 Who was Brian Poole's backing group?
3 What was on the other side of Boney M's "Rivers of Babylon"?
4 What was the Monkees' first and best-selling single?
5 Who was percussionist with the Police?
6 Who was vocalist with the News?
7 Which Irish group's name means "family"?
8 In which decade did Simple Minds have their first No. 1?
9 Who had a 1988 album called *Introspective*?
10 Which group's 1991 best-selling album was *Stars*?
11 Who had an *Appetite For Destruction* in 1987?
12 Which band's line-up included "Chrissie Boy" Foreman and Lee "Kix" Thompson?
13 Which band were *All the Way From Memphis* in 1973?
14 Who were Eric Clapton, Jack Bruce and Ginger Baker?
15 Which singer/guitarist published his autobiography *X-Ray* in 1995?
16 Which word follows Mad in the song title by Tears For Fears?
17 Paul Heaton formed which group after The Housemartins?
18 Which Gibb brother is the eldest Bee Gee?
19 Whose first No. 1 was "In the Summertime" in 1970?
20 Which two Tamla groups combined on "I'm Gonna Make You Love Me" in 1969?

Quiz 32 Late Greats

Answers – see page 236

LEVEL 2

1 The late Jerry Garcia was vocalist with which band?
2 Which musical instrument did Karen Carpenter play?
3 Which Billy had chart success with "Halfway To Paradise" in 1961?
4 Carl Wilson of which legendary band died in 1998?
5 Which disaster in 1988 claimed the life of Cockney Rebel Paul Jeffreys?
6 Michael Hutchence was born in and died in which city?
7 *The Rose* was a Bette Midler movie based on the life of which singer?
8 Which late great duetted with k.d. lang on his mega hit "Crying"?
9 The late Brian Connolly fronted which glam band?
10 Which song was "The Best Of Free" according to the 1991 re-released single?
11 Which Jimi Hendrix song hit No. 1 a few weeks after the singer's death?
12 What was the first name shared by Messrs Perkins and Wilson who both died of cancer at the beginning of 1998?,
13 How is Mary O'Brien who died in March 1999, better known?
14 Whose life story was recreated in the biopic Sweet Dreams?
15 How many UK No. 1s did Buddy Holly have during his lifetime?
16 Florence Ballard was a member of which group?
17 The husband of which 1998 chart topper died in a skiing accident at the beginning of that year?
18 Whose album *Rhymes And Reasons* included the classic "Leaving On A Jet Plane"?
19 Whose farewell note in 1995 read, "It's better to burn out than fade away"?
20 Which Marvin Gaye hit got into the top ten again after his murder?

Answers

Gone & Forgotten? (Quiz 28)
1 Boney M. 2 Wilson. 3 Dana. 4 Screaming Lord Sutch. 5 Cheryl Baker.
6 Barbara Dickson. 7 *Absolutely Fabulous*. 8 USA. 9 The Pogues.
10 Beverley Sisters. 11 Gerry Marsden. 12 The Full Monty. 13 Kiki Dee.
14 The MG's. 15 Three. 16 The Clash. 17 Righteous Brothers.
18 Cassidy. 19 Frank Sinatra. 20 Hot Gossip.

1 Which song was a No. 2 for both Nat King Cole and Rick Astley?
2 How is Clive Powell better known?
3 What did Jim Reeves follow "I Love You" with in 1964 and 1971?
4 Who sang "Anyone Who Had A Heart" in 1964?
5 Who was the female member of the Captain and Tennille?
6 Who had a No. 1 with "Let's Party"?
7 In which decade was Little Jimmy Osmond born?
8 Which colour Corvette provided a hit for Prince in 1983 and 1985?
9 Which song title links Dolly Parton and Sheena Easton?
10 Whose backing group were the All Stars?
11 Who sang with the Beatles on their 1969 No. 1 "Get Back"?
12 Who sang "Band Of Gold" in 1970?
13 Which singer/songwriter's wife was "Claudette" in the Everly Brothers'song?
14 Which port was a hit for Mike Oldfield?
15 Who sang with Robert Palmer on "I'll Be Your Baby Tonight" in 1990?
16 Whose first hit was "Pictures Of Matchstick Men"?
17 What was the nationality of Linda McCartney before she married?
18 Who had a 90s album called *Black Tie White Noise*?
19 In which decade did Meat Loaf have his first hit?
20 Which girl did Derek And The Dominoes sing about in 1972?

1 Which word followed Let's Get in the song title by Def Leppard?
2 Chris de Burgh's real name is Christopher John what?
3 Which group in the charts in the 90s sang "I'll Meet You At Midnight" in the 70s?
4 Which planet links Shocking Blue and Bananarama?
5 Judith Durham was the female member of which group?
6 What was the first top ten UK hit for Dr Hook?
7 Which word follows Causing A in the song title by Madonna?
8 What was The Style Council's follow-up to "Walls Come Tumbling Down!'?
9 In the song title where was Gallagher And Lyle's Heart ?
10 What was Boyzone's first No. 1 album called?
11 With which group did Susanna Hoffs gain recognition on guitar and vocals?
12 What city was Seal from?
13 Who had a 70s No. 1 with "Yes Sir, I Can Boogie"?
14 Which word follows The Killing in the song title by Echo And The Bunnymen?
15 Which Sinatra song became a hit for Elvis Presley in a live recorded version?
16 Who brought out an album called *The Wedding Album* in 1993?
17 How many of the Doobie Brothers were called Doobie?
18 Which word follows "The Only Rhyme That" in the song title by 808 State?
19 Which country did Celine Dion represent in the Eurovision Song Contest?
20 Who wrote the original theme music for Neighbours?

1 In which city was George Michael brought up?
2 What was his debut solo album called?
3 Who did he duet with on "I Knew You Were Waiting (For Me)"?
4 On whose version of "Nikita" did George sing backing vocals?
5 Where did George first meet Wham!'s Andrew Ridgeley?
6 What is George Michael's real first name?
7 In which decade was he born?
8 With which band did he record the *Five Live EP*?
9 Which female vocalist was on the same record?
10 From which newspaper did he receive damages in 1989 after accusations about gatecrashing a party?
11 What is the name of his autobiography?
12 Which item of his clothing is burned on his "Freedom 90" video?
13 What was his second solo album called?
14 Which Elton John song did he sing at the Live Aid concert?
15 Which 1990/91 conflict helped the fortunes of "Praying For Time" because of its lyric?
16 What was his 1996 comeback ballad?
17 Which album was released the same year?
18 Which Corporation became parent company of Epic Records, which caused a legal battle with George?
19 What was his first solo No. 1?
20 Which film soundtrack contained the controversial, sometimes banned single "I Want Your Sex"?

1 Which actor/singer wrote "Crocodile Shoes" and appeared in the TV series?
2 Who presented *The Word* after being a member of Faith, Hope & Charity?
3 Which group made the music for the 1999 Heinz ad?
4 Who tried to turn TV's *Birds Of A Feather* stars into opera singers in *Jobs For the Girls*?
5 Which TV presenter Michael made "Too Much For One Heart" in 1995?
6 Which sports presenter recorded "If" to the background of Fauré's Pavane for the 1998 World Cup?
7 Andy Williams' "Music To Watch Girls" by advertised which make of car?
8 Which Ben E. King hit was used in a Levi's ad in 1986?
9 Clannad's "Legend" was the theme from which TV series?
10 Which glam rock star did TV chef Gary Rhodes impersonate on his culinary roadshow?
11 Weetabix's TV ad plea to the referee is to the tune of which Bee Gees' hit?
12 Eric Idle and Richard Wilson charted with the theme from which sitcom?
13 Which 60s pop star starred in *Budgie* and *Love Hurts*?
14 What sort of Days was the name of Robson & Jerome's Best of album?
15 Which cult animation series featured the voice of Isaac Hayes?
16 What sort of clothes did Sam Cooke's "Wonderful World" advertise in 1986?
17 Which classic song did *London's Burning* star John Alford take into the charts in 1996?
18 Which Hot Chocolate 70s hit advertised Cadbury's Hot Chocolate?
19 Which song from the 60s introduced Absolutely Fabulous?
20 Which singer presented the British version of the American game show *The Dating Game*?

1 Which Spice Girl was Ginger Spice?
2 In which country was Roger Whittaker born?
3 Which surname is shared by Noel and George?
4 Which song title links Tammy Wynette and Billy Connolly?
5 How is Gaynor Hopkins better known?
6 What is Toyah's surname?
7 In which decade was Michael Bolton born?
8 Who was Dr Hook's backing group on "Sylvia's Mother"?
9 Who had UK top ten hits in 1983 and 1988 with"Blue Monday"?
10 Who has topped the charts with Slik and Band Aid?
11 Who closed the American side of the Live Aid concert?
12 What is Steve Hurley's "middle" nickname?
13 What does SWV stand for?
14 Who had a solo album called *Journeyman*?
15 Who experienced "Afternoon Delight" in 1976?
16 Whose first hit was "Give Me Just A Little More Time"?
17 Who celebrated April Love in 1957?
18 Who's Waiting according to Bananarama?
19 Who had a 60s hit with "Tobacco Road"?
20 Who sang "Don't Sleep In The Subway"?

1 Who had an 80s No. 1 with 19?
2 What was The Beautiful South's follow-up to "Song For Whoever"?
3 Which Chris Rea 90s album title gave him a UK No. 16 singles hit?
4 In which decade did Kool And The Gang first have a top ten single?
5 What was the title of Chris Rea's first No. 1 album?
6 Which word follows Dead Ringer For in the song title by Meatloaf?
7 What was the name of Buddy Holly's backing group?
8 Which group had a UK No. 2 hit with "Gudbuy T'Jane"?
9 Which pet was Loved by Cat Stevens in a 1966 single?
10 What were Pepsi and Shirley singing about in their No. 2 1987 hit?
11 Maddy Prior was the female member of which group?
12 Which word completes the song title by Mel and Kim, _____ Out (Get Fresh At The Weekend)?
13 Which *Grease* track was covered by Hylda Baker and Arthur Mullard?
14 Depeche Mode brought out a 90s album called Songs Of Faith And what?
15 Which country does Leonard Cohen come from?
16 Who had a 70s No. 1 with "You To Me Are Everything"?
17 Which word follows Praying For in the song title by George Michael?
18 Who were Lulu's backing group when she first hit the charts?
19 Which word completes the song title by Spandau Ballet, "I'll ____ For You"?
20 The Look was the first top ten single for which group?

1 Which No. 1 includes vocals by Captain Tobias Wilcock?
2 Who had a 1974 No. 1 with "Rock Your Baby"?
3 Which 70s No. 1 was about a nudist?
4 Who teamed up Under Pressure in 1981?
5 What was Brotherhood of Man's Mexican shepherd boy called?
6 Who had a 70s No. 1 with "Show You The Way To Go"?
7 What was on the other side of the Detroit Spinners' "Forgive Me Girl"?
8 Who wore a Pierrot costume for his "Ashes to Ashes" video?
9 Who had three No. 1's in the first two months of 1981?
10 Who had their first No. 1 with "This Ole House"?
11 Which No. 1 was based on the Zulu folk tune "Wimoweh"?
12 Who was the first German band to have a UK No. 1 in 1982?
13 Why did Stevie Wonder not receive full billing on his No. 1 with Paul McCartney?
14 Which 80s No. 1 was a song from the musical *South Pacific*?
15 Who had a 70s No. 1 album called *Horizon*?
16 Who had a 60s hit with "Fire"?
17 Which 60s group were named after an American Civil War battle and wore period army uniforms?
18 Who was the oldest ever artist at the time to have a No. 1 record in 1968?
19 Who was lead singer on the 1968 No. 1 "Mighty Quinn"?
20 Which 70s No. 1 had a French title?

Quiz 40 Movie Links
Answers – see page 244

LEVEL 2

---

1 Which 1996 movie featured the song "Seven Day Weekend"?
2 Which song from *Robin Hood: Prince Of Thieves* topped the UK charts?
3 Which Shania Twain hit came from the movie *Notting Hill*?
4 "Lovefool" was featured in which late 90s movie?
5 Which European group sang the theme song from the Bond movie *The Living Daylights*?
6 Which movie featured Robbie Williams' 'Man Machine"?
7 Which controversial director filmed Adam And The Ants for the punk movie Jubilee in 1978?
8 Which 1997 hit for Ash was a theme from a film of the same name?
9 Whose Theme was written by Burt Bacharach for the 1981 movie with Dudley Moore?
10 Which Dean Martin classic featured in the movie *Moonstruck*?
11 Which Beatles debut movie had an entirely self-composed soundtrack?
12 Which Chuck Berry song was revived for the movie *Pulp Fiction*?
13 Sleeper covered which Blondie track for the movie *Trainspotting*?
14 What was the name of the *Blues Brothers* sequel movie made in 1998?
15 Which Michael recorded the theme for Disney's *Hercules*?
16 Which Boyzone song featured in *Bean: The Movie*?
17 Which film with Susan Sarandon featured a musical contribution from Johnny Cash?
18 Which John Travolta film included Neil Diamond's "Girl, You'll Be A Woman Soon"?
19 Which Four sang "Loco In Acapulco" for the 1988 soundtrack for *Buster*?
20 Who was lead singer on the track "You Sexy Thing" from *The Full Monty*?

Answers

TV Links (Quiz 36)
1 Jimmy Nail. 2 Dani Behr. 3 Ladysmith Black Mambazo. 4 Lesley Garrett.
5 Barrymore. 6 Desmond Lynam. 7 Fiat (Uno). 8 "Stand By Me".
9 *Robin Of Sherwood*. 10 Gary Glitter. 11 "Tragedy".
12 *One Foot In The Grave*. 13 Adam Faith. 14 *Happy Days*.
15 *South Park*. 16 Levi jeans. 17 "Smoke Gets In Your Eyes'.
18 "Put You Together Again". 19 "This Wheel's On Fire'.
20 Cilla Black (*Blind Date*).

1 Whose first hit was "Rock With The Caveman"?
2 Which surname is shared by Tony and Lou?
3 In which decade was Petula Clark born?
4 Who wanted to be Bobby's Girl in 1962?
5 Who were Vic Reeves's backing group?
6 What is the home country of Paul Anka?
7 What was on the other side of Louis Armstrong's "What a Wonderful World"?
8 Which Beach Boys album included goats on the album cover?
9 Whose 1996 album was called *K*?
10 Dolores O'Riordan is lead singer with which band?
11 How is Vincent Furnier better known?
12 Who had Joe Strummer as lead vocalist?
13 A 1991 TV concert by Clannad was a tribute to which Irishman?
14 How are David, Stephen, Graham and Neil better known?
15 Which Gibb was not a Bee Gee?
16 Whose real surname is Gudmundsdóttir?
17 Whose first chart entry was "Chantilly Lace"?
18 Who was keyboard player with the Dave Clark Five?
19 In which decade did the Faces have their first hit record?
20 Whose album *Diva* topped the charts in 1993?

LEVEL 2

1   What was Tracy Chapman's first No. 1 album called?
2   In which English county was Paul Weller born?
3   What was Sheena Easton's first UK top ten hit?
4   Which word goes before Girl in the song title by New Kids On The Block?
5   What was Bad Manners' follow-up to "Special Brew"?
6   Which surname was added to Crosby, Stills and Nash?
7   Who had an 80s No. 1 album with *So*?
8   Which group included John Phillips and Dennis Doherty?
9   What did TV presenter Phillip Schofield ask us to Close in his 1992 hit?
10 Who had an 80s No. 1 with "Jack Your Body"?
11 What was the first No. 1 album of the 90s for The Rolling Stones?
12 Which word goes before Out in the song title by Odyssey?
13 Which black fabric provided Alannah Myles with a No. 2 hit in 1990?
14 What is Johnny Logan's real name?
15 Which word completes the song title by Jon and Vangelis, "I'll Find My Way _____'?
16 Which national football team released "Ole Ola (Muhler Brasileira)' in 1978?
17 Which 70s No. 1 artist appeared in his early days dressed as a circus clown?
18 The Everly Brothers were born in which decade?
19 "Dancing In The Dark" was the first top ten for which singer?
20 What was Bananarama's follow-up to "Cruel Summer"?

1 "Eye Level" was the theme music for which detective series?
2 Who had a 1962 No. 1 with "Nut Rocker"?
3 Which music by which composer was it based on?
4 What was the nickname of the Shadows' Brian Locking?
5 Which music was a No. 1 twice for Eddie Calvert and Perez Prado?
6 Who had a 50s hit with "Hoots Mon"?
7 What was Lieutenant Pigeon's only hit?
8 How is the instrumentalist Philippe Pages better known?
9 Which 60s instrumental is said to be a favourite of Lady Thatcher?
10 Which Shadows hit was a theme for a series of Edgar Wallace stories?
11 Who became the Shadows' drummer after Tony Meehan left?
12 Which 60s March became a minor hit for Joe Loss And His Orchestra?
13 Which No. 1 was accompanied by 1920s flappers?
14 Who had the longest name of any group to have a No. 1?
15 Which instrument did Fleetwood Mac's Mick Fleetwood play?
16 Who had a 1977 instrumental hit with "The Floral Dance"?
17 Who had a 1968 hit with "Classical Gas"?
18 Who was the soloist on the 1976 hit "Aria"?
19 Which pianist had a 50s hit with "Unchained Melody"?
20 To the nearest five, how many instrumental No. 1s were there between 1974 and 1994?

Quiz 44 Christmas Songs

Answers – see page 256

LEVEL 2

1 "Santa Claus Is Comin' To Town" was on the other side of "My Hometown" in 1985 for whom?
2 Which residents of Home Hill had an Christmastime No. 1 in 1997?
3 Which Welsh performer topped the charts in 1985 with "Merry Christmas Everyone"?
4 Who duetted with Cliff Richard on "Whenever God Shines His Light" in December 1989?
5 Which Mel was "Rockin' Around The Christmas Tree" with Kim Wilde?
6 Who sang "All I Want For Christmas Is You" in 1994?
7 Who took "Walking In The Air" from *The Snowman* into the charts?
8 Which weatherman was in the title of a song during the Christmas period in 1988?
9 What was Wham!'s classic Christmas hit?
10 Which duo's song was knocked off the top spot by Michael Jackson's "Earth Song" in 1995?
11 Which Glam Rock star sang "Another Rock And Roll Christmas" in 1984?
12 Who was the first non-human Christmas No. 1?
13 Who pleaded "Please Come Home For Christmas" in 1994?
14 Which pop classic has the line, "Well, here it is, Merry Christmas"?
15 Which ex-Beatle had an Christmas hit with "Wonderful Christmas Time"?
16 Whose "Christmas Through Your Eyes" reached No. 8 in 1992?
17 Which band's *Greatest Hits* album was at No. 1 at Christmas 1991?
18 Who had three consecutive Christmas No. 1s in the later half of the 90s?
19 Which David duetted with Bing Crosby in 1982?
20 Which Jive Bunny single was a Christmas No. 1 in 1989?

Answers

Albums (Quiz 48)
1 For Your Feet. **2** *Spiders*. **3** Jimmy Nail. **4** Paul Weller. **5** Pink Floyd.
6 Celine Dion. **7** Abba Gold. **8** Revelation. **9** Carole King. **10** Lauryn Hill.
11 Annie Lennox. **12** Madonna. **13** Sunday 8 p.m. **14** Horses.
15 "Stand By Your Man". **16** Ladysmith Black Mambazo. **17** Alisha's Attic.
18 Kate Bush. **19** Kula Shaker. **20** *More Monty*.

1 In which decade did the Smurfs have their first hit record?
2 How was Walden Robert Cassotto better known?
3 Which song title links Scott Walker and Kool And The Gang?
4 Whose first hit was "Shake, Rattle and Roll" in 1954?
5 Who was lead vocalist with The Zombies?
6 Whose album *Shepherd Moons* topped the charts in 1992?
7 How many hit singles did Frank Zappa have in the 70s?
8 Whose debut album was *No Parlez*?
9 How was Alvin Stardust previously known in the charts?
10 Which group's members included Neil Innes and Vivian Stanshall?
11 In which country were Boney M based?
12 In which decade was Dolly Parton born?
13 Whose first hit was "Get Down And Get With It"?
14 Who had an 80s hit with "Got My Mind Set On You"?
15 What is Clarence Henry's nickname?
16 What is the home country of Bjorn Again?
17 Who took part in the Eurovision Song Contest as a member of separate groups, Co-Co and Bucks Fizz?
18 Who did Sarah Brightman sing with on her first chart hit?
19 Which record label did Herb Alpert co-found?
20 What name was given to the new country stars of the 1990s?

1 What was Black Box's follow-up to "Ride On Time"?
2 Which group includes Pete Buck on bass?
3 What was En Vogue's first chart success?
4 Who backed early rocker Johnny Kidd?
5 In what year did Carter – The Unstoppable Sex Machine release the No. 1 *Love Album*?
6 Which word goes before Box in the song title by OMD?
7 Who took *Crazy* into the 1994 album chart?
8 What is the first name of US vocalist Benatar?
9 Which song sung by Ronan Keating contains the line, "There's a truth in your eyes"?
10 Who had a 70s No. 1 with "Matchstalk Men And Matchstalk Cats And Dogs"?
11 Which title has been used for hits by MC Hammer and Take That?
12 Which surname is shared by jazz singer Cleo and 50s hitmaker Frankie?
13 Who played Madonna's night club singer lover in *Evita*?
14 What colour was Betty in Ram Jam's Top 20 UK hits from 1977 and 1990?
15 What is Meatloaf's real name – Marvin Lee what?
16 Steve and Muff Winwood were in which Group?
17 What was The Beat's follow-up to "Hands Off – She's Mine"?
18 Which word follows My One in the song title by Mica Paris?
19 Who had an 80s No. 1 with "We Are The World"?
20 Which Alley took The Mamas And The Papas up the late 60s charts?

1   Which solo singer had a hit with "Spirit in the Sky"?
2   What was Des O'Connor's first No. 1 hit?
3   Who had a 90s No. 1 with "The Real Thing"?
4   Which singer was named after the Wind in "Paint Your Wagon"?
5   Who wrote Take That's "Babe" before pursuing a solo career?
6   Who was the first soloist to have a No. 1 hit with the same name as himself?
7   How is Londoner Ms Bobb better known?
8   Whose first single "The One and Only" went to No. 1 in 1991?
9   What is Wink Martindale's most famous hit?
10 Who took "Stairway To Heaven" into the charts in 1993?
11 Who had a 60s hit with "Where Do You Go To My Lovely?"?
12 Who has recorded with Richard Carpenter and the Pet Shop Boys?
13 Which singer's songs ranged from "Little Green Apples" to "You Can't Roller Skate In A Buffalo Herd"?
14 Who was famous for having a rabbit's foot swinging from his belt?
15 Who had a best-selling album called *Tapestry*?
16 Who went to No. 1 in her first-ever week in the charts in 1994?
17 Who had the first-ever No. 1 in the UK?
18 Which female soloist has recorded on at least nine different record labels in a 30-year career?
19 Who sang about "Me And Mrs Jones" in 1973?
20 Which American had a 1989 hit with "The Wind Beneath My Wings"?

1 On *Ladies And Gentlemen*, "For Your Heart" was the ballad section. What was the upbeat section called?
2 What was Space's debut album?
3 Which *Evita* star made the album *Tadpoles In A Jar*?
4 Whose 90s Greatest Hits album was called *Modern Classics*?
5 Who released the classic *Ummagumma* album?
6 Which Canadian singer sang with the legendary Paul Anka on "It's Hard To Say Goodbye" on *A Body of Work*?
7 Which Abba album was No. 1 again in 1999 seven years after its release?
8 Genesis's debut was called Genesis To what?
9 Celine Dion's *Tapestry Revisited* was a tribute to which singer-songwriter?
10 Whose Miseducation album featured the track "Superstar"?
11 Whose solo debut album was *Diva* in 1992?
12 Whose collection of love songs was called *Something to Remember*?
13 What date and time was Faithless's second album?
14 Which animals featured on the cover of Catatonia's *International Velvet*?
15 In the tribute album *Tammy Wynette Remembered* what song does Elton John sing?
16 Whose Best Of album was called *The Star And Wiseman*?
17 Which duo released the album *Illumina*?
18 Whose *The Whole Story* included "The Man With the Child In His Eyes"?
19 Whose second album was *Peasants, Pigs And Astronauts*?
20 Which Party album was a follow-up to *The Full Monty* soundtrack?

1 In which country was Neneh Cherry born?
2 Who sang "Billy Don't Be A Hero" in 1974?
3 How is Ernest Evans better known?
4 Which record label shares its name with a nautical aid?
5 Who were All Out Of Love in 1980?
6 Whose album *High OnTthe Happy Side* topped the charts in 1992?
7 Who took "Charmaine", "Diane" and "Ramona" into the top ten?
8 Who did Kate Bush duet with on "Don't Give Up"?
9 Which song was a hit for Elvis Presley and Andy Williams?
10 Who had the "Bell Bottom Blues" in 1954?
11 In which decade was Frankie Valli born?
12 Which song title links The Three Degrees and Barbra Streisand?
13 Whose first hit was "Hong Kong Garden"?
14 What was Midge Ure's first solo No. 1?
15 What is the home country of Berlin?
16 What was Cilla Black's first single?
17 Which surname is shared by Ronnie and Dina?
18 Whose singles include "Call Up The Groups" and "Pop Go The Workers"?
19 Who had their second No. 1 with "Spirit In The Sky"?
20 In which decade did Genesis have their first hit record?

1   Who decorated the room shown on the *Definitely Maybe* album cover?
2   What was Bon Jovi's follow-up to "Livin' On A Prayer"?
3   What was David Essex's first UK top ten single?
4   Who had a 90s album called *Woodface*?
5   Who had an 80s No. 1 with "Seven Tears"?
6   Who had a No. 2 UK hit in 1982 with "Heartbreaker"?
7   Who released the 80s album *Never Forever*?
8   Where was Demis Roussos Happy To Be On in his 1975 hit?
9   What was the name of the first album to chart for Jim Diamond?
10 Which word follows We Are in the song title by Gary Numan?
11 In which decade did Gladys Knight first have a top ten single?
12 In which film did Van Morrison sing "Brown-Eyed Girl"?
13 To whom did Kenny Rogers ask "Don't Take Your Love To Town" in 1969?
14 Which word completes the song title by Peter Gabriel, "Don't ___ Up"?
15 Which female signer had a 70s No. 1 with "Free"?
16 *Flesh And Blood* was an 80s No. 1 album for which group?
17 Who took "Eloise" to a UK No. 3 in 1986?
18 Who had a 70s No. 1 album called *Million Dollar Babies*?
19 In which decade did Charles Aznavour first have a top ten single?
20 Which word goes before Of Love in the song title by Fun Boy Three?

1 Which Bob Dylan composition was a US hit for Peter, Paul and Mary and Stevie Wonder?
2 What was his first UK hit single?
3 What was the first chart-topping composition by Dylan?
4 Which album includes the lengthy "Sad-Eyed Lady Of The Lowlands"?
5 Why was Dylan booed off stage in 1965 and 1966?
6 Which Dylan song was a hit for Manfred Mann in 1968?
7 Which album did he record with the help of Johnny Cash?
8 To the nearest £1,000 how much did Dylan receive for a one-hour session at the Isle of Wight Festival in 1969?
9 What was the title of the novel he published in 1970?
10 Which album was said to have been due to the end of his marriage?
11 Which Dylan song was a hit for Eric Clapton and Guns N' Roses?
12 Which film did he act in and provide the music for in Mexico?
13 When asked what were the most overrated and underrated books of the last 75 years, what did he reply?
14 What was the name of his own record label?
15 Which UK guitarist co-produced "Infidels"?
16 Which religion did he embrace in the late 70s?
17 Which Dylan song was a hit for Jimi Hendrix in 1968?
18 For which film did he write "Lay Lady Lay" – though it was not chosen?
19 Which Dylan band also included George Harrison and Roy Orbison?
20 Which cricketer added Dylan to his first names?

1   What was their 1999 album called – their first of original material for over five years?
2   In 1976 they signed a ground-breaking contract to promote what clothes item?
3   Which royals attended their live show at the NEC in 1982?
4   Which No. 1 album shared its name with a magazine?
5   Who joined them on vocals for "All Around My Hat"?
6   Who had the original hit with "The Wanderer"?
7   Fun Fun Fun was a 1996 collaboration with which group?
8   On their *Rock Til You Drop* tour, the Quo playing four venues in a day, where did they play in Scotland?
9   What was their first No. 1 album of the 80s?
10 In 1984 where was their Live album recorded?
11 In an early hit what went before "I melt away"?
12 How many Gold Bars featured in their 1984 album?
13 What sort of Work was a 1994 album title?
14 They opened the 1985 Live Aid concert but with which song?
15 Which member of the band is famous for his ponytail?
16 In which city were Status Quo founded?
17 Which Tom had a minor hit with Quo's "Something 'Bout You Baby I Like"?
18 Which 1990 single was released in Parts 1 & 2?
19 What was released to promote The Race Against Time?
20 What followed Burning Bridges in the title of the song?

1   Which country did Baccara come from?
2   How is Stuart Goddard better known?
3   Which actor was Under The Boardwalk in 1987?
4   Who had a 60s No. 1 with "Where Are You Now (My Love)"?
5   Whose album *Innuendo* topped the charts in 1991?
6   Who had a 1969 hit with "Melting Pot"?
7   Who had a Total Eclipse Of The Heart in 1983?
8   In which decade did Neil Sedaka have his first hit record?
9   What was the Byrds' debut No. 1?
10   Which car was Natalie Cole's first hit record?
11   How many members of D:Ream are there?
12   What are the home countries of the members of Los Bravos?
13   Who was a Sunshine Superman in 1966?
14   Whose first hit was "House Of Love"?
15   Who recorded the original "This Wheel's On Fire"?
16   In which decade was Enya born?
17   Who had a Horse With No Name in 1971?
18   Which song title links Kylie Minogue and Sonia?
19   Which day of the week did The Easybeats have on their mind in 1966?
20   Which numbers were a 60s hit for Len Barry?

1   What was The Prodigy's follow-up to "Charly"?
2   Which word follows Slave To in the song title by Bryan Ferry?
3   Who had a 90s No. 1 album called *Very*?
4   Complete the title of the classic Black Sabbath song, "The Children Of The ____"?
5   Who helped the sex and rock'n'roll image by making a 13-year-old his third wife when he was aged 22?
6   Which US state does Jewel come from?
7   Who released a 90s album titled *In Utero*?
8   Sandy Denny was the female member of which group?
9   Who had a UK No. 2 hit with "Lazy Sunday" in 1968?
10 Which word follows Get The in the song title by Electronic?
11 What is Marty Wilde's real name?
12 In which decade was singer and pianist Gilbert O'Sullivan born?
13 What part of the body were the Pet Shop Boys singing about in 1988?
14 Which word completes the song title by The Specials, "Do Nothing"/"_____ Farm"?
15 "Weather With You" was the first top ten hit for which group?
16 Who had a 70s No. 1 with "Don't Cry For Me Argentina"?
17 The Kemp brothers were in which band?
18 Who had a 90s No. 1 with "End Of The Road"?
19 In which decade did Barron Knights first have a top ten single?
20 What was the title of Simon And Garfunkel's first No. 1 album?

1 Who sang "Something Outa Nothing" with Paul Medford in 1986?
2 Who was Just This Side of Love in 1990?
3 How was Michelle Gayle known in *EastEnders*?
4 Which "Street" couple sang "Somethin' Stupid"?
5 How is Bill Tarmey better known?
6 What was the title of the song based on the *EastEnders* theme tune?
7 Who had a hit with it in 1986?
8 Who had an album called *Emmerdance*?
9 Who sang "Passing Strangers" with Joe Longthorne in 1994?
10 Wendy Richard, a.k.a. Pauline Fowler, was heard on which 1962 No. 1?
11 Who was the male vocalist on the record?
12 Who replaced Shane Richie in *Grease* in 1997?
13 How was Sean Maguire better known in Albert Square?
14 Which song did Mike Reid, alias Frank Butcher, take into the charts?
15 Which *Coronation Street* character was originally a singer in the soap's storyline?
16 Which 60s singer played Len Fairclough's son Stanley?
17 Whose grandson in *Coronation Street* was played by the future Monkee Davy Jones?
18 What was the title of Nick Berry's 1986 chart topper?
19 Cindy from *EastEnders* was formerly a backing singer for which artist?
20 Which musical star once played Kevin Webster's rival Malcolm Nuttall?

1   What was Erasure's next top ten hit following "Abba—Esque"?
2   The Lemonheads' chart debut in the UK was It's A Shame About who?
3   Which duo twice entered the charts with "Boss Drum"?
4   What sort of Blonde was a 1990 hit for INXS?
5   Who had a 1998 hit with "Avenging Angels"?
6   Who followed up "Ocean Drive" with "Postcards From Heaven"?
7   Which song with Stone in the title was the first to chart for The Stone Roses?
8   What is Jamiroquai's Jay Kay's real first name?
9   Whose 1996 hit was "Trash" – according to the single's title?
10 Which name featured in the title of Supergrass's first top ten hit?
11 2 Unlimited are based in which country?
12 Whose *Sound Of Drums* album heralded their 1998 tour?
13 Which band famous for their "Joyrider" were the most successful 90s Scandinavian act on the US singles chart?
14 What is the baby swimming towards on the cover of Nirvana's *Nevermind*?
15 Which Ocean Colour Scene album featured "The Day We Caught The Train"?
16 What sort of Karma was a 90s hit for Radiohead?
17 What were Jamiroquai Travelling Without doing in 1996?
18 Who provided Music For The Jilted Generation?
19 Which Pulp single was accompanied by a video where celebrities described losing their virginity?
20 Gwen Stefani was lead singer with which band?

1 In which decade did Shakin' Stevens have his first hit record?
2 Which villain was a 70s hit for Boney M?
3 Who took "Ma He's Making Eyes at Me" into the Top Ten in 1974?
4 Whose first chart hit was "Wild Thing"?
5 Whose album "Sleeping With The Past" topped the charts in 1990?
6 Who said "Please Mr Postman" in 1975?
7 Which comedian sang "Don't Laugh At Me" in 1954?
8 Who pleaded to Honey to Come Back in 1970?
9 Who was Terry Dactyl's backing group?
10 Who spent "Seven Drunken Nights" in 1967?
11 In which decade was Suzi Quatro born?
12 What was Simon Dupree's backing group?
13 Whose first hit was "Planet Earth"?
14 Who made a hit Easy in 1977?
15 Who had a 60s hit with "Rescue Me"?
16 What is the home country of The Cranberries?
17 Who sang "Come And Get It" in 1970?
18 What was Tori Amos's first Top Ten hit?
19 Which word completes the song title by Public Image Ltd, 'This Is Not A ___ Song'?
20 Who was John Fred's backing group?

1 In what year did Bob Marley die?
2 Who had a 90s album called *Elegant Slumming*?
3 Which word follows Dancing On The in the song title by Lionel Richie?
4 What is Georgie Fame's real name?
5 The Best Of *Everything But The Girl* album of 1993 also had which title?
6 Which song starts, "When I find myself in times of trouble, Mother Mary comes to me"?
7 What was The Real Thing's follow-up to "Can't Get By Without You"?
8 What goes before I'm Only The Piano Player in an early Elton John album title?
9 Which word goes before Without You in the song title by King?
10 Who had an 80s No. 1 with "You Spin Me Round (Like A Record)'?
11 Which word completes the song title by Queen, "It's a ____ Life"?
12 Which 60s group were named after an American Civil War battle?
13 Who had a 70s No. 3 with "48 Crash"?
14 Which colour links a No. 2 from Spandau Ballet to a No. 10 hit from Prince?
15 Which word follows Crazy Crazy in the song title by Kiss?
16 Elkie Brooks was the female member of which group?
17 Who were in a Dead End Street in the 60s?
18 Who were the backing group for Paul Revere?
19 In which decade did Tony Bennett first have a top ten single?
20 Who had an early 80s album called *Absolutely*?

1   What was M.C. Hammer's debut single?
2   How was the 1990 "Geordie Boys" subtitled?
3   How is Alison Moira Clarkson better known?
4   In which city did rap originate?
5   Who said "(You Gotta) Fight For Your Right (To Party)" in 1987?
6   Which singer's and band's bass-line music features on "Ice Ice Baby"?
7   What does KRYME stand for in Partners in Kryme?
8   What was their first No. 1?
9   Which duo had a hit with "Whatta Man" in 1994?
10   What is the home country of the Rapper Derek B?
11   Who backed Queen Latifah on "Mama Gave Birth To The Soul Children"?
12   What was En Vogue's first chart success?
13   Which Mattel product did M.C. Hammer help launch in 1991?
14   Which Rap was an 80s hit for MC Miker "G" and Deejay Sven?
15   Who backed Morris Minor on "Stutter Rap"?
16   Who had a 1993 No. 1 with "Boom! Shake The Room"?
17   Who had a Top Ten album called *Fear Of A Black Planet*?
18   Which Blondie single features the name of Grandmaster Flash?
19   Which blond rapper's real name was Robert Van Winkle?
20   What was Liverpool F.C.'s 1988 Rap single?

1 Candy Girl was a No. 1 for which New band?
2 Who duetted with East 17 on "If You Ever"?
3 What was Take That's first No. 1?
4 Hanson's first No. 1 "Mmmbop" first featured on which album?
5 Which 1998 hit for 911 was a cover of a 70s hit by Tavares?
6 What is the name of Mrs Ronan Keating of Boyzone fame?
7 Which night of the week is featured on a 1997 hit from 911?
8 What was Ronan Keating's first solo No. 1?
9 Esther Bennett married which member of a boy band in 1998?
10 Which part of the body featured on the second and third top ten hits for Backstreet Boys?
11 How were New Kids On The Block styled on *Dirty Dawg*?
12 Which Bee Gees hit did Take That cover in 1996?
13 Who had the original hit with 911's cover "A Little Bit More"?
14 Which London borough was the title of an album by East 17?
15 Which boy band is managed by Boyzone's Ronan Keating?
16 Which 1997 hit was a No. 1 on both sides of the Atlantic for Hanson?
17 Which Mr was a top 20 hit for New Edition?
18 "Father and Son" was originally a hit for which singer before Boyzone took it into the charts?
19 Which boy band were the first to release eight singles entering at No. 1, the first in 1993?
20 What was on the other side of Boyzone's "Baby Can I Hold You"?

1 What was Joan Baez's first top ten hit?
2 Which song was a hit for Shirley Bassey and Harry Belafonte in 1957?
3 Whose album *But Seriously* topped the charts in 1990?
4 Who duetted with Frank Sinatra on the 1993 single "I've Got You Under My Skin"?
5 Who sang "The Sun Ain't Gonna Shine Any More" in 1966?
6 Which conservationists' "Minuetto Allegretto" charted in 1974?
7 Who was lead singer with The Troggs?
8 Which two 80s Wimbledon tennis champions had a Top 100 hit in 1991?
9 Who were Echo's backing group?
10 According to Edison Lighthouse, what happens Where My Rosemary Goes?
11 In which decade was Donny Osmond born?
12 Which fellow-Western actor was on the flip side of Lee Marvin's "Wandrin' Star"?
13 Who had Magic Moments in 1958?
14 Whose first hit was "One Of These Nights"?
15 Who was a Yesterday Man back in 1965?
16 Which day of the week was Beautiful to Daniel Boone in 1972?
17 How is Arnold Dorsey better known?
18 Which song title links Don Partridge and Elton John?
19 In which decade did Jackie Wilson have his first hit record?
20 What is the home country of Jimmy Cliff?

Answers

Pot Luck 29 (Quiz 57)
1 1980s. 2 Rasputin. 3 Lena Zavaroni. 4 The Troggs. 5 Elton John.
6 The Carpenters. 7 Norman Wisdom. 8 Glen Campbell. 9 The Dinosaurs.
10 The Dubliners. 11 1950s. 12 The Big Sound. 13 Duran Duran.
14 The Commodores. 15 Fontella Bass. 16 Ireland. 17 Badfinger.
18 Cornflake Girl. 19 Love. 20 The Playboy Band.

1 Where was Billy Ocean's birthplace?
2 Who sang with UB40 in 1990 on "I'll Be Your Baby Tonight"?
3 In which decade did Black Lace first have a top ten single?
4 What type of red car gave Prince a hit in 1985?
5 What was M People's follow-up to "Don't Look Any Further"?
6 Which dance is mentioned in the lyrics of "Bohemian Rhapsody"?
7 Mike Love was a member of which long lasting American group?
8 Who had a 90s album called *Zeitgeist*?
9 Who charted in 1989 with "Get A Life"?
10 In which decade did Ben E. King first have a top ten single?
11 Who were the backing group for Junior Walker?
12 What word follows Electric in the song title by Eddy Grant?
13 Who had a UK No. 3 in 1976 with "Portsmouth"?
14 Which No. 1 was accompanied by dancing 20s-style flappers?
15 What was Linda McCartney's home country?
16 Who had a 70s No. 1 with "Mississippi"?
17 Which song title links Freda Payne with Don Cherry?
18 Which word follows White in the song title by Billy Idol?
19 What was Paul McCartney's follow-up to "No More Lonely Nights"?
20 Who had an 80s No. 1 with "Save Your Love"?

1 Which charities benefited from the Five Live EP in 1993?
2 Which comedienne featured on the B side of "The Stonk" for Comic Relief?
3 Which disaster prompted the release of "Ferry 'Cross the Mersey"?
4 Which newspaper created Ferry Aid?
5 Which album was a reinterpretation of songs from *Sgt Pepper*?
6 Who sang "With A Little Help From My Friends" for Childline?
7 Which male artist sang "She's Leaving Home" for the same charity?
8 Where was the fire which prompted the release by the Crowd?
9 Which two Motown stars wrote "We Are The World" for USA For Africa?
10 What did Rod Stewart release in aid of the Zeebrugge ferry disaster?
11 Who sang "Ave Maria" in aid of the Malcolm Sargent Cancer Fund for Children?
12 Who was lead vocalist with The Crowd?
13 Which charity record reached No. 1 twice?
14 Who released "Ben" as a charity single?
15 Who have produced three charity singles?
16 Which Dionne Warwick single raised money for AIDS research?
17 What was the Dunblane single called?
18 Which charity benefited from "Live Like Horses"?
19 Who wrote "With A Little Help From My Friends"/"She's Leaving Home"?
20 Which Cliff Richard single helped famine relief?

1　Which country singer wrote "I Will Always Love You" which became a huge hit for Whitney Houston?
2　Who had a record-breaking eight posthumous albums in the UK charts in the 60s?
3　What is the first word of Charlie Rich's classic "The Most Beautiful Girl In The World"?
4　Which girl gave Kenny Rogers his first UK No. 1?
5　Which best-selling country singer became the first country singer to enter the US pop album chart at No. 1 in 1991?
6　Which member of Steeleye Span sang "All Around My Hat" with Status Quo in 1996?
7　Who appeared on stage with Elton John and the Backstreet Boys in 1999 and sang "That Don't Impress Me Much"?
8　Whose orchestra charted with "Riverdance"?
9　Who duetted with Glen Campbell on "All I have To Do Is Dream"?
10　According to Faith Hill, Love Will Always what?
11　Who had hits with "El Paso" and "Devil Woman"?
12　Which band included Alan Hull?
13　Who married fellow country star George Jones in 1969?
14　For which 1996 film with a prison theme did Johnny Cash contribute to the soundtrack?
15　Who first charted with "Talking In Your Sleep"?
16　Which pop festival's name was in the title of a song by The Waterboys?
17　How is Robin described in the Clannad song?
18　Which Highway was Revisited in a classic 60s album by Bob Dylan?
19　Which traditional lover did Mindy McReady appeal to on her first trip into the UK singles chart?
20　Which Harris sang with Linda Ronstadt and on the tribute album to Tammy Wynette?

1   Which surname is shared by Debby and Pat?
2   What is the home country of Doop?
3   Whose album *Take Two* topped the charts in 1996?
4   In which decade did Sonia have her first hit record?
5   Whose first hit was "In The Midnight Hour"?
6   Who had a No. 1 in 1967 with "Let The Heartaches Begin"?
7   Who sang "The Letter" in 1967?
8   What was Clifford T. Ward's only top ten hit?
9   What did "Paloma Blanca" become – Wurzels style?
10 Who was in "Nutbush City Limits" in 1973?
11 Who were "On the Road Again" in 1968?
12 Which James Bond married the 1950s singer Dorothy Squires?
13 Who was the most long-haired of the Eurythmics?
14 Which Shakespeare play was the title of a David Essex hit?
15 Who took the "Legend of Xanadu" to No. 1 in 1968?
16 Who had "A Little Love And Understanding" in 1975?
17 Who was vocalist with Aphrodite's Child?
18 In which decade was Chuck Berry born?
19 Who were Reparata's backing group?
20 Who were singing about "Lady Lynda" in 1979?

Answers

Pot Luck 35 (Quiz 69)
1 The Beatles. 2 Stevie Wonder. 3 1970s. 4 1941. 5 Kiki Dee.
6 "When I Fall In Love". 7 The Devotions. 8 Joe Brown.
9 "Anyone Who Had a Heart". 10 Ricky Valance. 11 1940s.
12 "Private Dancer", "What's Love Got to Do With It?". 13 "Could It Be Forever?".
14 Julie Covington. 15 Detroit. 16 Austria. 17 "Crazy". 18 (Ruby) Tuesday.
19 Midnight In Moscow. 20 Their bodies were stolen after their deaths.

1 Meatloaf achieved his first hit in which decade?
2 Which Big group first hit the charts with "Blame It On The Boogie"?
3 Who had a late 80s album called *Sonic Temple*?
4 What is Bonnie Tyler's real name?
5 In which decade was soul vocalist Michael Bolton born?
6 Who joined Dr Hook on the UK No. 2 "Sylvia's Mother"?
7 Who links Slik with Band Aid?
8 Who had a 90s album called *Protection/No Protection*?
9 Which word follows Being in the song title by Human League?
10 Who had a 70s No. 1 with "Barbados"?
11 Which word starts song titles which end in Friend and Touch?
12 "Manic Monday" was the first top ten hit for which group?
13 In which country was easy listening singer Roger Whittaker born?
14 Who called his first solo album *Mr Bad Guy*?
15 Which word completes the song title by Hot Chocolate, "What Kinda ____ Are You Looking For (Girl)'?
16 Who had an 80s album called *Picture Book*?
17 Who had an 80s No. 1 with "Easy Lover" with Phil Collins?
18 What word completes the Moody Blues album Days Of Future ____?
19 What was the first name of Mr Palmer from Emerson, Lake and Palmer?
20 "Seven Days And One Week" was the first top ten hit for which group?

1   What was Engelbert Humperdinck's first single?
2   Who had a hit with "Sugar Sugar"?
3   Which 60s band started life as The Mann-Hug Blues Brothers?
4   Who took "You Really Got Me" to No. 1 in 1964?
5   Which group included Tony Hicks and Graham Nash?
6   Who recorded the album *Pet Sounds*?
7   Which group had Judith Durham as lead singer?
8   Which trio included the two Clusky brothers?
9   Who was Tommy James's backing group?
10 Who were famous for their Tottenham Sound?
11 Which satellite was a hit for the Tornados?
12 Which 60s group included Carl Wayne and Roy Wood?
13 Whose first No. 1 was "Sweets For My Sweet"?
14 Which instrumentalist in the Honeycombs was female?
15 Who had a 1965 No. 1 with "Go Now"?
16 Which Group included Steve and Muff Winwood?
17 How many people sang "Concrete and Clay"?
18 What was Wayward on Frank Ifield's 1963 No. 1?
19 Who spent the early part of her career with brother Tom plus Tim Field before going solo?
20 Who was lead singer with Amen Corner?

1   Which Jackson duetted with Luther Vandross on The Best Things In Life Are Free in 1992 and 1995?
2   What did Jocelyn Brown Keep On Doing in 1996?
3   Who recorded "Angel Street" from the album Fresco?
4   Which hit for LaBelle in the 70s was huge success for All Saints 20 years later?
5   Who found the album *Situation Critical* to be a success in the late 90s?
6   Who did Betty Boo tell that she couldn't Dance To The Music You're Playing?
7   What did Freakpower do after Turn On Tune In?
8   Who charted with M-Beat on "Do U Know Where You're Coming From" in 1996?
9   How is Roberto Concina, who had Europe's 1996 top seller, "Children", better known?
10 Who accompanied Rod Stewart on "Da Ya Think I'm Sexy" in 1997?
11 Which Virtual song charted for Jamiroquai in 1996?
12 Gianfranco Bortollotti of "U Got 2 Know" and "U & Me" fame is better known as what?
13 Which songwriter/producer released a surreal self-titled album featuring "songs" such as "I've Got No Chicken (But I've Got Five Wooden Chairs)" and "Listen To Edward"?
14 After Depeche Mode and Yazoo which duo was Vince Clarke's most successful group?
15 Which album did Vengaboys' third hit "Boom Boom Boom Boom" come from?
16 C & C Music Factory's "Everybody Dance Now" said I'm Gonna make You what?
17 What was the South if the North was Naughty in the hit by E:Motion?
18 Which Flat puppet advertised Levis to the music of "Mister Oizo"?
19 Which D:Ream hit was used as the Labour Party anthem in the 1997 election?
20 Which quintet were the youngest act to top the UK album chart with *Silk And Steel* in 1987?

1   Whose album *Live At The BBC* topped the charts in 1994?
2   Whose first hit was "Uptight"?
3   In which decade did Squeeze have their first hit record?
4   What year was the Bee Gees' "New York Mining Disaster"?
5   How is Pauline Matthews better known?
6   What was on the other side of Rick Astley's "My Arms Keep Missing You"?
7   Who was Belle's backing group?
8   Who took A Picture Of You in 1962?
9   With which song did Cilla Black beat Dionne Warwick to the top spot?
10   Who said "Tell Laura I Love Her" in 1960?
11   In which decade was Robin Gibb born?
12   Which two Tina Turner singles are also the names of albums?
13   What was on the other side of David Cassidy's "Cherish"?
14   Who had the original No. 1 with "Don't Cry For Me, Argentina"?
15   Which city links Spinners and Emeralds?
16   What is the home country of Falco, who had a No. 1 with "Rock Me Amadeus"?
17   Which song title links Patsy Cline and Mud?
18   Which day of the week is included in a Rolling Stones song title in 1967 and again in 1991?
19   In 1961 where was Kenny Ball and at what time?
20   What is the link between Evita and Charlie Chaplin?

1   What was Madonna's follow-up to "The Look Of Love"?
2   What was the name of the horse owned by Ernie, The Fastest Milkman In The West?
3   In which decade did Ivy League first have a top ten single?
4   Which word follows Big in the song title by Gap Band?
5   Who had a 90s No. 1 album simply called *Album*?
6   Who had an 80s No. 1 with "Spirit In The Sky"?
7   I "Feel Love (Medley)" was the first top ten hit for which singer?
8   Which superstar closed the Live Aid Concert in America?
9   Who released a solo album called *Journeyman*?
10 Which Vocal Band had chart success with "Afternoon Delight" in 1976?
11 What was Chairmen Of The Board's first UK top ten hit?
12 Which month of Love took Pat Boone to a UK No. 7 in the 50s?
13 Which Road were Nashville Teens on in 1964?
14 Where did Petula Clark say Don't Sleep?
15 What word completes the song title by Heaven 17, "Come ___ With Me"?
16 What was the title of Status Quo's first No. 1 album?
17 Which group was Jerry Garcia linked with?
18 "Slight Return" was the first top ten hit for which group?
19 With which group did TV personality Bill Oddie have a number of chart hits?
20 Under what name did Will Smith first get to No. 1 in the UK?

LEVEL 2

1 Which Roy Orbison single peaked at No. 3 after his death?
2 Which Eddie Cochran hit was re-released in 1988?
3 Who had the quickest hat trick of No. 1's in 1981?
4 Which soul singer died in 1964 during a shooting incident at a motel?
5 Who was the subject of *Lady Sings the Blues*?
6 Which contemporary of Marty Wilde and Tommy Steele died aged 41 in 1983?
7 Which member of Free died in 1976?
8 Who was bass guitarist with Thin Lizzy?
9 Which late Motown great was married to Berry Gordy's sister?
10 Who was famous for a banned single in French at first intended for Brigitte Bardot?
11 Which late great's songs were the subject of Jeff Beck's *Crazy Legs* album?
12 Who was the subject of the 80s biopic *La Bamba*?
13 Whose first No. 1 was "It's Only Make Believe"?
14 In which Parisian cemetery is Jim Morrison buried?
15 Who had a UK hit with "Mack The Knife"?
16 Who wrote and sang "I Guess The Lord Must Be In New York City"?
17 Which former Animal and Jimi Hendrix manager died in 1996?
18 What type of car was Marc Bolan in when he met his death?
19 *Hellooo Baby* was a Greatest Hits album of which late great?
20 Whose "Winter Dance Party" tour ended in tragedy?

Answers

The 60s (Quiz 67)
1 "Release Me". 2 The Archies. 3 Manfred Mann. 4 The Kinks.
5 The Hollies. 6 The Beach Boys. 7 The Seekers. 8 The Bachelors.
9 The Shondelles. 10 The Dave Clark Five. 11 "Telstar". 12 The Move.
13 The Searchers. 14 The drummer. 15 The Moody Blues.
16 The Spencer Davis Group. 17 Six (Unit Four Plus Two). 18 Wind.
19 Dusty Springfield. 20 Andy Fairweather-Low.

1   Who did R.E.M. ask What's The Frequency in 1994?
2   Which band had No Surprises in 1998?
3   What did Marillion base their group name on?
4   Which fellow-guitar great joined Brian May on "We Are The Champions" in 1992?
5   Who said "Janie Don't Take Your Love To Town" in 1997?
6   What did Meat Loaf add to I'd Lie For You in his 1995 single?
7   Which Platter hit was a solo success for Freddie Mercury in 1987 and after his death?
8   In which month of 1999 did Oasis lose two of their original members?
9   Whose early hits were under the name Tubeway Army?
10 Vincent Furnier was in which US rock group that had a UK No. 1 in the 70s?
11 Robert Palmer recorded "I'll Be Your Baby Tonight" with which band?
12 What colour was the Haze in the title of the Jimi Hendrix classic?
13 Who was the original singer with Genesis?
14 Nick Cave hails from which country?
15 Which colour was the title of Hole's second UK top 20 hit?
16 Who went solo from his usual band to sing solo with Michael Jackson in 1984 on State Of Shock?
17 Who is mentioned by name by The Faces on "You Can Make Me Dance Sing Or Anything"?
18 During their mega-successful years with albums in the 60s, 70s, and 80s how many Pink Floyd singles reached the UK top ten?
19 Which late 90s female chart topper duetted with Iggy Pop on "Well Did You Evah" in 1991?
20 Which Sonny And Cher hit was a No. 1 for Chrissie Hynde with UB40?

1   Who had the 50s Top Ten hit with "Seven Little Girls Sitting In The Back Seat"?
2   Whose album *Daydream* topped the charts in 1995?
3   In which decade was Noel Gallagher born?
4   Who duetted with Celine Dion on "Beauty And The Beast"?
5   Who was leaving Durham Town in 1969?
6   Who joined John Travolta and Olivia Newton-John on "Grease – The Dream Mix" in 1991?
7   Whose first hit was "Kids In America"?
8   Which former model hit the charts with "Here I Go Again"?
9   In which decade did Lisa Stansfield have her first hit record?
10 Who charted with "Harvest for the World" in 1988?
11 Who has duetted with the future Princess Grace of Monaco and David Bowie?
12 Which song title links Marcella Detroit with Robson and Jerome?
13 Who had a 60s hit with "This Little Bird"?
14 Who was "Wide-Eyed And Legless" in 1975?
15 What is the home country of Foster and Allen?
16 Which surname is shared by Howard and Paul?
17 Who sang about Victoria in 1970?
18 Who were Disco Tex's backing group?
19 Who joined Bananarama on their first two hits?
20 How is George Benson nicknamed on his first hit single?

1 Who had a 90s album called *This Way Up*?
2 'Wishing I Was Lucky' was the first top ten hit for which group?
3 Who had a late 80s album called *Ancient Heart*?
4 In which decade did Imagination first have a top ten single?
5 Which word comes before In My Side in the song title by Eurythmics?
6 Who had a 80s No. 1 album called *Keep Your Distance*?
7 What was Elton John's follow-up to "Sad Songs (Say So Much)"?
8 Who had an early 80s album called *British Steel*?
9 Who had a hit with "Les Bicyclettes de Belsize"?
10 Who had a 70s No. 1 with "Save Your Kisses For Me"?
11 "It Ain't What You Do It's The Way That You Do It" was the first top ten hit for which group?
12 Who had an 80s No. 1 album called *Sparkle In The Rain*?
13 Which song title completes the song title by Bruce Springsteen, "I'm On ____'?
14 "Rock With The Caveman" was the first hit for who?
15 Which word completes the song title by Cyndi Lauper, "I ____ All Night"?
16 In which decade was Petula Clark born?
17 Whose Girl did Susan Maughan want to be in 1962?
18 Who had an 80s No. 1 with "Candy Girl"?
19 Which country is the birthplace of singer/songwriter Paul Anka?
20 In which decade did David Bowie first have a top ten single?

1 Which film title provided a hit for Ray Parker Jr?
2 Which film other than *The Bodyguard* featured "I Will Always Love You"?
3 "The Shoop Shoop Song" was heard at the end of which Cher film?
4 In which film did Kylie Minogue play Lola Lovell and sing on the soundtrack?
5 In which film did Phil Collins revive the 60s hit "Groovy Kind of Love"?
6 Which River Phoenix film sent Ben E. King to the top of the charts?
7 Which film does "The John Dunbar Theme" come from?
8 For which film did Van Morrison sing "Brown-Eyed Girl"?
9 Which Woody Allen film starring Peter Sellers had Tom Jones singing the theme song?
10 Who sang the title song from *Grease* in 1978?
11 Who sang "Raindrops Keep Falling On My Head" in the film?
12 Which film had the theme "Take My Breath Away"?
13 Who sang "Be Prepared" in *The Lion King*?
14 Who played Madonna's night-club-singer lover in *Evita*?
15 "You'll Never Walk Alone" appears in which film musical?
16 Which song is the most famous on the *Woman in Red* soundtrack?
17 Who won an Oscar for "Flashdance – What a Feeling"?
18 What is the link between Barbra Streisand and the film *M*A*S*H*?
19 In which movie did Madonna sing "Into The Groove"?
20 Who sang "Up Where We Belong" from *An Officer And A Gentleman*?

1 Which 1992 hit features the artist's own name?
2 What was his UK chart debut that made the top 50?
3 When he was still at school Prince was a member of a band named after which drink?
4 What is Prince's surname?
5 Which Scottish singer performs uncredited on "U Got The Look"?
6 How is he credited on The Holy River?
7 Who was his backing group in 1981?
8 "Purple Rain" charted in the 80s – which Purple reached the top 40 in the 90s?
9 Who are credited along with Prince on "Cream" and "Gett Off"?
10 Which 1985 top 20 single was also the name of his own record label?
11 "Pop Life" came from which album?
12 In the name TAFKAP what did K stand for?
13 What was on the other side of "Sexy MF"?
14 Which 1986 Bangles hit was written by Prince under the pseudonym Christopher Tracy?
15 What was Prince's first album?
16 Dialogue by Michael Keaton and Jack Nicholson on a single came from which movie?
17 Which album featured "The Ballad Of Dorothy Parker"?
18 Who had a No. 1 in 1984 with Prince's "I Feel For You"?
19 Which Tour began in 1990?
20 What was his only top ten hit of 1995, with "The New Power Generation"?

1   In which decade did Stevie Wonder have his first hit record?
2   How is Concetta Rosemarie Franconero better known?
3   How did Charles Aznavour Dance in the 70s?
4   Who were Acker Bilk's backing band?
5   Whose first hit was "Year Of Decision"?
6   Which musical instrument does Larry Adler play?
7   Whose album *Nobody Else* topped the charts in 1995?
8   What was the Who's first chart hit?
9   Who was like a Rubber Ball in 1961?
10 Who thought Elenore was swell in 1968?
11 Who sang "Nice One Cyril" in 1973?
12 Who was Out of Time in 1966?
13 What is the home country of Boris Gardiner?
14 Which song title links Len Barry and Gloria Estefan?
15 Whose first hit was "Love Is Like A Violin"?
16 Who was on the Marrakesh Express in 1969?
17 How many times in the 80s did "Do They Know It's Christmas?" enter the charts?
18 In which decade was Sade born?
19 Which animals are on the cover of the Beach Boys album *Pet Sounds*?
20 Which creature links song titles by Elton John and Jimmy Nail?

1   What was MC Hammer's first UK chart success?
2   Who recorded the No. 1 album *Steeltown*?
3   The late Bon Scott was lead singer with which band?
4   What was Bryan Adams' follow-up to '(Everything I Do) I Do It For You"?
5   What was Bob Dylan's first chart-topping composition?
6   Who had a mid-80s album called *Signing Off*?
7   Who was percussionist with The Police?
8   Who left the Go Go's to become a solo vocalist?
9   Who had an album of *Greatest Hits* before their *Arrival* album?
10   Who had an 80s No. 1 with "I Should Have Known Better"?
11   In which decade did the Sensational Alex Harvey Band have their only top ten single?
12   What was Marc Bolan's real surname?
13   "Do the fairies keep him sober for a day" comes from which Christmas song?
14   What was the name of Billie's first No. 1?
15   "New Year's Day" was the first top ten hit for which group?
16   What was A-Ha's follow-up to "The Living Daylights"?
17   Which word goes after Running Up That in the song title by Kate Bush?
18   Who was lead vocalist of The Clash?
19   Who recorded the album Spellbound in 1991?
20   How is Alison Moira Clarkson better known?

1   What was Cliff's Eurovision Song Contest entry in 1973?
2   In which West End musical by Dave Clark did Cliff star?
3   Which film did Cliff make after *Summer Holiday*?
4   What was Cliff's first hit album called?
5   In which film did Cliff play the role of Bongo Herbert in 1959?
6   In 1976 Cliff recorded an album called *I'm Nearly...* what?
7   Why did Cliff sing at Buckingham Palace in May 1995?
8   Which record producer signed Cliff to the Columbia label in 1958?
9   How are the Shadows known on the hit "Move It"?
10 What does Blue Turn To in the 1966 hit written by the Rolling Stones' Jagger and Richards?
11 Which Woman gave Cliff his first top ten US hit?
12 What was Guaranteed according to the title of Cliff's 1987 album?
13 Who co-wrote "Bachelor Boy" with Bruce Welch?
14 Which future *It Ain't Half Hot Mum* actor starred with Cliff in *The Young Ones* and *Summer Holiday*?
15 Which TV puppet did Cliff co-star with on TV in 1969?
16 How was Cliff Travellin' in his 1959 No. 1?
17 Which evangelist did Cliff join on stage at Earl's Court in 1966?
18 Which member of the Shadows produced "Miss You Nights" in 1976?
19 "Little Town" was an up-tempo version of which Christmas carol?
20 Which soul star played all the instruments on "She's So Beautiful"?

1   Which Bachelors hit was a 90s No. 1 for Robson and Jerome?
2   Who had the very first UK No. 1 with "Unchained Melody"?
3   Which Doris Day hit, also recorded by Tracey Ullman did The Times vote the top easy-listening track of all time?
4   Who is the only female Frank Sinatra has duetted with and entered the charts?
5   Which band did Herb Alpert lead?
6   In which African country was Roger Whittaker born?
7   Whose "Music To Watch Girls By" was re-released in the 90s after achieving popularity through TV ads?
8   Jackie Trent charted in the 80s but which TV theme she co-wrote was heard around the world?
9   "He Was Beautiful" or "Cavatina" was the theme from which war movie?
10 Which violin player had a Red Hot tour in 1996?
11 Which show did Michael Ball's No. 2 hit "Love Changes Everything" come from?
12 Barbra Streisand's "As If We Never Said Goodbye" came from which Lloyd-Webber musical?
13 Which Carpenters song was the name of a food dish?
14 Whose "Guaglione" charted in 1995 nearly 40 years after being No. 1?
15 Which ever-popular live performer sang "Whatever Happened To Old-Fashioned Love" in 1993?
16 Which regular 90s TV presenter sang "The Skye Boat Song" with Roger Whittaker in 1986?
17 Which Louis Armstrong classic was re-released in 1994 after TV ad coverage?
18 Whose uncredited vocals feature on Natalie Cole's "Unforgettable"?
19 Which singer, a former child star, was the first British female to win a Grammy?
20 Which John Denver song did an Irish flautist take to No. 3 in 1978?

1 Where was Pat Boone's gold mine in 1957?
2 Who replaced Brian Jones when he left The Rolling Stones?
3 What was the Osmonds' only No. 1 UK hit?
4 Who released an album titled *No Parlez*?
5 What novelty song was the only UK No. 1 single for Chuck Berry?
6 How old was Elvis Presley when he died? 41, 42 or 43?
7 Where are Aria electric guitars produced?
8 Which US State did the Bee Gees sing about?
9 Which Buddy Holly hit asks: "Oh misery, misery, what's gonna become of me"?
10 Who released a million-selling album in 1983 titled *Let's Dance*?
11 Which film featured the song "Bright Eyes"?
12 How is Paul Hewson better known?
13 Who was Jimmy James's backing group?
14 In which decade was David Essex born?
15 Which band shares its name with an instrument of torture?
16 Which song title links Elvis Presley and Bobby Brown?
17 Which Spice Girl is Posh Spice?
18 Which UK female singer had two records in the top ten in the same week in 1980?
19 Who was lead singer with The Sugarcubes?
20 Who released the album *Goodbye Cruel World* in 1984?

LEVEL 2

1 Which Verve album came before *A Northern Soul*?
2 Mike Smith was keyboard player with which band?
3 Which superstar released the top-selling album *Diva* in 1993?
4 Who had a UK No. 4 hit in 1996 with "I've Got A Little Puppy"?
5 "Goldfinger" was the first top ten hit for which group?
6 Which girl gave Kool And The Gang a UK No. 2 hit in 1984?
7 Who released a top-selling album in 1992 called *Shepherd Moons*?
8 What was Neneh Cherry's follow up to "Manchild"?
9 Which word follows Vision Of in the song title by Mariah Carey?
10 Who had a 70s No. 1 with "No Charge"?
11 Who recorded the 90s hit album *Pump*?
12 In which decade did Al Green first have a top ten single?
13 Which word follows Pearl in the song title by Howard Jones?
14 Who released the 80s album *The Sensual World*?
15 As writers of "Don't Go Breaking My Heart", Elton John and Bernie Taupin were credited as Anne Orson and who?
16 Who took Margate into the charts for the first time?
17 Who had an 80s No. 1 with "Never Gonna Give You Up"?
18 Which word completes the song title by Bronski Beat, "Hit That ___ Beat"?
19 In which decade did Chris Rea first have a top ten single?
22 What goes with Rattle And in the U2 album title?

1 Which Hollies hit was used in a 1997 campaign by Boots?
2 Who had the ad hit "Jeans On"?
3 Which song to advertise jeans showed two young women holding a guy's jeans as he takes a swim?
4 Who sang it?
5 Which Steve Miller Band single hit the top after being used by Levi's?
6 Which band went to No. 1 with "Should I Stay or Should I Go" after it was used in an ad?
7 In which decade did Levi's begin to use classic hits to advertise?
8 Which was the first such record used in the UK?
9 Which Eddie Cochran hit has been used?
10 Which superstar advertised Diet Coke in 1991?
11 Who sang "It Takes Two" as part of a Pepsi TV ad deal?
12 The melody of "O Sole Mio" has been used to advertise which treat?
13 Who used Elvis's "You Were Always On My Mind" to advertise their services?
14 Whose "Guaglione" advertised Guinness?
15 The tune from "I Can't Let Maggie Go" advertised what?
16 Which product did "Like A Prayer" advertise?
17 Which Ben E. King single was used in a jeans ad?
18 Who sang "What A Wonderful World" to advertise the same product?
19 Out of the first five songs used to advertise Levi's how many were from performers already dead?
20 Who was dropped from an advertising campaign by Coca-Cola after publicity about his private life?

LEVEL 2

1   What was Phil Collins' first UK No. 1 album?
2   "Take A Look At Me Now" follows which words, which are also the title of the film it was taken from?
3   Which instrument did he play on "Do They Know It's Christmas"?
4   Throughout the 80s Phil Collins recorded on which label?
5   Which US cop series did he appear in as Phil the Shill?
6   Whose departure from Genesis in 1975 pushed Phil Collins forward as the band's vocalist?
7   What was his second UK album?
8   Which 1985 hit and US No. 1 was from the film *White Nights*?
9   Which album won him the Best British album award in 1986?
10 Which UK singer guitarist made the album *August*, which Collins produced?
11 Which character did he play in the film where he sang "A Groovy Kind Of Love"?
12 Which Royal lady did Collins describe as a "pretty good jiver" at Prince Charles's 40th birthday bash?
13 Collins played Uncle Ernie in which rock musical work in 1989?
14 The soundtrack of *Buster*, which Collins put together, was of songs from which decade?
15 From which album does "Sussudio" come?
16 His song "Another Day In Paradise" was about which social problem?
17 Which country did Collins move to in the 1990s?
18 Which 1989 album was the then biggest-selling album in UK chart history?
19 What was the name of his world tour after *But Seriously* hit No. 1?
20 In the 90s which Disney film was he commissioned to write the music for?

1 Whose first single "I Think I Love You" sold in excess of four million copies?
2 What Beatles song begins "You think you've lost your love ... "?
3 Who co-produced "Do They Know It's Christmas?"?
4 In which year was Cliff Richard's first album released?
5 Who had the nickname Pearl?
6 In which decade was the Grammy award introduced?
7 What are John Lennon and Yoko Ono doing on the cover of the *Milk And Honey* album?
8 Who recorded the Heavy-Metal album *Hysteria*?
9 Who was commemorated on Jamaican stamps in 1982?
10 Where were Doris Day's Black Hills?
11 Who was the subject of the film tribute *Hail! Hail! Rock 'N' Roll*?
12 Who formed the rock band Tin Machine in 1989?
13 Who was Wishing He Was Lucky in 1987?
14 Which TV personality did Tribe Of Toffs celebrate in song in 1988?
15 What was Deborah Harry doing In the USA in 1986?
16 Who sang "The Last Farewell" in 1975?
17 Which Summer song was a 1974 hit for the Bay City Rollers?
18 What is the nationality of the "Do It Again" singer Raffaella Carra?
19 Which Spice Girl is Scary Spice?
20 What was Buddy Holly's real first name?

1   Who recorded the album The Visitors?
2   Who had an 80s No. 1 with "Don't Turn Around"?
3   Which group went on the Gluttons For Punishment Tour?
4   Which word completes the song title by Big Fun, "Can't __ The Feeling"?
5   What was Culture Club's follow-up to "It's A Miracle"?
6   "Serious" was the first top ten hit for which female singer?
7   What was Ace Of Base's first No. 1 album called?
8   Which word follows Foolish in the song title by Debbie Gibson
9   Which country was base for Boney M?
10 Where do Bjorn Again originate from?
11 Whose first hit was "I Lost My Heart To A Starship Trooper"?
12 Which country was the birthplace of Neneh Cherry?
13 What is Chubby Checker's real name?
14 What were Air Supply All Out Of in their UK No. 11 hit in 1980?
15 Which group released an album in 1992 called *High On The Happy Side*?
16 In which decade did A Flock Of Seagulls first have a top ten single?
17 Who recorded "The Oldest Swinger In Town"?
18 Which word completes the Shakin' Stevens' song title, "A _____ To You"?
19 "Addicted To Love" was the first top ten hit for which singer?
20 What was The Cure's follow up to "Love Cats"?

1 Which Spice Girl is Baby Spice?
2 Who was the "Acid Queen" in the film *Tommy*?
3 Whose first hit was "Lost In France"?
4 Who had a hit with "Remember (Walkin' In the Sand)"?
5 Whose "Breathe Again" won a US award for Song of the Year in 1995?
6 Who said "Do It Do It Again" in 1978?
7 How many girls were in Ace Of Base?
8 Whose real name is Elaine Bookbinder?
9 Whose first album was *The Kick Inside*?
10 Which musical instrument did Lynsey De Paul play?
11 Which Page Three girl hit the charts in 1986?
12 Which group has Susanna Hoffs on guitar and vocals?
13 Which group scrapped a video made as part of the "In At the Deep End" TV show?
14 On which 90s movie soundtrack did Brenda Lee feature?
15 Whose debut album was called *Alf*?
16 Which country did Celine Dion represent in the Eurovision Song Contest?
17 Whose top-selling album featured the Red Hot Chili Peppers's bassist Flea on one track?
18 What was Lulu's only 70s hit?
19 Who participated in the opening of Euro Disney in Paris in 1992?
20 Who had a top-selling album called *Guilty* in 1980?

Answers

TV Ads (Quiz 83)
1 "I'm Alive". 2 David Dundas. 3 "Inside". 4 Stiltskin. 5 "The Joker".
6 The Clash. 7 1980s. 8 Marvin Gaye – "I Heard It Through the Grapevine".
9 "C'Mon Everybody". 10 Elton John. 11 Rod Stewart, Tina Turner.
12 Cornetto ice cream. 13 BT. 14 Perez Prado. 15 Nimble bread. 16 Pepsi.
17 "Stand By Me". 18 Sam Cooke. 19 Three. 20 Michael Jackson.

1   What was his first UK hit?
2   Where did Elvis have Fun in 1963?
3   Which album released after his death gave his full name?
4   What was his mother's name?
5   In which country was Elvis stationed to do his National Service?
6   What was the name of his private jet, named after a member of his family?
7   What was his first album which was a film soundtrack?
8   Which 1975 top 40 entry was a big hit for Tom Jones?
9   In which state was Elvis born?
10   What was his first hit with Christmas in the title?
11   Which single shot to No. 1 immediately after Elvis death?
12   Which hit for Elvis in the 90s had been a Cliff Richard 60s success?
13   In a live recording of which Elvis classic does he stop singing because he is laughing so much?
14   What was the name of Priscilla Presley's book of her life with The King?
15   In 1988, "Stuck On You" was used in an ad in the UK for what product?
16   *Elvis – That's The Way It Is* was a documentary about his concerts where?
17   Which medley included the Battle Hymn Of The Republic?
18   Where was Elvis Presley Boulevard, the location for his 1976 album?
19   What was his first million-seller?
20   Which Elvis single was the first ever to go straight to No. 1 in 1958?

1 Who had a highly successful album titled *Never Forever*?
2 Which Spice Girl is Sporty Spice?
3 Who pleaded "Hold Me Close" in 1975?
4 Which artist originated the rock classic "Tutti Frutti"?
5 Who has recorded under the name Kris Carson?
6 Which group included Mick Avory and Pete Quaife?
7 Which Eddie Cochran hit did the Sex Pistols do a cover version of in 1979?
8 Which Boney M single sold over 2 million copies on the UK?
9 In which decade was Bryan Adams born?
10 Which song title links Petula Clark and S.W.V.?
11 Who was going to Dress You Up in 1985?
12 Which TV show opened to Manfred Mann's "5-4-3-2-1"?
13 Which Wild West hero features on a Cher single?
14 Who had a late 80s album called *Viva Hate*?
15 Who rightly sang "We Are Family" in 1979?
16 Who had a 1996 album called *Everything Must Go*?
17 Who in 1997 said drug taking was as normal as having a cup of tea?
18 What was on the other side of Boney M's "Oh My Lord"?
19 Which two Fleetwood Mac albums are two of the best sellers of all time?
20 Which band leader is the one with the most chart albums in the UK?

1   Who recorded the 90s hit album Get A Grip?
2   Which word follows Dead in the song title by Shalamar?
3   In which movie did Madonna sing "Into The Groove"?
4   Blue Moon was the first top ten hit for which male singer?
5   What was Celine Dion's follow-up to "Think Twice"?
6   Which comedienne featured on the B-side of Comic Relief's "The Stonk"?
7   What was Midge Ure's first solo UK top ten hit?
8   Who had a 90s No. 2 album called *Between The Lines*?
9   Who played bass with Thin Lizzy?
10 Who had a 70s album called Journey To The Centre Of The Earth?
11 What was Mark Owen's first solo hit?
12 Who had an 80s No. 1 with "You'll Never Stop Me From Loving You"?
13 Which word completes the song title by The Smiths, "Heaven Knows I'm _____ Now"?
14 In which decade did 5000 Volts first have a top ten single?
15 Who had a huge 1994 album hit with *The Glory Of Gershwin*?
16 Who did Peter Gabriel duet with on "Don't Give Up"?
17 Which Blues were suffered by Alma Cogan in 1954?
18 What was Siouxsie And The Banshees' first UK top ten hit?
19 In which decade did Nina Simone first have a top ten single?
20 Which word follows All The Things She in the song title by Simple Minds?

LEVEL 2

1 What was Elton John's first chart album called?
2 What was the name of his first solo No. 1?
3 In which north London suburb was Elton born and brought up?
4 Which Beatles song did Elton have a hit with in 1974?
5 Which song from *High Society* did Elton record with Kiki Dee in 1993?
6 Which tabloid paid £1 million damages to Elton John in 1988?
7 Which UK singer did Elton duet with on "Slow Rivers"?
8 Which blues singer provided Elton with his surname?
9 What completes the album title, *Don't Shoot Me...*?
10 Which middle name did Elton choose when he changed his name legally in 1972?
11 What kind of problem caused Elton to miss the David Beckham/Posh Spice wedding?
12 Which album was recorded at Château d'Herouville in 1972?
13 Which song won Elton his Best Original Song Oscar in 1995?
14 What follows in brackets after "Breaking Hearts" in the 1985 hit?
15 Who, with her friends, joined Elton on "That's What Friends Are For"?
16 Which instrumental record was dedicated to a motor-cycle messenger boy who died in an accident?
17 What follows "Sad Songs" in the title of the 1984 hit?
18 In 1991 he was the central figure in an ad campaign for which drink?
19 In 1976 where did Elton John become the first rock star to be immortalized since the Beatles?
20 Which very big star did Elton duet with in 1996?

LEVEL 2

1 Rod's fan club takes its name from which one-word 1974 album?
2 "Sailing" featured on which album?
3 What was the other A side on "I Don't Want To Talk About It"?
4 Rod has a UK home with a football pitch out the back near which forest?
5 In which decade did he release a solo album called *Greatest Hits*?
6 Which eyesight peculiarity does he share with William Hague and Paul Newman?
7 In 1991 which singer/songwriter came on stage dressed as Rod's then-new wife Rachel Hunter?
8 What was the first of his six consecutive No. 1 albums?
9 The Complete Anthology 1964–1990 had which title?
10 In the 1960s, Rod was thrown out of which country on a charge of vagrancy?
11 "Have I Told You Lately" on *Vagabond Heart* was a cover of which artist's song?
12 Which song was released with the Scottish Euro 96 football team?
13 Which 1998 album featured material from current bands?
14 Which Stone did he make *Unplugged... And Seated* with in 1993?
15 Who was credited on "I've Been Drinking" in 1973?
16 Which 1993 hit included the name of his daughter with Kelly Emberg?
17 Which soccer side did he have a trial with in the 60s?
18 "You Wear It Well" originally came from which album?
19 Rod was born during which war?
20 Which 1990 hit with Tina Turner was originally a success for Marvin Gaye and Tammi Terrell?

1 Where does Susie fall asleep in the hit "Wake Up Little Susie"?
2 Which artist had a No. 3 hit in 1972 with "You're A Lady"?
3 What Killed The Radio Star according to the Buggles?
4 On which Neil Diamond album is the track "Play Me"?
5 What was Golden for the Tremeloes?
6 Which rock guitarist first set a guitar ablaze at the '67 Monterey Pop Festival?
7 In which West End musical did David Essex play the role of Jesus?
8 Who sang "Papa's Got A Brand New Bag"?
9 Where did Supertramp have Breakfast?
10 Which German phrase did Ian Dury rhyme with "Rhythm Stick"?
11 Which group included Al Jardine and Mike Love?
12 Which Sheryl Crow song was Grammy Record of the Year in 1994?
13 Who sang "How Am I Supposed to Live Without You?" in 1989?
14 Who had an instrumental version of "Don't Cry For Me Argentina"?
15 Which comedy actor appeared on Annie Lennox's *Walking on Broken Glass* video?
16 Which "group" was founded by Ian Broudie?
17 Who was Frankie Lymon's backing group?
18 Which song with Love in the title was a hit for the Beatles and Ella Fitzgerald?
19 What was the home city of Bob Marley's father?
20 How many Vandellas were there?

1   What was the follow-up album by Bryan Adams to *Waking Up The Neighbours*?
2   Which animal had no name according to the UK No. 3 from America?
3   Who had a hit in 1966 with "Friday On My Mind"?
4   Which Ma gave Boney M a UK No. 2 hit in 1977?
5   Who released the chart-topping album *Sleeping With The Past* in 1990?
6   Which word follows Breakfast In in the song title by UB40?
7   What did Glen Campbell ask Honey to do in 1970?
8   "It's Too Late" was the first top ten hit for which singer?
9   In which decade was female vocalist Enya born?
10 What was Depeche Mode's follow-up to "People Are People"?
11 Who had an 80s No. 1 with "Move Closer"?
12 Under what name did Paul Gadd have a string of hits?
13 What took Honor Blackman and Patrick MacNee into the 1990 charts?
14 In which decade did Neil Diamond first have a top ten single?
15 Which word follows Thunder In The in the song title by Toyah?
16 Which Norman had a hit with "Don't Laugh At Me"?
17 Who recorded the best-selling album *A Night At The Opera*?
18 Who had a 70s No. 1 with "Forever And Ever"?
19 Ali and Robin Campbell are in which band?
20 Who had a 90s album called *Conversation Peace*?

1 Who sang "We've Got Tonight" with Kenny Rogers?
2 How were Ms Forest and Ms Reid better known?
3 Who was Gordon Waller's singing partner?
4 Which duo were Roger Cook and Roger Greenaway?
5 Who were originally known as Tom and Jerry?
6 Godley and Creme were members of which chart-topping group?
7 How are Bill Medley and Bobby Hatfield better known?
8 What were Robson and Jerome's characters called in "Soldier, Soldier"?
9 How were Linda Greene and Herb Fame better known?
10 What was the surname of the twins Hal and Herbert?
11 How were the Danish duo Baron and Baroness van Pallandt known in the pop charts?
12 What is the surname of the Brothers Iain and Gavin?
13 Who had a 70s hit with "Whispering Grass"?
14 Who were Passing Strangers back in 1957?
15 Who recorded with Mary Wells, Kim Weston and Tammi Terrell?
16 Which Daryl and John took "Maneater" into the charts?
17 Whose first hit was "Labour of Love"?
18 Who had a 1981 No. 1 with "It's My Party"?
19 Who sang "It's Raining Men" in 1984?
20 Who recorded "I'm Leaving It (All Up to You)" in 1974?

1 "We're In This Together" was released for which sporting event?
2 A songwriting partnership with Lamont Dozier was credited to Hucknall Dozier Hucknall in honour of whom?
3 Which album was the top British seller in 1991 and 1992?
4 "Thrill Me" came from which album?
5 Where was Mick Hucknall born?
6 What was the 1994 biography of Simply Red's lead singer called?
7 Which single topped the US charts for just one week in 1986?
8 "Fairground" featured on which album?
9 Which tennis star's name was linked with Mick Hucknall's in the 1990?
10 Which early band of Mick Hucknall's were named after a classic Jimi Hendrix song?
11 What was their first hit with the colour red in the title?
12 With which band did Mick Hucknall sing "Angel" on the Greatest Hits album?
13 The reggae classic "Night Nurse" also features Sly and who?
14 Which colourful album did "Say You Love Me" first feature on?
15 What was their first top ten album called?
16 Why were the band called Simply Red?
17 In which European city does Mick Hucknall have a second home?
18 What was the name of the 1998 radio series which was about the band and their 1998 album?
19 How many people feature on the cover of *Stars*?
20 Mick Hucknall took a university degree in what subject?

1 What was Smokey Robinson And The Miracles 1970 No. 1 hit?
2 What company had a No. 2 hit in 1968 with "Simon Says"?
3 Who played the title role in *Tommy*?
4 Which rocker had a kiss-curl over his forehead as his trademark?
5 Who is almost naked on a bed, on the cover of his *1999* album?
6 Which group were giving "Lessons in Love" in 1986?
7 Where was Gene Chandler the Duke of?
8 Who was lead singer with the Spencer Davis Group?
9 What was the name of the priest in "Eleanor Rigby"?
10 What four people are on the front cover of the *Saturday Night Fever* album?
11 Which film did the theme "A Whole New World" come from?
12 How are Chris Lowe and Neil Tennant better known?
13 Which Street is named on a 10 c.c. single?
14 Which song with Love in the title was a 1980 hit for Neil Diamond?
15 Who was lead singer with the Bluesbreakers?
16 Candida Doyle plays keyboards with which group?
17 In which decade was Chris Rea born?
18 Who left Velvet Underground in 1970?
19 Which musical instrument does Bryan Ferry play?
20 In which country were The Shamen founded?

1 Who had a 1994 hit album Under The Pink?
2 "Uh La La La" was the first top ten hit for which singer?
3 What went with Spiders in a 70s hit by Jim Stafford?
4 Which word goes after Let's in the song title by Earth, Wind and Fire?
5 In which decade did the Damned first have a top ten single?
6 Which film featured the song "Up Where We Belong"?
7 What was Prince's follow-up to "Controversy"?
8 Whose backing band were The Dinosaurs?
9 How many Drunken Nights did The Dubliners spend in 1967?
10 In which decade was female rocker Suzi Quatro born?
11 Whose backing group were the Big Sound?
12 What was Duran Duran's first UK Top 20 hit?
13 Who told us to Sail On in 1979?
14 What did Fontella Bass ask us to do in 1965?
15 Who had a 70s No. 1 with "January"?
16 Which big 70s band released the successful album *Union* in the 90s?
17 Which word completes the song title by Sheena Easton, "For Your ___ Only"?
18 Who had an 80s No. 1 with "True"?
19 Who had early 90s hits about Trancentral?
20 Glen Tilbrook and Chris Difford were in which band?

LEVEL 2

1 Who is the famous mum of Crispian in Kula Shaker?
2 Whose daughter did Jermaine Jackson marry?
3 Who were Marion Ryan's sons?
4 Who is the sister of Peter from Peter and Gordon?
5 Under what name had Peter Sarstedt's elder brother had a chart hit?
6 What is Julian Lennon's mother called?
7 Who has been married to George Harrison and Eric Clapton?
8 Which rock star's daughter has Heavenly and Tiger Lily among her first names?
9 Which member of the *Spitting Image* voice team is a cousin of Paul McCartney?
10 Which pop star was married to top hairdresser John Frieda?
11 Which clothes designer did Sandie Shaw marry?
12 Which fellow country singer was a sister of Crystal Gayle?
13 Which comic record-maker's daughter plays the late John Archer's girlfriend Hayley in *The Archers*?
14 What were the first names of the Bellamy Brothers?
15 Which 50s hit-makers were Joy, Babs and Teddy?
16 How were Veronica and Estelle Bennett, plus cousin Nedra Talley, better known?
17 Which group was made up of sisters Debbie, Kathie, Kim and Joni?
18 Who is Mrs Bobby Brown?
19 Who was Liza Minelli's mother?
20 Shane Ritchie was married to a member of which Irish singing sisters group?

1 Which label did he sign with in the UK after his court battle with Sony?
2 In which year did "Star People" chart?
3 What was his childhood nickname?
4 In 1992 it was rumoured he would replace the lead singer in which band?
5 Who was the only artist to have more US No. 1s than George Michael in the 80s?
6 Which album had two parts – For Your Heart and For Your Feet?
7 Which album was issued as *Volume 1*?
8 Which animal title from *Faith* was one of four US No. 1's from that album?
9 Members of which profession featured on the video of *Freedom 90*?
10 Which company did he say saw its artists as "little more than software"?
11 What was his first hit with Wham!?
12 What was his comeback single after the dispute with Sony?
13 Which track on *Ladies & Gentlemen* is sung with Queen?
14 "Spinning The Wheel" came from which album?
15 Which track on *Ladies & Gentlemen* is sung with Elton John?
16 Who featured on "Waltz Away Dreaming"?
17 Which No. 1 followed "Jesus To A Child"?
18 Which George said, "I'll wear anything as long as it hasn't been on George Michael's back"?
19 What was on the other side of the single "Older"?
20 "Wake Me Up Before You Go Go" originally featured on which album?

1   What group had a No. 1 album entitled *Once Upon A Time* in 1986?
2   Who do Chas and Dave say "You've got more rabbit than…"?
3   In which decade was Dusty Springfield born?
4   Which David released *David Live* in 1974?
5   Which state is "almost heaven" for John Denver?
6   Which group had a hit with "Son Of My Father"?
7   Which member of the group Genesis left in 1975?
8   Whose second No. 1 album was *A Day At The Races*?
9   How many "vestal virgins" were leaving in "Whiter Shade Of Pale"?
10   Who sang the official "Sport Aid" song?
11   Brian Eno was a member of which group?
12   In which decade did Billy Joel have a hit with "Just the Way You Are"?
13   Who were Joan Jett's backing group?
14   Who was "Doin' The Do" in 1990?
15   Who has recorded with Barry Gibb, Neil Diamond and Don Johnson?
16   Who released the album *Jagged Little Pill*?
17   How is Yvette Stevens better known?
18   What were Ant and Dec previously known as?
19   Who sang "I'd Really Love to See You Tonight"?
20   What was Gary Barlow's first solo single after leaving Take That?

1   Which group sang "Behind Blue Eyes"?
2   Who recorded the 1990 album *Choke*?
3   Who had the first No. 1 with "This Ole House"?
4   Which word follows Sign Your in the song title by Terence Trent D'Arby?
5   What was the title of Neil Young's first album to chart in the UK?
6   Which song has the words, "And just like the guy whose feet were too big for his bed...'?
7   Brett Anderson is in which group?
8   At the end of which film did Cher sing "The Shoop Shoop Song"?
9   What was Linda Greene known as when singing with Herb?
10 Who had an 80s No. 1 with "Give It Up"?
11 Which word follows Tell It To My in the song title by Taylor Dayne?
12 In which decade did Roger Daltrey first have a solo top ten single?
13 Who duetted with Bono on "I've Got You Under My Skin" in 1993?
14 "I'll Be There For You – You're All I Need To Get By" was the first top ten hit for which singer?
15 Which country is home to The Cranberries?
16 Which Girl gave Tori Amos her first top ten hit?
17 Whose backing group were The Playboy Band?
18 Who had a UK No. 8 hit with "There But For Fortune" in 1965?
19 Who released and topped the album charts with *But Seriously*?
20 Which word follows The Magic In the song title by De La Soul?

1   What is Paul McCartney's first name?
2   What were The Beatles known as immediately before acquiring their final famous name?
3   Who was their bass player in the early 60s?
4   Who did Ringo replace as drummer?
5   Where did they have their first gig as The Beatles?
6   To 100 either way, how many people went to The Beatles' first gig in southern England?
7   What completes the LP title *A Collection of Beatles Oldies…*?
8   What was the name of their first EP?
9   Which song was the group's first US No. 1?
10   Which song did the Beatles perform first on nationwide TV?
11   Who sang lead vocal on "Yellow Submarine"?
12   In which film did John Lennon play the role of Private Gripweed?
13   In 1969 John changed his middle name from what to what?
14   George and Patti Harrison were arrested for marijuana possession in 1969 on which special day for Paul McCartney?
15   Who was the first ex-Beatle to have a No. 1 album?
16   What was the Beatles' second album?
17   Which children's TV series did Ringo begin narrating in 1984?
18   Which previously unreleased Beatles single came out in the mid-90s?
19   Who did Ringo marry in 1981?
20   Which album was the first to have track lyrics on the sleeve?

1 Who did Janet sing "The Best Things In Life Are Free" with?
2 Which one-word song was a 90s hit with brother Michael?
3 Janet is the youngest of how many Jacksons?
4 Janet starred in which TV series about a school?
5 Which British superstar did she duet with on "Dream Street"?
6 Which Paula choreographed "Control The Video"?
7 Which album did "Til It's Gone" come from?
8 What was her follow-up to "Together Again" in 1998?
9 Which Canadian star featured with her on "Got Til It's Gone" in 1997?
10 Which year featured on the title of her *Rhythm Nation* album?
11 What was her first US No. 1, which reached 10 in the UK?
12 Her first world tour shared a name with which album?
13 Which record label did she sign to in 1991 in a $50 million deal?
14 Who succeeded Janet Jackson in signing a record-breaking record contract a week after she signed in 1991?
15 "Let's Wait Awhile" came from which album?
16 Which 1993 album debuted at No. 1?
17 Which daughter of a famous star became her sister-in-law in 1994?
18 In which film did the ballad "Again" feature?
19 What was her first UK hit – which reached No. 3?
20 Which 1993 hit had a two-letter title?

1 How is Marie McDonald McLaughlin Lawrie better known?
2 Who plays Magaldi in the film *Evita*?
3 Which musical instrument does Ravi Shankar play?
4 Who were Johnny Kidd's backing group?
5 What does UHF mean on a radio dial?
6 Which group was often known as P.I.L.?
7 In which decade was Lionel Richie born?
8 Who starred as Bongo Herbert in a film?
9 Who had an album called *My People Were Fair And Had Sky In Their Hair But Now They're Content To Wear Stars On Their Brows*?
10 Which song title links The Cars and R.E.M.?
11 Which comic chat show host used an Abba song for his show's title?
12 What could Barry Manilow not do in 1978?
13 Who were the *Top of the Pops* dancers for nine years until 1976?
14 How were Danny, Joe, Donnie, Jon and Jordan better known?
15 Whose first album was *Born to Run*?
16 What is the surname of the Spice Girls' Geri?
17 Which number links a 70s hit by Ringo Starr and a 60s hit by Neil Sedaka?
18 Which "drink" was the Four Seasons' first hit?
19 Which Wet Wet Wet single has "Home And Away" in brackets?
20 In which decade was Chris Rea's first top ten hit?

LEVEL 2

1 "Animal Nitrate" was the first top ten hit for which group?
2 "Unbelievable" provided which group with a 90s US No. 1?
3 Which group from the 60s got to No. 2 in 1990 with the album Summer Dreams?
4 Which word goes before In The Sand in the song title by Belinda Carlisle?
5 In which decade did Curiosity first have a top ten single?
6 Which group issued the statement: 'As soon as we are able, we would like to celebrate his life in the style to which he was accustomed"?
7 How is instrumentalist Philippe Pages better known?
8 What was Michael Jackson's follow-up to "Bad"?
9 Under what name does Saul Hudson perform?
10 "From the day we arrive on the planet and blinking step into the sun" is the first line of which film song?
11 Who had an 80s No. 1 with "A Good Heart"?
12 In which decade was teenage idol Donny Osmond born?
13 Which movie helped "Unchained Melody" into the 90s charts?
14 Which actor was on the other side of "Wandrin' Star" by Lee Marvin?
15 Which word follows Stool in the song title by Kid Creole And The Coconuts?
16 Who had an 80s US No. 1 with "It's Still Rock And Roll To Me"?
17 "How Am I Supposed To Live Without You?" was the first top ten hit for which singer?
18 What was Madonna's follow-up to "Dear Jessie"?
19 Who had a 70s No. 1 album called Rollin"?
20 In which decade did Chuck Berry first have a UK top ten single?

Answers

Pot Luck 56 (Quiz 110)
1 Arrest. 2 Eternal. 3 "The Lion Sleeps Tonight". 4 "Sweet Child O' Mine".
5 Thinking. 6 Simple Minds. 7 Paula Abdul. 8 "The Ugly Duckling".
9 Bananarama. 10 ZZ Top. 11 World. 12 Kajagoogoo. 13 Billie Holiday.
14 AC/DC. 15 The Shondelles. 16 Blur. 17 "Don't Cry For Me Argentina".
18 "Warriors". 19 Beatles. 20 70s.

LEVEL 2

1 Which 60s Beatles song was a chart hit for The Overlanders?
2 Who took "No Woman No Cry" into the charts in 1996?
3 Who had the first hit with "Walk On By"?
4 Who covered "Strawberry Fields Forever" in 1990?
5 What was an important date for Donny Osmond and Cliff Richard?
6 Which song has been a hit for Bing Crosby and Jim Davidson?
7 Who got higher in the charts first time out with "My Girl" – Otis Redding or The Temptations?
8 Who covered Roy Orbison's "A Love So Beautiful"?
9 Who had the UK version and covered "Singing The Blues"?
10 Who had the original version of Boyzone's "Father And Son"?
11 Which Tommy Roe song was covered by Vic Reeves and the Wonder Stuff?
12 Which female sang on "I Got You Babe" in 1985?
13 Who had a hit with "Everything I Own" in the 80s?
14 Which instrumental was a 50s hit for Perez Prado and Eddie Calvert?
15 Which song has been a hit for Elvis Presley and the Stylistics?
16 Who covered Jennifer Rush's "The Power Of Love" in 1994?
17 Which song links Willie Nelson and the Pet Shop Boys?
18 Who had the original "This Wheel's On Fire", covered by Siouxie and the Banshees in 1987?
19 Which Kinks song did the Stranglers cover in 1988?
20 Who had the original version of "Love Is All Around"?

1   What is Bowie's real surname?
2   With which band did he record "Under Pressure"?
3   Whose puppet creations featured in the movie *Labyrinth*?
4   Which song contains the line, "And the papers want to know whose shirts you wear"?
5   What was Bowie's first No. 1 album?
6   What name did Bowie's son originally have which rhymed with his surname?
7   What were the first three words of the title of his single with Bing Crosby?
8   Which film title gave him a hit in 1986?
9   What or who was Laughing in an early novelty number?
10 Which hit was the first ever to get to No. 1 as a reissue?
11 Bowie wrote "All the Young Dudes" for which act?
12 In 1984 what was his Greatest Hits album called?
13 What followed *Black Tie* in the title of a 90s album?
14 Which supermodel did Bowie marry in 1992?
15 Which major space event was "Space Oddity" timed to coincide with in 1969?
16 What was Bowie's first top ten hit of the 90s?
17 What sort of Dogs featured in the title of a 70s album?
18 Which record label did Bowie join in 1995?
19 Which Rick played synthesizer on "Space Oddity"?
20 Who recorded *Transformer* which was co-produced by Bowie?

1 In which decade was Prince born?
2 Who recorded with San José calling himself Rodriguez Argentina?
3 Who was Sam the Sham's backing group?
4 Whose first chart album was *In Dreams*?
5 Which country is Johnny Halliday from?
6 How was Yusef Islam known when he was in the pop charts?
7 How are the pop composers Burt and Hal better known?
8 What did Clive Sarstedt change his name to for the pop charts?
9 Which Nick Berry single was the best seller of 1986?
10 The Singing Nun had a hit record in which language?
11 In which decade were LPs first sold in the UK?
12 Which Michael Jackson album was the best-selling album of 1987?
13 Who were Hunting High And Low in an 80s album?
14 What was special about the paintwork of John Lennon's 1965 Rolls-Royce?
15 Who had the best-selling 1984 album *Can't Slow Down*?
16 What was first unveiled at the Palais Royal Saloon in San Francisco in 1889?
17 In which show did Samantha Juste play the records?
18 Whose 70s instrumental album sold over two million copies in the UK?
19 Which Portuguese singing sensation was created by Steve Coogan?
20 Which Irish singer released "Don't Cry For Me Argentina" as a single in 1992?

1 Which word follows House in the song title by Krush?
2 Who recorded the album *Different Light*?
3 Under what title did the Zulu folk tune "Wimoweh" make No. 1?
4 What was Guns N'Roses' follow-up to "Paradise City"?
5 Which word follows Wishful in the song title by China Crisis?
6 Who had an 80s No. 1 album called *Live In The City Of Light*?
7 Who brought out the album *Forever Your Girl* in 1989?
8 Which novelty song was a hit for Mike Reid, alias EastEnder Frank Butcher?
9 Who managed to get Robert De Niro into the title of a chart hit?
10 Who had a big 80s album success with *Eliminator*?
11 Which word follows Harvest For the in the song title by Christians?
12 Who had an 80s No. 1 with "Too Shy"?
13 Who was the subject of the musical movie *Lady Sings The Blues*?
14 Who made the 80s No. 1 album *Back In Black*?
15 Which group backed Tommy James?
16 "There's No Other Way" was the first top ten hit for which group?
17 Which song from *Evita* took The Shadows back to the charts?
18 What was Frankie Goes To Hollywood's follow-up to "Rage Hard"?
19 Which group had the album Live At The BBC at No. 1 in the 90s?
20 In which decade did Elkie Brooks first have a top ten single?

1 Which show does "Love Changes Everything" come from?
2 Who had a hit with "I Don't Know How To Love Him" in 1972?
3 Which show does the song come from?
4 Which musical includes the classic "Send In The Clowns"?
5 "One" comes from which long-running stage show?
6 Who had a hit single with "All I Ask of You" but did not star in the show?
7 Who had a hit with "As If We Never Said Goodbye" in 1994?
8 "With One Look" features in which West End and Broadway show?
9 Which show features "Let the Sun Shine In"?
10 What are the nationalities of the Elaine Paige and Barbara Dickson characters portrayed in "I Know Him So Well"?
11 Who duetted with Diana Morrison on "The First Man You Remember"?
12 In which musical does Mrs Johnstone sing "Tell Me It's Not True"?
13 Which song from *Oliver!* did Shirley Bassey take into the charts?
14 Who had a hit with "If I Were A Rich Man" in 1967?
15 Who sang "Wishing You Were Somehow Here Again" in 1987?
16 Which musical does "You'll Never Walk Alone" come from?
17 Which *Evita* song provided Barbara Dickson with a top twenty hit?
18 Which show does "You're The One That I Want" come from?
19 Who had a hit with "Aquarius" in 1969?
20 Who had chart success with "Oh What A Circus" in 1978?

1 In which decade did the Jackson 5 sign to Motown?
2 Which Jones was highly involved in Jackson's material from 1975?
3 Jackson's first son shared a name with which star?
4 "Man In The Mirror" first featured on which album?
5 Who did he duet with on an album of *Love Songs* in 1987?
6 Which movie did he make in 1988?
7 What was his debut hit away from the Jackson 5?
8 Which city's police department investigated Jackson's involvement with children?
9 Which anthem beat The Beatles' "Free As A Bird" to the Christmas No. 1 spot?
10 Which British star duetted with Jackson on the co-penned "The Girl Is Mine"?
11 What was the name of Jackson's second wife?
12 Which band consisting of his nephews did he help launch in the 1990s?
13 Michael's reunion with which brother resulted in the album Victory in 1984?
14 Which musical did he take part in in 1977?
15 "Black Or White" came from which album?
16 A career-changing move to which label did he make in 1975?
17 Which soccer Wanderers could not use "The Wanderer" as a club anthem because Jackson held the copyright?
18 What was his immediate follow-up to "Off The Wall"?
19 Which actress married for the seventh time on Jackson's ranch in 1991?
20 What was the name of his autobiography written in 1988?

1   What was the Bob Marley hit compilation album called?
2   In which decade did Olivia Newton-John have her first hit record?
3   Who had the best-selling album *Oxygène*?
4   Which was the only group to have an album among the top ten of the decade in the 70s and the 80s?
5   How much did an LP measure across?
6   In which language was Falco's "Rock Me Amadeus" sung?
7   "Money For Nothing" and "So Far Away" featured on which album?
8   Which Boys featured on the Fat Boys' "Wipe Out" in 1987?
9   Which record label used by Daniel O'Donnell shares its name with a famous London Hotel?
10 In which decade was Neil Diamond born?
11 Who had the best-selling record of 1974 with "You Won't Find Another Fool Like Me"?
12 Which pop show did Cathy McGowan regularly present?
13 Who recorded the Grammy-winning "Don't Worry Be Happy"?
14 Who was B. Bumble's backing group?
15 How was the controversial James Marcus Smith better known?
16 Who sang with Paul Miles-Kingston on "Pie Jesu"?
17 Who had a 1996 hit with "Mysterious Girl"?
18 Which group did Paul Heaton form after the Housemartins?
19 What is Leonard Cohen's home country?
20 Who teamed up with Natalie Cole on a 1983 tribute album to her father?

1 In which decade did The Clash first have a top ten single?
2 What was The Eagles' first UK hit?
3 Who had a hit with "Beautiful Sunday' in 1972?
4 Who released a chart-topping album in 1996 called *Take Two*?
5 What was Wilson Pickett's first UK hit?
6 Who was Clifford T. Ward singing about in his UK No. 8 in 1973?
7 Which song starts, "She packed my bags last night, pre-flight"?
8 What was Michael Ball's first album called?
9 What was Iron Maiden's follow-up to "The Evil That Men Do"?
10 Who had a 70s No. 1 with "I Love To Love (But My Baby Loves To Dance)'?
11 Which word follows I Don't Know Anybody in the song title by Black Box?
12 What was Chris Andrews' only UK top ten hit in 1965?
13 What was the first No. 1 for Mungo Jerry?
14 In which decade did Randy Crawford first have a top ten single?
15 What sort of Dreams gave Jimmy Nail a 90s hit?
16 Which 60s band was once known as The Mann-Hug Blues Brothers?
17 Who had an 80s No. 1 with "Down Under"?
18 "Livin' On A Prayer" was the first top ten hit for which group?
19 Which word goes before The Conga in the song title by Black Lace?
20 What was Janet Jackson's follow-up to "The Best Things In Life Are Free"?

Quiz 115 Place the Place

Answers – see page 327

LEVEL 2

1   Who were going to Barbados in 1975?
2   Which Asian country provided Kim Wilde with an 80s hit?
3   In which US state might you be Dreamin' of Girls or a Man in a Hotel?
4   Patsy Gallant was From where to where in 1977?
5   Which city was the title of a Simple Minds EP in 1989?
6   Which geographical group had China, Tokyo and Cantonese in chart titles?
7   Who had a 60s hit with "Do You Know The Way to San Jose?"?
8   Which city has given hit songs to Frank Sinatra, Gerard Kenny and Sting?
9   Who was in Africa in 1983?
10 It was a Rainy Night and The Devil Went Down To where?
11 Who was Leavin' Durham Town in 1969?
12 Wichita and Galveston provided hits for whom?
13 Which location was a hit for Bobby Bloom in 1970?
14 Where was Michael Jackson a Stranger in 1996?
15 Which Queen was a hit for Billy Ocean?
16 Where did Tony Christie ask the Way To in the 70s?
17 Which US city links Elton John and Bruce Springsteen in song?
18 Which tropical paradise was the subject of a David Essex hit?
19 Which US state was a 70s hit for Pussycat?
20 Who were All the Way From Memphis in 1973?

1 What was Madonna's surname at birth?
2 In 1998 Madonna appeared live on which TV show?
3 What was Madonna's first No. 1 album?
4 What is Madonna's record label called?
5 "Frozen" appeared on which album?
6 Which film star's face does Madonna have tattooed on her bottom?
7 In which state was Madonna born?
8 Which original song from the movie *Evita* charted in 1996?
9 What was Madonna's first UK No. 1 single?
10 Which Boys supported Madonna on her *Like A Virgin* Tour?
11 Which album first featured the track "Papa Don't Preach"?
12 What item of lingerie from the 1993 *Girlie Tour* sold at auction for £4,600?
13 Which 1987 hit was also the title of a movie?
14 Which Madonna single and video were condemned by the Vatican in 1989?
15 In which movie did she sing "I'm Breathless"?
16 What are the forenames of her first daughter?
17 "Into The Groove" came from which movie in which she starred?
18 What was the name of her controversial 1990 tour?
19 Which album to accompany the book *Sex* included "Deeper And Deeper"?
20 What was on the other side of the single "The Power Of Goodbye"?

1 Who sang the theme song from *Watership Down*?
2 In which decade did CDs first go on sale in Europe?
3 In which decade did Kenny Rogers first have a top ten single?
4 How is LaDonna Andrea Gaines better known?
5 Who had a hit with "Nothing's Gonna Change My Love for You" aged 18?
6 Which comedian had the best-selling record of 1965?
7 What was on the other side of the Beatles' "We Can Work It Out"?
8 Which single of 1977 was the first ever to sell two million in the UK?
9 Who sang "Don't You Want Me?" in 1981?
10 Who were the only two Americans to have million-selling singles in the 80s in the UK?
11 Who made *Private Investigations* in 1982?
12 What is Mick Jagger's middle name?
13 In which decade did John Lennon's "Imagine" hit the top spot?
14 Whose "Tell Laura I Love Her" was banned in 1960?
15 Which Cliff Richard record before 1997 has the longest title?
16 How many r.p.m. did an LP have?
17 Who had the 1981 album *Face Value*?
18 What is Marianne Faithfull's real name?
19 In which decade was Bryan Adams born?
20 Which veteran had a 70s album *And I Love You So*?

1 What was Kylie Minogue's follow-up to "Step Back In Time"?
2 Who recorded the 90s hit album *Ballbreaker*?
3 In which decade did Jimmy Cliff first have a top ten single?
4 Which word follows Holdin' Out For A in the song title by Bonnie Tyler?
5 Which Blondie single gives a credit to Grandmaster Flash?
6 Gloria Gaynor's hit "I Am What I Am" comes from which musical?
7 What was Canned Heat's first UK hit in 1968?
8 Which 50s singer married 007 Roger Moore?
9 Vocalist and instrumentalist Chuck Berry was born in which decade?
10 Which Lady did the Beach Boys sing about in their UK No. 6 in 1979?
11 Who released a chart-topping album *Live At The BBC* in 1994?
12 What was Stevie Wonder's first hit?
13 What is Kiki Dee's real name?
14 Who had an 80s No. 1 with "Japanese Boy"?
15 Who did Mark Knopfler record "Neck And Neck" with?
16 What was George Michael's follow-up to "Faith"?
17 Who had a spiky 80s album called *Porcupine*?
18 Which word completes the song title by Ultravox, "Dancing With ____ In My Eyes"?
19 In which decade did The Carpenters first have a top ten single?
20 Which charity benefited from "Live Like Horses"?

1 Which Gibb brothers are twins?
2 Where in the UK were the Gibbs born?
3 What was their first UK hit?
4 What was the sleeve to "Odessa" made from?
5 Who did Maurice marry in 1969?
6 In 1969 which brothers did the Bee Gees consist of?
7 Which song is about a man about to be electrocuted on Death Row?
8 Which song from *Saturday Night Fever* did Yvonne Elliman record?
9 How many Bee Gees songs were in *Saturday Night Fever*?
10 Which Barry Gibb song was a hit for Frankie Valli in 1979?
11 Who had a No. 1 UK and US hit with Barry Gibb's "Woman in Love"?
12 What was their last No. 1 of the 70s and their last for eight years?
13 Which 80s hit meant they were the first group to have a No. 1 in each of three decades?
14 Which of their songs was a hit for Dionne Warwick in 1982?
15 What was the sequel to *Saturday Night Fever*?
16 Which Bee Gee had a solo album called *Secret Agent*?
17 Which cricketer contributed to "We Are The Bunburys" about a group of cricket-mad rabbits?
18 Which Gibb made a cameo appearance in "Only Fools and Horses"?
19 Which group used a Gibb song as their swan song?
20 Who did they pay tribute to in *Tapestry Revisited*?

Answers

Place the Place (Quiz 115)
1 Typically Tropical.   2 Cambodia.   3 California.   4 "From New York To LA".
5 Amsterdam.   6 Japan.   7 Dionne Warwick.   8 New York.   9 Toto.
10 Georgia.   11 Roger Whittaker.   12 Glen Campbell.   13 Montego Bay.
14 Moscow.   15 Caribbean.   16 Amarillo.   17 Philadelphia.   18 Tahiti.
19 Mississippi.   20 Mott The Hoople.

1　Who sang "I've Never Been To Me"?
2　Who was backed by a Music Theatre?
3　Do you remember who sang "I Remember Elvis Presley"?
4　Fern Kinney's only hit said that "Together We Are...' what?
5　Which school choir sang "There's No One Quite Like Grandma"?
6　Whose only hit was "My Resistance Is Low"?
7　Which Minnie had the 70s hit with "Loving You"?
8　It's Raining what according to the Weather Girls?
9　Which song contained the words, "You are my candy girl, And you got me wanting you"?
10　Whose hit "The First Time" was the last time in the charts?
11　What completes the title of Althia and Donna's Up Town?
12　Which 70s hit was about Coconut Airways?
13　Whhat was the number of The Fruitgum Company who played "Simon Says"?
14　What was coupled with Jasper Carrott's "Magic Roundabout"?
15　"Little Things Mean A Lot" was a 50s No. 1 for who?
16　Whose only hit was "Groovin' With Mr Bloe"?
17　What is the only one-hit No. 1 to be sung in French?
18　Which singer with lots of hits charted once with Python Lee Jackson?
19　What was Mary MacGregor Torn Between in a 70s hit?
20　Which artist gave Brian and Michael their only hit?

LEVEL 2

1 Which religious political leader were the Clash referring to in "Rock The Casbah"?
2 Which group received a gold record for "Baby I'm A Wanting You" in 1972?
3 Which No. 1 for the Platters was a hit for Brian Ferry in 1974?
4 Who had the original hit in 1963 with "It's My Party"?
5 Who duetted with Georgio Moroder on "Together In Electric Dreams"?
6 Who sang "Wonderful World Beautiful People" in 1969?
7 Who was the manager of the Dave Clark Five?
8 Which John Cougar hit has the lyric "two American kids growin' up in the heartland"?
9 What is Ringo Starr holding on the cover of the *Sgt Pepper* album?
10 What was the title of Freda Payne's No. 1 from 1970?
11 Which breakfast cereal was advertised with the song "Spirit in the Sky" in early 1997?
12 In which decade was Tori Amos born?
13 Who were Bobby Boris Pickett's backing group when they first charted?
14 Whose first hit was "Can't Stand Losing You" in the 70s?
15 Which drink was Berni Flint singing about in 1977?
16 Who spent her early years in radio in *Meet The Huggetts*?
17 Whose second manager and first husband is Bobby Willis?
18 What was Andy Newman's nickname?
19 What is Love according to Pat Benatar in 1984?
20 Who was the Man With The Golden Trumpet?

1   What was Oasis' follow-up single to "Cigarettes And Alcohol"?
2   What kind of costume did David Bowie wear for his "Ashes To Ashes" video?
3   Which word goes before With Knives in the song title by Bizarre Inc?
4   In which decade did Petula Clark first have a top ten single?
5   Which country was Brotherhood of Man's shepherd boy Angelo from?
6   In Partners In KRYME what did the letter E stand for?
7   Whigfield's first ever week in the charts was spent at what position?
8   Who had a 90s album called *Swagger*?
9   What is Wink Martindale's most famous hit?
10 "Get Ready For This" was the first top ten for which group?
11 Andy Fairweather-Low was lead singer with which group?
12 Who had a 80s album called *3 Sides Live*?
13 Who had a 70s No. 1 with "Tears On My Pillow"?
14 What was on the other side of Rick Astley's "When I Fall In Love"?
15 Whose backing group were the Devotions?
16 What was Joe Brown and the Bruvvers' first UK top ten hit?
17 Who did Cilla Black beat to No. 1 with her version of "Anyone Who Had A Heart"?
18 To whom did Ricky Valance Tell I Love Her in 1960?
19 What was on the other side of David Cassidy's "Could It Be Forever"?
20 My Prerogative was the first top ten hit for which singer?

1 What did Dora Bryan want for Christmas in 1963?
2 In which decade did Bing Crosby's "White Christmas" first enter the UK charts?
3 What did John Lennon's "Happy Christmas" have in brackets in 1980?
4 According to Adam Faith, what was in a Christmas Shop in 1960?
5 Who said "Please Come Home for Christmas" in 1994?
6 Which Christmas Rock has been a hit for Max Bygraves and Chubby Checker with Bobby Rydell?
7 Who wished It Could Be Christmas Every Day in 1973?
8 What was Johnny Mathis's 1976 Christmas hit?
9 What kind of Merry Christmas did a band of environmentalists wish us in 1974?
10 Who said "All I Want For Christmas is You" in 1994?
11 Which comedian was "Rockin' Around The Christmas Tree" in 1987?
12 Which Snowman did the Cocteau Twins sing about in 1993?
13 Who covered the Carpenters' "Santa Claus Is Comin' To Town" in 1985?
14 Where was Santa Claus according to Spitting Image in 1986?
15 Who pleaded with Santa Baby in the 1990s?
16 Who sang with the Smurfs on "Christmas in Smurfland" in 1978?
17 Whose "Christmas Alphabet" went to No. 1 in 1955?
18 Who had a Wonderful Christmas Time in 1979?
19 What is the theme song from *The Snowman*?
20 Who had "White Christmas" on the other side of "Too Risky"?

1 What did the Wind cry according to Jimi Hendrix?
2 Which word completes The Yardbirds hit, "Over Under Sideways ____"?
3 Who went "Down Town"?
4 Which song starts, "Dirty old river must you keep rolling, Rolling into the night"?
5 Who first hit the top ten with "Wild Thing"?
6 Which word was the whole of a Mark Hopkin hit and half a Beatles hit?
7 Which group became known as the ones with the girl drummer?
8 Who had a huge hit with "In The Ghetto"?
9 Bob Dylan had what type of Homesick Blues?
10 Who sang about a Swiss Maid?
11 Which Move hit "sampled" a phrase from the 1812 Overture?
12 Paradoxically, who sang "I Love My Dog"?
13 What other words described Tom Jones' Funny Forgotten Feelings?
14 Who were in Bits And Pieces?
15 What was the first UK hit for The Supremes?
16 Where did you have to go to find the House Of The Rising Sun?
17 "Do You Want To Know A Secret" was a first chart hit for who?
18 To whom did the Hollies say Sorry in 1969?
19 Which song finishes, "And I can never, never, go home again"?
20 In a song title what Has A Thousand Eyes?

1 What time was it for Status Quo in a 1983 No. 3 hit?
2 Who launched The Really Useful Company in 1986?
3 Which disco group was formed by Nile Rodgers and Bernard Edwards?
4 Who were Ready Or Not in 1996?
5 What was On the Run for Manfred Mann in 1968?
6 Who was No. 1 with "Singing The Blues" in 1956?
7 What are shaking and rattling in "Great Balls Of Fire"?
8 What is David Bowie wearing on his hands on the cover of the *Let's Dance* album?
9 Which *Dallas* star released his *And I Love You So* album in 1984?
10 Where was Johnny Duncan's Last Train going to in 1957?
11 In which decade was Joan Armatrading born?
12 Which city features in the title of the 1978 Darts hit?
13 Which Summer was a 1985 hit for Bryan Adams?
14 Whose first album was *The Lexicon of Love*?
15 Who's On the Road Again according to Manfred Mann's Earth Band in 1978?
16 What is Barry Blue's real name?
17 Who is known as the Divine Miss M?
18 Whose first hit was "Stop Your Sobbing" in the 70s?
19 Who were Craig McLachlan's backing group?
20 Who had *Breakfast At Tiffany's* in 1996?

1 Who had a 90s album called *Rid Of Me*?
2 Which song title links Mud and Eternal?
3 Which singer/songwriter had a 1995 autobiography called *X-Ray*?
4 What was the Pet Shop Boys' follow up to "Rent"?
5 "You're History" was the first top ten hit for which group?
6 Which song has the words, "Daylight. I must wait for the sunrise, I must think of a new life. And I mustn't give in"?
7 Which word follows Give Me Back My in the song title by Dollar?
8 Which band included Bob Dylan, George Harrison and Roy Orbison?
9 What is the main image on the cover of Prodigy's *Music For The Jilted Generation*?
10 Who had an 80s No. 1 with Dave Stewart with "It's My Party"?
11 In which decade did Chicory Tip first have a top ten single?
12 Whose first No. 1 was "Sweets For My Sweet"?
13 Which title was used for hits by BabyBird and New Edition?
14 What was Simon and Garfunkel's first UK top ten hit?
15 Which word follows Look in the song title by Big Country?
16 What was Mariah Carey's follow up to "I'll Be There"?
17 Which TV soap link group had an album called *Emmerdance*?
18 Who sang and wrote "I Guess The Lord Must Be In New York City"?
19 "Vision Of Love" was the first top ten hit for which singer?
20 Which city links Marcella with the Spinners?

1 Who was Carole King's songwriting partner?
2 Who wrote "Anyone Who Had A Heart" which was a Cilla Black hit?
3 Who was the lyricist on "A Whole New World" from *Aladdin*?
4 Who had a hit with "I Write The Songs" in 1975?
5 Who wrote "Love Is All Around"?
6 Which member of Take That also wrote "Everything Changes"?
7 Who wrote the music for Phillip Schofield's first hit single?
8 Which singer wrote Sinead O'Connor's "Nothing Compares 2 U"?
9 Which two Rogers' many hits include "Something's Gotten Hold Of My Heart"?
10 Who co-wrote with Mike Chapman on over 50 Top Ten hits of the 70s?
11 Who wrote "Chain Reaction" for Diana Ross?
12 Who was Dusty Springfield's song-writing brother?
13 Which Cliff Richard No. 1 was written by Lionel Bart?
14 Which 1985 No. 1 was written by Rodgers and Hammerstein?
15 Who co-wrote "I Know Him So Well" with Tim Rice?
16 Whose first No. 1 as a writer was with the Monkees' "I'm A Believer"?
17 Which singer/songwriter was Bette Midler's pianist and arranger?
18 How are songwriters Doc and Mort better known?
19 Who was the first act, other than The Beatles, to take a Lennon and McCartney composition to No. 1?
20 Who wrote Whitney Houston's "I Will Always Love You"?

1 Which No. 1 has the lines, "Come all without, Come all within"?
2 Which No. 1 title contained in brackets the words "Be Sure To Wear Some Flowers In Your Hair"?
3 Who took "Dizzy" to the top?
4 Which Beatles No. 1 contains the line, "Let it out and let it in"?
5 Who duetted with Nancy Sinatra on "Something Stupid"?
6 What is the next word to follow "Do Wah Diddy"?
7 What was The Monkees' first UK No. 1?
8 In the 60s Denny Laine made it to No. 1 with which group?
9 Which lady reached the top with "I'll Never Fall In Love Again"?
10 Which No. 1 started with the French national anthem?
11 What Was Rising at No. 1 the week before "Je T'Aime" took over?
12 What creatures sang "House Of The Rising Sun"?
13 Which No 1 contained the line, 'They're going to crucify me'?
14 What was the only 60s No. 1 for Jim Reeves?
15 What completed the hat trick of No. 1s for The Searchers?
16 Who had the 60s No. 1 with "Mony Mony"?
17 What follows the line, "If Paradise Is…"?
18 What was the colour of the Moon for The Marcels?
19 Chart-topping "Moon River" came from which film?
20 Which line follows "Ob-La-Di, Ob-La-Da"?

1 Who had a 1996 hit with "Flava"?
2 Who joined East 17 on "If You Ever" in 1996?
3 What nickname did the DJ Steve Wright give Prince?
4 What is Andy Summers doing on the cover of the *Synchronicity* LP?
5 What did Mrs Brown have according to Herman's Hermits?
6 Which Rod Stewart album had "Blondes" in the title?
7 What was a hit for Neil Sedaka and then the Partridge Family?
8 In which city was Eartha Kitt Under the Bridges Of in 1955?
9 What was the title of Paul McCartney's first solo album?
10 Who sang "Unbreak My Heart" in 1997?
11 In which decade was Michael Bolton born?
12 Whose first hit was "Letter From America" in the 80s?
13 Who was told Don't Be A Hero by Paper Lace in 1974?
14 Which type of Summer was an 80s hit for the Style Council?
15 Whose first album was *Soul Provider*?
16 Whose nickname was Lady Leather?
17 Which country star's initials are J.R.?
18 How is Christopher Geppert better known?
19 Which city features in the title of the Clash hit?
20 Who are Harold Melvin's backing group?

Quiz 130 Pot Luck 66

Answers – see page 342

LEVEL 2

1 TV producer Mike Leggo helped create which performer?
2 Who had an 80s No. 1 with *The Special AKA Live!* (EP)?
3 Who released the 80s album *The Dreaming*?
4 Which Irish band led a TV tribute concert to Brian Keenan in 1991?
5 What did David Bowie suggest in the title of his 1983 million-selling album?
6 What was Cher's follow-up to "If I Could Turn Back Time"?
7 Which word follows Chocolate in the song title by Bros?
8 "Axel F" was the first top ten hit for which group?
9 Which animal appears in hit titles for both Jimmy Nail and Elton John?
10 "Smells Like Teen Spirit" was the first top ten hit for which group?
11 Who had an early 90s album called Growing Up In Public?
12 How old was Elvis Presley when he died?
13 Which song from *High Society* was a 1993 Christmas hit for Elton John and Kiki Dee?
14 What was added to the name of Manfred Mann in 1971?
15 Which word completes the song title by The Beastie Boys, "She's _____ It"?
16 Who had a 90s No. 1 album called *Step By Step*?
17 What was Duran Duran's follow-up to "A View To A Kill"?
18 In which decade did Nazareth first have a top ten single?
19 What was Chris Farlowe Out Of in his 1966 hit?
20 What was Ken Dodd's first UK hit?

1   Who was lead singer with The Sweet?
2   Which dance-hall group banned The Sweet due to their suggestive stage act?
3   What was Marc Bolan's real name?
4   Which former glam rocker is the father of the producer Paul Gadd Junior?
5   Whose second album was *Rock 'N'Roll Dudes*?
6   What was Alvin Stardust's first No. 1?
7   What was T. Rex's first No. 1 album?
8   For which song did The Sweet dress up in native American costumes and make up?
9   What was David Bowie's first hit with "star" in the title?
10 Which song did Bowie give to Mott the Hoople?
11 Who wrote an autobiography called *Leader*?
12 Who did Alvin Stardust feature as in the charts in 1961?
13 Which glam rock writers were referred to as Chinnichap?
14 What was Mud's first No. 1?
15 Who was Mud's lead singer?
16 What was the debut single of Tyrannosaurus Rex?
17 Who played Leather Tuscadero in the TV series *Happy Days*?
18 Which band had two each of vocalists, drummers, guitarists and bass players?
19 Mickey Finn was part of which band?
20 Who took "The Cat Crept In" to No. 2?

1   Who sang 'I'll Be Home'?
2   What was Lonnie Donegan's first No. 1?
3   In which year were the first charts published in the UK?
4   Which song has the words, "She was too young to fall in love, And I was too young to know"?
5   Which No. 1 was the first to have the word Rock in its title?
6   Which 50s No. 1 was revived as a 70s hit for Barbara Dickson?
7   Who was "Just Walkin' In The Rain"?
8   "On The Street Where You Live" featured in which musical?
9   What was Jimmy Young's second No. 1?
10 What was "She" wearing in the 1953 hit from Guy Mitchell?
11 Who was the featured vocalist with The Teenagers on "Why Do Fools Fall In Love"?
12 What was on the other side of the Everly Brothers' 'All I Have To Do Is Dream"?
13 Who were credited as Cliff's backing group on "Living Doll"?
14 A theme from the Russian composer Borodin was used in which No. 1?
15 Who had the No. 1 with "It's Only Make Believe"?
16 Who is the first person to have a UK No. 1?
17 Which line comes after, "Putting On The Agony"?
18 What was Russ Conway's first No. 1?
19 What particular type of White went with Cherry Pink?
20 Which was the only 50s No. 1 to have Roman numerals in the name of the performers?

1   Which film heroine was born in 1919 and died in 1952?
2   Who is "a star in the face of the sky" in an Elton John hit?
3   Who joined Joe Cocker in the 1983 hit "Up Where We Belong"?
4   What couldn't Petula Clark Live Without in her 1966 hit?
5   Which group had a No. 1 in 1985 with "I Wanna Know What Love Is"?
6   What did Ray Charles have "On his mind" in the 1960 hit?
7   What group went Atomic in 1980?
8   Which Police album cover had coloured stripes superimposed with photos?
9   Which No. 1 is sometimes referred to as "Starry Starry Night"?
10 Who had a No. 1 hit with "Down Down"?
11 How is Doris Kappelhoff better known?
12 Who had a hit with "Oh Superman" in 1981?
13 Who's In Love according to Rickie Lee Jones in 1979?
14 Who had the 1987 hit "Never Can Say Goodbye"?
15 Which city features in the title of the 1964 hit with a sporting link by Helmut Zacharias?
16 Who were Echo's backing group?
17 Whose first top ten album was *52nd Street*?
18 Which Summer was an 80s hit for Bananarama?
19 Whose first hit was "You To Me Are Everything" in the 70s?
20 In which decade was Jon Bon Jovi born?

1   What was Erasure's follow-up to "The Circus"?
2   Who had a late 80s album called *Raindancing*?
3   "Nothing Can Divide Us" was the first top ten hit for which singer?
4   In which decade did Cher first have a solo top ten single?
5   Which word follows Keep The in the song title by Bon Jovi?
6   Who were Bill Medley and Bobby Hatfield?
7   Which song begins, "Trailer for sale or rent, Rooms to let 50 cents"?
8   Which singer said, "It costs a lot to make me look so cheap"?
9   Which word follows Room In Your in the song title by Living in a Box?
10 Who had an 80s No. 1 with "Eye Of The Tiger"?
11 What is Connie Francis' real first Christian name?
12 Who had the Paramount Jazz Band as his backing band?
13 What was the Three Degrees first UK hit?
14 Who released a chart-topping album in 1995 called *Nobody Else*?
15 Which word completes the song title by Rick Astley, "She Wants To _____ With Me"?
16 What object was Bobby Vee like in a UK No. 4 in 1961?
17 Who was swell according to The Turtles' 1968 hit?
18 Who was a Nice One according to Cockerel Chorus in 1973?
19 Which word goes before Nights in the song title by London Boys?
20 Perez Prado charted in the 90s but in which decade did he first have a top ten single?

1 In which decade was Sinatra born?
2 What was his nickname?
3 Which is the only decade in which Sinatra has not had a Top Ten album?
4 What was his first UK No. 1 in 1954?
5 What was Sinatra's middle name?
6 For which 50s film did Sinatra win an Oscar?
7 What was Sinatra's own record label, set up in 1961?
8 Which 1966 hit won a Grammy that year?
9 Which song was dedicated to his elder daughter?
10 Who wrote the English lyric for Sinatra's signature tune "My Way"?
11 Which song did he take into the charts with Bono in 1993?
12 In which film did Sinatra sing his famous "The Lady Is A Tramp"?
13 Of which co-star did he say on her death, "She was a princess from the day she was born"?
14 Which of Sinatra's wives went on to marry Andre Previn?
15 In which decade was "My Way" first released?
16 Which of Sinatra's children was kidnapped?
17 Which city gave Sinatra a 50s hit?
18 Which city gave him a hit single 23 years later?
19 Who played the character loosely based on Sinatra in *The Godfather*?
20 In addition to *Sinatra-Basie*, which album did he make with Count Basie in 1964?

Answers

Glam Rock (Quiz 131)
1 Brian Connolly. 2 Mecca. 3 Mark Feld. 4 Gary Glitter.
5 The Glitter Band. 6 "Jealous Mind". 7 *Electric Warrior*.
8 "Wig Wam Bam". 9 "Starman". 10 "All The Young Dudes".
11 Gary Glitter. 12 Shane Fenton. 13 Chapman and Chinn.
14 "Tiger Feet". 15 Les Gray. 16 "Debora". 17 Suzi Quatro.
18 Showaddywaddy. 19 T. Rex. 20 Mud.

1   What was All Saints' first million-seller?
2   Which million-seller was written by Reg Presley?
3   Aqua's first No. 1 sold a million – what was it?
4   Which was the first million-seller with Christmas in the title by a solo singer?
5   Which TV detective sold a million with "Don't Give Up On Us"?
6   What was Frank Ifield's only million-seller?
7   Who was the first Canadian to sell a million in 1991?
8   What was the first Eurovision Song Contest winner to sell a million?
9   The Simon Park Orchestra's "Eye Level" was the theme from which TV series about a European detective?
10 Boyzone's first million-seller was written by whom?
11 Who holds the 20th-century record for most UK million-sellers?
12 How many million-selling singles have The Rolling Stones had?
13 "The Power Of Love" only sold a million for whom?
14 Who was the first person to leave Take That to have a million-seller?
15 "Mary's Boy Child" has been a million-seller for Boney M and who else?
16 What was Celine Dion's second million-seller?
17 Which Cliff Richard million-seller was the title of a film?
18 Who had two million-sellers in one year – 1995?
19 How many million-sellers did Robbie Williams have with Take That?
20 Who was the first non-human act to have a million-seller?

Quiz 137 Pot Luck 69

Answers – see page 349

LEVEL 2

1 Which group had a hit with "Rag Doll" in 1964?
2 Which 1977 hit told of "four hungry children and a crop in the field"?
3 Which song was highest in the charts for the Spice Girls at the beginning of 1997?
4 In which month was Pat Boone in love, in a 1957 song title?
5 What is on the cover of the *Brothers In Arms* album?
6 Which female was Shakin' Stevens singing about in his 1982 No. 1?
7 What sort of wind did Frank Ifield and Jimmy Young sing about?
8 What was Blur's first No. 1 of 1997?
9 Which Small Faces song asks "What did you do there?"?
10 What did Guy Mitchell have "by the number" in his final hit in 1959?
11 Which Summer was a 1990 hit for Belinda Carlisle?
12 Which Michael Jackson/Paul McCartney hit is one word three times?
13 In which decade was Bob Geldof born?
14 What game were the Pet Shop Boys Dancing to in 1988?
15 Which late singer was born Ellen Naomi Cohen?
16 Who was Dear according to Siouxsie And The Banshees in 1983?
17 Whose first album was *Heaven On Earth*?
18 Which town features in the title of the 1988 Four Tops hit?
19 Whose first hit was "Daddy Cool" in the 70s?
20 Who were Eddie's backing group?

Answers

Pot Luck 71 (Quiz 141)
1 "Talk To The Animals". 2 Mary. 3 1952. 4 A tubular bell.
5 Stewart Copeland. 6 Andy Stewart. 7 Good Vibrations.
8 *Elton John's Greatest Hits*. 9 Peter Noone. 10 Jamiroquai.
11 The Heartbreakers. 12 Boyz II Men. 13 1960s. 14 New York.
15 Marti Pellow. 16 Marilyn Martin. 17 Violin. 18 Cher.
19 Darren Day. 20 Lynda.

1 "Don't Make Me Wait" was the first top ten hit for which group?
2 What was the Charlatans' follow up to "The Only One I Know"?
3 Which name links Freedom with Vanessa?
4 What was The Christians' first UK top ten hit?
5 Who had a 60s hit with "Come And Stay With Me"?
6 Andy Fairweather-Low was Wide-Eyed and what in his 1975 hit?
7 Which surname is shared by Rickie Lee and Quincy?
8 Which Queen was a 1970 hit for The Kinks?
9 What is the main colour on the album cover of Blur's *The Great Escape*?
10 Which word follows Love And in the song title by Cher?
11 In which decade did Stevie Wonder have his first UK hit?
12 Who was the Glam Rock writing partner of Chapman?
13 In which decade did Clarence Frogman Henry first have a top ten single?
14 Who had an 80s No. 1 with The Model?
15 What was The Fine Young Cannibals' follow-up to "She Drives Me Crazy"?
16 Which word goes before Gunn in the song title by Art Of Noise?
17 What was Kim Wilde's first UK hit?
18 In which decade did The Pioneers first have a top ten single?
19 Which word follows Winter In in the song title by Bomb The Bass?
20 Where was Roger Whittaker leaving in 1969?

1 Which ballad began life as "Comme D'Habitude"?
2 Which song has charted for Frankie Laine, plus Robson and Jerome ?
3 Which 50s singer of big ballads was nicknamed the Sultan of Sob?
4 Connie Francis had a 1958 No. 1 with "Who's Sorry Now?", but in which decade was the song written?
5 Who had a 60s hit with "As Long As He Needs Me"?
6 Which song from *La Cage Aux Folles* was a hit for Gloria Gaynor?
7 Which Platters hit begins "They asked me how I knew"?
8 Which song charted for Doris Day and Kathy Kirby?
9 Which two acts have had a No. 1 with "You'll Never Walk Alone"?
10 Who got to No. 2 with "You've Lost That Lovin' Feeling", pipped at the post by the Righteous Brothers?
11 Who had a UK No. 1 with the English version of a French hit "La Dernière Valse"?
12 Which 6' 9" chart topper sang "Let The Heartaches Begin"?
13 Which 1970 No. 1 for Elvis was recorded live in Las Vegas?
14 Who was the biggest selling artist in the 1967 "Summer Of Love"?
15 Which Diana Ross ballad reached No. 1 after Tony Blackburn played it every day on his breakfast show in 1971?
16 What was Madonna's first hit of 1997?
17 Who had a 1965 No. 1 with "Where Are You Now (My Love)?"?
18 Which song took Whitney Houston to the top of the charts in 1988?
19 Which ballad first took the Walker Brothers to No. 1 in the mid 60s?
20 Which 1996 album did Celine Dion's "All By Myself" come from?

LEVEL 2

1 What was Madonna's first No. 1 after making Evita?
2 Which group were the first chart-toppers named after a European city?
3 Who featured on the 1992 chart topper which included "Take A Chance On Me" and "Voulez-Vous"?
4 Which Kinks classic starts, "The taxman's taken all my dough"?
5 Which UB40 No. 1 began "Wise men say only fools rush in"?
6 Hale and Pace's No. 1 "The Stonk" was written to raise money for which charity?
7 Who featured on Tamperer's No. 1 "Feel It"?
8 The Spice Girls had three consecutive Christmas No. 1s but what was their first?
9 Which Peter and Gordon record was No. 1 in the US and the UK?
10 What was Whitney Houston's second UK No. 1?
11 What was Cher's first 90s No. 1?
12 What is the only No. 1 to have Wind in the title?
13 Which Anne Murray hit from the 70s was a 90s chart-topper for Boyzone?
14 What was the first UK Eurovision song of the 90s to top the UK chart?
15 What followed Dreams on Gabrielle's debut single?
16 What went along with Robson and Jerome's "What Becomes Of The Broken Hearted"/ "Up On The Roof"?
17 Who had a 1962 No. 1 with "Nut Rocker"?
18 What was Steve Hurley's middle name on "Jack Your Body"?
19 What was SClub7's debut single which went straight to No1?
20 Who had a 60s No. 1 and appeared in *EastEnders* as a car-dealer in the late 90s?

1   What song from *Dr. Dolittle* won an Oscar in 1967?
2   Who did the Everly Brothers ask a message to be taken to in 1959?
3   In which year was the first UK record chart published: 1952, '53 or '54?
4   What, on the cover of *Tubular Bells*, is set against the sky?
5   Who was the tallest member of the Police?
6   Who had "A Scottish Soldier" in the charts for nine months in 1961?
7   What do the Beach Boys get from "the way the sunlight plays upon her hair"?
8   Which Elton John album cover shows him sitting in a white suit at a piano?
9   Who was Herman's Hermits' lead singer?
10 Who had a 1996 album called *Travelling Without Moving*?
11 Who are Tom Petty's backing group?
12 Whose first hit was "End Of The Road" in the 90s?
13 In which decade was Boy George born?
14 Which city features in the title of the 1988 Sting hit?
15 How is Mark McLoughlin better known?
16 Who sang with Phil Collins on the 1985 hit "Separate Lives"?
17 Which musical instrument did Stephane Grappelli play?
18 Whose first album was *All I Really Want To Do*?
19 Who starred in the 1996 revival of *Summer Holiday* on stage?
20 Who were Hue and Cry Looking for in 1989?

Answers

Pot Luck 69 (Quiz 137)
1 The Four Seasons.   2 "Lucille".   3 "2 Become 1".   4 April.
5 A steel guitar.   6 Oh Julie.   7 A wayward wind.   8 "Beetlebum".
9 "Itchycoo Park".   10 Heartaches.   11 "Summer Rain".   12 "Say Say Say".
13 1950s.   14 Domino.   15 Mama Cass.   16 Prudence.   17 Belinda Carlisle.
18 Acapulco.   19 Boney M.   20 The Hotrods.

1   What was Michael Jackson's follow-up to "Heal The World"?
2   House Of Love was the first top ten hit for which group?
3   Which group took their name from a number in A Hitch Hiker's Guide To The Galaxy?
4   In the late 60s who was the oldest ever artist to have a No. 1 record?
5   Which word goes before Control in the song title by Laura Branigan?
6   In which decade did Johnny Nash first have a top ten single?
7   Which 90s top ten film hit has the words, "The truth is I never left you"?
8   Which title links different songs by Blondie, Go West and Spanga?
9   Who had an 80s No. 1 with "Use It Up And Wear It Out"?
10   Where do Memories Light The Corners Of on the single "The Way We Were"?
11   On which album cover is Michael Jackson wearing a white suit?
12   Where were Dire Straits Twisting By in a hit from 1983?
13   Which Sting hit advertised Rover cars?
14   Who appears on the *Guilty* album cover with Barbra Streisand?
15   What colour was my lipstick on Connie Francis' 'Lipstick On Your Collar"?
16   Which all-boy band released *A Different Beat* in 1996?
17   Who had a 1996 hit with the Simon and Garfunkel song "Cecilia"?
18   Which word completes the song title by U2, "Where The _____ Have No Name"?
19   Who was vocalist with The News?
20   What was The Jam's follow-up to "Just Who Is The Five O'Clock Hero"?

Quiz 143 Novelty Songs

Answers – see page 347

LEVEL 2

1 Who sang with Arthur Mullard on "You're the One That I Want"?
2 Who backed Paul McCartney on "We All Stand Together"?
3 Who were The Firm singing about when they said " 'E's Alright"?
4 Who sang about The Funky Gibbon in 1975?
5 What was the name of Ernie, The Fastest Milkman In The West's, horse?
6 Which clothes were Honor Blackman and Patrick MacNee singing about in 1990?
7 Which song did the adult comedian Mike Reid take into the pop charts?
8 Which seaside resort provided Chas and Dave with a 1982 hit?
9 Who was The Oldest Swinger in Town in 1981?
10 Which two 80s Wimbledon champions were backed by the Full Metal Rackets on their 1991 record?
11 Which all-girl pack was Billy Connolly in, in 1979?
12 Which Ballad was a 1965 hit for Peter Cook?
13 Which late radio DJ recorded "Oh, My Father Had a Rabbit" in 1986?
14 Who used his catchphrase "You Are Awful" in a chart hit?
15 Which record did Claire and Friends chart with in 1986?
16 Who announced "John Wayne Is Big Leggy" in 1982?
17 Which song did the Turzels record to "Una Paloma Blanca"?
18 Which record has the line "Sing, Lofty"?
19 Which comedy duo were on the Trail of the Lonesome Pine in 1975?
20 Who sang the Monster hit which begins "I was working in the lab late one night"?

1 Which Take That song knocked Mr Blobby off the top only to be replaced by him the next week?
2 How many weeks did Elton John's "Sacrifice"/"Healing Hands" remain at No. 1?
3 What was Madonna's first No. 1 of the 90s?
4 Who knocked Whitney Houston and "I Will Always Love You" off the top?
5 Which group had the first new No. 1 of the 90s?
6 How many weeks did The Simpsons stay at No. 1 with "Do The Bartman"?
7 Who featured on Beats International's "Dub Be Good To Me"?
8 What was the longest-running No. 1 of 1994?
9 Who knocked "(Everything I Do) I Do It For You" off the top of the charts?
10 What was Snap!'s second No. 1?
11 Who knocked Rednex's "Cotton Eye Joe" off the top of the charts?
12 Whose No. 1 "I Want It That Way" was from the album Millennium?
13 Who had the Christmas No. 1 in 1991?
14 What was the first No. 1 of 1994?
15 How many weeks did Kylie Minogue's "Tears On My Pillow" stay at No. 1?
16 Who knocked Oasis and "Some Might Say" off the top of the charts?
17 Who featured on "Love Can Build A Bridge" with Cher, Chrissie Hynde and Neneh Cherry?
18 Who spent three weeks at No. 1 with Deeply Dippy?
19 How many No. 1 hits did Queen have in 1991?
20 Who knocked "Three Lions" off the top of the chart and then were replaced by the same song four weeks later?

1 Who was "bound to die" in Lonnie Donegan's 1958 hit?
2 Whose names also feature on the album title *Two Rooms*?
3 Who took "Bye Bye Baby" to the top in 1975?
4 What instrument is on the back cover of Stevie Wonder's *Hotter Than July* LP?
5 Who was singing about "My Guy" in 1964?
6 What Buddy Holly song goes: "Oh misery, misery, what's gonna become of me"?
7 Who narrated Jeff Wayne's *War Of The Worlds* album?
8 What sort of entertainment were Simply Red enjoying in 1995?
9 Which group made No. 5 with "De Do Do Do, De Da Da Da?
10 Who told us he was *An Innocent Man*?
11 Who took "Two Can Play at That Game" to No. 2 in the charts?
12 Which George Michael video featured the supermodel Linda Evangelista?
13 How is Roberta Streeter better known?
14 What was Jimi Hendrix's first top ten hit in the UK?
15 Who had Something In Common in 1994?
16 Who said "Don't Turn Around" in 1988?
17 What did Bobby Goldsboro say Hello to in 1974?
18 Which colours did Michael Jackson take to the top in 1991?
19 Who had a hit with "The Fly" the same year?
20 Which song begins "Close your eyes and I'll kiss you, Tomorrow I'll miss you"?

1 "Pacific State" was the first top ten hit for which group?
2 In which decade did Barry Manilow first have a top ten single?
3 Which word goes before Vibes in the EP title by Apache Indian?
4 New Order was formed from the remains of which group?
5 Who had a UK No. 3 hit in 1969 with "Melting Pot"?
6 What was Inner City's follow-up to "Big Fun"?
7 Which female singer released "Ave Maria" in aid of The Malcolm Sargent Cancer Fund for Children?
8 Who had a 90s album called *Cover Shot*?
9 Whose first hit was "Two Princes"?
10 What was Sinead O'Connor's first UK hit?
11 In which film did Kylie Minogue play Lola Lovell?
12 "Come As You Are" and "Lithium" appeared on which album?
13 Which word follows Burning in the song title by Survivor?
14 What was New Kids On The Block's follow-up to "Cover Girl"?
15 In which decade did Johnny Mathis first have a top ten single?
16 Who had an 80s No. 1 with "Merry Christmas Everyone"?
17 Who had an early 90s album called The White Room?
18 What was the name of Ray Charles' backing group?
19 Who released an album in the 70s called *Crepes And Drapes*?
20 Which word completes the song title by The Style Council, "Big _____ Groove"?

1 Which Patrick Swayze film had a top-selling soundtrack album in 1987?
2 Who took "Dr Love" into the top ten in 1976?
3 In which decade were the *Dance Mix* albums first released?
4 Who had a 1986 album called *Disco?*
5 Who sang "He's The Greatest Dancer" in 1979?
6 Who took "Yes Sir, I Can Boogie" to the top of the charts?
7 Who was "Dancing On A Saturday Night" in 1973?
8 Who sang with the Sex-O-Lettes?
9 Who was heard to Rock his Baby in 1974?
10 Who was "Happy Just to Be With You" in 1995?
11 Who had an 80s hit with "Ooh La La La (Let's Go Dancin')"?
12 Who were in a "Gangsta's Paradise" in 1995?
13 What completes the title of Chic's "Dance Dance Dance"?
14 Which word follows Dance Yourself in the song title by Liquid Gold?
15 Which Brothers went "Boom Boom Boom" in the 90s?
16 Which Donna Summer disco hit was at No. 1 when Elvis Presley died?
17 Who were a "Sight For Sore Eyes" in the 90s?
18 Which dance record was the Bee Gees' first 70s No. 1?
19 Which Bee Gees song did N Trance take to the charts nearly 20 years after the original?
20 Who had a 1974 No. 1 with "You're My First, My Last, My Everything"?

1 Kylie Minogue and Prodigy both had hits with different songs that had which common title?
2 What was Whitney Houston's follow-up single to the mega hit "I Will Always Love You"?
3 Which solo singer joined Tina Turner on "On Silent Wings"?
4 Who was the first person to take "Wind Beneath My Wings" into the UK top three?
5 What kind of Suit did Paul Weller sing about?
6 Ben and Tracy hit the charts with "Wrong" under what name?
7 Which George Michael chart success was also a hit for the newly-solo Robbie Williams?
8 What was the next Hot Chocolate re-issue to make the top 20 after the success of "You Sexy Thing"?
9 Which Joan was One Of Us in 1996?
10 What was the first 90s top ten hit for Human League?
11 Which Girl was a follow-up to Babybird's "You're Gorgeous"?
12 Who teamed up with Zucchero on "Senza Una Donna (Only A Woman)'?
13 What was White Town's follow-up to their No. 1 "Your Woman"?
14 How many Seconds featured in the 1994 chart success for Neneh Cherry and Youssou N'Dour?
15 Which Bryan Adams chart success in 1997 was also the title of his then-current album?
16 What followed All Night in the title of Peter Andre's top 20 hit?
17 Which chart hit for Louise was also the title of her debut solo album?
18 "Goodbye Heartbreak" was a third 90s chart success for which duo?
19 How were Cast travelling in October 1996?
20 Who has had hits with both Nick Cave and Keith Washington?

1 What do You Make Me Feel according to the Stylistics?
2 Who had "Sexy Eyes" at No. 4 in 1980?
3 What did Freak Power do after "Turn On" in 1995?
4 What was John Denver's only solo hit single in the UK?
5 What was a No. 2 hit for Andy Williams and a No. 3 for The Beat?
6 Who was Paul McCartney's girlfriend from 1963 to 1966?
7 Who sang with the uncredited Little Eva on "Swinging On A Star"?
8 Who partnered John Oates on "Maneater"?
9 What were them "good ole boys drinkin" in "American Pie"?
10 What is following Cat Stevens in his 1971 hit?
11 What is the real first name of Noddy Holder of Slade?
12 Which song begins "When the moon is in the seventh house, and Jupiter aligns with Mars"?
13 In which decade was Steve Harley born?
14 Who was lead vocalist with Yazoo?
15 Which recording and musical star has written under the pseudonym of Al Grant?
16 How were the Motown writers Eddie, Lamont and Brian better known?
17 Who recited "A Hard Day's Night" dressed as Richard III?
18 How were Limmie, Jimmy and Martha Snell known?
19 Whose first hit was "Get Out of Your Lazy Bed"?
20 How is William Broad better known?

1   "Hold On" was the first top ten for which group?
2   What was Tammy Wynette's real name?
3   Who had an early 90s album called *Home*?
4   Who produced the late 80s album *Black Tie White Noise*?
5   Who had a top ten hit in 1967 with "Tin Soldier"?
6   Whose biopic was called *What's Love Got To Do With It*?
7   What was the title of the Oscar-winning song from *The Little Mermaid*?
8   Which old-timer released an album in 1996 called *Strong Love Affair*?
9   Who had a UK No. 6 in 1984 with "Your Love Is King"?
10 Which word follows When We Were in the song title by Bucks Fizz?
11 Who had an 80s No. 1 with "Nothing's Gonna Stop Us Now"?
12 What was The Human League's follow-up to "Mirror Man"?
13 Who had the ad hit "Jeans On"?
14 Which word starts song titles which end in Love and Surrender?
15 Who had a 90s album called *Laid*?
16 'Ain't Nobody' was the first top ten hit for which singer?
17 What was Imagination's follow up to 'Just An Illusion'?
18 Which suit of cards gave Lonnie Donegan a UK hit in 1957?
19 Which word follows Every Little in the song title by Bobby Brown?
20 Which country star recorded the album *Images*?

1 In which decade did Status Quo have their first Top Ten hit?
2 Which 50s/60s singer co wrote "Ice in the Sun"?
3 Which Dion hit did they record in 1984?
4 How many US No1 singles did they have in the 70s?
5 In 1988 Status Quo apologized to the UN for performing where?
6 What was Status Quo's first UK hit (no a No. 1) album?
7 What were their 1990 medleys of rock 'n' roll classics called?
8 Which rerecorded song was used for the Race Against Time in 1988?
9 Where was their 1982 hit "Caroline" recorded live?
10 What sort of car was Rick Parfitt driving when he was involved in an accident in 1995?
11 Which game between Great Britain and Australia was about to be played when they sang "Rockin' All Over the World" in 1995?
12 What was the title of their first No. 1 album?
13 In which year did they release no singles, breaking a run of a Top 20 single per year for 12 years ?
14 Which first BBC 2 pop show did they appear on in 1994?
15 Who has been with Quo from the beginning along with Rick Parfitt?
16 Which soccer team did Quo help to the top of the charts in 1994?
17 Which Quo song was the football song based on?
18 What was the name of a single and an album in 1986?
19 Who refused to play Status Quo in 1996 saying they were too old?
20 Who wrote the *Status Quo* autobiography in 1993?

1 What was coupled with Wham's "Everything She Wants'?
2 What was John Lennon's first No. 1?
3 What was the last No. 1 of the 80s?
4 What was the Christian name of the poor guy considered to be the "Coward Of The County"?
5 What was Kylie Minogue's second solo No. 1?
6 Which line goes before, "And I'll cry if I want to, cry if I want to"?
7 Blondie's "The Tide Is High" came from which album?
8 Volver A Empezar were the bracketed words in which title?
9 Which No. 1 had a video featuring Ian McKellan as a Dracula-like figure?
10 What was on the other side of "Going Underground"?
11 Who became the only performer to have No. 1s in the 50s, 60s, 70s and 80s?
12 Loleatta Holloway's disco anthem "Sensation" was shamelessly sampled on which hit?
13 Don McLean took "Crying" to No. 1 in 1980 but who had the original?
14 Which newspaper helped the Ferry Aid project that took "Let It Be" to No. 1?
15 Which No. 1 had the line, "Life, Jim, but not as we know it"?
16 What was the first No. 1 for ELO?
17 Under which title did a remix of the *Doctor Who* theme make No. 1?
18 Which Blondie No. 1 came from the soundtrack of *American Gigolo*?
19 Under what name did Christopher John Davidson have a No. 1?
20 Joe Loss' "March Of The Mods" featured on which No. 1?

LEVEL 2

1 Which song begins "Why do birds suddenly appear, ev'ry time you are near"?
2 Who had the No. 1 "Don't Give Up On Us"?
3 What is the logo of the British record label Parlophone?
4 Who had the first instrumental No. 1 hit in 1953?
5 Who resigned as a Radio 1 DJ when he couldn't have Fridays off?
6 In which decade was Roberta Flack born?
7 Who was "Dancing On The Ceiling" according to his 1986 hit?
8 Who was a "junkie" according to Bowie's "Ashes To Ashes"?
9 On which tube station were the New Vaudeville Band in 1967?
10 Which *Mary Poppins* song won an Oscar in 1964?
11 Which bathroom item was advertised by "Raindrops Keep Falling On My Head" in 1997?
12 Which song has been a hit for Doris Day and Tracey Ullman?
13 Which part of which day features in song titles by Cat Stevens and Barry Blue?
14 What was the Miami Sound Machine's first UK hit?
15 Which country does Eddy Grant originate from?
16 Which London store refused Jason Donovan entry because he was improperly dressed?
17 Who were Frankie Lymon's youthful backing group?
18 In which country was Peter Andre brought up outside the UK?
24 Which Chris's classic is 'Driving Home For Christmas'?
20 Who sang about "The Living Years" in 1989?

1 Which actor sang the TV theme song "I Could Be So Good For You"?
2 Which method of transport appears on the *Bat Out Of Hell* album sleeve?
3 Which river gave The Piranhas a hit in 1982?
4 Who took "True Love" to No. 4 in 1956 with Bing Crosby?
5 In which decade did Michael Jackson first have a top ten single?
6 Which Osmond was married in June 1982 before 3,000 Mormons?
7 "Run To The Hills" was the first top ten hit for which group?
8 Which group released an 80s album called *Outlandos D'Amour*?
9 Which word follows Love In The First in the song title by Bananarama?
10 What was Rick Astley's follow-up to "Hold Me In Your Arms"?
11 Which song starts, "I was working in the lab late one night"?
12 What was the first name of Mr Lake from Emerson, Lake and Palmer?
13 Who had an 80s No. 1 with "I Just Can't Stop Loving You"?
14 Up to his death in the mid-70s Paul Kossoff was a member of which band?
15 Who sang with Kenny Rogers on the 1983 hit "Islands In The Stream"?
16 Which word goes before Harmony in the song title by Beloved?
17 Who had a late 70s album called *Give 'Em Enough Rope*?
18 Who had a minor 1994 hit with a cover of Nirvana's "Smells Like Teen Spirit"?
19 In which decade did Jean-Michel Jarre first have a top ten single?
20 Who was the Beautiful South's first female vocalist?

1   What is Reba McEntire's Best Of album called?
2   What is Johnny Cash's singing daughter called?
3   Who had a 60s hit with "Harper Valley P.T.A."?
4   Who was *Sittin' On The Top Of The World* with her successful album?
5   Which three country stars feature on "Honky Tonk Angels"?
6   Who wrote Emmylou Harris's only UK hit, "Here, There And Everywhere"?
7   Whose life was portrayed in the film *Your Cheatin' Heart*?
8   Whose first album hit in the UK was *Good 'N' Country* in 1964?
9   Which country singer wrote a piece for the soundtrack of *Dead Man Walking*?
10 Who recorded the album *Images*?
11 Who is Loretta Lynn's youngest sister?
12 Who did Don Williams Recall in his UK hit?
13 Who wrote "By the Time I Get To Phoenix"?
14 Who sang "Thank God I'm A Country Boy" in the 70s?
15 Whose "The Battle" in 1975 told of the split from his wife Tammy Wynette?
16 Whose *Red River Valley* topped the album charts in 1977?
17 Whose "I'm A Lonesome Fugitive" reflected his life in prison and on the run?
18 Who are referred to as the "first family" of American country music?
19 Which specialist type of singing is Slim Whitman famous for?
20 Which country star recorded an album of ballads called *Time Piece*?

Answers

Stateside (Quiz 159)
1 "White Christmas".   2 Four.   3 Little Eva.   4 Debby Boone.
5 Mariah Carey.   6 "I Want To Hold Your Hand".   7 "I Will Always Love You".
8 Debbie Gibson.   9 Tiffany.   10 Boston.   11 "Hound Dog".   12 America.
13 Johnny Mathis.   14 1980s.   15 Billy Preston.   16 Ella.
17 Bacharach and David.   18 Texas.   19 Tennessee.   20 Elvis Presley.

1 "Mirror Man" was a big 1982 hit for which band?
2 Embarrass yourself and try to complete the French title of Kylie Minogue's 1988 hit "Je Ne Sais Pas"?
3 Alison Moyet went Weak In The Presence Of what?
4 Which Heavy Metal mob charted with "The St Valentine's Day Massacre"?
5 Who sang about the Last Of The Famous International Playboys?
6 What type of Gold invited you to Dance Yourself Dizzy?
7 Supertramp recorded "It's Raining Again" but which solo singer sang "It's Raining"?
8 What was in brackets in the title of Wet Wet Wet's "Angel Eyes"?
9 Who visited the Club Tropicana?
10 How many top ten hits did the Bee Gees have in the 80s?
11 Yazz sang that you should Stand Up For Your what?
12 Which was the only act to have Strawberry as the first part of its name?
13 Which movie gave Ray Parker Jr a big 80s hit?
14 Who sang about Julie and Shirley?
15 Which Ms Williams said Let's Hear It For The Boy?
16 Who took "The Clairvoyant" into the charts?
17 What was Culture Club's follow up to "Do You Really Want To Hurt Me"?
18 What was the year of the Eurythmics' "Sexcrime"?
19 Who declared "We Are Detective"?
20 Which Doris Day hit was revived by Tracy Ullman?

1 Who had a hit with "Mouldy Old Dough"?
2 Which country star is backed by the "Tennessee Two"?
3 Which Welsh singer stipulated that two songs per album be recorded in Welsh?
4 Who does Paul Anka ask "Oh, please, stay with me"?
5 What were the Isley Brothers behind in the title of a hit from 1969?
6 Who had a 1970 hit with a cover version of "I Hear You Knocking"?
7 What was the first UK No. 1 hit for Diana Ross as a solo artist?
8 Which Beatles LP includes "Only A Northern Song" and "Hey Bulldog"?
9 Which single gave the Shadows their first hit without Cliff Richard?
10 Which comedian had a hit with "Splish Splash" in 1958?
11 In which decade was M.C. Hammer born?
12 Who sang "Let's Get Rocked" in 1992?
13 Whose *Private Collection* album consisted of hits from 1977–1988?
14 Who featured with Robert Miles on the 1996 hit "One and One"?
15 Whose 1996 debut single was "Anything"?
16 Which record label do the Spice Girls record on?
17 Which song begins "Wise men say only fools rush in"?
18 Who had *Breakfast At Tiffany's* in 1996?
19 Which food was a 60s hit for Peter Sellers and Sophia Loren?
20 Who played Che in the film *Evita*?

1   "I Need Love" was the first top ten hit for which rapper?
2   Who had a 90s No. 2 album called *Dummy*?
3   Which word goes before Cash in the song title by The Adventures Of Stevie V?
4   Who had a 70s No. 1 with "Whispering Grass"?
5   Which song won Elton John the Best Original Song Oscar in 1995?
6   In which decade did Aretha Franklin first have a top ten single?
7   Which toy product did Hammer help promote in 1991?
8   Who co-wrote "We Are the World" for USA For Africa with Lionel Richie?
9   Which hit song was based on the *EastEnders* theme tune?
10 Who released the album Circle Of One and single "Get Here"?
11 Who had a 60s hit with "Heroes And Villains"?
12 Which group had a 1984 hit called "Michael Caine"?
13 Who had a No. 11 UK hit with "Michelle" in 1966?
14 Who gave the Supremes a hit in 1971 and Bananarama a hit in 1988?
15 On whose Farm was Paul McCartney in a 1974 hit?
16 Who had a 90s No. 1 with the album *Only Yesterday*?
17 What was Five Star's follow-up to "Find The Time"?
18 Who asked for "Two Pints Of Lager And A Packet Of Crisps Please" in 1980?
19 Who had a 80s No 1 album called *The Final Cut*?
20 In which decade did Focus first have a top ten single?

1 Which song has been a bestseller in the US every year since 1942?
2 How many members of Boyz II Men are there?
3 Who was only 17 when she had a US hit with "The Locomotion"?
4 Who had the 70s US best seller "You Light Up My Life"?
5 Who sang with Boyz II Men on "One Sweet Day"?
6 What is the Beatles' best-selling single in the US?
7 Which female vocalist's No. 1 was the first to top 4 million US sales in the 1990s?
8 Which American starred as Sandy in *Grease* in London in the 90s?
9 Whose debut single was "I Think We're Alone Now"?
10 Which US group are named after a US town and had a debut album of the same name in 1977 and another in 1981?
11 What is on the other side of Elvis's "Don't Be Cruel"?
12 Who recorded "A Horse With No Name"?
13 Who had a 50s album called *Heavenly*?
14 In which decade did Garth Brooks first top the US country charts?
15 Which American joined the Beatles on "Get Back"?
16 Which US jazz singer recorded "Can't Buy Me Love" as a single?
17 Which Americans wrote "Walk On By", a 90s hit for Gabrielle?
18 In which US state was The Best Little Whorehouse in the musical film?
19 What was Ernie Ford's nickname?
20 Who has had most chart albums in the US?

1 Which 70s No. 1 gave Steps a huge 90s hit?
2 What were the main instruments featured in the No. 1 version of "Amazing Grace"?
3 With which group did singer Tony Orlando make it to No. 1?
4 Which "singing tent" made No. 1?
5 Which No. 1 tackled the delicate subject of inability to consummate a marriage?
6 Which song took a Dad's Army star to No. 1?
7 Who took a reworking of The Crickets' song "Oh Boy" to No. 1?
8 Which No. 1 mentions the character Heathcliff?
9 Which 70s No. 1 provided Boy George with an 80s No. 1?
10 Which song sticking at 3 stopped Abba having seven consecutive No. 1s?
11 Which No. 1 has the words, "I kept my promise, Don't keep your distance"?
12 What was Gary Glitter's first No. 1?
13 Who was the only artist to have a No. 1 mentioning Liverpool?
14 What was the first word uttered on "Mouldy Old Dough"?
15 How many No. 1s did Slade have in the 70s?
16 Where did Suzi Quatro Come Alive?
17 What was T-Rex's last 70s No. 1?
18 Which No. 1 had the literary gem of a line, "We don't need no education"?
19 Who had two No. 1s both with Eyes in the title?
20 What was the theme from TV's *Seven Faces Of Woman* that reached No. 1?

1　Which playing card gave Lonnie Donegan a hit in 1957?
2　Who was born Wynette Pugh in 1942?
3　Which religious ballad was a No. 1 for Elvis in 1965?
4　Who was doing A Whole Lotta Shakin in 1957?
5　What album did "Candle In The Wind" come from?
6　Whose only UK No. 1 was "She"?
7　What is Herb Alpert's home country?
8　What type of soldier was a hit for the Small Faces?
9　In which decade was Marvin Gaye born?
10　Who else is mentioned by name in "Eleanor Rigby"?
11　On which ill-fated flight was the Everly Brothers' Ebony Eyes?
12　Which husband-and-wife team wrote "Don't Sleep in the Subway"?
13　"Girls On Film" was the first top ten hit for which group?
14　Whose first No. 1 was "Go Now" in 1964?
15　Which comedy group invited us to "Always Look On The Bright Side Of Life" in 1991?
16　Which 1989 film was the Oscar-winning "Under The Sea" from?
17　Whose recording names have included Bonnie Jo Mason and Cherilyn?
18　In which decade did Art Of Noise first have a top ten single?
19　Which half of a duo celebrated his 60th birthday on February 1, 1997?
20　What was the name of the film in which Elvis Presley appeared as himself?

1 Who was the first German band to have a UK No. 1 in 1982?
2 "What Have You Done For Me Lately" was the first top ten hit for which singer?
3 Who went on a Day Trip To Bangor?
4 Who released the album *Love Over Gold*?
5 Who was lead vocalist of the Three Degrees?
6 What was the theme song from *Aladdin*?
7 Which band released the *Out Of The Blue* album?
8 What type of heart does everybody have according to Bruce Springsteen?
9 Which member of The Beatles was the eldest?
10 A-Ha were on a Train Of what?
11 Who had an 80s No. 1 with "Star Trekkin"?
12 In which decade did The Elgins first have a top ten single?
13 What was Bucks Fizz's follow-up to "If You Can't Stand The Heat"?
14 How many girls were in Ace Of Base?
15 "We skipped the light fandango,' is the first line of which 60s world smash?
16 Whose first hit was "Lost In France"?
17 Which word completes the song title by Altered Images, "I Could Be ____'?
18 In which film did Phil Collins sing "Groovy Kind Of Love"?
19 Which Prime Minister said that the 60s instrumental "Telstar" was a favourite of theirs?
20 Which band came sang "Honaloochie Boogie, yeah" in a 70s hit?

1   What is the name of Jackson's second wife?
2   Which part in *The Wiz* was Jackson chosen to play in 1977?
3   What was his first solo No. 1?
4   Which record label did he move to with his brothers after leaving Motown?
5   What was the first hit he had with Paul McCartney?
6   Who is credited with Jackson on the sleeve of "I Can't Stop Loving You" but not on the label?
7   What type of creature is his pet Muscles?
8   "Happy" was the love theme from which film?
9   Which horror film actor raps on the album *Thriller*?
10 Which particular item of clothing did the Michael Jackson doll have?
11 What is the name of Jackson's pet chimpanzee?
12 What was his autobiography called?
13 What was Jackson's next No. 1 album after *Bad*?
14 Which film were "Scream" and "Childhood" from?
15 Who duetted with Michael on "Scream"?
16 What were Lisa Marie Presley's grounds for divorce from Jackson?
17 Which other male vocalist appears on the ...*Very Best Back to Back* album?
18 Who else is on the 1983 Greatest Hits album?
19 What was his 1995 No. 1 album called?
20 What is the youngest Jackson brother called?

1   Which band sang about Brother Louie?
2   What was the first of Showaddywaddy's top ten hits?
3   Who managed to get a Cat and a Tiger into hit titles?
4   Jimmy Lea co-wrote the hits for which band?
5   Who had a huge 1970 hit with "Question"?
6   Which Lady did Cat Stevens sing about?
7   Who led The Wombles?
8   What type of game did Andy Williams play in a big hit from 1973?
9   Which group had a top three hit with "Part Of The Union"?
10 What was the first top ten hit for KC and the Sunshine Band?
11 Who wanted to do The Bump?
12 "Have you seen the old man outside the seamen's mission" comes from which song?
13 Who had a hit with "Father Christmas Do Not Touch Me"?
14 Which band was fronted by Jeff Lynne?
15 Who took "One Man Band" into the charts?
16 Who did Donna Summer team up with for "No More Tears (Enough Is Enough)'?
17 Who sang about a Silver Lady?
18 Under which name did Jonathan King record "Loup Di Love"?
19 What was Paul McCartney's first solo hit?
20 Which group had Ray Dorsey on vocals?

Answers

Queen (Quiz 168)
1 Freddie Mercury.   2 Hyde Park.   3 Montserrat Caballé.   4 *Queen's First EP*.
5 *News Of The World*.   6 "Under Pressure".   7 The Beatles.   8 *Innuendo*.
9 "Flash".   10 "Bohemian Rhapsody".   11 Brian May.   12 Made In Heaven.
13 Bicycle.   14 Five Live.   15 Knebworth.   16 Freddie Mercury.
17 Drums.   18 "Bohemian Rhapsody".   19 White.   20 70s.

1 Which film gave Cliff Richard his first lead role and fifth British No. 1?
2 Who had a No. 1 in 1954 with "Secret Love"?
3 What was "your love" according to Sade?
4 Who was the lead singer with the Union Gap on "Young Girl"?
5 What Human League hit was the only single to sell over a million in the UK in 1981?
6 In which decade was k.d. lang born?
7 What colour ribbons was Harry Belafonte singing about in 1957?
8 Which Barbra Streisand hit starts "Memories light the corners of my mind"?
9 What colour suit is Michael Jackson wearing on the cover of the *Thriller* album?
10 Who treated Neil Sedaka "cruel" in his No. 3 hit from 1959?
11 Which song begins "What would you do if I sang out of tune"?
12 Who had a No. 1 hit with "Rose Marie"?
13 Whose combined age was over 100 when they had a hit with "Unchained Melody"?
14 Which Dire Straits hit is the title of a Shakespeare play?
15 In which language did Charles Aznavour sing his only UK No. 1?
16 Who had a hit with "Distant Drums"?
17 Which make of car did Sting's "Englishman in New York" advertise?
18 Which film did "The Harry Lime Theme" come from?
19 Whose "Mannish Boy" was used in a jeans ad?
20 What type of music was Scott Joplin famous for?

1 After a quarter of a century gap Shirley Bassey was back in the top 20 featured with which act?
2 "Dr Beat" was the first top ten hit for which singer?
3 Which word follows The Space in the song title by Adamski?
4 In which decade did an England World Cup squad first have a top ten single?
5 What was the title of the first No. 1 album for Fine Young Cannibals?
6 What was David Bowie's follow-up to "Peace On Earth"/"Little Drummer Boy"?
7 Which Shakespearean character gave Petula Clark a UK No 3?
8 Who had a Midlife Crisis in 1992?
9 What was Lynsey De Paul's first UK top ten hit?
10 What is Billy Ocean's real name – Leslie Sebastian what?
11 Who established The Mothers Of Invention in 1966?
12 Who had a UK No. 9 hit in 1983 with "Love On Your Side"?
13 Which word follows Thought I'd Died And Gone To in the song title by Bryan Adams?
14 Who had an 80s No. 1 with "Nothing's Gonna Change My Love For You"?
15 Which River links Danny Williams and Andy Williams?
16 Who released the 80s album The Whole Story?
17 Which Free single was a top ten hit in both 1970 and 1991?
18 What was the real name of the late, great Billy Fury?
19 Who had a 70s No. 1 album called " ?
20 What was Bronski Beat's follow-up to "Why"?

1 Who felt we were on the "Eve of Destruction" in 1965?
2 Which Joan Baez hit became a civil rights anthem?
3 Maddy Prior has been linked with which band since the 70s?
4 In which language did Fairport Convention sing their first UK hit?
5 How are Yarrow, Stookey and Travers better known?
6 Who wrote "Leaving On A Jet Plane"?
7 In which decade was Pete Seeger born?
8 What was Joan Baez's first UK Top Ten hit?
9 Which song with words from the Old Testament was a 60s hit for the Byrds?
10 Who wrote the 1965 No. 1 for the Byrds, "Mr Tambourine Man"?
11 Who wrote "Streets Of London"?
12 Whose first hit was "Meet Me On The Corner" in 1972?
13 Which Rainy Day Women were a hit for Bob Dylan in 1966?
14 Which musical instrument did Martin Carthy play?
15 Who had a UK top ten hit with "Both Sides Now"?
16 What is the nationality of Leonard Cohen?
17 Who wrote "The Last Thing On My Mind"?
18 What was Simon and Garfunkel's first UK Top Ten hit?
19 Which folk singer's songs feature on the Joan Baez album *Any Day Now*?
20 Which five-piece group recorded "Light Flight"?

1 Who was the oldest member of Queen?
2 Where did Queen play a free concert in London in 1976?
3 Who did Freddie Mercury record "Barcelona" with to tie in with the 1992 Summer Olympic Games?
24 What was their first EP called?
5 Which 70s album shared its name with a newspaper?
6 Which hit with David Bowie featured on the album *Hot Space*?
7 By the end of the 90s who were the only band to have sold more albums than Queen?
8 Which album in 1991 was also the name of a No. 1 single?
9 Which 80s hit had the name of its film soundtrack in the title?
10 Which song was re-released to coincide with the movie *Wayne's World* where it was featured?
11 Which member of the band recorded the solo album *Back To The Light*?
12 Which 1995 album was dedicated to the "immortal spirit of Freddie Mercury"?
13 What sort of race was on the other side of "Fat Bottomed Girls"?
14 Which EP shared its name with a real-life radio station?
15 Which stately home was the scene of Queen's final live concert?
16 Which member of the band was born outside the UK?
17 Which instrument did Roger Taylor play?
18 What was the first track on A Night At The Opera?
19 What was the background colour of the cover of "Bohemian Rhapsody"?
20 Which decade's hits featured on the album *Live Killers*?

1 What was George Michael's first solo album?
2 Who won the British Rock and Pop Best Female Singer award in 1978 and 1979?
3 Which word links a Sinatra hit and an instrumental by Acker Bilk?
4 Who is on the cover of the *Guilty* album with Barbra Streisand?
5 What was Tommy Steele's first No. 1?
6 Who was Twistin' the Night Away in 1962?
7 What Connie Francis hit says: "Yours was red, mine was baby pink"?
8 What group's first No. 1 was "True"?
9 What is a beguine in the classic "Begin the Beguine"?
10 How many tears did the Goombay Dance Band sing about in 1982?
11 Who was the only American to have a UK No. 1 in 1963?
12 Who had a 70s No. 1 with "The Streak"?
13 Who had the original hit with "Matthew And Son"?
14 Which song begins "Desmond has a barrow in the marketplace"?
15 Who had a 1996 album called *A Different Beat*?
16 Which fictional doctor did Andy Stewart sing about?
17 What did Stephen Stills suggest doing if you "couldn't be with the one you love"?
18 Whose first hit was "Second Hand Rose"?
19 Who had a 1996 album called *Take Two*?
20 Which Simon and Garfunkel song was a 1996 hit for Suggs?

1 Who recorded the album *Miaow*?
2 In which decade did Dollar first have a top ten single?
3 Who had a top ten album called *Fear Of A Black Planet*?
4 Which word starts song titles which end in Jessie and Prudence?
5 Who took "You Really Got Me" to No. 1 in 1964?
6 A disaster at which soccer ground led to the fund-raising disc "Ferry 'Cross the Mersey"?
7 Which word completes the song title by Paul Young, "Love Of The _____ People"?
8 Who had a 90s album called *King For A Day, Fool For A Lifetime*?
9 What was the first Eternal single that failed to reach the top ten?
10 Which easy listening group included the two Clusky brothers?
11 What was Sid Vicious' real name?
12 "Touch Me" was the first top ten hit for which singer?
13 Who had an 80s No. 1 with "Doctorin' The Tardis"?
14 What was the Backstreet Boys' follow-up to "Get Down (You're The One For Me)"?
15 Which word starts song titles which end in Moon and Velvet?
16 "Johnny Come Home" was the first top ten hit for which group?
17 In which decade did Adam Faith first have a top ten single?
18 Which word follows Don't Turn in the song title by Ace Of Base?
19 Whose debut album was called City To City?
20 What was on the other side of the Sex Pistols' 'My Way"?

1   In which part of London was David Bowie born?
2   What was the name of his first No. 1 album?
3   Which novelty disc did he make imitating Anthony Newley?
4   Which new record label turned down Bowie in 1968?
5   In which important space year was "Space Oddity" first released?
6   Who was his first wife?
7   Which Bowie song was a hit for Lulu?
8   Which stage persona did Bowie introduce in 1972?
9   Why did Bowie leave on the *QE2* for the US in 1973?
10 Which Lou Reed hit was co-produced by David Bowie?
11 Which model appears on the album cover of *Pin-Ups*?
12 What was his son Joe originally called?
13 In which film did he play the title role in 1975?
14 Which role did he play on Broadway in 1980?
15 Which film did he make with Tom Conti?
16 Which song did he record for the Band Aid Trust?
17 In which film did he play the Goblin King?
18 Which record label did he sign to in 1995?
19 What was Serious in the title of his 1983 Tour?
20 Which music industry charity did he become patron of in 1994?

1 In 1996 Oasis filled which stadium – the home of their favourite football club?
2 Which 80s rock festival stars made the album *Who Made Who* in 1986?
3 What did Pink Floyd perform in Berlin in 1990 for a charity concert?
4 Whose stadium performances were documented on the video Electronic Punks?
5 Which Berkshire venue was Thin Lizzy's last UK show?
6 Who had a series of concerts at Wembley Stadium in 1995 after the success of their albums *Crossroads* and *These Days*?
7 What was R.E.M.'s follow up to *Murmur*?
8 Which single was the follow up to The Verve's first No. 1?
9 What was the name of Mark Knopfler's less famous Dire Straits brother?
10 What were Supergrass Pumping on in 1999?
11 What part of his body did Def Leppard drummer Steve Allen lose in a car crash in 1984 but returned to work two months later?
12 Which guitarist did Mark Knopfler make the album *Neck And Neck* with?
13 Which top live band of the 70s first performed live as Quiet Melon and charted with "Stay With Me"?
14 "Drive" was on which R.E.M. album?
15 What was The Who's famous live album called?
16 Who had ten consecutive top three albums in the 80s including *Duke* and *Abacab*?
17 Which band were "Born To Be Wild" in 1969 but still tour in the 1990s?
18 Where was the Essex V-99 festival, attended by Supergrass, Stereophonics and others?
19 What was the title of Bon Jovi's Christmas release in 1994?
20 Which member of U2 played the drums?

1   What is step three in "Three Steps to Heaven"?
2   Who have all the luck according to a Rod Stewart 1984 hit?
3   Who was backed by the Raelettes?
4   Which Boomtown Rats song goes "Walk, don't walk, talk, don't talk"?
5   Who is on the inside cover of the Who's *Quadrophenia* album?
6   In which decade was Des O'Connor born?
7   Which 70s band had an album called *Crepes and Drapes*?
8   Whose first chart hit was "Mandinka"?
9   What was Joe Cocker's first No.1?
10 Who did Buddy Holly love with a heart so rare and true?
11 Who was the only American soloist to have a UK No. 1 in 1964?
12 Who in 1968 were the second married couple to have a No. 1 hit?
13 Who were Dion's backing group?
14 Who were Young At Heart in 1993?
15 In which decade was Jose Feliciano born?
16 Which Brothers were Ronald, Rudolph and O'Kelly?
17 Which country is the orchestra leader Bert Kaempfert from?
18 Which "Fantasy League" stars featured on "Three Lions"?
19 Who was behind Sakkarin with the 70s hit "Sugar Sugar"?
20 Who represented the UK in the Eurovision Song Contest in 1996?

1 Which '60s Scottish folk singer was famous for his hat?
2 According to Elvis Costello in 1981 it was a Good Year for the what?
3 What did Boy George once say was preferable to sex?
4 Whose debut album was *Prodigal Sista*?
5 Who topped the US chart in the 70s with a cover of Bob Marley's "I Shot the Sheriff"?
6 Whose 1996 album was *William Bloke*?
7 Who was the biggest-selling country artist of the 90s worldwide?
8 What was Alanis Morissette's follow-up to *Jagged Little Pill*?
9 Which fellow-soloist did Bryan Adams sing with on "I Finally Found Someone" in 1997?
10 What was Gary Barlow's first solo album?
11 Who released *My Love Is Your Love* at the end of the 90s?
12 Who became Mrs Fatboy Slim in 1999?
13 Whose *Private Collection* was of hits from 1979-1988?
14 Who had a solo album *Golden Heart* in 1996 after going solo?
15 Who released an album of *The Globe Sessions*?
16 Whose debut solo album was *Shepherd Moons*?
17 Which Beatles star's ex-wife married Eric Clapton?
18 How was Stuart Leslie Goddard better known in the 80s?
19 Who released the album *Time* after appearing at the 1999 Party In The Park?
20 Whose *Simply The Best* includes "River Deep Mountain High"?

Quiz 175 Tom Jones

Answers – see page 379

LEVEL 2

1 In which decade was Tom Jones born?
2 How old was he when he first married?
3 What was his first album called?
4 Which song did he sing for a James Bond film?
5 Which city was the subject of a 1967 hit?
6 Who also features on his 1988 hit "Kiss"?
7 At which venue was he on a *Live* 1967 album?
8 Which Royal event was he invited to sing at in 1969?
9 What was his second chart-topper?
10 What was his first No. 1 album?
11 He produced a live album from which US city in 1969?
12 Which 70s hit had previously been recorded by Ben E. King and Shirley Bassey?
13 Who did he record "All You Need Is Love" with in aid of Childline?
14 According to an American critic, Tom Jones made which act possible?
15 In which style did he wear his hair in the early days?
16 Who was the projected musical *Matador* about?
17 Which Phyllis Nelson hit did he record in the 80s?
18 Which hit single came from *Matador*?
19 Which George Martin-produced recording did he feature on with other Welsh performers?
20 How many Smash Hits were on his 1967 album?

David Bowie (Quiz 171)
1 Brixton. 2 *Aladdin Sane*. 3 "The Laughing Gnome". 4 Apple. 5 1969.
6 Angela (Barnet). 7 "The Man Who Sold the World". 8 Ziggy Stardust.
9 He is afraid of flying. 10 "Walk On The Wild Side". 11 Twiggy.
12 Zowie. 13 *The Man Who Fell To Earth*. 14 The Elephant Man.
15 *Merry Christmas Mr Lawrence*. 16 "Dancing In The Street". 17 *Labyrinth*.
18 Virgin. 19 Moonlight. 20 War Child.

1 Who had the 1986 album *Appetite For Destruction*?
2 Which Wings hit was the title of a nursery rhyme?
3 Which group's "Our House" was used in 1999 in a docu-soap about estate agents?
4 What was Meat Loaf's first 80s hit?
5 Which band included Paul Heaton and Norman Cook among their line-up?
6 How was Newsworthy Hugh Cregg III better known?
7 Whose *Business As Usual* featured the No. 1 "Down Under"?
8 Which 90s Guns N'Roses hit shared its name with a James Bond movie?
9 Which 80s Manchester-based band included Peter Hook and Bernard Sumner?
10 Who did the Pet Shop Boys collaborate with in the charts and on the soundtrack of the movie *Scandal*?
11 "Every Little Thing She Does Is Magic" featured on which Police album?
12 Which Smokey Robinson hit took Japan to No. 9 in 1982?
13 Which Prefab Sprout album titled with the name of an actor was retitled in the US because his family objected?
14 Which Police CD set's title was reminiscent of an early hit single?
15 Who followed their first No. 1 with "Bed Sitter" in 1981?
16 Two members of which 80s success starred in *The Krays* in 1990?
17 Whose first top ten entry was "The Sun Goes Down (Living It Up)'?
18 Which band did three of The Specials form when they left ?
19 In The Smiths, what was Morrissey's first name?
20 What type of Drum was a chart album success for Japan?

1 What were the Moody Blues "in search of" in 1968?
2 Who produced the 1984 Lionel Richie hit "Hello"?
3 What was The Who's first top ten LP in the USA?
4 What group suggested "a great big melting pot"?
5 Who was the first on-stage Evita?
6 What does "everybody" have according to Bruce Springsteen?
7 What is on the front cover of the *Out Of The Blue* album by ELO?
8 Which movie had "Up Where We Belong" as its theme?
9 Whose face is on the cover of the *No Jacket Required* album?
10 There "ain't no way to hide" what according to the Eagles?
11 Who had an album called *Love Over Gold*?
12 Who was a Professional Widow in 1997?
13 Sheila Ferguson was vocalist with which group?
14 What was Fiddler's Dram's destination in 1979?
15 Who had a 1983 No. 1 with "Only You"?
16 Which number *Now That's What I Call Music!* topped the compilation charts at the beginning of 1997?
17 Which manager promoted the Four Tops on their early 60s visits to the UK?
18 What is Boris Gardiner's home country?
19 What was Art Garfunkel's first solo No. 1?
20 In which decade was Natalie Cole born?

1 What was Billie's follow up to "Because We Want To"?
2 How is Yvette Marie Stevens who had a hit with "I'm Every Woman" better known?
3 "Sunday Girl" featured on which Blondie album?
4 Who had The Voice Of An Angel?
5 How is Patricia Andrzejewski who made the 1997 album *Inamorata* better known?
6 At which airport did Björk famously assault a journalist?
7 Whose first No. 1 was the title of a Brontë novel?
8 Whose Best Of album was called *Tried And True*?
9 In the mid-90s Cerys Matthews became lead singer with which band?
10 Which female singer performed with the Miami Sound Machine?
11 On which Nights were Sheryl Crow's debut album recorded?
12 Who recorded "It Isn't, It Wasn't, It Ain't Never Gonna Be" with Aretha Franklin?
13 What followed "Nobody Love" on the title of Suzy Bogguss' album?
14 Which Gloria Gaynor No. 1 is one of the biggest karaoke hits of all time?
15 Who is Natalie's sister in All Saints?
16 Tracy Chapman's "Baby Can I Hold You" became a hit for which boy band?
17 How is Eithne Ni Bhraonain better known?
18 Whose debut album was *Pieces*?
19 Which then-supermodel girlfriend did Billy Joel dedicate "Uptown Girl" to?
20 Which singer was Mrs Andrew Lloyd-Webber but not Lady Lloyd-Webber?

LEVEL 2

1 Who was described as, "the tacky tattooed terror of the 20th century."?
2 Who said, "I would not want to be Bach, Mozart, Tolstoy ... or James Dean."?
3 Who said, "I can't picture Jesus doing a whole lotta shakin'."?
4 What did John Lennon tell people in expensive seats to do at a Royal performance, instead of applauding?
5 Who said, "Hair today gone tomorrow," when he joined the Army?
6 Who said, "I really wanted to be a soccer star."?
7 How did Elton John finish "I haven't met anyone I'd like to settle down with..."?
8 Who said, "I never had any problems with drugs, only with policemen."?
9 Who said, "If we hadn't been related we would probably never have gotten back together."?
10 Who said on announcing his second retirement, "I've rocked my roll."?
11 Who said about her early career, "I must have been a revolting little cow."?
12 Which rock star said, "People like their blues singers dead."?
13 Who dedicated his first solo record to his parents: "5 minutes ... for 21 years"?
14 On whose death was the statement made, "As soon as we are able, we would like to celebrate his life in the style to which he was accustomed."?
15 Which band was Mick Taylor referring to when he said he left them because he wanted to be a rock-and-roll star?
16 Who said he let Frank Sinatra have "My Way" because he didn't want to find a horse's head in his bed?
17 Who said, "Marriage is a wonderful invention but so is the bicycle repair kit."?
18 Who was Marvin Gaye referring to when he said, "If he refuses to release me then you'll never hear any more music from Marvin Gaye"?
19 Which female singer said in a song, "Mother stands for comfort"?
20 Dolly Parton said, "It costs a lot to make me look so" what?

1. What was on the other side of Texas's "Say What You Want"?
2. What went after "Popped In" on the title of Wet Wet Wet"s album?
3. Which Glasgow-based band had a 1992 hit with "Reverence"?
4. Which Scots band featured Wu Tang Clan on a 1998 chart success?
5. Which White Band enjoyed 70s success and released a 90s re-mix single?
6. Who backed Lulu in the 60s?
7. Which fashion item was the hallmark of The Bay City Rollers?
8. What is the first name of Texas's lead singer?
9. Which comedian joined Gerry Rafferty in The Humblebums?
10. What sort of town was Big Country's No. 1 1984 album?
11. Who left Bronski Beat to form The Communards?
12. Simple Minds star Jim Kerr expressed an interest in the late 90s in buying which soccer club?
13. Which Twins from Grangemouth charted in 1990 with the album *Heaven Or Las Vegas*?
14. Which Scottish sextet had the million-selling album *When The World Knows Your Name*?
15. After 10 years in the singles charts what eventually hit the No. 1 spot for Simple Minds in 1989?
16. Which Al Green hit was a success for Texas in 1992?
17. What was Big Country's Greatest Hits album called?
18. Ex-Skids member Stuart Adamson formed which band in the 80s?
19. Who were Best Newcomers at the 1988 Brit Awards, the year when "With A Little Help From My Friends" went to No. 1?
20. Which city did the Scottish half of The Eurythmics come from?

1   What word begins song titles that end with "Daddy," "Shack" and "Sugar" ?
2   Which city does the song "Three Coins In A Fountain" refer to?
3   Which Merseyside group got to No. 1 one month before the Beatles in 1963?
4   Who had a No. 1 hit with "Back Home" in 1970?
5   Which pop programme first appeared on screen in November 1982?
6   Which drink did Bob Geldof advertise in 1987?
7   Where, according to Ben E. King, is there a rose?
8   What word begins song titles that end "That A Shame" and "No Sunshine"?
9   On which record label did Cat Stevens record all but one of his LPs?
10 Which pianist had a fifties chart success with "Party Pops"?
11 How many bottles do the Police find "washed up" on the shore?
12 What girl is "always window-shopping but never stopping to buy"?
13 What was Tina Turner's autobiography called?
14 Which song has been a hit for George Michael and Bobbie Williams?
15 Who was the oldest Beatle?
16 In which decade was Noel Gallagher born?
17 Who had a live album *Under A Blood Red Sky*?
18 Which country does Enigma come from?
19 How is Leslie Sebastian Charles better known?
20 Which band did Frank Zappa establish in 1966?

Answers

Pot Luck 88 (Quiz 177)
1 The Lost Chord.   2 Lionel Richie.   3 *Tommy*.   4 Blue Mink.   5 Elaine Paige.
6 A Hungry Heart.   7 A flying saucer.   8 *An Officer Aand A Gentleman*.
9 Phil Collins'.   10 Your lyin' eyes.   11 Dire Straits.   12 Tori Amos.
13 Three Degrees.   14 Bangor.   15 The Flying Pickets.   16 35.
17 Brian Epstein.   18 Jamaica.   19 "I Only Have Eyes For You".   20 1950s.

1 In the US, a record by Ann Orson and Carte Blanche was Elton duetting with which female singer?
2 Which animal lent its name to a 1974 No. 1 album?
3 Who sang an Elton/Bernie Taupin song as a Eurovision choice when "Boom-Bang-A-Bang" won?
4 Which child of a Beatle is Elton a godfather to?
5 Which 1972 album owes its name to where it was made at the Château d'Herouville?
6 In 1997 his costume from which album cover originally featuring "Candle In The Wind" fetched £11,500 at auction?
7 What was the nationality of Elton's wife whom he married in 1984?
8 Which tribute album was celebrating the songs of Elton & Bernie Taupin?
9 Which album featured the Melbourne Symphony Orchestra?
10 Which lyric writer did he team up with in 1967?
11 Who was he Sleeping With according to a 1989 album title?
12 Which middle name did Elton John include when he ceased being Reginald Kenneth Dwight?
13 Which flower was on the front of "Candle In The Wind 97"?
14 Who duetted on "Runaway Train" and appeared with him on a concert tour?
15 Which song from *The Lion King* won an Oscar?
16 Who did Elton duet with on the 90s version of "Don't Go Breaking My Heart"?
17 Which Take That member provided backing vocals for "Can You Feel The Love Tonight"?
18 To whom did he send a letter, "To the queen of country music from the queen of England"?
19 In 1976 he became the first pop star to be immortalised at Madame Tussaud's since whom?
20 Who duetted with him on "True Love" which featured on the album *Duets*?

1   What was Queen's first hit single?
2   Who was the band's bass player?
3   What was the band's first hit album?
4   What was on the other side of "Bicycle Race" in 1978?
5   On which record label did they make their early recordings?
6   Which album was "Killer Queen" on originally?
7   "Bohemian Rhapsody" lasts just under how many minutes?
8   Which album followed *Sheer Heart Attack*?
9   Who was the first member of the group to release a solo disc?
10 Which record tied with "Bohemian Rhapsody" as best-selling single of the period of the Queen's reign, 1952–77, honouring her Silver Jubilee?
11 Freddie Mercury contributed to whose album *Puttin' On the Style*?
12 Which film soundtrack did they record in 1980?
13 Which continent did they visit on their *Gluttons For Punishment* tour?
14 Who used their "I Want to Break Free" for TV commercials?
15 Which South African political group also used "I Want to Break Free"?
16 What was on the other side of "We Will Rock You"?
17 What was Freddie Mercury's first solo album called?
18 Which song did he take to No. 5 in March 1987?
19 What was on the other side of "Bohemian Rhapsody" after its re-release following Freddie Mercury's death?
20 Which album topped the charts in its first week in 1995?

1 Who did Hermann Love on the title of Super Furry Animals' 1997 hit?
2 Who suffered an attack of Road Rage in 1998?
3 Who sang "(If Paradise Is) Half as Nice"?
4 What relation are Manics Sean Moore and James Dean Bradfield?
5 What won the Best Album award at the 1997 Brit Awards for Manic Street Preachers?
6 Which Welsh songstress Mary formed a group called Oasis with Peter Skellern and John Williams long before the Gallagher Brothers?
7 Which Welsh actress formed a duo with David Essex on "True Love Ways" in 1994?
8 What was the first hit Stereophonics had from their album *Performance And Cocktails*?
9 What was the Manic Street Preachers' first hit without Richey Edwards?
10 Which Catatonia album shared its name with a film about horses with Tatum O'Neal?
11 Which duo teamed up for "A Rockin' Good Way" in 1984?
12 Which singer had a huge late 60s hit with the big ballad "This Is My Song"?
13 Which album featured Catatonia' s "You've Got A Lot To Answer For"?
14 Which band suggested "Something 4 The Weekend" in 1996?
15 Which book was the title of the Manic Street Preachers' third chart album?
16 What was the last No. 1 for Shakin' Stevens?
17 What relation is Stereophonics' Kelly Jones to Richard Jones?
18 Which sport features on the title of a Super Furry Animals 1998 hit?
19 At which Welsh Castle did The Stereophonics play to 10,000 people in 1999?
20 Who featured with Tom Jones on "Kiss" in 1988?

1   What was "all over the world" according to The Carpenters in 1976?
2   Who had a hit in 1984 with "You Take Me Up"?
3   Which rock 'N' roll classic opens with: "Get out in that kitchen and rattle those pots and pans"?
4   Who had a No. 5 with "Sugar Me" in 1972?
5   In which film did The Platters perform "Only You" and "The Great Pretender"?
6   Which Chicago hit gave them a Grammy award in 1976?
7   What group consisted of Godley, Creme, Stewart and Gouldman?
8   Which two Williamses had No. 1 hits with "Moon River"?
9   Which song by Barry Manilow starts: "I've been alive forever"?
10 Where were the lights brighter for Petula Clark?
11 Whose autobiography was called *Is That It?*?
12 Who were "All Right Now" in the 70s and again in the 90s?
13 How was the 50s/60s star Ronald Wycherly better known?
14 Which film featured the music "Lara's Theme" which was used in the song "Somewhere My Love"?
15 What was Telly Savalas's only UK No. 1?
16 What was the title of Gerry Rafferty's first album?
17 Who asked, "Ullo John, Got a New Motor?" in 1984?
18 What was Seal's first UK hit?
19 Whose first No. 1 was "Ebeneezer Goode"?
20 What was on the other side of the Sex Pistols's "No One Is Innocent"?

1 Which Irish band contributed "Haunted" to the movie Sid And Nancy?
2 What is the real name of U2's The Edge?
3 In what year did Boyzone first chart?
4 Which member of Clannad featured on Chicane's Saltwater?
5 Which U2 album included "Discotheque" and "Wake Up Dead Man"?
6 In a good week for Ireland who topped the singles chart when Boyzone went to No. 1 with "Where We Belong"?
7 Maire Brennan originally joined Clannad to play which traditional musical instrument?
8 Who duetted with U2 on "When Loves Come To Town"?
9 Whose second album was *No Need to Argue* which featured the single "Zombie"?
10 Which member of U2 recorded with Frank Sinatra?
11 Who was lead singer with Thin Lizzy?
12 Who were "So Young" in 1998?
13 Which Ash single shares its name – but nothing else – with a Bond movie?
14 In what language did Clannad sing their early songs?
15 Who were The Pogues Waiting For on the title of their 1993 album?
16 Which 80s solo singer featured on Clannad's "Both Sides Now" in 1991?
17 Which No. 1 preceded The Boomtown Rats' 'I Don't Like Mondays"?
18 Which original member of Pulp's line-up was born in Belfast?
19 What is the name of the only male member of The Corrs?
20 The first retrospective U2 album featured the best of which years?

1 Who had a 1969 hit with "Frozen Orange Juice"?
2 What was Procul Harum's follow-up to "A Whiter Shade of Pale"?
3 Which solo singer had the best-selling single of 1966?
4 Which Georgie Fame hit was the first No. 1 of 1968?
5 Which group was Paul McCartney's brother in?
6 Which tearjerker was on the other side of "Walk Right Back"?
7 In "A Whiter Shade of Pale" who were leaving for the coast?
8 What was the longest No. 1 single of the 60s?
9 Which song includes the lines "I could be handy mending a fuse, When your lights have gone"?
10 Which two cities are mentioned in "Trains and Boats and Planes"?
11 In which TV show did Mary Hopkin find fame?
12 Who had 1969's best seller "Sugar Sugar"?
13 Who are the two main characters in "Ob-La-Di, Ob-La-Da"?
14 How was "Je Ne Regrette Rien" known in English?
15 What comes after "I've lived a life that's full" in "My Way"?
16 Who did Steve Winwood have a No. 1 with in 1966?
17 Who had a No. 1 "With A Girl Like You"?
18 Which song did the Hollies take to the top twice in 1965?
19 What was on the other side of Cliff Richard's "The Next Time"?
20 Who wrote Petula Clark's "This is My Song"?

1   Which then *Coronation street* husband and wife recorded "Something Stupid" in 1995?
2   Which role in *Coronation Street* did Adam Rickitt play before launching his pop career?
3   Which Leo Sayer hit did Will Mellor chart with in 1998?
4   Which character did Sensational singer Michelle Gayle play in *EastEnders*?
5   Whose first single on leaving *Coronation Street* was "The Heart's Lone Desire"?
6   Denise Welch recorded "You Don't Have To Say You Love Me" in 1995 but how is she better known in Weatherfield?
7   Which soap was Sue Nicholls – aka Audrey in *Coronation Street* – appearing in when she charted in 1968?
8   Which Australian soap star took Bo Diddley's "Mona" into the charts in 1990?
9   Ian Kelsey – *Emmerdale's* David Glover – toured with which show on leaving the Yorkshire soap?
10 Which soap star was the biggest-selling female vocalist of the late 80s?
11 How was Jack Duckworth styled when he had chart success with "One Voice"?
12 Who sang "Where The Wild Roses Grow" with Kylie Minogue in 1995?
13 Which star of *Emmerdale* was the then-youngest *New Faces* winner in the mid 70s?
14 Whose first single on leaving *EastEnders* was "Someone to Love"?
15 The actor who plays *EastEnders* character Steve Owen was in which 80s band?
16 Which pop star name did Tiffany – Martine McCutcheon – give her daughter in *EastEnders*?
17 What, from the musical *Joseph*, was Jason Donovan's third UK No. 1?
18 Which actress who played Sharon in Albert Square charted in 1986 with "Something Outa Nothing"?
19 Which *EastEnders* couple recorded "Better Believe It (Children In Need)" in 1995?
20 Whose top ten hit on leaving *EastEnders* was "Sweetness"?

1 Which word starts song titles which end in "Surrender" and "Music"?
2 Who made his stage debut in 1980 as the *Elephant Man*?
3 Which sixties TV pop show was co-hosted by the boxer Freddie Mills?
4 What sleeps tonight according to the Tokens and Tight Fit?
5 Who was the lead singer for the Bay City Rollers?
6 Who was a Woman In Love according to her 1980 No. 1 hit?
7 What was the title of Chicago's 13th album?
8 Who took "Donna" to No. 3 in 1959?
9 Which Beatles song goes "sont les mots qui vont très bien ensemble"?
10 Who wrote "It Doesn't Matter Anymore"?
11 Stevie Nicks and Christine McVie were in which band in the 70s?
12 Who won the Grammy award for Best Soul Singer from 1967 to 1974?
13 Who had a 90s album called *Bilingual*?
14 How is John Beverley better known?
15 In which decade was the ex-Shadow Jet Harris born?
16 Which actress has been married to recording stars Don Johnson and Antonio Banderas?
17 Who sang about the "Jean Genie" in 1972?
18 How many *letters* are there in the title of Kirsty MacColl's first top twenty hit?
19 Which soundtrack was the top-selling album of 1965, '66 and '68?
20 Who sang "I Could Be So Good For You" from *Minder*?

1   Most members of Abba were born in which decade?
2   Which Kraftwerk album celebrated motorways?
3   Which Swedish band's second top 20 hit was called "Hit"?
4   Which country do The Cardigans hail from?
5   Which 1997 film included "Lovefool" on its soundtrack from The Cardigans?
6   What sort of ride did Roxette have in 1991?
7   Daft Punk came from which country?
8   What colour were The Smurfs from Holland?
9   In 1990 Snap sang Mary Had A Little what?
10 Who insisted, Music Sounds Better with You in 1998?
11 Which country won the last Eurovision Song Contest of the 20th century?
12 "U Got To Know "was the first top ten hit for whom?
13 Who won the Eurovision Song Contest twice for Ireland?
14 Where was Air's 1998 album *Safari*?
15 How many made up the production act Age Of Love?
16 Ace Of Base signed with a Danish record label in the early 90s but where are they from?
17 Which toy gave Aqua chart success?
18 What did Björk Play in 1993 according to her top 20 single?
19 Which Scandinavian group recorded a tribute single to a British soap opera?
20 Which country did Black Box hail from?

1   Which duo's album was the bestseller of 1970 and 1971?
2   Who had a 1970 No. 1 with "Spirit in the Sky"?
3   Which musical did Lee Marvin's "Wandrin' Star" come from?
4   Whose lead singer was Ray Dorset?
5   What was Elvis's first 70s No. 1?
6   Which Beatle had the bestselling single of 1971?
7   What was Elton John's top-selling album of 1973?
8   Who had a hit with "Love Grows (Where My Rosemary Goes)"?
9   What was Gary Glitter's bestseller of 1973?
10 Who wrote *Woodstock* though she only watched the festival on TV?
11 Which chart-topper's catchphrase was "They don't like it up 'em"?
12 Whose album *And I Love You So* was a 1973 best-seller?
13 Who was born Michael Anthony Orlando Cassavitis?
14 Who had a No. 1 with "Chirpy Chirpy Cheep Cheep"?
15 What was Supertramp's best-selling 70s LP?
16 What was "I'd Like To Teach The World To Sing" originally called?
17 Who were Lennie and Di?
18 Who had a compilation LP of their singles from 1969–1973?
19 Which city was home to Paper Lace and gave them their name?
20 Which song had the line "Don't look, Ethel"?

1 Which Girl hails from Yorkshire?
2 Who played their manager in *Spiceworld*?
3 Geri reached No. 1 with a solo single at which attempt?
4 Who couldn't attend the Posh/Beckham wedding due to ill health?
5 Which magazine invented the Sport, Ginger, Baby, Posh and Scary nicknames?
6 What was Geri's debut solo album?
7 What was on the other side of "Who Do You Think You Are"?
8 At which 1999 concert did Mel C launch her solo career?
9 What was the first track on *Spice*?
10 Who is the youngest Spice Girl?
11 What label was their second single recorded on?
12 What is Mel short for in Mel B's name?
13 "Step To Me" advertised which drink?
14 What colour were Posh and David Beckham's wedding reception outfits?
15 Out of their first nine singles which didn't go to No. 1?
16 Which brand of crisps had the five Spice Girls on different flavours?
17 Who was their real-life manager when they first hit the top of the charts?
18 What is Mel B's daughter called?
19 What colour did all the guests have to wear at Mel B's wedding?
20 Which Spice Girl is the only one with a single first name?

1 What type of vehicle is featured on the album sleeve of Meat Loaf's *Bat Out Of Hell*?
2 Which African river gave a hit title to Lou Busch and Eddie Calvert?
3 Who once performed as Artie Garr?
4 EMI used the record-number prefix "Marc" from 1972–77 for which group's releases?
5 Who accompanied Bing Crosby with a 1956 top ten hit "True Love"?
6 What did Lily the Pink invent?
7 Whose first hit which reached No. 1 in 1974 was "Sugar Baby Love"?
8 What is the main colour of the *Brothers In Arms* album cover?
9 Which group got to the top of the charts with "Start"?
10 Who was married in silk taffeta before 3,000 Mormons in June 1982?
11 Which major 60s event was held at the farm of Max Yasgur?
12 Which Pilot hit reached No. 1 on February 1, 1975?
13 Which chart-topper's catchphrase was "Who loves ya, baby?"?
14 How many marriages had Tammy Wynette had when she advised "Stand By Your Man"?
15 Who were the first male/female vocal duo to have two No. 1 hits?
16 "My Sweet Lord" was accused of being like which Chiffons hit?
17 Which Jackie Wilson hit topped the charts two years after his death?
18 Which band was named after a song by Bernard Cribbins?
19 What did Free's "All Right Now" advertise in 1991?
20 Which Rolling Stones hit has the longest title?

1 Who was the youngest Beatle?
2 What sort of Men were John Lennon's skiffle group?
3 In which country did John say the Beatles were more popular than Jesus?
4 Which honour did they receive from the Queen in the mid 60s?
5 "Lucy In the Sky With Diamonds" featured on which album?
6 Who was the last member to join the band?
7 What was their first US No. 1?
8 Which soul singer featured with them on "Get Back"?
9 Which Beatle wrote the classic "Something"?
10 What type of shop did Brian Epstein own near the Cavern?
11 Which band had their first top 20 hit with the Beatles' "I Wanna Be Your Man"?
12 Who became known as the fifth Beatle?
13 Which children's TV show did Ringo narrate?
14 Which song by The Beatles was the first released in the 1990s from a tape recorded by John in the 70s?
15 Which Beatle was left-handed?
16 In which city was Yoko Ono born?
17 Which peace anthem did John and Yoko record at the "bed in"?
18 Where in Germany did The Beatles have bookings in the early 60s?
19 Why was John Lennon threatened with deportation from the USA?
20 "Hey Jude" was their first recording on which label?

1 Who had the album *Eat to the Beat*?
2 Who sang "Together We Are Beautiful"?
3 Who was the Police's drummer?
4 What was the No. 1 sung by St Winifred's School Choir?
5 What was Roxy Music's first No. 1?
6 How many members of Bucks Fizz were there?
7 Which 80s No. 1 was recorded in Spanish?
8 Who wrote and produced "Under Pressure"?
9 Which Motown trio wrote Phil Collins' chart-topper "You Can't Hurry Love"?
10 How many members of Kajagoogoo were there?
11 Whose second album was *Cargo*?
12 What was David Bowie's first No. 1 not to mention Major Tom?
13 Which band included the Kemp brothers?
14 Who sang "I Want to Know What Love Is" in 1985?
15 Who duetted with Philip Bailey on "Easy Lover"?
16 Which single referred to the average age of US soldiers in the Vietnam War?
17 Who were Pal, Mags and Morten?
18 Which part did Nick Berry play in "EastEnders"?
19 What was Madonna's third No. 1?
20 What was the nationality of Aneka who had a hit with "Japanese Boy"?

1 Which author rhymes with Prozac in the line created by Blur's Damon Albarn?
2 Who wrote "Leaving On A Jet Plane"?
3 What were Madness Waiting For in 1986?
4 Which solo singer wrote "I'm A Believer" for The Monkees?
5 Which word follows Double in the 1983 song by Malcolm McLaren?
6 What was Robert Palmer Addicted To in 1986?
7 Which Madonna hit begins, "It won't be easy"?
8 What was the first musical Tim Rice wrote the lyrics for with Lloyd-Webber?
9 Rod Stewart told us "I Don't Want To Talk About It" in 1977 but who expressed the same feeling 11 years later?
10 Who wrote the classic "Streets Of London"?
11 What kind of Minds have been shared chartwise by Fine Young Cannibals and Candi Staton?
12 Which word follows I Second That in the Smokey Robinson song covered by Japan?
13 Which Motorhead single used their own name in the title?
14 Which word goes before Addict in the song by the Pearson family, Five Star?
15 Which song has the line, "Bismillah, no! We will not let you go"?
16 In 1983, Phil Everly said She Means what To Me?
17 What were Australians Flash And The Pan Waiting For in 1983?
18 What was Alison Moyet In The Presence of Beauty in 1987?
19 According to The Jam, in 1983 they had The Bitterest what (I Ever Had To Swallow)?
20 Which prolific song writer penned "By The Time I Get To Phoenix"?

1 Which group were asking "Baby Come Back" in 1968?
2 Which song was a No. 1 for both Tommy Steele and Guy Mitchell in 1956?
3 Where does Bill Haley want to be "when the chimes ring five and six and seven"?
4 Which girl's name gave Kenny Rogers a Grammy Award in 1977?
5 Who started Manfred Mann's Earth Band in 1971?
6 Who, in 1965, got Tired Of Waiting For You?
7 Who released an album entitled *Outlandos D'Amour*?
8 What were the first names of Emerson, Lake and Palmer?
9 Which Beatles record begins and ends with the sound of a jet?
10 Which song includes the lines "Sweet Loretta Martin thought she was a woman, but she was another man"?
11 Who had the album *Circle of One*?
12 In which decade was Bryan Ferry born?
13 Who had a 60s hit with "God Only Knows"?
14 How old was Karen Carpenter when she died?
15 Which film star was the title of a single by Madness?
16 Who had a 60s hit single with "Michelle"?
17 Which two groups had hits with "Nathan Jones"?
18 Who was on Junior's Farm in 1974?
19 Which song title links James Taylor, and Big Fun and Sonia?
20 What did Splodgenessabounds ask for in 1980?

The Hard Questions

This, of course, is where you sort the sheep from the goats. To succeed in this section requires a detailed knowledge of your subject and only the very best contestants will be able to stay afloat. This section is used to grind down the remaining contestants until only the very best remain. Let's face it, even to want to know some of the strange facts contained in this section requires a somewhat quirky view of reality.

Unless you're dealing with hardened quiz fanatics, use this section sparingly because you don't want to spoil people's fun by firing off a string of unanswerable questions.

1 In the 1990s Sweet's Brian Connolly discovered which TV detective was his natural brother?
2 In which film did Elvis play the role of Clint Reno?
3 Who released an album entitled *The Dream of the Blue Turtles*?
4 What was Russ Conway's second No. 1?
5 Who wrote "World Without Love" for Peter and Gordon?
6 Who was Capital Radio's choice as Best London Artist from 1978–80?
7 Who is the biopic *La Bamba* about?
9 Which 90s chart-topper had a fitness video called *A New Attitude*?
9 Who had a hit in 1981 with "Shaddap you face"?
10 Who wrote the lyric to the theme from Exodus?
11 Who said, "If music be the food of love, let's have a Beethoven butty"?
12 In which town was Marc Almond born?
13 Who backed Graham Parker?
14 What was Glenn Medeiros's debut album called?
15 Why did Donovan spend two weeks in Strangeways Prison in Manchester in the early 60s?
16 In which sport did Billy Joel excel when at school?
17 Which band was once called the Ravens?
18 Which group's name is the German for "power plant"?
19 Who won the Logie Award for Best New Talent in Australia in 1987?
20 Which two bands have President Bill Clinton's middle name in their names?

1   Which 90s album contains the tracks "Sour Times" and "It Could Be Sweet"?
2   "Flowers In The Rain" was famously the first record played on Radio 1; what was the second?
3   Whose band The Bar Keys perished in a 60s plane crash?
4   What was the first top ten hit for The Adventures Of Stevie V?
5   Who had an early 90s album called *Enchanted*?
6   What was Amen Corner's follow-up single to "(If Paradise Is) Half As Nice"?
7   Who had a 80s album called *Dada*?
8   Who said "I Love Your Smile"?
9   Who is in the letter P on the cover of the album Spice World?
10 What was Abba's follow-up to "Waterloo"?
11 Which No. 2 hit was the theme from TV's *Life And Times Of David Lloyd George*?
12 What is the last word of "The Power Of Goodbye" by Madonna?
13 Which song was at No. 1 at the time of the 1997 general election?
14 Which album contains the track "Die Young And Stay Pretty"?
15 What breed of dog was Madonna's Chiquita?
16 Who followed up a No. 1 with "Ohh To Be Ah"?
17 What is the last word of "Good Enough" by Dodgy?
18 What was All About Eve's first top ten hit?
19 On whose US show did The Simpsons first appear?
20 Which 1999 chart-topper used to be in a band called Wind In The Willows?

Answers

Pot Luck 4 (Quiz 6)
1 Leeds.   2 "Black Or White".   3 PWL Continental.   4 NW8.
5 *Dog Man Star* by Suede.   6 "I Swear".   7 More.   8 "Sky Pilot".
9 "Red Red Wine".   10 Chumbawamba.   11 Betty Everett.
12 "What Do You Want To Make Those Eyes At Me For".   13 Right.
14 "Lady Lynda".   15 Deuce.   16 Louise Jameson.   17 Shaggy.
18 "Gangsta's Paradise" by Coolio featuring LV.   19 Dexy's Midnight Runners.
20 Big Audio Dynamite.

1   Where was Emile Ford born?
2   Which chart-topper appeared on BBC TV's *Drumbeat*?
3   Who had a 50s No. 1 with "Here Comes Summer"?
4   Who played the piano on Bobby Darin's "Dream Lover"?
5   How was Terence Perkins better known?
6   What was Marty Wilde's highest chart hit?
7   Which female singer starred in *It's Trad Dad*?
8   What was Cliff Richard's middle name when he was Harry Webb?
9   Who was the first solo instrumentalist to have consecutive No. 1 hits?
10   Which female had four top ten hits in 1952?
11   Who sang the English version of "Le Jour Où La Pluie Viendra"?
12   Who was the resident band on "Oh Boy"?
13   Who had the 50s hit with "It's All In The Game"?
14   Which brothers replaced which brothers at No. 1 in 1958?
15   Which Cherokee Indian was in the charts in 1958?
16   Which 1950s artist had a TV show *Relax With Mike*?
17   Who was the first British female singer to have a No. 1 in the 50s and what was it called?
18   What was Conway Twitty's real name?
19   How many records made up the charts in 1952 and 1953?
20   Which song was recorded by Al Hibbler, Les Baxter, Liberace and Jimmy Young?

1 Which song was at No. 1 when David Beckham got sent off in France 98?
2 Who produced "The Stonk" for Hale and Pace and the Stonkers?
3 What was the longest-running Christmas No. 1 of the 90s?
4 Marcella Detroit was part of which No. 1 act?
5 What was Norman Cook's first 90s No. 1, although his name did not appear as such?
6 What did Oasis' first No1 replace at the top of the charts?
7 Only one record entered the singles charts at No. 1 in 1992. What was it?
8 Who co-wrote "Killer" with Adamski and was an uncredited vocalist?
9 What is the last word of "Mama" by The Spice Girls?
10 Which 90s chart-toppers consisted of James Alpern and Richard Usher?
11 What did Right Said Fred's first No. 1 replace at the top of the charts?
12 Which rapper featured on "3 A.M. Eternal"?
13 Which big No. 1 did Graeme Duffin produce?
14 What was No. 1 the week before "It's Like That" took over?
15 The first No. 1 for Manchester United Football Club was released on which record label?
16 Which song gave 80s favourite Nik Kershaw his first No. 1 as a writer?
17 Apart from "Never Ever", which only other No. 1 did not enter the charts at No. 1 in 1998?
18 How many singles entered the charts at No. 1 in 1993?
19 Which song gave 60s No. 1 artist Peter Asher his first No. 1 as a producer?
20 Which song was at No. 1 when Nelson Mandela was released from prison?

1 Who won the 1973 Grammy for Best New Artist?
2 What album contains the tracks "Whole Lotta Love" and "The Lemon Song"?
3 What was Bryan Adams's debut album called?
4 Who wrote "Blackberry Way"?
5 What colour was the MGM label in the 60s?
6 What was the follow-up single to the Rolling Stones' "(I Can't Get No) Satisfaction"?
7 How is David Grundy better known?
8 Which group released an album titled *Outlandos d'Amour*?
9 Whose only UK top ten hit was "Tell Me When"?
10 Which song by the Coasters recommends "Calomine Lotion"?
11 Who starred as Ulysses S. Grant in *Hair* in Los Angeles in 1969?
12 Which singer, known only by her first name, has the surname Safka?
13 How were Berry and Torrence better known?
14 Which actress married Jean-Michel Jarre?
15 In which city was Paul Anka born?
16 Who backed Mitch Ryder?
17 Who wrote under the pseudonym of Bernard Webb?
18 Which record label did Charles Aznavour have his hit records on?
19 What was "Doc" Shuman's real first name?
20 Which group included the Batt brothers?

1   Mark Knopfler was awarded an honorary doctorate at which university?
2   What was Michael Jackson's first single release from Dangerous?
3   The first No. 1 for 2 Unlimited was released on which record label?
4   What is the first half of the postcode for the Abbey Road Studios made famous by The Beatles?
5   Which album contains the tracks "Introducing The Band" and "Still Life"?
6   What was All-4-One's first top ten hit?
7   What is the last word of "Ooh...Aah Just A Little Bit" by Gina G?
8   What was The Animals' less successful follow-up to "San Franciscan Nights"?
9   Which Neil Diamond song became a No 1 for UB40?
10 Who had a 90s album called *Swingin' With Raymond*?
11 Who originally recorded "The Shoop Shoop Song"?
12 What was the last top ten hit for Shakin' Stevens?
13 What is the last word of "Don't Stop Movin'" by Livin' Joy?
14 Which Beach Boys song is based on Bach's "Jesu Joy Of Man's Desiring"?
15 Who had a 90s album called *On The Loose*?
16 Which *EastEnders* actress was born on exactly the same day as Luther Vandross?
17 Who had a 1993 No. 1 on the Greensleeves label and a 1995 No. 1 on the Virgin label?
18 What replaced Fairground at the top of the charts?
19 Who had an 80s album called *Geno*?
20 Which band did Mick Jones form after The Clash disbanded?

1 Who had a 1961 album called *21 Today*?
2 Which major world event took place when Gerry and the Pacemakers were at No. 1 with "You'll Never Walk Alone"?
3 Which was the most successful Mersey group not managed by Brian Epstein?
4 Whose 1969 album was called *Goodbye*?
5 What did the J. stand for in Billy J. Kramer's name?
6 Which film did the Dave Clark Five make?
7 Who were originally called The Harmonichords?
8 Which Stones album was No. 1 in the album charts in 1966?
9 Which 60s chart-topper went on to manage James Taylor and Linda Ronstadt?
10 Which town did the Four Pennies come from?
11 What was the drummer Ann Lantree's group?
12 Who was originally offered "It's Not Unusual" before Tom Jones?
13 How old was Sonny when he had his first No. 1 record with Cher?
14 Who were Messrs Engel, Maus and Leeds?
15 Who had a 1968 album, ...*Rocks But Gently*?
16 Which group did Steve Marriott leave to form which band in 1969?
17 How many different bands had a No. 1 album in 1964?
18 Which single topped the charts when England won the World Cup?
19 Which song was subtitled "Exordium And Terminus"?
20 Which group sold more singles than The Beatles in the US in 1968?

1 The 1993 album *Jump Back* was a greatest hits compilation of which years?
2 What was their first album with Darryl Jones?
3 Which Rolling Stones album contains the tracks "Dear Doctor" and "Parachute Woman"?
4 What was their first No. 1 album of the 70s?
5 What was their first US No. 1?
6 Which Rolling Stones album cover has the band members wearing women's wigs?
7 How many UK million-selling singles have they had?
8 Which art school did Keith Richards attend?
9 What was their first album which did not include their name?
10 Which Stone used the pseudonym Elmo Lewis in his early days?
11 Which 80s hit reached the highest chart position?
12 *Steel Wheels* won which album award from the readers of Rolling Stone magazine?
13 Which group did Jagger and Richards belong to before the other member of the band created The Rolling Stones?
14 What was the only hit from *Dirty Work*?
15 What was their first 90s hit to reach the top 20?
16 What was their first single not to chart?
17 Which cover of a Dylan song featured on *Stripped*?
18 Which label did they record on immediately before their Rolling Stones label?
19 In 1978 as a penalty for drugs offences Keith Richards had to play a benefit concert for a charity for what?
20 Their first gig with the famous five line-up was a matter of days before which Beatles hit entered the chart?

1   Who is Bob Dylan arm in arm with on the cover of *The Freewheelin' Bob Dylan*?
2   Who backed Gary Lewis?
3   At whose party did Rod Stewart meet Britt Ekland?
4   On what single and album did Marc Almond join Bronski Beat?
5   Which music paper published Britain's first-ever record chart?
6   What was Tori Amos's debut album called?
7   What was Matt Monro's first UK hit?
8   Which guitarist formed a group called the Band Of Gypsies?
9   Who did Sid Vicious replace in the Sex Pistols in 1977?
10   Which group included Derek Leckenby and Keith Hopwood?
11   In which town was Rick Astley born?
12   How are the Bramlett family duo better known?
13   Which song won the first Grammy Record of the Year in 1958?
14   Which TV show did Al Jarreau's "Since I Fell For You" feature in?
15   Which musical instrument did Jethro Tull's Ian Anderson play?
16   Who complete Grandmaster Flash's group?
17   Which two artists have recorded albums called *Tapestry*?
18   Who left home to hitch-hike through Canada with her dog Sparkle?
19   Where did John Lennon marry Yoko Ono?
20   Which group previously called themselves History Of Headaches?

1   "Too Good To Be Forgotten" was the first top ten hit for which group?
2   Which comedian appeared in The Farm's video "Don't Let Me Down"?
3   The first No. 1 for Right Said Fred was released on which record label?
4   Which charity did Tasmin Archer's October 1992 hit raise money for?
5   Which album contains the tracks "Legend In My Living Room" and "Keep Young And Beautiful"?
6   What is the last word of "Slight Return" by The Bluetones?
7   What was Long John Baldry's follow-up to "Let The Heartaches Begin"?
8   Who had a 90s album called *Merry Christmas*?
9   Which Beatles song mentions Mao Tse Tung?
10   What replaced "Believe" at No. 1?
11   "Spanish Flea" was the first top ten hit for which performer?
12   Who was England boss when "Englandneworder" made No. 1?
13   Who other than Climie Fisher had a hit called "Love Changes Everything"?
14   Who had a late 80s album called *Girls Girls Girls*?
15   What is the last word of "Peacock Suit" by Paul Weller?
16   What was the first Bananarama song to hit No. 1 in the US but fail to do so in the UK?
17   Which 80s top ten star was in the same regiment as Elvis Presley 30 years later?
18   Whose debut album was called *Life's A Riot With Spy Vs. Spy*?
19   Who had a 80s album called *No Sleep At All*?
20   What was The Barron Knights" follow-up to "A Taste Of Aggro"?

1 Which duo had the first reggae No. 1 in 1971?
2 Which ex-Hoochie Coochie Men vocalist went on to have great success in the 70s and beyond?
3 Which 1972 single was the first major hit to feature a synthesizer?
4 Which singer/songwriter was "Killing Me Softly" written about?
5 Which song was about babysitting for the singer's manager?
6 Which hit featured Rob and Hilda Woodward?
7 Which 70s group leader died on February 10, 1997?
8 What was the first No. 1 for Jonathan King's UK record label?
9 Who accompanied Nottingham Forest FC on "We've Got the Whole World in Our Hands" in 1978?
10 Which group was famous for its white berets in 1974?
11 Who was the "Queen Of The Blues" in the 1971 hit by Ray Stevens?
12 Who was mentioned in a 1974 song title but not in the song itself?
13 Which part did David Essex play in *That'll Be The Day*?
14 Which was the third of Mud's three 70s No. 1s?
15 Which group were Jeffrey Calvert, Max West plus session musicians?
16 Whose version of "No Charge" was called "No Chance"?
17 Who was the heaviest individual chart-topper in the 70s?
18 What was Elton John's first release on Rocket?
19 What nationality were Pussycat?
20 What was Deniece Williams's profession before singing?

Answers

1   What was his first double A-side No. 1?
2   A live show from where in 1973 – made into an album – had more viewers than the moon landings?
3   What was his first album which did not have his name in the title?
4   What was the last album to chart before his death?
5   What did the B stand for in his TCB ring he wore?
6   What was Elvis's last No. 1 in his own lifetime?
7   What was his first No. 1 on both sides of the Atlantic?
8   What was the first new single to be released after his death?
9   Which Bond girl co-starred with Elvis in *Fun In Acapulco*?
10   Who played the older Elvis in Jack Good's *Elvis* in the West End in 1996?
11   Where was "The Wonder Of You" recorded live?
12   What was his first UK million-seller?
13   Where did his daughter marry her second husband?
14   In his very early days Elvis sang jingles for the radio for what product?
15   What was his first single which went straight to No. 1?
16   What was Peter Guralnick's biography called?
17   What song did he sing on his first TV appearance?
18   Which 1992 movie featured a group of sky-diving Elvis impersonators?
19   Which Elvis product had the ad line, "America has had 41 Presidents... but only one King"?
20   What was the first digit of his army number?

1 Which Stevie Wonder LP won a 1973 Grammy for Album of the Year?
2 Who had a million-seller in 1967 with "Here Comes My Baby"?
3 What were Status Quo originally called prior to 1968?
4 Which other musical personality, apart from Paul and Linda McCartney, is on the cover of the *Band On The Run* album?
5 Who married Julianne Phillips in Oregon in May 1985?
6 Who had hit albums called *The Slider* and *Futuristic Dragon*?
7 What was Aswad's debut album called?
8 Who beat Madonna to take the 1985 Best New Artist Grammy award?
9 Who recorded under the name Sallyangie?
10 What soundtrack album from 1986 showed a black-and-white photo of David Bowie?
11 Other than the USA, in which country was Joan Baez brought up?
12 Who won four out of the first five Grammy awards for Best Pop Female Vocal Performance?
13 Who were originally known as the Elgins?
14 Whose book of poems was called *Songs For While I'm Away*?
15 Who was drummer/vocalist with Traffic?
16 Where did the US part of the Live Aid concert take place?
17 Who backed Danny?
18 In which film did Elvis play the role of Deke Rivers?
19 Who said, "The trouble with some women is they get all excited about nothing – then they marry him"?
20 Howard Kaylan was lead vocalist with which group?

1   Who had an early 90s album called *Lovelines*?
2   What replaced B*Witched's first No. 1 at the top of the charts?
3   What was the first top 20 hit for Sunscreem?
4   Who had a 80s album called *Stutter*?
5   The first No. 1 for Shaggy was released on which record label?
6   Which album contains the tracks "Smooth Operator" and "Your Love Is King"?
7   What was The Beach Boys' follow-up to "Do It Again"?
8   What is the background colour of Alisha's Attic's *Illumina*?
9   What is the last word of Suggs' version of "Cecilia"?
10 Whose black felt hat was auctioned at Sotheby's for £14,300?
11 What did the Spice Girls' third No. 1 replace at the top of the charts?'
12 Who wrote "Woodstock" which gave Matthews' Southern Comfort their only UK No. 1?
13 Who had an 80s album called *Exorcising Ghosts*?
14 What was the first top ten hit for Angry Anderson?
15 What was Shirley Bassey's unsuccessful follow-up to "What Now My Love"?
16 Which song contains the words, "… I've had a few, but then again, too few to mention"?
17 Which 70s US chart-topper was born on exactly the same day as MP Virginia Bottomley?
18 What is the last word of "Charmless Man" by Blur?
19 What were The Who called in their early days?
20 Which album contains the track "Strange Brew"?

LEVEL 3

1 Which was the largest group to have a chart-topper in 1981?
2 Who played the Fairy Godmother on Adam and the Ants' "Prince Charming" video?
3 In which decade was Julio Iglesias's first solo hit written?
4 Which band included Philip Oakey and Susanne Sulley?
5 How did Demis Roussos hit the headlines in 1985?
6 Which 80s hit was based on a Zulu folk tune?
7 Which double-sided No. 1 replaced which double-sided No. 1 in 1982?
8 How did Mark Chapman find notoriety in the 1980s?
9 Which video by which band featured Ian McKellen as Dracula?
10 Which band's name means "black" in Arabic?
11 How is the American Ms Darwisch better known?
12 Which album was T'Pau's "China In Your Hand" from?
13 What was the Bee Gees' first 80s No. 1?
14 Which country are Europe from?
15 How was Ray Burns known as an 80s soloist?
16 What did The Real Thing's Chris Amoo win in 1987?
17 Which country were The Goombay Dance Band based in?
18 Who, in which song, sang "I've been undressed by kings and I've seen some things a woman ain't supposed to see"?
19 Which city are Berlin from?
20 Which Radio 1 DJ first refused to play Frankie Goes to Hollywood's "Relax"?

1   Which fellow-rock star inducted him into the Rock and Roll Hall of fame in 1994?
2   What was his follow-up to the N Trance Featuring Rod Stewart version of "Do Ya Think I'm Sexy"?
3   Which band did he join in 1964?
4   What did "Baby Jane" replace at the top of the charts?
5   Which album featured "Handbags And Gladrags"?
6   The 90s album is the best of which years with The Faces?
7   Who features on "People Get Ready"?
8   What was the second of his six consecutive No. 1 albums?
9   What was his first US No. 1?
10   In 1989 which body awarded him a Living Legend Award?
11   At which football stadium did he open the UK leg of his Vagabond Heart Tour?
12   Which album featured "You Wear It Well" which got to No. 1 in the singles charts?
13   What was the first US No. 1 he had which was not a No. 1 over here?
14   Whose "In A Broken Dream" had uncredited vocals by Rod Stewart?
15   Which hit kept The Sex Pistols off the top spot with "God Save The Queen"?
16   Which member of Duran Duran co-produced *Out Of Order*?
17   Who was the mother of his child who appeared in the "Forever Young" video?
18   Which song did he contribute to the *Two Rooms* tribute album?
19   Which album featured his duet with the subject of the biopic *What's Love Got To Do With It*?
20   Which cover of a Van Morrison single reached US No. 5 in 1993?

1 In which town was Barry Gibb born?
2 What is in the baby's mouth on the cover of Van Halen's 1984 album?
3 Who organizes Buddy Holly Week each year?
4 What type of car was used by Madness in their video for "Driving In My Car"?
5 Which fifties singer married Millicent Martin?
6 What label did the Police record all their hit albums on?
7 What Beatles movie was originally going to be called *Eight Arms To Hold You*?
8 Which California group toured with Maharishi Mahesh Yogi?
9 Who backed Captain Beefheart?
10 What shape is the sleeve of the Rolling Stones' *Through The Past Darkly* album?
11 Who is lead singer with UB40?
12 Which Steve Winwood song was Grammy Record of the Year in 1986?
13 Who were first formed as Tiger Lily in 1973?
14 Which veteran was behind the US fundraiser by USA For Africa?
15 Which role did Tina Turner play in *Mad Max: Beyond Thunderdome*?
16 Who was President Reagan writing to when he said, "Your deep faith in God and adherence to traditional values is an inspiration to us all"?
17 How is Jiles Perry Richardson better known?
18 What was Bananarama's debut album called?
19 What were The Troggs initially called?
20 What is U2's The Edge's real name?

1 How many people are seen standing up on the cover of The Best Of M People?
2 What was The Bee Gees' follow-up to "Words"?
3 What is the last word of "One Of Us" by Joan Osborne?
4 What was Joan Armatrading's first top ten?
5 On which Michael Jackson hit did Eddie Van Halen play heavy metal guitar?
6 The first No. 1 for Shakespear's Sister was released on which record label?
7 Which fellow rock star produced Chris Farlowe's 60s No. 1 "Out Of Time"?
8 What replaced Hanson's first No. 1 at the top of the charts?
9 Which album contains the track "She Came In Through The Bathroom Window"?
10 Which lady described Madonna as, "a woman who pulled herself up by her bra straps"?
11 Which Gerry And The Pacemakers hit was at No. 1 at the time John F Kennedy was assassinated?
12 What was the title of Mary Hopkin's debut album?
13 Who had a 90s album called Praise?
14 What is the last word of "Trash" by Suede?
15 What happened to Black Box in 1996?
16 Which Beatles song contains the line, "What do you see when you turn out the light?'
17 Who had a late 80s album called Liquidizer?
18 Who was the heaviest person to make No. 1 in the 70s?
19 What was The Beatles' follow-up to "From Me To You"?
20 What is Joni Mitchell's real name?

1   Which band was started with a loan from the alleged Mafia member James Martorano?
2   Which band presented the 1994 Christmas edition of "Top Of The Pops"?
3   Who did the 52-year-old manager Rene Angelil marry in 1994?
4   Who went on a *Zoo TV Tour* in 1992?
5   Where was it suggested Elton John be listened to through headphones otherwise noise regulations could be broken?
6   Who was the album *No Prima Donna* a tribute to?
7   Why didn't Englandneworder make a follow-up to the 1990 "World in Motion"?
8   What are the first names of the original Spice Girls?
9   Which album was Madonna's "Vogue" taken from?
10   Which band included Keymaster Snow and MC Golden Voice?
11   Who was named as executive producer of "Itsy Bitsy Teeny Weeny Yellow Polka Dot Bikini"?
12   Who was the first female vocalist with Beautiful South?
13   Which two movies did "The One And Only" feature in?
14   How is Jim Moir better known?
15   Who, in the early 1990s, would make records only in aid of charities?
16   Who featured on the soundtrack of *In The Name Of The Father*?
17   How many weeks was Wet Wet Wet's "Love Is All Around" at No. 1?
18   Which 90s band included Wanya and Nathan Morris?
19   Who made the album *Growing Up In Public*?
20   Whose suicide note said, "It's better to burn out than to fade away"?

1   What was the name of his first band in the early 60s?
2   What was the first single to go straight to No. 1?
3   Who sang "Rocket Man" on the *Two Rooms* tribute album?
4   What was the name of the publishing company he formed in 1974?
5   Which was his sole 80s hit on the Arista label?
6   What was the B-side of "Candle In The Wind" on the original UK single?
7   What was his first album without Taupin's lyrics?
8   What was his first US No. 1?
9   Which Lionel Richie album prevented *The One* from entering the album charts at No. 1?
10 A 1993 Melbourne concert was cut short when the stage was invaded by what?
11 What was his first UK million-selling single?
12 What was his first American label?
13 Who was his tennis partner against Martina Navratilova and Bobby Riggs at a 1993 charity event?
14 What was his first hit credited to The Elton John Band?
15 What was his first album chart success with a title not containing his name?
16 Who was his co-host when he hosted the 1994 Brit Awards ceremony?
17 His manager of 28 years had been manager of which US label in the UK?
18 What replaced "Sacrifice" at the top of the charts?
19 What was his first hit on his own label?
20 Who was the producer on his third UK No. 1?

1 What shape was the Small Faces' *Ogden's Nut Gone Flake* album cover?
2 Who backed Country Joe?
3 Which animal appears on the cover of Tina Turner's *Private Dancer* album?
4 Who wrote the first two No. 1 songs for Gerry And The Pacemakers?
5 Who backed Lloyd Cole?
6 What group was Steve Winwood a member of before joining Traffic?
7 What is Michael Jackson leaning on, on the cover of *Thriller*?
8 Who was the first artist to have three consecutive UK No. 1 singles?
9 Who did Lennon and McCartney write "Goodbye" for?
10 Which city saw the most Elvis performances?
11 What is Björk's surname?
12 What type of waitress was Debbie Harry?
13 In which part of London was Damon Albarn born?
14 What was Bette Midler's 1989 Grammy Record of the Year for?
15 What is the real name of Bono of U2?
16 What is a Fender Stratocaster?
17 Who did Buddy Holly's guitarist Tommy Allsup give up his seat for on the ill-fated last flight?
18 How is Evangelos Papathanassiou better known?
19 How did the Velvet Underground get their name?
20 What was Pat Benatar's debut album called?

1 What replaced "(Everything I Do) I Do It For You" at No. 1?
2 What is on the cover of ELO's Greatest Hits album cover?
3 Ali Campbell is lead singer with which group?
4 The first No. 1 for Take That was released on which record label?
5 Which Jimi Hendrix album contains the tracks "Foxy Lady", "Can You See Me" and "Fire"?
6 "If music be the food of love" what did John Lennon say he would have?
7 What is the last word of "How Bizarre" by OMC?
8 What was Hamilton Bohannon's first top ten hit?
9 What was Dave Berry's follow-up to "The Crying Game"?
10 Who had an early 90s album called *Whaler*?
11 Who was lead vocalist with Marillion when they first hit the charts?
12 What was Black Sabbath's first top ten hit?
13 Which album contains the track "Zoo Station"?
14 Who had an early 80s album called *Best Moves*?
15 Which song was at No. 1 at the time of the 1992 general election?
16 What was the cause of Billie Holliday's death in July 1959?
17 The Columbia record label was the first to have 50 of what?
18 What is the last word of "Ocean Drive" by The Lighthouse Family?
19 Fairport Convention sang their first UK hit in which language?
20 Who had a 70s album called Midnight Lightning?

1   What are Madonna's two middle names?
2   What was her first major film role?
3   What name was given to the clothing outlet in Macy's US stores?
4   Which album included the song "Rain"?
5   Who did Madonna describe as "the coolest guy in the universe"?
6   Which knight did Madonna star with in *Who's That Girl*?
7   Who was said to have beaten Madonna to the *Evita* role in 1988?
8   Which role did Madonna play in *Dick Tracey*?
9   Who designed her clothes for the *Blonde Ambition* tour?
10   Why was Madonna sued by her neighbour in 1990?
11   Which 1991 video shows a steamy bedroom scene filmed in black and white?
12   Where was Madonna when she was interviewed on *Wogan*?
13   What was the name of her company founded in 1992?
14   What was her first album on her own record label?
15   Which controversial "sport" features in her "Take A Bow" and "You'll See" videos?
16   Which two roles did Carlos Leon have in Madonna's life?
17   Who directed Madonna in *Evita*?
18   Which instrument did Madonna play in the rock band Breakfast Club?
19   Who produced "Shanghai Surprise"?
20   Which album was "Papa Don't Preach" originally on?

1 Which track on *Ladies And Gentlemen* is sung with the singer who took "Mary Jane" into the charts in 1995?
2 What was the name of his first band formed with Andrew Ridgeley and others?
3 What did "Careless Whisper" replace at the top of the charts?
4 Which single featured on the soundtrack of *Beverly Hills Cop II*?
5 How many UK No. 1s feature on *Ladies And Gentlemen*?
6 In which city did he perform his first new song for five years in 1994?
7 How was "Careless Whisper" credited when it was first released in the US?
8 What was his first UK million-seller?
9 For which Elton John album did George do backing vocals on "Nikita" and "Wrap Her Up"?
10 Which is the only track on *Ladies And Gentlemen* where he duets with a band rather than another soloist?
11 What replaced "Don't Let The Sun Go Down On Me" at No. 1?
12 In which city did his *Faith* tour open?
13 In the 80s George was second only to whom as having most No. 1 hits in the States?
14 On which Jody Watley album did he feature in 1989?
15 Which live cover version was on the B-side of "Praying For Time"?
16 What was his 1990 autobiography called?
17 What was his last single on the Epic label?
18 In what year did he make his first solo tour?
19 Which album kept *Listen Without Prejudice* off the top of the US album charts?
20 What was his second single to be at No. 1 on both sides of the Atlantic.?

Answers

Elton John (Quiz 20)
1 Bluesology. 2 "Don't Let The Sun Go Down On Me". 3 Kate Bush.
4 Big Pig Music. 5 "Through The Storm". 6 "Bennie And The Jets".
7 *A Single Man*. 8 "Crocodile Rock". 9 *Back To Front*. 10 Crickets.
11 "Candle In The Wind 1997". 12 Uni. 13 Billie Jean King.
14 "Philadelphia Freedom". 15 *Tumbleweed Connection*. 16 RuPaul.
17 Motown. 18 "Turtle Power" by Partners In Kryme.
19 "Don't Go Breaking My Heart". 20 George Michael.

430

1   Whose stabbed head appears on the cover of her first solo album?
2   Which country pioneered pirate radio ships in the late 1950s?
3   Which guitarist went from Barnstorm toThe Eagles?
4   What was Manfred Mann's last single with Paul Jones on vocals?
5   Who started his career with "I Go Ape" in 1959?
6   Who composed the soundtrack for *Deathwish II*?
7   Who backed Archie Bell?
8   Who did Jerry Hall have a long relationship with before Mick Jagger?
9   What is Mike Oldfield standing on, on the *Incantations* album cover?
10   Who formed the Straight and Barking Pumpkin labels?
11   What was Boy George's debut album called?
12   Whose autobiography was called *X-Ray*?
13   Who were made up of a cowboy, an Indian, a policeman, a biker, a GI and a builder?
14   How was Vincent Eugene Craddock better known?
15   In which year was Bert Weedon born?
16   In which film did Elvis play the role of Vince Everett?
17   In 1997 who issued bonds in his name for people to invest in?
18   What relation is Pat Boone to the Western pioneer Daniel Boone?
19   In which part of Manchester was Elkie Brooks born?
20   In which immortalized road in Woking did Paul Weller live as a child?

1 Who had an early 80s album called *Reproduction*?
2 What did The Spice Girls first No. 1 replace at the top of the charts?
3 What was the first top ten for The Isley Brothers?
4 Which football team does Elvis Costello support?
5 Who won Grammy Record of the Year in 1986 with *Higher Love*?
6 Which deceased *EastEnders* actress had a hit with "Love's Unkind"?
7 Whose backing group were The Rumour?
8 What was the name of No Doubt's first No. 1?
9 Which Kenny Rogers hit inspired a film of the same name in which he starred?
10 What was Cilla Black's follow-up to "Something Tells Me (Something Is Gonna Happen Tonight"?
11 What is the last word of "Female Of The Species" by Space?
12 Who had a No. 10 hit with "Sheila Take A Bow"?
13 Who wrote the autobiography *And The Beat Goes On* published in 1991?
14 Gwen Dickey was lead singer with which group?
15 In which city did the *Blonde Ambition* tour by Madonna commence?
16 What was Pat Boone's follow-up to "Johnny Will?
17 Who released the LP *She's So Unusual*?
18 What was the first top ten for Jo Boxers?
19 Which Duran Duran single video was shot in Sri Lanka?
20 Who had a 90s album called *Truth And Love*?

LEVEL 3

1 Which song has a line based loosely on one from Shakespeare's *As You Like It*, "You know someone said that all the world's a stage"?

2 What does Celine Dion sing after "I think of all the friends I've known" in "All By Myself"?

3 How many times does Gabrielle sing "Walk On By" in the first chorus?

4 Which song has the line "Will all those having relatives on Flight 1203 please report to the chapel across the street"?

5 Which 1960s song has the line "Wearing smells from lab'ratories, facing a dying nation of moving paper fantasy."?

6 Who does Bob Dylan tell "Don't block up the hall" in "The Times They Are A-Changin'"?

7 Which song starts, "What goes up must come down."?

8 Which month is it in Paul Simon's "I Am A Rock"?

9 In "My Way" what goes before "I did what I had to do."?

10 Which song says "I love your chin-ey chin chin."?

11 Which line follows the unforgettably tasteless "I'm as serious as cancer"?

12 Which island does Madonna lament in "La Isla Bonita"?

13 What colour did Vincent "paint his palette" in the Don McLean hit?

14 Which song goes "I've never done good things, I've never done bad things."?

15 Where would you find the lines "Ev'ry summer we can rent a cottage in the Isle of Wight"?

16 Which song has the lines "I got up to wash my face, When I come back to bed, Someone's taken my place."?

17 Which song starts "When I was a little girl I had a rag doll"?

18 Where will you hear the line "Tried to hitch a ride to San Francisco"?

19 Which song says "The world is like an apple whirling silently in space"?

20 What is the answer to "What do you see when you turn out the light?"?

1 Which member of Guns N' Roses performed on the original "Black And White"?
2 Which minor hit was the love them from *Lady Sings The Blues*?
3 What was his first solo hit after he left Tamla Motown?
4 Who was the first group he had a hit with after he left the Jacksons to go solo?
5 Who wrote the words for "Ben" and suggested Michael sing it rather than Donny Osmond as first suggested?
6 The purchase of which music publishing catalogue gave Michael the right to more than 250 Beatles songs?
7 Which Michael-penned hit for Diana Ross was named after his pet snake?
8 In 1984 what was he filming when his hair caught fire and he was hospitalised?
9 What replaced "Billie Jean" at the top of the charts?
10 How many top ten singles came from the album *Thriller*?
11 Which brother did he duet with on "Tell Me I'm Not Dreaming" from that brother's solo album?
12 Which second-generation pop star appeared on Moonwalker?
13 1983 saw the release of an album with a booklet of pictures of Jackson cuddling who?
14 Who duetted with Michael on the first single from the *Bad* album?
15 What was the original name of the ranch in California, which has its own zoo and theme park, which he bought in 1988?
16 What was his first No. 1 to top the charts on both sides of the Atlantic during the same week?
17 On which Stevie Wonder album did the two sing "Get It"?
18 At which UK race course did he perform in 1988?
19 Who became Jackson's new manager in 1990?
20 What was his first UK No. 1 which did not make it to No. 1 in the US?

1 Who had a No. 1 hit with "Young Love" 16 years before Donny Osmond?
2 Who took the cover photo for Paul McCartney's first solo album?
3 In which city was Joe Cocker born?
4 Who had a 1973 hit with "Gaye"?
5 Who married the heiress Anne Friedman in 1984?
6 Which Rod Stewart album cover features him sitting in an armchair?
7 What was Boyz II Men's debut album called?
8 What rag was Winifred Atwell celebrating in 1953?
9 What did Ringo Starr have removed in November 1964?
10 How many albums did David Bowie have in the charts in July 1983?
11 Which Doobie Brothers song was Grammy Record of the Year in 1979?
12 An imitator of which pop star won the 1996 *Stars in Their Eyes*?
13 Why was Barry White imprisoned in 1960?
14 Which vocalist links Deep Purple and Whitesnake?
15 Who backed Mike Batt on "Summertime City"?
16 Who said, "Too much of a good thing is simply wonderful"?
17 Who was brought up in the bordello run by his aunt Handsome "Honey" Washington?
18 Which singer shares her birthday with Emily Brontë?
19 Which band includes Bob "The Bear" Hite and Al "Blind Owl" Wilson?
20 Who was the youngest-ever recipient of the Songwriter of the Year trophy at the Ivor Novello awards in 1985?

1 Which album was David Bowie's track "Space Oddity" taken from?
2 Which novelty song was a hit in 1980 for Keith Michell?
3 Which Elton John song did Jeffrey Archer choose on *Desert Island Discs*?
4 The first No. 1 for Prodigy was released on which record label?
5 Which Rolling Stones album contains the track "When The Whip Comes Down"?
6 What did Celine Dion sing in a Eurovision Song Contest?
7 What replaced "I Will Always Love You" at No. 1?
8 Whose debut album was called *Not Me*?
9 Which Beatles song mentions Edward Heath and Harold Wilson?
10 David Ball left Soft Cell to form which 90s band?
11 Who had a 80s album called *Turbo*?
12 What is the last word of "It's All Coming Back To Me Now" by Celine Dion?
13 Whose backing group was The FBI in 1989?
14 In his Radio 1 DJ days Mike Read's refusal to play which record helped the publicity as it became a huge No. 1?
15 "Take A Chance On Me" and "The Name Of The Game" first appeared on which Abba album?
16 What is the last word of 'Walkaway' by Cast?
17 What was The Carpenters' follow-up to "Only Yesterday"?
18 Who was vocalist in the band Chicago?
19 Who had a 80s album called *Piano Man*?
20 What replaced Take That's last No. 1 at the top of the charts?

---

1. Who were originally called The Saxons?
2. Which group was Keith Potger in and which group did he form?
3. What was the home country of Bachman-Turner Overdrive?
4. What was the Boomtown Rats' first hit?
5. Whose songs are on Deacon Blue's 1990 EP?
6. Vince Clarke left one successful band for another in 1981–82. Which?
7. Whose single "The Cover of *Rolling Stone*" was banned by the BBC because they said it was advertising?
8. What did the group change the title to?
9. Who is Hot Chocolate's lead vocalist?
10. Who links Bananarama and Shakespear's Sister?
11. What was the home town of The Housemartins?
12. Which band took its name from *The Hitch-Hiker's Guide to the Galaxy* and the answer to the question "What is the meaning of life?"?
13. Whose first top ten hit was "Love Missile F1–11"?
14. How many Stray Cats were there?
15. Whose first album was called *Boy*?
16. Who signed a deal to sponsor Clydebank Football Club in 1993?
17. Roland Gift was lead singer with which group?
18. Which group released "Songs in the Key Of X" in 1996?
19. Who first performed as Ripples And Waves Plus Michael?
20. What did REO Speedwagon name themselves after?

1   Which soap star charted with the same song that took Steven Houghton to No. 3 in 1997?
2   Which soap star had a minor chart hit with "Happenin' All Over Again"?
3   Which duo had a US TV series called *Make Your Own Kind Of Music*?
4   Which Elvis hit was first used by BT to promote their phone services?
5   Which TV Western star recorded "Welcome To The Ponderosa" from which Ringo topped the US chart?
6   Village People sang which of their hits on *The Rikki Lake Show* in 1997?
7   Which Heavy Metal Kids singer starred in *Auf Wiedersehen Pet*?
8   Who had a hit with "I'm Gonna Be A Country Girl Again'
9   Which female vocalist presented *Sesame Street* for over five years and made a guest appearance in the sitcom *Bread*?
10 Which chart duettist with Wendy Richard appeared as a drug smuggler in *The Knock* in 1997?
11 Which 70 chart-topper appeared in *The Grimleys* in 1997 with Nigel Planer and Jack Dee?
12 His first chart success was "Someone To Love" but what was his character's name in *EastEnders*?
13 Which soap actress backed the so-called Neasden Queen Of Soul?
14 Which Corrie character was Posh among the Corrie Babes who aped The Spice Girls on *Celebrity Stars In Their Eyes*?
15 Who duetted with Tina Turner as part of an early 90s Pepsi TV ad deal?
16 What was Michelle Gayle's top ten follow-up to "Sweetness"?
17 Whose "Blue Velvet" was used in a 90s commercial?
18 Which 60s star played a drug-pushing DJ in the Nick Berry series *Heartbeat*?
19 Which singer of "Ruby Tuesday" wrote the music for the *Beauty And The Beast* TV series?
20 Who wrote the music for the 60s pop series *Ready Steady Go*?

1 In which country was Chris de Burgh born?
2 What label did Buddy Holly record on?
3 How old was Bobby Darin when he found out that the woman he thought was his mother was his sister?
4 What is the Yardbirds' only hit to get in the Top 10 in the US and UK?
5 Who left Roxy Music to form Obscure Records?
6 Who left the Go-Go's to go solo?
7 Whose alter ego was The Thin White Duke?
8 Which Stones album commences with "Sympathy For The Devil"?
9 Who backed Freddy Bell on "Giddy-Up-A-Ding-Dong"?
10 What record label was founded by Ahmet Ertegun and Herb Abramson?
11 What was Billy Bragg's debut album called?
12 Who won the Grammy Record of the Year in 1967 with "Up Up And Away"?
13 Who were called the High Numbers in their early days?
14 Which UK vocalist joined Michael Jackson on his *Bad* tour in Europe?
15 How is Roberta Anderson better known?
16 In which city was Steve Winwood born?
17 Which band had Fish on lead vocals?
18 What is Bob Marley's eldest son called?
19 What was Barry Manilow's "Mandy" originally called in the US?
20 Which 1977 chart-topper was sung in French?

1 What is the background colour of The Carpenters' *Love Songs* album?
2 What did The Manic Street Preachers' first No. 1 replace at the top of the charts?
3 What was Cher's follow-up to "Bang Bang (My Baby Shot Me Down)"?'
4 The first No 1 for Vic Reeves was released on which record label?
5 Who had an early 80s album called *Flush The Fashion*?
6 What was Eddie Cochran's first top ten hit?
7 Which famous singer used to be in a band called Kat Kool And The Kool Cats?
8 In 1976 whose record about a trucker trying to run a police blockade was made into a film by Sam Peckinpah?
9 Who was voted the Best Newcomer at the 1999 Brit Awards?
10 Which band started life as The Warlocks?
11 What was Ray Charles' follow-up to "Take These Chains From My Heart"?
12 What is the last word of "Just A Girl" by No Doubt?
13 What was the last word of "Call The Man" by Celine Dion?
14 What replaced "Ice Ice Baby" at the top of the charts?
15 Which album first contained the track "Drive-In Saturday"?
16 Who released a reunion album in 1994 titled *Hell Freezes Over*?
17 Which Michael Jackson song was originally intended for Donny Osmond?
18 Who had a 70s album called Come Again?
19 Which movie included Elvis' "Can't Help Falling In Love"?
20 What was the first top ten for Arthur Conley?

Answers

Pot Luck 20 (Quiz 38)
1 Go. 2 *All Mod Cons* by The Jam. 3 "Don't Sleep In The Subway".
4 "You'll Never Walk Alone" by The Crowd. 5 Jiles Perry Richardson.
6 Celine Dion. 7 Elgar. 8 "Tell Him". 9 Again. 10 Billy Joel.
11 *Satan*. 12 Humble Pie. 13 Systematic. 14 Neil Diamond.
15 "Over And Over". 16 Curved Air. 17 DJ Jazzy Jeff and Fresh Prince.
18 Lemonheads. 19 "Love Me Or Leave Me". 20 In the virgin snow.

1. Penny Ford and Turbo B were vocalists in which 90s dance group?
2. In which city did House Music originate?
3. Where is Perez "Guaglione" Prado from?
4. Whose first single was "Dance Stance"?
5. Which Madonna dance hit was her first No. 1?
6. What follows the Outhere Brothers' "Don't stop"?
7. Who had a party hit about "Atmosphere"?
8. Whose "Sideboard Song" was subtitled "Got My Beer in the Sideboard Here"?
9. Who sang about "Reggae Like It Used to Be"?
10. What gave the Brothers Johnson their first top ten hit?
11. Ottawan who had an 80s hit with "D.I.S.C.O" were from where?
12. Who sang "I Haven't Stopped Dancing Yet" in 1989?
13. Who are credited with "Boogie Wonderland" in 1979?
14. Who said Dance Yourself Dizzy in 1980?
15. Which disco queen's first album was *Heart And Soul*?
16. In which year did Barry White's "You're My First, My Last, My Everything" hit the top?
17. Whose first album was *Party Party 16 Great Party Icebreakers*?
18. What did the party hit "Hoots Mon" advertise when it was re-released in 1993?
19. Which disco band included Maizie Williams, Bobby Farrell and Marcia Barrett?
20. Which two stars are credited on the cover of *Dirty Dancing*?

1 Which album featured her UK No. 1 "Chain Reaction"?
2 On which top 20 single is she credited as simply Diana?
3 What was her first No. 1 album?
4 What were the The Supremes called when Diana Ross joined them?
5 What was her first solo No. 1 in the US?
6 Whose arrival in The Supremes meant they were now called Diana Ross And The Supremes?
7 What was Diane Ross's middle name?
8 MC Lyte's "Cold Rock A Party" was based on which Diana Ross hit?
9 Who directed her second feature film *Mahogany*?
10 Which album did she make with two opera giants?
11 Which part did Michael Jackson play when Diana Ross played Dorothy in *The Wiz*?
12 Who wrote "Muscles" from the Silk Electric album?
13 Which film soundtrack on which she sang reached No. 1 in 1972?
14 The ballad "Missing You" was dedicated to whom?
15 "Love Hangover" featured on which album?
16 Which product did she advertise with her daughter Tracee in the early 90s?
17 Which Briton was the principal producer behind "The Force Behind The Power"?
18 Notorious BIG's "No Money Mo Problems" was based on which Diana Ross hit?
19 In July 1992 which Radio 1 DJ did she sit in for?
20 What was her last hit on Motown before moving to Capitol at the start of the 80s?

1 How many older brothers and sisters does Celine Dion have?
2 Who was the lead singer of The Shirelles?
3 Which label's first releases included Mary Hopkin and James Taylor?
4 Who backed Boyd Bennett on "Seventeen"?
5 What were the real names of Paul and Paula?
6 What is George Benson's nickname?
7 Who made his mark in the 60s act John's Children?
8 Which group's own record label uses the reference number prefixes COC and CUN?
9 What type of transport was on Elton John's Rocket record label?
10 Who had Britain's first-ever double-sided No. 1 in the 1950s?
11 What was Garth Brooks's debut album called?
12 Who won the Grammy award for Best Male Vocal Performance in 1984 and 1985?
13 What did "5-4-3-2-1" replace as theme music for *Ready Steady Go!*?
14 What name was given to the open-air concerts by Madness at Finsbury Park in 1992?
15 Who said, "I'm the innovator. I'm the emancipator. I'm the originator. I'm the architect of rock 'n' roll"?
16 How is Otha Ellas Bates better known?
17 In which city was Mark Knopfler born?
18 In which film did Elvis play the role of Danny Fisher?
19 Who formed the Spiritual Cowboys?
20 Who did Joe Cocker's parents name him after?

1 What is the last word of "Tell Him" by Celine Dion and Barbra Streisand?
2 Which album contains the track "Down In The Tube Station At Midnight"?
3 What was Petula Clark's follow-up to "This Is My Song"?
4 What replaced "19" at the top of the charts?'
5 What was the Big Bopper's real name?
6 Who had a 90s album called *Unison*?
7 Which composer opened the EMI studios in Abbey Road in 1931?
8 What was the first top ten for Billie Davies?
9 What is the last word of the 'Day We Find Love' by 911?
10 Which American Innocent Man excelled at boxing at school?
11 Which Orbital video was banned?
12 Which group did Steve Marriott form when he left the Small Faces in 1969?
13 The first No. 1 for Whigfield was released on which record label?
14 Who had an early 80s album called *Heartlight*?
15 What was The Dave Clark Five's follow-up to "Catch Us If You Can"?
16 Before The Police, Stewart Copeland was drummer for which group?
17 Who had a late 80s album called *Rock The House*?
18 Who had a 90s album called *It's A Shame About Ray*?
19 What was the first top ten hit for Sammy Davis Jr.?
20 Where is the bloody rose lying crushed and broken in the song "Vincent"?

Answers – see page 448

Answers

Pot Luck 18 (Quiz 34)
1 White.   2 "No Matter What" by Boyzone.   3 "I Feel Something In The Air".
4 Sense.   5 Alice Cooper.   6 "C'mon Everybody".   7 Paul Young.
8 CW McCall.   9 Belle And Sebastian.   10 The Grateful Dead.   11 "No One".
12 Here.   13 Here.   14 "Saviour's Day" by Cliff Richard.
15 *Aladdin Sane* by David Bowie.   16 The Eagles.   17 "Ben".
18 Peter Cook and Dudley Moore.   19 *Blue Hawaii*.   20 "Sweet Soul Music".

1 Who was the only performer to have a No. 1 in 1952?
2 What was Elvis Presley's first double-sided No. 1?
3 Who sings the backing "ook-a-chunka, ook-a-chunka" with George Jones on Johnny Preston's "Running Bear"?
4 With which record did Cliff first replace Elvis at the No. 1 spot?
5 What was The Beatles' last No. 1 on Parlophone?
6 Which 80s No. 1 was about the love between a teacher and pupil?
7 Who recorded the 1988 No. 1 which advertised Coca-Cola?
8 What was Cliff Richard's first self-produced No. 1?
9 What was the first record to be No. 1 over two separate Christmases?
10 What was the first No. 1 with "rock and roll" in the title?
11 What was at No. 1 when the first heart transplant took place in 1967?
12 Who were Messrs Pettigrew and Chacon who had a No. 1 in 1992?
13 Who had a record go straight to No. 1 in 1995 while in hospital?
14 Which two acts had No. 1s with cover versions in autumn 1996?
15 What was a No. 1 for Sargeant Major Williams and Private Sugden?
16 Which phrase used by John Wayne in *The Searcher* inspired a 50s No. 1 hit?
17 Which chart-toppers had Canon Colin Bowles and Sheikh Haroun Wadi el John R.T. Davies among their number?
18 Which animal was in the title of No. 1s by David Cassidy and Donny Osmond?
19 How did Women's Lib change the title of the 1975 hit by The Tymes?
20 Who was the first British act to have a No. 1 and what was it called?

1 What was his first No. 1 album of the 90s?
2 In 1994 he became a patron of which charity?
3 What did "Ashes To Ashes" replace at the top of the charts?
4 Who opened Bowie's *Outsiders* UK tour which began at Wembley?
5 What was his first US No. 1?
6 Who did he play in *The Last Temptation Of Christ*?
7 What replaced "Let's Dance" at the top of the charts?
8 Who did he record the theme from *The Falcon And The Snowman* with?
9 Two major film titles were the titles of 1997 minor hits, but which got to the higher placing?
10 In 1998 he sold a self-portrait and a portrait by him of whom on the Internet?
11 Which single was No. 1 on both sides of the Atlantic?
12 Which Bowie hit did Puff Daddy base his "Been Around The World" on?
13 Who did he play in the movie *Basquiat*?
14 What was his first UK million-seller?
15 Which 70s album was a selection of 60s cover versions?
16 Which album recorded his last 70s tour?
17 In what year did he receive the BRIT award for outstanding contribution to British Music?
18 What was he wearing on the cover of *The Man Who Sold The World*?
19 Which album came from his musical version of *1984*?
20 What was the first of his chart albums to mention his name?

1   What producer's label had the slogan "Tomorrow's Sound Today"?
2   What was the lady wearing on the front and back covers of Rod Stewart's *Blondes Have More Fun* album?
3   Who recorded "Daydream Believer (Cheer Up Peter Reid)" in 1996?
4   Who was the first group at No. 1 with Roman numerals in its name?
5   What did Pink Floyd's 1977 *Animals* tour feature an inflatable of?
6   Whose first album was *Natty Dread*?
7   Whose deaths were recalled in the Stones' "Sympathy For The Devil"?
8   Which group was formerly Linda Ronstadt's backing band?
9   Who wrote Lulu's hit "The Boat That I Row"?
10 Which British female singer had three song titles on the first UK chart?
11 How is Michael Lubowitz better known?
12 What do the Beverley Sisters, the Bee Gees and the Shangri-Las have in common?
13 Who links the Beatles in Hamburg, Elvis's "Wooden Heart" and "Strangers In The Night"?
14 How is the US producer Jazzie B better known?
15 What are the grandchildren called in "When I'm Sixty-Four"?
16 Who was the first female performer to have four UK No. 1s?
17 What did the Bluebells' "Young At Heart" advertise in 1993?
18 Who were John McGeoch, Steve Severin and Budgie?
19 Who are the five named people in "Fifty Ways To Leave Your Lover"?
20 Which 50s chart-topper was at one time Paul Simon's father-in-law?

1 What replaced Cliff's "Mistletoe And Wine" at No. 1?
2 What was Marv Johnson's first top ten?
3 What was Eddie Cochran's follow-up to "Three Steps To Heaven"?
4 What is the last word of "Flava" by Peter Andre?
5 Which veteran performed at *Party In The Park 1998* along with All Saints, Boyzone and Natalie Imbruglia?
6 Whose debut album was called *Deep Sea Skiving*?
7 Which album contains the track "Pigs On The Wing"?
8 Which fellow-rock star produced the No. 1 "Something In The Air" for Thunderclap Newman?
9 What was the name of the perfume launched by a Beatle spouse?
10 Who had a 90s album called *All Around The World*?
11 What were The Kinks known as before they changed their name?
12 In which year did the Erasure first have a No. 1 single?
13 In 1977 whose record about a love triangle was made into a film of the same name with Lee Remick and George Peppard?
14 Whose debut solo single was called "This Is The World Calling"?
15 What are the first names of producers Gamble and Huff?
16 What is the last word of "If You Ever" by East 17 Featuring Gabrielle?
17 Which song was at No. 1 at the time of the October 1974 general election?
18 Which singer had a late 70s album called *Some Of My Best Friends Are Songs*?
19 What was Nat King Cole's follow-up to "When I Fall In Love"?
20 Which album contains the tracks "Everybody Loves Me Baby" and "Winterwood"?

1   Which instrumental was the first to have a mother and son at No. 1?
2   Which orchestra leader recorded as Manuel And His Music Of The Mountains?
3   What was the guitarist John Williams's first solo single?
4   Who had an album called *Rockin' With Curly Leads*?
5   Which group included the music writer Benny Green?
6   Which film theme was the first to top the charts in 1953?
7   Who played "A Taste of Honey" with the Leon Young String Chorale?
8   Which city were Doop from?
9   In which year did Fleetwood Mac's "Albatross" enter the charts?
10 Which musical instrument did Floyd Cramer play?
11 Which instrumental took over from which instrumental at the top of the charts in 1962?
12 Whose backing group had The Tornados been?
13 Who had a 1960s instrumental hit with "Love is Blue"?
14 On which album did "Amazing Grace" first appear?
15 Which hit included electric violin, ocarina, piccolo, trumpet and electronic harmonica?
16 What was the first TV theme to be a chart-topper?
17 Who had a 1997 top ten hit with "Toxygene"?
18 Which Kenny Ball hit had an oriental-sounding title?
19 Who was the first person to have a hit with "Classical Gas"?
20 Who had the album *Music From Riverdance – The Show*?

LEVEL 3

1 What was his first single after he left The Beatles which was not on the Apple label?
2 In what year did he receive his knighthood?
3 What type of record did The Guinness Book of Records give him to honour outstanding sales achievements?
4 What was his first post-Beatles album on Parlophone?
5 What was his first album credited to Paul and Linda McCartney?
6 What replaced "Ebony And Ivory" at No. 1?
7 How many ex-Beatles had reached No. 1 solo before Paul?
8 Which single was accompanied by a video of Paul in the trenches of WWI?
9 Which song did Paul write for the fashion premiere of one of his daughters?
10 In what year did he receive a Lifetime Achievement Grammy?
11 *Pipes Of Peace* was the sequel to which album?
12 What guise did he take on to promote his Liverpool Institute of the Performing Arts?
13 Who was the Bond girl in the film where Wings sang the title track?
14 Where is The Paul McCartney Kindergarten where children are taught English through his songs?
15 Whose record did he beat by performing in front of a record 184,000 in Brazil?
16 What was his first solo US No. 1?
17 What was the name of his late 80s/early 90s world tour?
18 In 1988 he received an honorary doctorate from which university?
19 Who duetted with him on his first song that reached No. 1 on both sides of the Atlantic?
20 Where did his world tour which began in 1989 begin?

1   Which Free member was brought back to life after 35 minutes in 1975?
2   Which group had three members pay £5 fines for urinating against a London petrol station?
3   Who followed up her No. 1 hit with a song called "Ring Of Ice"?
4   Which society collects performance royalties for British composers?
5   Which TV cop series theme tune was a hit in 1953 for Ray Anthony?
6   Which gift to the royal family inspired HMV to manufacture the world's smallest working gramophone records?
7   How is Trevor Sandford DSM better known?
8   Which song begins "Midnight, one more night without sleeping"?
9   What do drummers play the high hat cymbals with?
10   Which brothers are singing on the flip side of Cliff Richard's "Saviour's Day" in 1990?
11   How is David Spencer better known?
12   Which song title links Frankie Laine and Jimi Hendrix?
13   Which country are Crash Test Dummies from?
14   Which Paul Simon song begins "Wish I was a Kellogg's Corn Flake"?
15   Who won a 1982 Grammy as Best Pop Female Vocal Performance for "You Should Hear How She Talks About You"?
16   Which band included Ron "Pigpen" McKernan?
17   Which singer/presenter/actor is also the name of a Victorian dance?
18   What were Chicago called on their first album?
19   Who has not made an album – Ronald Reagan, Pope John Paul II or Winston Churchill?
20   Who organizes the Grammy awards?

1   Who had 80s hits with "Piece Of The Action" and "Run For Your Life"?
2   What was Perry Como's follow up to "Delaware"?
3   Which album contains the track "Married With Children"?
4   What was Dr Feelgood's first top ten hit?
5   Who had a 80s album called Down In The Groove?
6   What is the last word of "Se A Vida E" by the Pet Shop Boys?
7   Who is David Evans better known as?
8   Which album contains the track "The Man's Too Strong"?
9   What subject did Chrissie Hynde study at university?
10 What followed the Pet Shop Boys' "Always On My Mind" at the top of the charts?
11 What was John Lennon's first posthumous hit that was not a re-entry?
12 What does the group Kraftwerk's name actually mean?
13 What was the first top ten for Fats Domino?'
14 What was the title of Cockney Rebel's debut album?
15 Sri Lankan-born Keith Potger was a member of which 60s hitmakers still touring in the 90s?
16 What was Adam Faith's autobiography called?
17 Who had a late 80s album called *Motormouth*?
18 Who had 70s hits with "I Don't Wanna Go To Chelsea" and "Radio Radio"?
19 What was The Commodores' follow-up to "Easy"?
20 Whose debut album was called *Ropin' The Wind*?

1 Who sang "Beauty School Dropout" in the film *Grease*?
2 Which fellow-singer did Bryan Ferry name his son after?
3 Who wrote the children's opera *Romulus Hunt*?
4 Who celebrated her 21st birthday party in the Chamber of Horrors in 1968?
5 Which number was a top 40 hit for Wilson Pickett?
6 Whose second album was called *You Want It, You Got It*?
7 Who made the album *Irish Heartbeat* with the Chieftains?
8 What was Donny Hathaway's cause of death?
9 Whose first UK hit was "I Wanna Love My Life Away"?
10 Which singer starred in a film with Laurence Olivier in 1979 and received the largest-ever fee for a debut role?
11 Who had a 1980s album called *Spanish Train And Other Stories*?
12 What are the forces of good and evil called on Prince's "Lovesexy"?
13 Who was the first person to take "Yesterday" into the top ten?
14 Which singer was Leo Sayer's manager?
15 Who made a comeback album, *Spirit*, in 1989?
16 Which musical instrument does Oleta Adams play?
17 Which singer's supposed 75th birthday was commemorated on a Tanzanian stamp in 1994?
18 In 1980 who did CBS say was the world's top-selling male singer?
19 What was Smokey Robinson's first solo No. 1 single?
20 Which 60s chart-topper compered Buddy Holly's only UK tour?

LEVEL 3

1 What was Cliff's first self-produced No. 1 hit?
2 With which single did Cliff score his century – his 100th chart hit?
3 What was Cliff's first single on the Rocket label?
4 The year Cliff first sang at Eurovision he released an album, *Cliff In* where?
5 Which band did he form while still at school?
6 Who duetted on "The Wedding" in 1996?
7 In what year was Cliff's first No. 1 album?
8 Which top seed was playing when rain delayed a Wimbledon match and Cliff staged an impromptu singalong concert?
9 How many weeks did his first No. 1 spend at the top of the charts?
10 What was his first album, which was from a pantomime he was appearing in?
11 Where did his 1994 *Heathcliff* UK tour begin?
12 What was Cliff's first No. 1 without The Shadows?
13 Between 1988 and 1990 he was involved with three Christmas No. 1s; what was the middle one?
14 What was the name of his 1989 video hits package?
15 Who did he write the book *Which One's Cliff*? with?
16 Which song did Cliff's "Daddy's Home" fail to topple from the No. 1 spot and make it a Christmas No. 1?
17 Which chart ballad from *Summer Holiday* did Cliff sing against the background of the Acropolis?
18 Cliff celebrated his 47th birthday with a top ten hit with which song?
19 On whose show did he sing the Eurovision selection of songs when he represented the UK for the second time?
20 Who co-wrote "Bachelor Boy" with Cliff Richard?

1 Which group's first UK hit was called "Candida"?
2 Which Rolling Stone plays dulcimer on "Lady Jane"?
3 Which Janis Joplin album was posthumously released?
4 Who was the only British girl singer to have three No. 1 hits in the 1960s?
5 What is Cliff Richard sporting on the cover of his *I'm No Hero* album?
6 Who did Brian Bennett replace in which group in 1961?
7 Whose *Bop 'Til You Drop* was the first digitally-recorded rock album?
8 Which was the second group with Roman numerals in its name to have a No. 1?
9 Who was the first British artist to enter the US top 20?
10 Whose debut album was called *Tops With Me*?
11 In which decade was David Bowie's "Laughing Gnome" recorded?
12 Which TV series did the 1981 No. 2 hit "Chi Mai" come from?
13 What was the name of the group made up of Mary Hopkin, Peter Skellern and Julian Lloyd-Webber?
14 What was Barry Manilow's first top ten hit?
15 What did Shakin' Stevens call himself between his real name Michael Barratt and his later stage persona?
16 Who other than Michael Ball had a hit called "Love Changes Everything"?
17 Whose first solo album was *Talk Is Cheap*?
18 Which item of Jimi Hendrix's was auctioned at Sotheby's for £14,300?
19 How is Frederick Heath better known?
20 In which film did Elvis play the role of Tulsa McLean?

1   What was Al Green's 1972 hit single?
2   Who had an early 90s album called *Changing Faces*?
3   Which superstar won the Grammy award in 1984 and 1985 for Best Male Vocal Performance?
4   What is the last word of "Rotterdam" by The Beautiful South?
5   What was Russ Conway's follow-up single to "More And More Party Pops"?
6   Who had a 80s album called *Wonderland*?
7   Who had a 90s album called *Cha Cha Cha*?
8   Who was backed by The Fish?
9   Which album contains the tracks "Gates Of Eden" and "It's Allright Ma (I'm Only Bleeding)"?
10   Whose backing band was The Magic Band?
11   What was Bing Crosby's follow-up to "Around The World"?
12   Who had 80s minor hits with "La Luna" and "World Without You"?
13   Which Logie Award was won by Jason Donovan in 1987?
14   What replaced Bros' first No. 1?
15   What was The Beloved's only chart hit?
16   What is the next year after 6565 to have a prediction in Zager & Evans' 1969 No. 1 hit "In The Year 2525"?
17   "Silver Machine" was the first top ten for which group?
18   Who was bound in chains lying naked on the floor?
19   Who had 70s hits with "Get It" and "Duke Of Earl"?
20   Which album contains the tracks "Gone Hollywood" and "Another Nervous Wreck"?

LEVEL 3

1   Who were at No. 1 when Princess Margaret married Anthony Armstrong-Jones?
2   Which US band featured on the first-ever *Old Grey Whistle Test*?
3   Who were Chynna, Carnie and Wendy?
4   Which first name did Jackie Wilson use as an amateur boxer?
5   What is Bobby Vinton's real first name?
6   Who was criticized for singing "The Star-Spangled Banner" in a Latin style before a baseball match in 1968?
7   Whose only UK hit was "Time For Living"?
8   How is Kevin Donovan better known?
9   Which vocalist is a former Miss America?
10 Which musical instrument did Connie Francis perform with as a child?
11 In which country was Fugee McLef Jean born?
12 What was Bill Haley's follow-up to "Rock Around the Clock" after it had first been No. 1?
13 Who established their own Brothers record label?
14 Who made the double album *Black Moses*?
15 Whose debut album was *Stompin' At the Savoy*?
16 Which band was Kim Carnes a member of in the late 60s?
17 Which film did Brenda Lee's "Speak To Me Pretty" come from?
18 Which group's name is Spanish for 'wolves'?
19 Before 1997 which was the best-selling UK album in the US charts?
20 Who named their group after a steamroller they had seen repairing a road?

1 Which of their songs was considered for Eurovision before "Waterloo" won?
2 "Mamma Mia" ended the nine-week reign of which chart-topper?
3 "The Winner Takes It All" first appeared on which Abba album?
4 Abba won with Waterloo in 1974 but in which venue?
5 What was their first No. 1 on both sides of the Atlantic?
6 On which solo album by one of the band did "S.O.S." first appear?
7 What did "Super Trouper" replace at the top of the charts?
8 *Abba The Movie* was filmed after a tour where?
9 Which Bjorn and Benny song was No. 1 in 1985?
10 Which Abba song did U2 perform on their *Zoo TV* Tour?
11 Which two-colour album sleeve included the stars' autographs?
12 What was their fifth single with a repeat in the title?
13 What part did Andersson play at Bjorn and Agnetha's wedding?
14 "Voulez-Vous" was on the other side of which single?
15 What was the penultimate No. 1 in their run of seven successive No. 1 albums?
16 What was their top ten follow up to "Waterloo"?
17 Which was their first album for six years that did not hit No. 1 after a run of chart-toppers?
18 What was the subtitle of their third hit of 1979?
19 Which Abba single was Australia's top seller in 1976?
20 Which was their biggest hit single in the US?

1 Who did Jon Landau produce in the 1970s and call the "future of rock 'n' roll"?
2 Which blues artist died in July 1959 of liver failure?
3 Who did The Chieftains record with on their first album?
4 Who's dancing in a red dress on the LP cover of *She's So Unusual*?
5 Peter Cetera was vocalist with which band?
6 Who had a 1960s album called *Blues Breakers*?
7 Which Elvis movie featured "Can't Help Falling In Love"?
8 Which British group's US LP cover was deemed in such bad taste in 1966 that 750,000 copies were recalled?
9 Which song refers to a bloody rose lying crushed and broken in the virgin snow?
10 Who signed James Taylor to Apple in 1968?
11 Who were Graham Russell and Russell Hitchcock?
12 Whose debut album was *Isn't It Grand Boys* in 1966?
13 Which forename is shared by Paul McCartney's father and son?
14 Which group takes its name from a 1950s Bette Davis film?
15 Who is the songwriting brother-in-law of the 1960s singer Julie Rogers?
16 Which country were Teach-In from?
17 Which concert was a follow-up to Live Aid and raised funds for the unemployed in the Irish Republic?
18 What were Roxy Music named after?
19 Whose son is called Edan?
20 How is Vito Farinola better known?

1. "If I Had A Hammer" was the first top ten for which singer?
2. Which album contains the track "Rocket Queen"?
3. Who provided the music for the TV show *Scully*?
4. Who had a 1976 album called On Tour?
5. Who had a late 80s album called *Inspirations*?
6. What was Doris Day's follow-up to "Whatever Will Be Will Be"?
7. Who had an early 90s album called *A Fond Kiss*?
8. What was Julie Covington's next chart single after "Don't Cry For Me Argentina"?
9. What is the last word of "If You're Thinking Of Me" by Dodgy?
10. What replaced "Karma Chameleon" at No. 1?
11. What was Peter Noone of Herman's Hermits name when he appeared in *Coronation Street*?
12. Lynda Turner and Shirley Porter missed out on a No. 1 when they left which group?
13. Who had 80s hits with "Go Wild In The Jungle" and "I Want Candy"?
14. Which Grammy was won by Bette Midler in 1973?
15. What is the last word of "Don't Dream It's Over" by Crowded House?
16. Which amazing event took place when "Let The Heartaches Begin" was at No. 1?
17. Who had 70s hits with "Long As I Can See The Light" and "Have You Ever Seen The Rain"?
18. Which Bob Dylan song covered by Jimi Hendrix reached the charts?
19. What was the first top ten hit for Lovin' Spoonful?
20. What was Bobby Darin's follow-up to "Lazy River"?

1 Which duo were resident songwriters with McGuinness Flint?
2 Which singer/songwriter did Little Eva babysit for?
3 On which album was James Taylor's "You've Got A Friend"?
4 What was Neil Diamond's best-selling single from *The Jazz Singer*?
5 Who was the musical "They're Playing Our Song" based on?
6 Whose autobiography was called *Laughter in the Rain*?
7 Whose album *Out Of The Blue* was a reaction to punk rock?
8 Which David Essex song was his last No. 1 of the 70s?
9 Who started out with the group Smile in the early 70s?
10 Who wrote the music for the Worzels' "Combine Harvester"?
11 How long were the Bee Gees given to come up with the songs for *Saturday Night Fever*?
12 Who was leader of Kilburn And The High Roads?
13 How is Gary Webb better known?
14 Who wrote "One Day At A Time", a 1970s hit for Lena Martell?
15 Who did Mungo Jerry's Ray Dorset write "Feels Like I'm In Love" for and why did he not record it?
16 What was Shakin' Stevens's first No. 1 that he wrote himself?
17 Who was Guiot who co-wrote "Stay" for Shakespears Sister?
18 Who are credited with writing "Don't Go Breaking My Heart"?
19 Who wrote "Both Sides Now", a hit for Judy Collins?
20 Who died of a heroin overdose the same month as John Lennon was murdered?

1   What were they called when they performed in Australia in the early 60s?
2   What did they sing on their first appearance on *Top Of The Pops*?
3   Who in addition to Bill Good was an early promoter from whome they got their name?
4   Who co-produced the album *Main Course* with them?
5   What was their first US No. 1?
6   In 1978 whose version of "Emotion" meant Gibb compositions held the top three places in the US charts?
7   The Bee Gees wrote and Barry co-produced which best-selling country single?
8   Who covered their "To Love Somebody" in 1992?
9   What replaced "You Win Again" at the top of the UK charts?
10 "Nobody's Child" raised money for which cause?
11 In 1992 they went to which record label after a spell with Warner Bros?
12 What was the title of Barry's No. 1 in Australia before they returned to the UK?
13 Which Carole King song did they perform on the tribute album *Tapestry Revisited*?
14 What was their last US No. 1 of the 70s?
15 Which 1996 Jack Lemmon film featured "Stayin' Alive"?
16 What was Robin's second solo album called?
17 For which Kathleen Turner movie did Maurice contribute the soundtrack?
18 What was their first hit on both sides of the Atlantic?
19 Which 1985 Diana Ross album did Barry co-produce?
20 Which No. 1 gave them the record of being the first group to have a No. 1 in three different decades?

1   Which Beatles album includes "Eight Days A Week"?
2   What is Diana Ross's middle name?
3   Who starred in the Western featuring the No. 1 "Man From Laramie"?
4   Who was chosen to play a classical concert by Arthur Rubenstein?
5   What does the instrumentalist in Captain and Tenille play?
6   Who persuaded Connie Francis to update "Who's Sorry Now?"?
7   Which Beach Boys single took six months, 90 hours of tape and four studios to make?
8   Who was the first woman to study philosophy at the Gukushuin University?
9   Who wrote "The First Cut Is The Deepest" for P.P. Arnold?
10 What was Roy Orbison's last No. 1 in his lifetime?
11 Which was the third group with Roman numerals in its name to have a No. 1?
12 Which chart-topper was in *Sister Act II*?
13 Which group was made up of Maria Mendiola and Mayte Mateus?
14 Which word was in both Art Garfunkel's No. 1 hits?
15 According to "19" what was the average age of a soldier in World War II?
16 How is Arthur Kelm better known?
17 Who worked at Luton's Vauxhall car plant and was a member of Kat Kool And The Kool Kats?
18 What is Dave Stewart's middle initial on some songwriting credits?
19 In UB40's "If It Happens Again" what was "It"?
20 Who played guitar on "Wuthering Heights"?

1 Which album contains the tracks "I Am The Law" and "Love Action"?
2 What was Dave Dee, Dozy, Beaky, Mick and Tich's follow-up to "Last Night In Soho"?'
3 What is the last word of "Marblehead Johnson" by The Bluetones?
4 Who had a 90s album called *Neverland*?
5 What replaced 'There's No-one Quite Like Grandma' at the top of the charts?
6 What was the first top ten hit for The Byrds?'
7 Who had a 90s album called *Evergreen*?
8 Who had a 70s album called *In For The Kill*?
9 Which drummer produced "Love Don't Live Here Anymore" for Jimmy Nail in 1985?
10 Who was backed by The Commotions?
11 What is the last word of "The Riverboat Song" by Ocean Colour Scene?
12 Which author of a celebrated tear-jerking film co-wrote The Beatles' movie *Yellow Submarine*?
13 What did Elvis's ex-wife call her son?
14 Who had 70s hits with "Our World" and "Stay With Me"?
15 Whose debut album was called *Reckless*?
16 Which role was played by Elvis Presley in the film *Love Me Tender*?
17 The first No. 1 for Aqua was released on which record label?
18 What was Neil Diamond's follow-up solo single after "You Don't Bring Me Flowers"?
19 Who had a 60s album called *Axis: Bold As Love*?
20 Which hit by Mungo Jerry did not have a drummer?

1   What did "Three Times A Lady" replace as Motown's UK best-seller?
2   Which instrument did Lionel Richie play with The Commodores?
3   Who was Linda Womack's father?
4   Which group was Ronnie White in?
5   Who appeared in the films *Muscle Beach Party* and *Bikini Beach*?
6   Who was the eldest Jackson brother?
7   Who did Berry Gordy sell Motown to in 1988?
8   Where was Gamble and Huff's record label based in the 70s?
9   Which record label did Lionel Richie go to after leaving Motown?
10 Which Jackson's real name was Toriano Adaryll?
11 Who was the first major star to leave Motown in 1964?
12 Which song did Lou Rawls make after the Budweiser beer he advertised?
13 Who left Motown in 1967 to set up their own labels?
14 Where in the US were Gladys Knight And The Pips all from?
15 Who made an album called *The Wildest Organ In Town*?
16 Where did Motown relocate to in 1971?
17 Who did Randy Taraborelli write a biography of in 1991?
18 Who wrote "Reet Petite" with Jackie Wilson's cousin?
19 Who was Miss Wright – and Miss Right – for Stevie Wonder in 1970?
20 Which song did Lionel Richie write for Kenny Rogers?

Answers

Novelty Songs (Quiz 63)
1 Laurel and Hardy.   2 Cadillac.   3 Anthony Newley, Joan Collins.
4 *The Millionairess*.   5 Roland Rat Superstar.   6 Wink Martindale.   7 Kevin Keegan.
8 "My Old Man's A Dustman".   9 Joan Collins Fan Club (Julian Clary).
10 Craig Johnston.   11 Harry Secombe, Peter Sellers and Spike Milligan.
12 "You're A Pink Toothbrush, I'm A Blue Toothbrush".   13 Barron Knights.
14 "No Chance".   15 René and Yvette (*'Allo 'Allo*).   16 The Krankies.
17 The Archies.   18 "Bloodnok's Rock 'N' Roll".   19 "The Old Payola Roll Blues".
20 Kevin the Gerbil.

1   Which of their 90s releases reached the highest spot?
2   Which 90s album topped the album charts?
3   Which Beatles song replaced a Beatles song at No. 1 – the first time in chart history that an act had replaced itself?
4   Who was the first Beatle to have a solo No. 1?
5   In 1991 which song was used as a wake-up call for the crew on the space shuttle flight?
6   What is the name of Paul's studio in Sussex?
7   What was their first No. 1 on both sides of the Atlantic?
8   Where was "Free As A Bird" first played by a DJ?
9   Which album kept the 1995 Anthology Volume I off the top album spot?
10 Of their first nine albums which didn't reach No. 1?
11 What was the name of the hospital in which John Lennon lost his fight for life?
12 Which chart position did "Love Me Do" reach on the 20th anniversary of its original release?
13 Who sang the first Lennon and McCartney song to top the US country chart?
14 What was their first album on their Apple label?
15 Which 60s pop star settled out of court with the Beatles over *Ready Steady Go* videos in which The Beatles appeared?
16 What was their last No. 1 in the US in the 60s?
17 In which decade was the band's 16th US No. 1 album?
18 Which was their first album which mentioned them by name?
19 What was the name of the club they first played in Hamburg?
20 What was their first UK million-seller?

LEVEL 3

1 Who sang "Raindrops Keep Falling on My Head" in the film?
2 What colour was the Island 45 record label in the 60s?
3 Who was the first artist to have two Oscar-winning songs in the same decade?
4 Whose first UK hit was "I'm A Man"?
5 What was Engelbert Humperdinck's last No. 1 in the 60s?
6 From which film did "Rock Around The Clock" come from?
7 Which film had the song "The Morning After"?
8 What was The Bachelors' only No. 1?
9 Which London group failed an EMI audition and had 15 top ten hits?
10 What is the main colour on the *Beggar's Banquet* album?
11 Who was known as the Godfather of Rhythm and Blues?
12 Who wrote Jackie Wilson's "The Sweetest Feeling"?
13 On which label was Lionel Richie's 1992 album *Back To Front*?
14 Who was the first solo artist to have a No. 1 album?
15 Whose real surname was Ivanhoe?
16 Who had a 60s album called *Please Get My Name Right*?
17 In which film did Elvis play the role of Pacer Burton?
18 How is Charles Westover better known?
19 In which country was Danny Williams born?
20 Which hit was based on a stay by Justin Hayward in Jamaica?

Quiz 62 Pot Luck 32

Answers – see page 464

LEVEL 3

1 Who had a 90s album called *Life*?
2 What is the last word of "Milk" by Garbage?
3 What was Billy Fury's first top ten?
4 What replaced "Stand And Deliver" at No. 1?
5 What was Ken Dodd's follow-up to "Love Is Like A Violin"?
6 Which ecclesiastical-sounding group was formed by Dave Stewart?
7 Which album contains the tracks "Turn It On Again" and "Misunderstanding"?
8 Which band started life as The Pendletones?
9 In which year did UB40 first have a No. 1 single?
10 Who had a 80s album called *Original Masters*?
11 What group was Steve Winwood a member of after The Spencer Davis Group?
12 Which non-Beatles film did the second oldest Beatle appear in in 1967?
13 Who had 70s hits with "Homely Girl" and "It's Time For Love"?
14 What was Cliff Richard's first self-produced No. 1?
15 The first No. 1 for Peter Andre was released on which record label?
16 Which Way was written by Roy Wood?
17 What was the first top ten single for Transvision Vamp?
18 Who had 80s hits with "Mirror In The Bathroom" and "Too Nice To Talk To"?
19 Which song was at No. 1 at the time of the 1966 general election?
20 Who had a 90s album called *Done By The Forces Of Nature*?

1 Which duo sang with the Avalon Boys featuring Chill Wills on their 1975 hit?
2 What type of car did that Old Fashioned Girl Eartha Kitt want that would accommodate a bowling alley?
3 Which husband-and-wife team were on the album *Fool Britannia* about the Profumo affair?
4 Which film inspired the novelty hit "Goodness Gracious Me"?
5 Whose *Cassette Of The Album* reached 67 in the album charts?
6 Who had "Deck Of Cards" in the charts five times in 14 years?
7 Who was Head Over Heels In Love in 1979?
8 Which song had the lines "[It's] full of toadstools – How do you know? – There's not mushroom inside!"?
9 Who was Leader Of The Pack in 1988?
10 Which Australian was credited on Englandneworder's "World In Motion"?
11 Who had an album called *How To Win An Election* in 1964?
12 Which song ends with "When we both use the same toothpaste"?
13 Who had a hit with "Pop Go The Workers" in 1965?
14 What was Billy Connolly's response to J.J. Barrie's "No Charge"?
15 Who had a hit with "Je T'Aime" in 1986?
16 Who had a hit with "Fan'Dabi'Dozi" twice in 1981?
17 Whose first song, "Bang-Shang-A-Lang", launched their US TV show?
18 What was on the other side of the Goons' "Ying Tong Song" in 1956?
19 In which song did Stan Freberg introduce Clyde Ankle?
20 Who had a hit with "Summer Holiday" in 1984?

1 Where was Oasis's first gig in the south of England?
2 What is the last word of "Wonderwall" by Oasis?
3 At which New York club did they perform their first US gig?
4 What was the first year they appeared at the Glastonbury Festival?
5 What did Oasis' second No. 1 replace at the top of the charts?
6 Which band were Bonehead and Guigsy in before Liam Gallagher joined them as lead singer?
7 Who took over as their manager in 1993?
8 What was their first No. 1 to go straight to the top spot?
9 In which part of Manchester were the Gallagher brothers born?
10 How did Liam break his foot in 1994?
11 In 1994 which country expelled them after a riot on a ferry?
12 Which Paul, as well as McCartney and Noel, was part of The Smokin' Jo Filters on a charity recording?
13 Whose photograph is in the room on the cover of *Definitely Maybe*?
14 For what crime was Noel Gallagher put on probation at the age of 13?
15 The Mike Flowers Pops produced an easy listening spoof of which single?
16 Who finally produced *Definitely Maybe*?
17 Whose *PopMart* tour did they join in 1997?
18 Where did Alan White make his debut with the band?
19 What was the venue of their first professional gig?
20 At which London store did they give a midnight concert to promote *What's The Story (Morning Glory)*?

1 Whose last hit was "Cowboy Jimmy Joe"?
2 What song from *Dr Dolittle* won an Oscar in 1967?
3 Which David Bowie video was censored because of nudity?
4 Which Rolling Stone produced "The Art Of Chris Farlowe"?
5 Who made a comeback in 1979 with her album *Broken English*?
6 What is Neil Young wearing on the album cover of *After The Gold Rush*?
7 What 50's song goes: "Oo-ee oo-ah-ah ting tang walla walla bing bang"?
8 Whose first hit was "Leaving Las Vegas"?
9 What was the first song ever to win an Oscar?
10 Which Orchestra did Procul Harum make an album with in 1972?
11 Which country did Plastic Bertrand come from?
12 Who was lead singer with The Floaters?
13 How many No. 1 hits did Elvis Presley have before 1997?
14 Where did Marc Almond study music?
15 How old was Bryan Hyland when he had a US No. 1 with "Itsy Bitsy Teeny Weeny Yellow Polka Dot Bikini"?
16 Which Lisa Stansfield song was on the soundtrack of *Indecent Proposal*?
17 Where did Black Box come from?
18 Who had a 60s hit with "Don't Jump Off the Roof Dad"?
19 Which sitcom did Sonia appear in?
20 Which group was Michael Steele in in 1989?

1 Who had a 90s album called *Santa Monica '72*?
2 Which football team does Alison Moyet support?
3 What is the last word of "Woman" by Neneh Cherry?
4 What was Val Doonican's follow-up to "If The Whole World Stopped Loving"?
5 What was Michael Ball's character's name when he appeared in *Coronation Street*?
6 What is reggae singer Pliers' real name?
7 Who was Joe Cocker named after?
8 Which album contains the track "I Hate You (But You're Interesting')"?
9 What was the first top ten for The Merseybeats?
10 The first No. 1 for Tori Amos was released on which record label?
11 Which comic had a 70s album called One Man Show?
12 Which first was achieved by Frank Ifield in the early 60s?
13 Which group made a reunion album in 1994 called *Far From Home*?
14 Who had 70s hits with "I Want Your Love" and "Good Times"?
15 What was Ruby Murray's first top ten?
16 Which pop star said, "Women should be obscene and not heard."?
17 Still on 60s nostalgia, what name does David Grundy go under?
18 Who had 80s minor hits with "You Don't Know" and "Like Flames"?
19 Which children's author died on the same day that Johnny Rotten was born?
20 Who had an early 90s album called *Tongues And Tails*?

LEVEL 3

1   What was Graceland before it was a mansion?
2   What was the band with Elvis, Scotty Moore and Bill Black called?
3   The *Young World* newspaper of which country declared Elvis Public Enemy No. 1 in 1960?
4   Why did Americans put the wrong address on letters in 1993?
5   Which annual Ball commemorates Elvis in Memphis?
6   Who hosted the "Welcome Home Elvis" Show in 1960?
7   Who played the older Elvis in the 1996 revival of *Elvis* in London?
8   Which Harold Robbins novel was *King Creole* based on?
9   What was given away with the album *A Date With Elvis* in 1959?
10 Which Elvis magazine was first published in February 1960?
11 Who played the title role in the TV film *Elvis* in 1979?
12 Which was Elvis's only million-seller between 1962 and 1969?
13 What was Peter Guralnick's biography of Elvis called?
14 Which was the only Elvis single between November 1960 and May 1962 not to reach No. 1?
15 Who with Elvis made up the so-called Million-Dollar Quartet?
16 Which Elvis No. 1 is the only one for which he is credited with the writing?
17 Which Elvis hit was the first record ever to go straight to No. 1?
18 What did Elvis buy with the $5,000 he received on signing with RCA?
19 What was the first private record Elvis made in 1954?
20 What was Elvis's first hit after he left the Army?

1 The band whose first top ten entry was "She Makes My Nose Bleed" hails from which city?
2 How many singles had Wet Wet Wet released from *High On The Happy Side* before "Goodnight Girl" got to No. 1?
3 In what year did Shed Seven have their first top 20 hit?
4 What was Hanson's follow-up to "Where's The Love"?
5 What is the last word of Boyzone's "No Matter What"?
6 What did New Kids On The Block's second No. 1 replace at the top of the charts?
7 What was PJ and Duncan's first top 30 hit?
8 Which singer's Bond theme was sampled on Robbie Williams' first solo No. 1 after leaving Take That ?
9 What is in the background of 911's *There It Is* album?
10 Which member of East 17 contributed to their first hit which featured an artist from outside the band?
11 What was the title of Take That's debut single which missed the UK top 75?
12 The band whose first top ten entry was "All You Good Good People" hails from which town?
13 What was the first US No. 1 for New Kids On The Block?
14 Take That's top ten debut was a cover of whose hit?
15 What is Ronan Keating's very own baby boy called?
16 What was Take That's first US hit?
17 What item of clothing are Spike and Lee not wearing on the sleeve notes of *The Journey* which Jimmy is?
18 Who created and managed New Kids On The Block?
19 What was Wham!'s Best Of album called?
20 What was the first Backstreet Boys hit to make the top 20?

1   What song sees the joker tell the thief, "There must be some way out of here"?
2   What was Craig Douglas's occupation before "Only Sixteen"?
3   Where did the singers of "Cinderella Rockefella" come from?
4   Who backed Tony Sheridan on "My Bonnie (Lies Over The Ocean)"?
5   Which band consisted of the Duggans and the Brennans?
6   Which group was made up of Allan, Graham, Tony, Eric and Bobby?
7   Which hit links Ketty Lester and Elvis Presley?
8   Whose orchestra had a 1950s hit with "The Faithful Hussar"?
9   Who wrote "Orville's Song" for Keith Harris?
10 What is Lemmy's group?
11 Which film had the Oscar-winning song "We May Never Love Like This Again"?
12 Who had the original "The Only Way Is Up"?
13 Which DJ was behind S Express?
14 Which director's film backed stage performances of the Pet Shop Boys' "Heart"?
15 Which group were at No. 1 when Charles and Diana got married?
16 Which Mary Hopkin song was originally called "Darogoi Dlimmoyo"?
17 What language was it originally in?
18 Other than the Hollies hit, where else does Jennifer Eccles appear?
19 Who were originally Dean Ford And The Gaylords?
20 Which group had their own Big Frock record label?

1 Which album contains the track "Motownphilly"?
2 Who founded his own Respond record label?
3 What was Duane Eddy's 60s follow-up to "The Theme From Peter Gunn"?
4 What was Bob Dylan's follow-up to "Lay Lady Lay"?
5 What is the last word of "Flying" by Cast?
6 Who had a 1991 hit with "Love Rears Its Ugly Head"?
7 Who had a 80s album called V Deep?
8 In 1996, who did a cover of "Daydream Believer"?
9 Which Elton John song did Ian Botham choose on Desert Island Discs?
10 Which Doctor Who recorded "When I'm 64"?
11 What replaced "Earth Song" at No. 1?
12 Sting was awarded an honorary doctorate at which university?
13 In which US city did Elvis Presley make most of his live performances?
14 Who had an early 80s album called Can't Get Enough?
15 The first No. 1 for All Saints was released on which record label?
16 Who managed to get "Barabajagal" into a song title?
17 Who had 70s hits with "My Best Friend's Girl" and "Just What I Wanted"?
18 What was The Applejacks' only UK top ten hit?
19 What is the last word of "Beautiful Ones" by Suede?
20 What did Robbie Williams' first No. 1 replace at the top of the charts?

1   Who was sacked from Radio 1 because he said the Transport Minister's wife had probably passed her driving test by slipping the examiner a fiver?
2   Which Belgian station did Steve Wright work for?
3   What was Chris Evans's 1992 Sunday show on Radio 1 called?
4   Who has a wife Sheila, four children and lives near Stowmarket?
5   Who was the first Radio 1 DJ to be knighted in 1990?
6   Which 60s singer presents a radio R&B show?
7   Which Radio DJ presented *Confessions* on TV?
8   Who presented the UK top 40 show on Radio 1 at the start of 1997?
9   Who is the only BBC national daily radio DJ to have had a No. 1 hit?
10 Who sang with Liz Kershaw and Bruno Brookes on "It Takes Two Baby"?
11 Who sang with Bruno and Liz on "Let's Dance"?
12 How was the former DJ J.P. Richardson better known?
13 What is John Peel's real surname?
14 Who presented the Radio 1 Breakfast Show between 1973 and 1978?
15 Who has been called the instigator of so called "zoo-radio"?
16 Who introduced Radio Luxembourg's "Under The Bedclothes Club"?
17 Whose catchphrase was "Your royal ruler, I wouldn't fool ya"?
18 Who was born on April Fool's Day in Oldham and has been a Capital Radio and Radio 1 DJ?
19 How was Michael Pasternak better known?
20 Whose autobiography was called *The Custard Stops At Hatfield*?

1   What replaced "Under The Bridge" at No. 1 the first time it hit the top of the charts?
2   What was Eternal's first No. 1 which went straight to the top spot?
3   What is the last word of "Finally Found" by The Honeyz?
4   What was Eternal's follow-up to their first No. 1?
5   What is the surname of Karen and Shellie whose second album was *Illumina*?
6   What was the first baby All Saint called?
7   Which En Vogue album features "Damn I Wanna Be Your Lover"?
8   "I Wanna Be The Only One" first came from which Eternal album?
9   Which Eternal hit featured Eric Clapton on guitar?
10   Which band were *Saturday Night Divas* on one of their top-selling albums?
11   What was TLC's debut top 20 single?
12   A former member of which group had a 1999 follow-up to a No. 1 with "I Got You"?
13   What is the last spoken word of "Bootie Call" by All Saints?
14   What was The Crystals' first top 20 hit?
15   What was The Ronettes' follow-up to their first top ten hit?
16   What was B*witched's first No. 1 on the Epic label?
17   Which TV presenter was a member of a band called Faith Hope And Charity?
18   What was Cleopatra's follow-up to their debut single?
19   What is the background colour of B*Witched's B*Witched?
20   What was the Supremes' first No. 1 on both sides of the Atlantic?

1 Who designed the album covers for Velvet Underground and Nico?
2 Which song links Elvis, Dorothy Squires and the Sex Pistols?
3 Who got to No. 18 with "Shifting Whispering Sands" in 1956?
4 What Stones album cover shows them dressed as sorcerers?
5 Who co-wrote "Fame" with John Lennon?
6 Which Paul Simon song begins "When I think back on all the crap I learned in high school"?
7 What is Chet Atkins's real first name?
8 Which film did the Oscar-winning "I'm Easy" come from?
9 What former Bee Gees manager produced the film *Saturday Night Fever*?
10 What is Pete Townshend holding on the cover of *The Who Sell Out* album?
11 What is Nana Mouskouri's only chart hit up to 1997?
12 Whose final album was *Message From the Country*?
13 Whose first band was Vance Arnold And The Avengers?
14 Who did Billy J. Kramer work for before entering the music business?
15 Which poet was part of a 1969 No. 1 hit?
16 Which country were Mouth and MacNeal from?
17 Whose unsuccessful follow-up to a No. 1 was called "Accidents"?
18 Which group was named after characters in "Tin Tin"?
19 Who has starred as Frank N. Furter in *The Rocky Horror Show,* and in *Neighbours* and *Grease*?
20 How was William Howard Ashton better known?

1 What is the last word of "Always Breaking My Heart" by Belinda Carlisle?
2 How old was the man who sang "Rave On" when he died?
3 Who was Keith Richards talking about when he said, "He's a wimp in disguise; he should go home and shave."?
4 Who recorded "Bring Your Daughter To The Slaughter"?
5 Which album contains the tracks "Space Time" and "Boss Dub"?
6 What was The Electric Light Orchestra's follow-up to "Evil Woman"?
7 The first No. 1 for Ace Of Base was released on which record label?
8 What was the first top ten hit for The Dubliners?
9 Whose 1977 *Animals* tour featured an inflatable pig?
10 Who had an early 90s album called *Everything's Alright Forever*?
11 Which British actor was Belinda Carlisle's father-in-law?
12 Julio Iglesias's chart-topper "Begin The Beguine" came from which show?
13 What was the first George Michael song to hit No. 1 in the US but fail to do so in the UK?
14 Which solo vocalist's surname is Gudmundsdottir?
15 Who had a 80s album called *The Whisper*?
16 Which film did a chart-topping ex-Playboy Bunny appear in in 1982?
17 What is the last word of "Someday" by Eternal?
18 Which vocal group had 70s hits with "Everything's Tuesday" and "Working On A Building Of Love"?
19 Which song by the Lambrettas recommends Calomine Lotion?
20 What was David Essex's follow-up to "Lamplight"?

1 Who was the organist on "A Whiter Shade Of Pale"?
2 Who left The Strawbs to join Yes?
3 Which band was Gary Brooker in before founding Procul Harum?
4 Who played keyboards with Erasure?
5 How is Rod Argent credited on San José's 1978 "Argentine Melody (Cancion de Argentina)"?
6 Which 1978 Elton John hit was an instrumental?
7 Which suitably-titled album did Billy Joel make in the US in 1974 although it was 10 years later that it was a minor UK hit?
8 Which band did Rod Argent found while still at school?
9 Who was keyboards player with The Doors?
10 Which pianist was one of the first Western musicians to visit China in 1991 with his *Oriental Melody* tour?
11 Who won a piano scholarship to the Juilliard School of Music in 1957?
12 Which jazz pianist had hits with "Take Five" and "Unsquare Dance"?
13 Who was keyboard player with the Moody Blues on "Go Now"?
14 Which Hammond organ specialist became Van Morrison's musical director in the early 90s?
15 Who was the original keyboard player with Pink Floyd?
16 Whose debut solo album was *Between Today And Yesterday*?
17 How is Silsoe better known?
18 Which theme music did Silsoe record for ITV's coverage of the 1986 World Cup Finals?
19 Which 70s David Bowie album did Rick Wakeman work on as a backing session musician?
20 How is Ferdinand la Menthe Morton better known?

1 Which Spice Girl has the most northerly birthplace?
2 What were the band known as when Emma joined?
3 Where was Mel C's first solo album recorded?
4 Who did they replace at No. 1 with the last single Geri was involved with?
5 On World Book Day 1998, Geri and Liam Gallagher both nominated which book as their favourite?
6 What was their only US No. 1 as a fivesome?
7 Which song was used in the Pepsi campaign?
8 Who did Madonna say was her favourite Spice Girl?
9 Which single was released in the UK during their 1998 US tour?
10 How many weeks did "Wannabe" stay at No. 1?
11 Which of their hits entered the US charts at 5 – the highest new entry ever by a UK act?
12 What was the stop-over on the first leg of their 1998 US tour?
13 In how many countries did "Wannabe" top the charts?
14 What was the last track on their first album?
15 What colour are Emma's sunglasses on the cover of *Spice*?
16 Which role does Dave Laudat have in the Spice Girls support staff?
17 Where did Geri go to grammar school?
18 What was their first No. 1 that was not a UK million-seller?
19 What is the first word of "Naked"?
20 How many times does "If You Can't Dance" appear in the chorus of the song with the same name?

1   Where did the Beatles stay in New York in their first week in the US?
2   Who did Bing Crosby Zing A Little Zong with in 1952?
3   What follows "I don't want to talk about it", in Rod Stewart's 1977 hit?
4   Whose *Imperial Bedroom* album has a Picasso-styled front cover?
5   Which song has the chorus "Lie la lie…"?
6   Who wrote the soundtrack for the Francis Ford Coppola film *Rumble Fish*?
7   Which record label was used by The Kinks throughout the 60s?
8   What soundtrack album was the best-selling album of the 50s?
9   What stands where "the Palais used to stand" in the 1980 Kinks hit?
10   Whose debut album was *Child Is The Father Of The Man*?
11   Who were Larry Cunningham's backing group?
12   Which group named themselves after a 1956 John Wayne film?
13   Whose first hit was "Endless Sleep"?
14   Who was the only non-Londoner in the Kinks?
15   How was Dino Paul Crocetti better known?
16   Who wrote a children's book called *The Saga Of Baby Divine*?
17   Which US group's only hits mention Tracy then Julie?
18   What injuries did James Taylor sustain in a 1969 motorbike accident?
19   Which singer/actor was Great Britain Irish Dance Champion at the age of 14?
20   Whose first album was called *God Shuffled His Feet*?

1 Who had an early 90s album called *The Martyr Mantras*?
2 What was The Everly Brothers' follow-up single to "Problems"?
3 What was Jonathan King's first top ten hit?
4 What is the last word of "Love II Love" by Damage?
5 How many months did it take The Beach Boys to make the single "Good Vibrations"?
6 Who was the first non-athlete to be inducted into Madison Square Garden's Walk Of Fame?
7 Which album contains the tracks "Love Or Confusion" and "Manic Depression"?
8 Who had 80s hits with "We Belong" and "All Fired Up"?
9 What was the first top ten hit for The Yardbirds?
10 Whose debut album was called *Natty Dread*?
11 Which Beatles song was inspired by teenager Melanie Coe?
12 Which music star was Bob Geldof's first best man?
13 Who had a late-80s album called *Getahead*?
14 Who had hits called "Smooth Operator" and "Sweetest Taboo"?
15 Who won 1989 Grammy Record of the Year with "Wind Beneath My Wings"?
16 Who had 70s hits with "Love Me Like A Lover" and "Rendezvous"?
17 Who had a 90s album called *Born Into The 90s*?
18 What was the first top ten for The King Brothers?
19 What was the first top ten hit for The Young Rascals?
20 What was the surname of 70s vocalist Melanie?

1 Which Cliff film was called *Wonderful To Be Young* in the USA?
2 What was Cliff's first religious album called?
3 Which album was recorded completely in Spanish?
4 Which show saw Cliff's TV debut?
5 How many weeks was "Bachelor Boy" in the charts in the US?
6 Which *Coronation Street* character was responsible for Cliff going on a diet – describing him as "that chubby Cliff Richard"?
7 In 1986 Cliff had duets in the charts three times but which went to No 1?
8 Which two pantomimes did Cliff record soundtracks of in the 60s?
9 In the *Cliff Richard Rock Special* in 1981, what did the audience wear?
10 What was Cliff's first film?
11 What was Cliff's autobiography called?
12 In which year did Cliff sing possible Eurovision songs on Cilla Black's TV show for viewers to vote for?
13 When Cliff fell ill at the Palladium in 1974 who took over for three shows?
14 Which Goodie starred with Cliff in *The Case* in 1972?
15 Which 1981 hit was first recorded by Shep And The Limelites in 1961?
16 In which Peter Shaffer play did Cliff make his straight stage debut in 1970?
17 Where did *Cliff Richard – The Event* take place in 1989?
18 Who duetted with Cliff on "Whenever God Shines His Light" in 1989?
19 In 1996 what did the *Daily Telegraph* refer to as "Cliffstock"?
20 Who decided to release "Please Don't Tease" as a single in 1960?

1　Which Aretha Franklin hit does Rupert Everett sing in a scene in the 1997 movie *My Best Friend's Wedding*?
2　Which 1990 single came from its singer's movie role as Lola Lovell?
3　Which 1998 movie with Drew Barrymore has a soundtrack of 80s hits including The Smiths and The Cure?
4　Which Lionel Richie hit from the 1985 film *White Nights* won an Oscar?
5　Who played Whitney Houston's manager in *The Bodyguard*?
6　Which singer played Sharon in the film *The Commitments*?
7　"Sooner Or Later" from the Madonna/Warren Beatty movie *Dick Tracy* was written by whom?
8　Which film included the hit "All The Right Places" by Lisa Stansfield?
9　Which film included the Oscar-winning song "(I've Had The) Time Of My Life"?
10　Which Leonardo DiCaprio film had a soundtrack which included Garbage and Radiohead?
11　Which Iggy Pop composition was used on the *Trainspotting* soundtrack?
12　Who recorded "The Look Of Love" for *Casino Royale*?
13　Which Richard Gere movie used Blondie's "Call Me" on its soundtrack?
14　Who sang the Bond theme in the movie where Jonathan Pryce played media baron Elliot Carver?
15　Whose "Trouble" was reissued after it was used in the *Mighty Morphin Power Rangers* movie?
16　Which husband and wife duo starred in *Good Times* and *Chastity*?
17　Who directed the movie of the life of Jim Morrison?
18　Whose album *Themes* included soundtracks from his films such as *Blade Runner* and *Mutiny On The Bounty*?
19　Which Richard Gere movie had a 50s chart-topper on the soundtrack singing "I'll Be Seeing You"?
20　Which film did Malcolm McLaren make about The Sex Pistols?

LEVEL 3

1 Who played in the group Aphrodite's Child with Demis Roussos?
2 Which Rolling Stone served for two years in the RAF?
3 Who had a hit in 1956 with "Moonlight Gambler"?
4 Which boxer appeared on the album cover of *Band On The Run*?
5 Who had the original version of "Na Na Hey Hey Kiss Him Goodbye"?
6 Who were described as a "con" by Pete Murray on *Juke Box Jury*?
7 Which Ken Dodd hit was the third-biggest-selling UK 1960s single?
8 Which former Animal managed and produced Slade?
9 Which Canadian gave EMI their biggest-ever hit in 1957?
10 Which Gallagher and Lyle album shows them on rollerskates?
11 How is Florencia Bisenta de Casillas Martinez Cardona better known?
12 What was the Oscar-winning song from the 1976 film *A Star Is Born*?
13 A recording of whose singing at a 1957 church fête was sold at Sotheby's for £78,000?
14 Who were the first Scottish band to have three No. 1s?
15 Which town does Tony Di Bart come from?
16 Which song title links a hit by Kool And The Gang and The Gap Band?
17 Who was Tommy Bruce's backing group?
18 What was Joe Henderson's nickname?
19 Why was Wilson Pickett arrested in New York in November 1974?
20 Which raunchy dance troupe appeared on *The Kenny Everett Video Show*?

1   What is the last word of "Undivided Love" by Louise?
2   Which album contains the tracks "Love Tried To Welcome Me" and "Sanctuary"?
3   Who was the first non-Soviet to advertise a product on Russian television?
4   What was Georgie Fame's follow-up to "Get Away"?
5   Who had hits with "Banana Republic" and "Like Clockwork"?
6   What subject did Yoko Ono become the first woman to study at the Gukushuin University?
7   Who had a late 80s album called *The Eternal Idol*?
8   Who took "I Believe" to No. 1 the first time?
9   Who had 70s hits with "Walkin'" and "Brother"?
10 Who made No. 8 in the album charts in 1982 with *Shape Up And Dance (Volume II)*?
11 The Eagles were originally backing group for which vocalist?
12 The first No. 1 for Boyz II Men was released on which record label?
13 Who had a late 70s album called *Raw Meat For The Balcony*?
14 What were Ultravox originally called on formation in 1973?
15 What was Fourmost's first top ten?
16 Which country do Fool's Garden come from?
17 Who was the first pop musician to be made a Fellow of the Royal College of Music?
18 What was the first top ten for Freddie And The Dreamers?
19 What was Fleetwood Mac's follow-up to the original release of "Albatross"?
20 Who had an early 80s album called *Special Forces*?

1 In which year was the so-called Summer of Love?
2 Whose only hit was "Let's Go To San Francisco"?
3 Which song described the history of the Mamas and Papas?
4 Whose melody was "A Whiter Shade of Pale" based on?
5 On which show did The Beatles sing "All You Need is Love" live to five continents?
6 Who did The Mamas And The Papas back on their first recordings?
7 Where did The Beatles plus Mick Jagger and Marianne Faithfull first attend one of the Maharishi's courses?
8 What did Ringo Starr compare to a Butlin's holiday camp in February 1968?
9 What colour jacket is John Lennon wearing on the *Sgt Pepper* cover?
10 Who recorded "Like An Old-Time Movie" in November 1967?
11 Who was paid the most to play at Woodstock?
12 Who took their name from the punchline to the joke, "What's purple and lives at the bottom of the sea?"?
13 Where in San Francisco was the first "Human Be-In"?
14 Who enjoyed "San Franciscan Nights" in 1967?
15 Who wrote "San Francisco (Be Sure To Wear Some Flowers In Your H air)"?
16 Which band had Grace Slick on lead vocals?
17 How was Ellen Cohen better known?
18 Who wrote "A Whiter Shade Of Pale"?
19 What was Scott McKenzie's real name?
20 Which politician sued The Move over a promotional postcard for "Flowers In The Rain" which had a caricature of him in the nude?

1 What replaced The Verve's "The Drugs Don't Work" at the top of the charts?
2 What colour are Manic Street Preachers' suits on the cover of *This Is My Truth Tell Me Yours*?
3 What was the name of U2's debut EP, only released in Ireland?
4 Who supported The Pretenders on their first UK tour?
5 On which R.E.M. album was "Lotus" first recorded?
6 Who was on the cover of Supergrass's *Caught By The Fuzz* when it was sold in the US?
7 Which record producer joined Bono and The Edge on stage at Pavarotti's War Child concert in 1995?
8 What means of transport did Super Furry Animals use for their rock festival tours?
9 Which Status Quo album featured "Living On An Island"?
10 Whose 1996 *These Days* world tour included three UK dates?
11 Which R.E.M. album featured "E–Bow The Letter"?
12 Who produced Stone Roses' second top ten hit?
13 What was U2's first US hit?
14 Which was the first Prodigy album to go straight to No. 1 on both sides of the Atlantic?
15 What was Bon Jovi's first US No. 1?
16 What does Jon Bon Jovi have tattooed on his left shoulder?
17 What colour is the lettering on R.E.M.'s *Up*?
18 Who had a *World Violation* tour in 1990?
19 Which Manics album won the Best Album at the 1997 BRIT Awards?
20 Of Bon Jovi's 80s run of four No. 1 albums which was the second?

1   What is on David Bowie's face on the album cover of *Aladdin Sane*?
2   Which instrumental group had a hit with "Perfidia" in the 1960s?
3   Who played bass on Manfred Mann's "Pretty Flamingo"?
4   Who first played Dorothy and the Scarecrow in *The Wiz* on Broadway?
5   Which Isley Brothers song was recorded by the Beatles?
6   Which British trio released the gold album *Brain Salad Surgery*?
7   What was the first-ever UK reggae No. 1, in 1969?
8   Who wrote "Baby Come Back" for The Equals?
9   Who was the first French solo singer to get to No. 1 in the UK?
10 Which Stones album cover had peel-off sticky labels on the front?
11 Who recorded the title track for *Twins* with Philip Bailey?
12 What is Evelyn King's middle nickname?
13 Who had a minor hit with "Gin And Juice" in 1994?
14 Whose first album was called *Postcard*?
15 Which British pop festival was founded in 1968?
16 What was the Oscar-winning song from the 1985 film *White Nights*?
17 How is Apollo C. Vermouth, producer of "I'm The Urban Spaceman" by The Bonzo Dog Doo-Dah Band, better known?
18 About whom did John Lennon say "We might have had him in the group."?
19 Which severe illness did Joni Mitchell suffer from when she was nine?
20 Which song title links The Supremes and Dannii Minogue?

1   Who had a 90s hit with "Doctor Jones"?'
2   What is the last word of "When I Fall In Love" by Ant And Dec?
3   What was The Four Seasons' follow-up single to "Silver Star"?
4   Which fellow-rock star produced the No. 1 "A Good Heart" for Feargal Sharkey?
5   What was the first top ten for Heinz?
6   Which album contains the track "Penny Lover"?
7   Which song title links Rod Stewart and PP Arnold?
8   What was Bob Marley's first posthumous hit that was not a re entry?
9   What was Vince Hill's first top ten hit?
10 Who had a late 60s album called Sher-oo?
11 What was Duran Duran's first top ten single of the 90s?
12 Which Lulu top ten hit was written by Neil Diamond?
13 In which year did The Eurythmics first have a No. 1 single?
14 Who had an early 90s album called *Anything Is Possible*?
15 Who published the novel *Tarantula* in 1970?
16 What was The Four Tops' follow-up to "If I Were A Carpenter"?
17 How many Light Years were The Rolling Stones from Home?
18 Who had 80s hits with "Where The Rose Is Sown" and "The Teacher"?
19 Which Bob Dylan song did General Norman Schwarzkopf choose on *Desert Island Discs*?'
20 What replaced "19" at the top of the charts?

1   Who had an album called *Hormonally Yours*?
2   Who were only the second all-girl group to receive a star in the Hollywood Walk of Fame?
3   Which group was made up of the Weiss sisters and the Ganser twins?
4   Which country were Mai Tai from?
5   What was the Poni-Tails' follow-up to "Born Too Late"?
6   Whose only hit was "You Don't Have To Be A Baby To Cry"?
7   Who were La Na Nee Nee Noo Noo, who sang "Help!" with Bananarama in 1989?
8   Who had their own Downkiddie record label?
9   Who had a 1992 album called *Portrait*?
10 Which quotation did Shakespear's Sister use to announce their break up?
11 Who joined Frankie Vaughan on "Gotta Have Something in the Bank Frank"?
12 Who had an album *Gold* in 1980?
13 Whose debut single was "Ain't 2 Proud 2 Beg"?
14 Who were originally called The Poquellos?
15 Who interviewed The Beatles on their first US tour?
16 Who were provisionally called Little Miss And The Muffets?
17 Whose autobiography was called *Dreamland*?
18 Who were Phyliss, Dorothy and Christine?
19 What was S.W.V.'s debut album?
20 On which record label did The Marvelettes record on?

1   What was Iron Maiden's first single with Bruce Dickinson as lead vocalist?
2   Which single along with "Crazy Train" was credited to Ozzy Osbourne's Blizzard of Ozz?
3   Who did Joey Belladonna replace in Anthrax before the album *Spreading The Disease*?
4   What is the name of the drummer on Alice Cooper's *School's Out* album?
5   How many non-winged figures appear on the album cover of Iron Maiden's *The Number Of The Beast*?
6   From whose album did the track "Ringfinger" come from?
7   Who was the guitarist on Deep Purple's *Machine Head* album?
8   What was Kiss's second UK top ten entry?
9   What is on fire on the cover of Def Leppard's album *Pyromania*?
10   What was Alice In Chains' first single to reach the UK top 20?
11   Charting in the 90s, what year was the previous top ten hit for Foreigner?
12   Which top 20 hit for Poison gave them their first Us No. 1?
13   Who did Brian Johnson replace in AC/DC in 1980?
14   Which Heavy Metal band is the only act to hold the two No. 1 album spots in the UK and in the USA on the week of releasing both records?
15   Which name did Marilyn Manson leave behind to form the shock rock band that brought his notoriety?
16   Which former "wild child" contributed a backing vocal to Metallica's *The Memory Remains*?
17   From whose album did the track "Dead Horse" come from?
18   What is the real name of Motorhead's Lemmy?
19   Who left Metallica and created Megadeth?
20   Which album yielded "Love In An Elevator" for Aerosmith?

1 What is on the back cover of Bridge Over Troubled Water?
2 Which song title links Tears For Fears and Lulu?
3 Which UK record label was the first to have 50 No. 1 hits?
4 What did Frank Sinatra lose at the Copacabana on April 26, 1950?
5 Who had a No. 10 hit with "Heaven Knows I'm Miserable Now"?
6 What is Duane Eddy standing beside on the album cover *Twangin' the Golden Hits*?
7 Which Buddy Holly hit exclaims, "My love's bigger than a Cadillac"?
8 Who had four No. 1's between February 1971 and May 1972?
9 Who was originally a drummer for Curved Air?
10 What are the celebrities standing in front of on the *Band On The Run* cover?
11 Who played Paul McCartney's grandfather in *A Hard Day's Night*?
12 Where did Madonna's *Blonde Ambition* tour begin?
13 What was the title of the Eagles' 1994 reunion album?
14 Who was Michael Jackson's song "Ben" originally intended for?
15 Which US soccer team was co-owned by Paul Simon, Mick Jagger, Rick Wakeman and Peter Frampton?
16 Which song did Dusty Springfield record for *Casino Royale*?
17 Whose 1991 autobiography was called *And The Beat Goes On?*
18 What was the Oscar-winning song from the 1988 film *Working Girl*?
19 Where were the group Mezzoforte from?
20 Why did Harry Connick Jr walk out of a benefit concert in 1995?

Answers

Pot Luck 47 (Quiz 93)
1 "This Is The World Calling". 2 *Electric Ladyland*. 3 Horst Jankowski .
4 Gerry Monroe. 5 Two. 6 "I Am A Rock". 7 A gun and a guitar.
8 Synthesizer. 9 Granada. 10 Ryan O'Neal, Diana Ross. 11 Hot Chocolate.
12 Blackpool. 13 Ireland. 14 Barry Manilow. 15 Royal Guardsmen.
16 "How Much Is That Doggy In The Window". 17 FBI. 18 Sweden.
19 Keith Michell. 20 "(I've Had) The Time Of My Life".

1 What was the first top ten hit for Johnny Johnson And The Bandwagon?
2 What did "Shaddapa You Face" replace at the top of the charts?'
3 Which album contains the track "I Love You Like A Ball And Chain"?
4 Who had 80s hits with "Ghosts" and "Cantonese Boy"?
5 What is the last word of "Frozen" by Madonna?
6 What is Manfred Mann's real name?
7 Who had an 80s album called *7800 Fahrenheit*?
8 Which Roy Orbison hit followed the 1964 UK No. 1 "Pretty Woman"?
9 Who was singer/guitarist that the song "Killing Me Softly" was describing?
10 Which singer had a 70s album called *Let's Get It On*?
11 What was on the other side of 80s No. 1 "The Model"?
12 The first No. 1 for Pato Banton was released on which record label?
13 Who had 80s hits with "Forgotten Town" and "Ideal World"?
14 In which year did Alice Cooper last have a No. 1 single?
15 What was Brian Hyland's first top ten hit?
16 Which guitarist joined the 101st Airborne Paratroopers in 1961 but was discharged when he broke his ankle?
17 What were the main colours used in Madonna's "Justify My Love" bedroom scene video?
18 Whose debut album was *Precious Time*?
19 What was Aretha Franklin's follow-up to "Respect"?
20 Who had a 90s album called Let Love Rule?

1 Which band did Brian May and Roger Taylor form in 1967?
2 How was Freddie Mercury billed on "I Can Hear Music" in 1973?
3 Which album did "Las Palabras De Amor" come from?
4 Which song mentions Krushchev and Kennedy?
5 Which organization owned the record company Queen signed with in 1990?
6 Which band had Freddie Mercury been singing with before he joined May and Taylor in 1970?
7 What did Brian May study at Imperial College London in the 60s?
8 Where did Freddie Mercury study graphic art and design?
9 Who did Queen support on their first US tour?
10 Who was "Bohemian Rhapsody" leaked to when EMI were reluctant to release it as it was too long?
11 Which album featured "Radio Gaga"?
12 Which record had been longest at No. 1 before the nine-week run of "Bohemian Rhapsody"?
13 Which Queen film supported *The Hustle* in UK cinemas?
14 What was Queen's follow-up to "Bohemian Rhapsody"?
15 Who supported Queen at their free Hyde Park concert in 1976?
16 Where did Freddie Mercury appear with Wayne Eagling and Derek Dean in July 1979?
17 Who played rhythm guitar on "Crazy Little Thing Called Love"?
18 Who was Roger Taylor's band on his solo album *Shove It*?
19 Whose 1985 No. 3 hit was produced by Roger Taylor?
20 Which album featured "I Want It All"?

1 How old was Louis Armstrong when he had his first UK No. 1?
2 The first No. 1 for Robson and Jerome was released on which record label?
3 Who had an 80s album called *Crusader*?
4 With which song did Johnny Logan win his second Eurovision contest?
5 What was the only No. 1 for 50s favourite Alma Cogan?
6 Which Johnny Mathis album stayed on the US charts for almost ten years – a record for a solo performer?
7 What was Barry Manilow's first UK single released in the UK to get to No. 1 in the US?
8 Who had 60s hits with "How High The Moon" and "Desfinado"?
9 Who had 60s hits with "Sea Of Heartbreak" and "Lonesome Number One"?
10 Who had a 90s album called *25*?
11 Charting in the 90s what year was the previous top ten hit for Rolf Harris?
12 What was the last US No. 1 for The Carpenters?
13 In 1961 Billboard magazine named which British singer as Top International Act and Most Promising Male Singer?
14 For how many singles did the Mike Sammes Singers join Ronnie Hilton?
15 Other than *I Left My Heart In San Francisco*, which 60s Tony Bennett album shared its name with a song title?
16 Who had 50s hits with "Hot Diggity (Dog Ziggity Boom)" and "Nothin' To Do"?
17 Which Frank Sinatra album cover shows the singer as a clown with a tear falling down his cheek?
18 Gerry Monroe had a 1970 hit with which girls' name?
19 In which US state was Nat King Cole born?
20 Prior to charting in the 90s, when was Julio Iglesias' previous top ten hit?

1   What was Bob Geldof's first solo single called?
2   Which Jimi Hendrix album cover shows a group of naked women?
3   Who took A Walk In The Black Forest in 1965?
4   Who had a 1970 hit with "Sally"?
5   How many million sales constitute a platinum single in the USA?
6   Which song says "I have my books and poetry to protect me."?
7   What is the soldier on Tom Robinson's "Hope And Glory" carrying?
8   With which musical instrument has Giorgio Moroder had chart success as a performer?
9   Which Spanish town links Frankie Laine and Frank Sinatra?
10 Who were the stars originally lined up for *The Bodyguard* 20 years before the Whitney Houston/Kevin Costner version?
11 Who recorded a reggae version of "Give Peace A Chance" in 1969?
12 In which town was Graham Nash born?
13 Where did Jerry Lee Lewis move to live in 1993?
14 Who released a boxed album set *The Complete Collection And Then Some* in 1992?
15 Who sang about "Snoopy Vs. The Red Baron" in 1967?
16 When the England cricket team were asked to choose a piece of music to walk on to the pitch to in New Zealand, what did Jack Russell choose?
17 Who was Redhead Kingpin's backing group in 1989?
18 Which country do Roxette come from?
19 Who had a 1980 hit with "Captain Beaky"/"Wilfred The Weasel"?
20 What was the Oscar-winning song from the 1987 film *Dirty Dancing*?

LEVEL 3

1 Who had an early 90s album called *A Pocketful of Dreams*?
2 Who provided the music for the TV show *Brush Strokes*?
3 What is the name of Dexy's Midnight Runners' vocalist?
4 What was Johnny Cash's first top ten hit?
5 Which album contains the track "Leopard-Skin Pill-Box Hat"?
6 Which Beatles track did Star Trek's William Shatner record?
7 What is the last word of "Where Do You Go" by No Mercy?
8 What replaced "Saving All My Love for You" at No. 1?
9 Which film did Lauryn "L" Hill appear in with Whoopi Goldberg?
10 Who had an early 70s album called *Kiln House*?
11 How was Bonnie Jo Mason, who recorded "Ringo I Love You", better known?
12 What is the last word of "Don't Let Go (Love)" by En Vogue?
13 Who had 80s hits with "Do Not Disturb" and "I Heard A Rumour"?
14 Which female artist was the first to achieve four UK No. 1 hits?
15 Wet Wet Wet's "Love Is All Around" was at No. 1 for how many weeks?
16 Who had a track called "Cold Ethel"?
17 Who had a late 80s album called "I Wanna Have Some Fun"?
18 Which 90s female US chart-topper was born on exactly the same day as rugby player Rory Underwood?
19 Which US group included Joe Walsh on guitar?
20 What was Marvin Gaye's follow-up to "I Heard It Through The Grapevine"?

1   Which singing duo appeared in "The Man From U.N.C.L.E." in 1967?
2   What are the members of Alisha's Attic called?
3   How did Everything But the Girl get their name?
4   Which crisis inspired the Style Council's hit "Soul Deep"?
5   What was Clock's first album called?
6   Who said "Sorry I'm A Lady" in 1978?
7   Which duo's song was used as a theme for the 1980 film *Little Darlings*?
8   How are Esther Zaled and Abraham Reichstadt better known?
9   Whose "Shake Your Head" had uncredited backing vocals by Kim Basinger and Ozzy Osbourne?
10   Whose first album was called *Let's Push It*?
11   Which duo had the top-selling single of 1981?
12   Who duetted with Pavarotti singing "Nessun Dorma" on a US late-night TV show in 1996?
13   How were Kevin Parrott and Michael Coleman better known?
14   Who went One Step Further in 1982?
15   Who had a hit with "I'll Find My Way Home" in 1981?
16   Up to 1996 who had the most duet partners in the charts?
17   Who took "Surrender Your Love" to No. 7 in 1995?
18   Whose debut album was *1 Polish 2 Biscuits And A Fish Sandwich*?
19   Which country do Jam and Spoon come from?
20   Who had a hit with "Blue Guitar" in 1975?

1 The first No. 1 for Puff Daddy was released on which record label?
2 How is rapper Durron Butler of Snap! fame better known?
3 "Gangsta's Paradise" is based on a record by which artist?
4 Vanilla Ice had won three national championships in which sport?
5 The first No. 1 for The Outhere Brothers was released on which record label?
6 Which song did The Fugees' "Killing Me Softly" replace twice at the top of the charts?
7 What was the name of the first rap album ever to enter the US charts at No. 1?
8 Who duetted with Puff Daddy on his first UK million-seller?
9 What did "Ready Or Not" replace at the top of the charts?
10 The first No. 1 for LL Cool J was released on which record label?
11 Who had a 90s hit with "Another Boy Murdered"?
12 From whose album does the track "Rat-A-Tat-Tat" come from?
13 Who joined Keith Murray on the chart single which shared its name with a film with Macaulay Culkin?
14 What was Public Enemy's follow-up album to *It Takes A Nation Of Millions To Hold Us Back*?
15 What was Adamski's follow-up to his first UK No. 1?
16 How was Makaveli also known?
17 Whose "What's My Name" charted in the top 20 in 1993?
18 What replaced "Men In Black" at the top of the charts?
19 What was the first rap record to enter the UK chart at No. 1?
20 How was Christopher Wallace better known?

1 What colour is the title on Neil Young's *Harvest* album?
2 Who won Grammys in 1986 for Best Album, Producer and Male Vocalist?
3 Who did Sandie Shaw record "Hand In Glove" with?
4 Which blondes are on the cover of the Stones' *Some Girls* album?
5 What links Nino Tempo and April Stevens with Donny and Marie Osmond?
6 Who does Prince give thanks to on the inner sleeve of *1999*?
7 Whose first album was *First Take* in 1970?
8 Who was executive producer of the Monty Python film *Life Of Brian*?
9 What former Cream star backed Roger Waters on a 1984 tour?
10 Which China Crisis album cover shows a photo of an industrial area?
11 How is the reggae singer Everton Bonner better known?
12 Which organization were The Joy Strings in?
13 Whose music was used by David Puttnam in *The Frog Prince* in 1985?
14 Whose middle names are Peter George St John Le Baptiste de la Salle?
15 Who made a reunion album, *Far From Home* in, 1994?
16 Who played a lock-keeper in the BBC sitcom *The River* in 1986?
17 Which band is led by Ms Leskanich?
18 Whose father was in the Jim Mac Jazz Band?
19 What does LOD stand for on Billy Ocean's 1979 hit?
20 What was the Oscar-winning song from *The Thomas Crown Affair*?

1 Which album contains the track "Magic Pie"?
2 Which singer named his daughter Levi after Levi Stubbs of The Four Tops?
3 What was Genesis' follow-up single to "Follow You Follow Me"?
4 What was Ricky Nelson's first top ten hit?
5 What did "Freak Me" replace at the top of the charts?
6 What was Davy Jones of The Monkees name when he appeared in *Coronation Street*?
7 Who had an early 90s album called *High Civilisation*?
8 Who had 70s hits with "Could It Be I'm Falling In Love" and "The Rubberband Man"?
9 Who recorded "Ain't Nothing But A Houseparty" after The Showstoppers?
10 How many members were in Baccara?
11 Who had an 80s album called *A Child's Adventure*?
12 "Dance Stance" was whose first single?
13 Which album contains the track "Two Out Of Three Ain't Bad"?
14 What was Gary Glitter's follow-up to "Doing Alright With The Boys"?
15 Which Bluebells hit was used in a Volkswagen advertising campaign?
16 Which song has the lines, "Will you still need me, Will you still feed me"?
17 The first No. 1 for The Beautiful South was released on which record label?
18 Who had 80s hits with "If She Knew What She Wants" and "Walking Down Your Street"?
19 What is the last word of "Step By Step" by Whitney Houston?
20 What was Neil Sedaka's first UK top ten hit in the UK?

1 What was the name of Sonny and Cher's daughter born in 1969?
2 Who is the mother of the writer and producer Terry Melcher?
3 Who is John and Michelle Phillips's singing daughter?
4 Who is the sister of the Dakotas' drummer, Tony Mansfield?
5 Who had a daughter called Owen Vanessa in 1967?
6 What is the name of Steve Winwood's brother, who was also in the Spencer Davis Group?
7 Whose brother set up the label Illegal Records?
8 Which father and son had No. 1 hits in 1967 and 1991 respectively?
9 Which second-generation musical group's first hit was "Boys Will Be Boys"?
10 Which musical star was the mother of Larry Hagman, a.k.a. J.R. in *Dallas*?
11 Which father and son were both on the 1987 hit "Hey Matthew"?
12 On which single did Sam Brown's mother Vicki make the top ten?
13 Whose sons had a chart hit with "Don't Bring Me Your Heartaches"?
14 Who was born Gary Levitch and is the son of a famous comedian?
15 Who were the first father and daughter to top the charts separately and together?
16 Who was the father of the Wilson sisters in Wilson Phillips?
17 Who was the husband of Beverley Sister Joy?
18 Who is the son of Marnie Nixon who sang for Natalie Wood and Audrey Hepburn in *West Side Story* and *My Fair Lady* respectively?
19 Who is the pop star son of the former Mrs Roy Boulting?
20 Which two brothers were in The Bluebells?

1 In which year did Patsy Cline first make the UK top 20?
2 What was Glen Campbell's second US No. 1?
3 What is the last word of "Dreams" by The Corrs?
4 What is the middle name of Kenny Rogers?
5 Which country singer recorded "Green, Grass Of Home" before Tom Jones?
6 What replaced "Young At Heart" at the top of the charts when the same version charted for the second time?
7 Who wrote "The Last Thing On My Mind"?
8 Which album was said to have reflected the end of Bob Dylan's marriage?
9 Which five-piece group recorded "Light Flight"?
10 What was Hank Locklin's first top ten hit?
11 Which Suzanne Vega album features the transatlantic success "Luka"?
12 Which 1992 movie featured Tammy Wynette on the soundtrack?
13 Which UK guitarist co-produced Bob Dylan's *Infidels*?
14 Whose 1993 album *Little Love Letters* included songs by Bernie Taupin?
15 Which country star recorded an album of ballads called *Time Piece*?
16 What cartoon characters did Billy Ray Cyrus sing with on "Achy Breaky Heart"?
17 From which American place does the group who have had 80s hit with "Sylvia's Mother" and "A Little Bit More" come from?
18 Which Bob Dylan album featured Johnny Cash?
19 Prior to charting in the 90s what was the previous top ten hit for Bob Dylan?
20 How was country rock pioneer Ingram Cecil Connor III better known?

1   Where is Elton John standing on the album cover of *A Single Man*?
2   What was Adam Faith's autobiography called?
3   Whose debut album was called *The Psychomodo*?
4   Why were The Nice banned from the Royal Albert Hall?
5   Who was Bubblerock on "(I Can't Get No) Satisfaction" in 1974?
6   What was Lord Rockingham XI's follow-up to "Hoots Mon"?
7   How did Jim Croce die?
8   How is Christopher Geppert better known?
9   Who understudied for David Essex in *Evita* and had a No. 1 in 1986 ?
10 What was the first musical instrument Eddy Grant learned?
11 Which item of clothing of Michael Jackson's was sold for £16,500 in 1991?
12 Who had the best-selling UK album in 1988?
13 Which Beach Boys single was co-written by Scott McKenzie?
14 Who was the only female to have one of the top ten best-selling singles of the 80s?
15 Who has had more weeks at No. 1 than Bryan Adams with one single?
16 Who had the two best-selling albums of the 70s?
17 What was the Oscar-winning song from the 1978 film *Thank God It's Friday*?
18 Who was guest of honour at the Foyle's Literary Lunch to mark Shakespeare's 400th birthday?
19 Who was the drummer with Mungo Jerry on "In The Summertime"?
20 Where was the Seekers' Keith Potger born?

1 "I Was Made To Love Her" was the first top ten hit for which performer?
2 Which part of the body is on the cover of Alanis Morissette's *Supposed Former Infatuation Junkie*?
3 What is the last word of "Clementine" by Mark Owen?
4 Whose debut album was called *Little Earthquakes*?
5 What was Bill Haley and his Comets' follow-up to "Rockin' Through The Rye"?
6 Who had a 90s album called *Time*?
7 Which band started life as The Invaders?
8 What did "Dizzy" replace at No. 1?
9 Which Joni Mitchell album contains the tracks "This Flight Tonight" and "Blue"?
10 Who recorded "Ain't No Sunshine" after Michael Jackson?
11 Who had 90s hits with "What Time Is It" and "Mary Jane"?
12 What was Mark Wynter's first top ten hit?
13 Who had a mid-90s album called *Mellow Gold*?
14 After 1962, in what year did Dinah Washington make the charts again?
15 A Maynard's Wine Gums ad led to the re-release of which former No. 1?
16 Which bird was the nickname of a member of The Banshees?
17 What replaced "Breakfast At Tiffany's" at No. 1?
18 The first No. 1 for B*witched was released on which record label?
19 What was Steve Harley and Cockney Rebel's follow-up to "Make Me Smile (Come Up And See Me)"?
20 Who had an early 80s album called *Scissors Cut*?

LEVEL 3

1   On which show were the Beatles first seen live on nationwide TV?
2   Whose record did The Beatles vote a miss on *Juke Box Jury* although it knocked them off the top of the US charts eight weeks later?
3   Which society elected Ringo its vice-president in 1964?
4   What was the first song they sang on *Top of the Pops*?
5   What was John Lennon's second book called?
6   Who was the last Beatle to marry?
7   Who was Ringo drummer with before the Beatles?
8   Which instrument did George Harrison play on "You've Got to Hide Your Love Away"?
9   What did Ringo reply as the Queen asked him, "How long have you been together now?" when she presented them with their MBEs?
10   Which part did Patti Boyd play in *A Hard Day's Night*?
11   Who won an album in *Melody Maker* for saying Paul McCartney played lead guitar on "Ticket To Ride"?
12   What was the Beatles' first instrumental release?
13   Who was the first non-Beatle to be credited on a Beatles single?
14   Which word in "The Ballad Of John And Yoko" made it subject to radio censorship in the US?
15   Which Hywel Bennett film did Paul McCartney write the score for?
16   Which song did Sinatra say was the greatest love song in the last 50 years?
17   Who first starred in Willy Russell's *John, Paul, George, Ringo And Bert*?
18   What was the first cover version of a Beatles hit to make the charts?
19   What was the name of Eric Idle's TV parody of the Beatles' career?
20   Which new discoveries were named Lennon, McCartney, Harrison and Starr in 1990?

1 What is the last word of "Sweet Like Chocolate" by Shanks and Bigfoot?
2 The first No. 1 for Steps was released on which record label?
3 The featured vocalist on Beats International's March 1990 No. 1 had starred in which famous kids' TV series?
4 Which band did Norman Cook form when Beats International disbanded?
5 How is Beresford Rome better known?
6 Who had 80s hits with "Searching" and "Change Of Heart"?
7 Which disco queen's first album was *Heart And Soul*?
8 Which song took M People into the top ten for the second time?
9 What was N Trance's follow-up to "Set You Free" which also just failed to hit the top spot in the charts?
10 Which group was DJ Mark Moore behind?
11 Who had a 90s album called *Northern Soul*?
12 What is the last word of "There's Nothing I Won't Do" by JX?
13 What was Primal Scream's first hit on their *Vanishing Point* album?
14 What was Prodigy's second million-seller in the UK?
15 How are Alex Gifford and Will White better known?
16 In which city were The Shamen formed?
17 Which Altern 8 single was the next to enter the top ten after Activ 8?
18 What was Paula Abdul's top ten follow-up to "Straight Up" which also went right to the top in the US?
19 Alex Party's "Read My Lips" is a remix of which previous minor hit?
20 What was Outhere Brothers' follow-up to their second UK No1?

1 Who drew the album cover for *The Who By Numbers*?
2 Who won a Grammy in 1970 for Best New Artist?
3 Whose pet boa constrictor died in 1977 stopping his plans for his first tour for two years?
4 Where was Duran Duran's video for "Hungry Like The Wolf" shot?
5 What is on the cover of Huey Lewis And The News' *Sports* album?
6 Which 50s pop star used to wear a hearing aid?
7 Which 1985 song won an Ivor Novello award for Elton John and Bernie Taupin?
8 Who was at No. 6 in 1958 with "Mad Passionate Love"?
9 Which Everly Brother has the lower voice?
10 On which Beatles album cover does George Harrison sit on top of the first letter of the title?
11 What is Whitney Houston's character called in *The Bodyguard*?
12 Who did Michael Jackson escort to her 65th birthday party in 1997?
13 Who was lead singer with Rose Royce?
14 What was The Manic Street Preachers' first solo single?
15 Which country was Manfred Mann himself from?
16 What was the Oscar-winning song from the 1979 film *Norma Rae*?
17 Who was asked to write the music for the Disney *Tarzan* film?
18 What were Ziggy Marley's backing group called?
19 Who won the Grammy Best Pop Male Vocal Performance in 1961 for "Lollipops And Roses"?
20 Which musical won the Oscar for Best Picture in 1958?

1 What is the last word of "Professional Widow" by Tori Amos?
2 Which album contains the tracks "You Shook Me All Night"?
3 What was Jet Harris and Tony Meehan's follow-up to "Diamonds"?
4 Which football team does Michelle Gayle support?
5 Whose first UK top ten hit was "Portrait Of My Love"?
6 What did "You Are Not Alone" replace at the top of the charts?
7 What was Donnie Elbert's first top ten hit?
8 Who had an 80s album called *Whammy!*?
9 Who had a hit with "Achy Breaky Heart" after Billy Ray Cyrus?
10 Who sang "My Bonnie" with The Beatles in 1963?
11 Who had a 90s album called *Songs From The Mirror*?
12 Who had 90s hits with "Big Gay Heart" and "My Drug Buddy"?
13 The first No. 1 for Culture Beat was released on which record label?
14 Which DJ and personality was born on the same day that Harry Houdini died?
15 In which year did Prince have his first No. 1 single?
16 Who had 80s hits with "Hard Habit To Break Girl" and "Hard To Say I'm Sorry"?
17 Which Paul Simon hit names Jack, Stan, Roy, Gus and Lee?
18 Which Roxy Music album first contained the track "Street Life"?
19 What was the first top ten hit for Wayne Fontana And The Mindbenders?
20 Who had a 90s album called *Essex*?

LEVEL 3

1. Who had a top ten hit with Marie Osmond's "Paper Roses" in 1960?
2. Who made a cover version of "Reet Petite" in 1993?
3. Which British artist previously recorded UB40 and Chrissie Hynde's "Breakfast In Bed"?
4. What did Rozalla sing in 1994 that The O'Jays had in 1976 and 1978?
5. Who had the original chart hit with "Caravan Of Love"?
6. Who had the first hit with "It's All In The Game" in 1958?
7. Who also had a hit with "When I Fall In Love" between Nat King Cole, the first time, in 1958 and Rick Astley in 1987?
8. Who did Johnny Mathis duet with on "When A Child Is Born" five years after his solo hit?
9. Who before Take That took "Could It Be Magic?" into the top 40?
10. Who joined The Troggs on a rerecording of "Wild Thing" in 1993?
11. Who had a top ten single hit with "Twist And Shout" 30 years before Chaka Demus and Pliers' 1993 No. 1?
12. Whose version of "This Old Heart Of Mine" got higher in the charts?
13. Who did the cover of "Too Busy Thinking 'Bout My Baby" in 1972?
14. Who had the '95 version of "Always Something There To Remind Me"?
15. Who had a "Total Eclipse Of The Heart" in 1995?
16. Who released the Beach Boys' "I Can Hear Music" in 1973?
17. Who made an EP of "Only Living Boy In New York" in 1993?
18. What was on the others side of KWS's No. 1 "Please Don't Go", a 1979 hit for KC And The Sunshine Band?
19. Who released the Kinks' "Waterloo Sunset" in 1997?
20. Who revived "Hazy Shade Of Winter" for the film *Less Than Zero*?

1   Who had 90s hits with "Where It's At" and "Devil's Haircut"?
2   What is the name of the drummer with the band who have had 80s hits with "Hardest Part Is The Night" and "Never Say Goodbye"?
3   What is the last word of "Hey God" by Bon Jovi?
4   What was Radiohead's first UK No 1 album?
5   Which artist started his chart career by creeping in the top 50 with "Marjorine"?
6   Prior tocharting in the 90s what year was the previous top 20 hit for Bono?
7   Who featured Billy Bragg on their 80s hit "Won't Talk About It"?
8   In 1996 Ocean Colour Scene had three top ten hits; which was the second?
9   Who had 90s hits with "I Need" and "What Would Happen"?
10 Power Station's most successful single was also the title of a famous film; what was it?
11 From what two countries do the group who have had 90s hits with "Straight To You" and "What A Wonderful World" come?
12 Who had 90s hits with "Circus" and "Motherless Child"?
13 What was Gary Numan's follow-up to his second successive No. 1, which charted at No. 6?
14 Which British guitarist worked on Tina Turner's *Break Every Rule* album?
15 What label did Edwyn Collins record his first charted single on?
16 What was Bon Jovi's first US No. 1?
17 What was Nirvana's last UK top ten single before Kurt Cobain's death?
18 Before re-charting in the 90s, what year was the previous top ten hit for Creedence Clearwater Revival?
19 Argent's Jim Rodford and Robert Henrit left the band to join which other group?
20 What was R.E.M.'s first album to go straight to No. 1 in the US and the UK?

1 What is Paul McCartney holding in his right hand on the cover of *Abbey Road*?
2 Which Madness video featured a van dropping out of a plane?
3 Which James Bond theme did Duran Duran sing?
4 Who was singing "If you'll be my bodyguard" in 1986?
5 What song title was a No. 1 for Frankie Laine and Barbra Streisand?
6 What word begins song titles that end with Cherry and Horses?
7 What was The Move's only No. 1?
8 Which song won the Oscar for the 1965 film *The Sandpiper*?
9 Whose debut album was *Time And A Word*?
10 What are the Beach Boys doing on the album cover of *Pet Sounds*?
11 Which song won a Grammy for Frank Sinatra for Best Pop Male Vocal Performance in 1965?
12 Who had the original UK hit with "Oh No Not My Baby"?
13 Who wrote "Don't Bring Me Down" a hit for The Animals?
14 Who had an album called *Blue Light Red Light*?
15 What was the Oscar-winning song from the 1970 film *Lovers And Other Strangers*?
16 Who was the subject of the biography *He's A Rebel*?
17 Who first played the title role in *Imagine – The John Lennon Story*?
18 Whose son is called Giacomo Luke?
19 How many Oscars was *My Fair Lady* nominated for in 1964?
20 Who felt like Buddy Holly in 1984?

1   Who had a late 80s album called *Paul's Boutique*?
2   "Because You're Mine" was the first top ten hit for which singer?
3   Which Rolling Stones album contains the track "Lady Jane"?
4   Who was the lead singer/guitarist in The Screaming Blue Messiahs.
5   Guitarist Jimi Hendrix formed a group called the Band Of what?
6   What is the last word of "Natural" by Peter Andre?
7   Who had a minor hit with a cover of "All Or Nothing" by The Small Faces?
8   Who had 80s hits with "Labour Of Love" and "Looking For Linda"?
9   What did the 80s "Spirit In The Sky" replace at the top of the charts?
10   Who had an 80s album called *Pornography*?
11   In which year did The Rolling Stones last have a No. 1 single?
12   The first No. 1 for New Kids On The Block was released on which record label?
13   Which car manufacturer did Paul Young work for?
14   What was Steve Lawrence's first top ten hit?
15   Which 60s group starred in the film known, in the US, as *Having A Wild Weekend*?
16   The first No. 1 for Boyzone was released on which record label?
17   Who had a 70s album called *Rainbow*?
18   What relation was Eddie Fisher to Paul Simon?
19   Which album contains the tracks "Drift Away "and "Stone Cold Sober"?
20   What was Herman's Hermits' follow-up to "I'm Into Something Good"?

LEVEL 3

1 Who spent Another Weekend in 1988?
2 Who sang about "August October" in 1970?
3 Where was the A-Bomb on The Jam's 70s double-A-sided record?
4 Which day has been recorded more than any other?
5 What was Earth, Wind And Fire's first single?
6 Which year features in a minor Bryan Adams hit?
7 Who were under "April Skies" in 1987?
8 Who had a "Three-Minute Hero" in 1980?
9 Who had a 1956 No. 1 with "It's Almost Tomorrow"?
10 Who backed Chris Farlowe on "Out Of Time"?
11 Whose second album was subtitled *1990 A New Decade*?
12 Who wrote the English lyric for "Seasons In The Sun"?
13 Whose only No. 1 was "One Day At A Time"?
14 Who turned down the title role in *Midnight Cowboy*?
15 Who had a "Morning Danc"e in 1979?
16 Which song's third line is "If woman can survive"?
17 Which song won the Oscar for Best Song in 1960?
18 What was Status Quo's fourth No. 1 album?
19 Who made a cover version of "Morning Has Broken" in 1992?
20 Who sang "Midnight At The Oasis" in 1974?

1   What was Abba's only Transatlantic No. 1?
2   In what year did both Frank and Nancy Sinatra have separate transatlantic No. 1's?
3   What was Madonna's third transatlantic No. 1?
4   What was the last transatlantic No. 1 for The Beatles?
5   What was Blondie's second transatlantic No. 1?
6   "I'm Walking Behind You" was the only transatlantic No. 1 for which singer?
7   What was Doris Day's only transatlantic No. 1?
8   What was the last US No. 1 of the 70s for The Bee Gees?
9   Which transatlantic No. 1 starts, "I'm So Young And You're So Old"?
10 How many transatlantic No. 1s did Phil Collins have in the 80s?
11 Coolio and LV's transatlantic No. 1 "Gangsta's Paradise" was the first single to pass how many million in the US?
12 How many US No. 1s did Ringo Starr have?
13 How many transatlantic No. 1s did The Rolling Stones have in 1965?
14 "Cathy's Clown" was the second transatlantic No. 1 for which act?
15 How many transatlantic No. 1s did Madonna have in the 80s?
16 In what year did Elvis Presley have his last transatlantic No. 1?
17 What was Elvis Presley's third transatlantic No. 1?
18 Before "Candle In The Wind 1997"/"Something About The Way You Look Tonight" how many transatlantic No. 1s had Elton John had?
19 How many transatlantic No. 1s did Brenda Lee have?.
20 In what year did Whitney Houston's first transatlantic No. 1 chart in the UK?

Quiz 113 Pot Luck 57

Answers – see page 523

1   What is Roger Daltry covered in on *The Who Sell Out* album?
2   Which song says "Check out Guitar George – he knows all the chords"?
3   What was Guns N' Roses' best-selling 80s album?
4   Who swapped autographs and soccer chat with Lech Walesa in 1984?
5   Where was Jumpin' Jack Flash born according to The Stones?
6   Who proposed to Maria Elena Santiago on their first date?
7   What was Madonna's best-selling UK album in the 1980s?
8   Who had the first UK hit with "Will You Still Love Me Tomorrow?"?
9   Who were going to Montego Bay in 1986?
10 Which US producer plays guitar on the Stones' "Play With Fire"?
11 Which film had an Oscar nomination for "Let's Hear It For the Boy"?
12 Who was "another man" in "Get Back"?
13 What are Holland, Dozier and Holland's first names?
14 Which song has the line "Tell me, will this *déjà vu* never end"?
15 Who were the first act after the Beatles to have a US hit with "I Want To Hold Your Hand"?
16 Which 30-year-old garment of John Lennon's was sold for £24,200 in 1992?
17 What was the top UK single of 1979?
18 Which song from the 1961 film *Breakfast At Tiffany's* won an Oscar?
19 Which Vanessa Williams song was used to advertise Bisto Gravy?
20 Who played solo recorder on Marvin, Welch and Farrar's "Music Makes My Day"?

1 Which album contains the track "Speed Demon"?
2 What is the last word of "You Might Need Somebody" by Shola Ama?
3 Jerry Lee Lewis moved to which country to live in 1993?
4 Which group included Glen Matlock until 1977?
5 What is the nationality of the duo who have had 90s hits with "Spending My Time" and "Fireworks"?
6 What replaced "I'd Do Anything For Love (But I Won't Do That)" at No. 1?
7 Who had a late 70s album called *It's A Game*?
8 What was Nick Lowe's first top ten hit?
9 Where did the acts from the cancelled Phoenix festival appear as bonus acts?
10 What were The Young Ones singing when their bus fell over a cliff at the very end of their TV series?
11 Who had a 90s album called *Homebase*?
12 Frank Sinatra and Frankie Laine both had hits with which Spanish town?
13 The first No. 1 for Mariah Carey was released on which record label?
14 On some songwriting credits Dave Stewart has a middle initial of what?
15 What was Bob Luman's first top ten hit?
16 Who had a 90s album called *Sense*?
17 What is the last word of "Let Me In" by OTT?
18 Which female vocalist suffered from polio at the age of nine?
19 What is the name of the keyboard player with the act who have had 90s hits with "Someday" and "Excited"?
20 Who had a late 70s album called *Morning Comes Quickly*?

1 Which Matt Monro hit has a country in the title?
2 In which year did the Beatles hit the top ten with "Back In The USSR"?
3 What was U2's second hit of 1988?
4 Where did The Council Come To in 1985?
5 What was The Gibson Brothers' first UK hit?
6 What was Tom Browne in the charts with in 1980 and in 1992?
7 Where did the Bee Gees try to hitch a ride to in "Massachusetts"?
8 Which song has the line "If only you'd started ringing your bell"?
9 Where is Paul Simon "counting the cars" in "America"?
10 Which musical includes a character called Nathan Detroit?
11 Which 1985 chart-toppers had a country and continent in their name?
12 Where were Christie after "Yellow River" in 1970?
13 Where was Marty Robbins in 1960?
14 Which Lassie was a 50s hit for Tommy Steele and Freddy Cannon?
15 Where were The Piranhas in 1982?
16 Which city links Ronnie Hilton and Max Bygraves within song titles?
17 Where was Perry Como's 1960 hit?
18 Where were Arrested Development in 1992 and 1993?
19 What was Tony Christie's first solo UK hit?
20 Who were on the "Ventura Highway" in 1972?

1   What did Aqua's third No. 1 replace at the top of the charts?
2   The surnames Engel, Maus and Leeds were the real names of which 60s chart-toppers?
3   What relation were the 50s No. 1 act The Kalin Twins?
4   What was the first three-track single to become a UK No. 1?
5   How many No. 1 hits did Elvis Presley have before 1990?
6   Who recorded the 1988 No. 1 which advertised Coca-Cola?
7   Shirley Bassey was knocked off the No. 1 spot in 1959 by a song she famously sang on the Morecambe And Wise show; what was it?
8   Who wrote Boy George's No. 1 "Everything I Own"?
9   What was the first UK No. 1 to be written, produced and recorded by the same person?
10   What was the first No. 1 for Jonathan King's UK record label?
11   Remember vinyl discs? What was the last vinyl EP to make No. 1?
12   Which singer had a record go straight to No. 1 in 1995 while in hospital?
13   Who recorded the first No. 1 for the label Parlophone in 1959?
14   What did Cornershop's first No. 1 replace at the top of the charts?
15   Who was the first teenager to win a UK gold disc?
16   CJ Makintosh mixed his way to No. 1 with which outfit?
17   Which No. 1 featured Rob and Hilda Woodward?
18   Who became the first solo instrumentalist to record consecutive No. 1 hits?
19   What language was Mary Hopkin's "Those Were The Days" originally in?
20   Which No. 1 was the first single to sell two million copies in Britain?

1 What have Genesis on their heads on the *Foxtrot* album cover?
2 What was Bobby Vinton's first million-seller?
3 Who co-wrote the songs for Disney's *The Lady And The Tramp*?
4 Who launched his chart career with the instrumental "Rebel Rouser"?
5 Which Coasters hit opens "Fee-fee fi-fi fo-fo fum"?
6 Which Stones album cover has holes in it with movable pictures?
7 Which group did Peter Noone join in 1980?
8 What did Jimmy Page play until Jeff Beck left The Yardbirds ?
9 Who had a No. 3 album in 1983 entitled *Nobody's Diary*?
10 What was Europe's best-selling 80s single?
11 What is Spice Girl Mel C's surname?
12 Which Survivor hit was used in *Rocky III*?
13 Whose singles "Big Seven" and "Big Six" were banned by the BBC?
14 Whose first solo album was *Armchair Theatre*?
15 Who was Best New Artist in the 1993 Grammy awards?
16 Who are the parents of Bobbi Kristina?
17 Who did Sonny and Cher have a private audience with in 1966?
18 What was the Oscar-winning song from the 1963 film *Papa's Delicate Condition*?
19 Which Bob Dylan song became a No 1 for Manfred Mann?
20 Who were responsible for *The Trial of Hissing Sid*?

1 Who was the first British female singer to have a No. 1 back in the 50s?
2 What was the name of the drummer in The Clash?
3 Who was Paul Young talking about when he said, "He reminds me of an aubergine: all shiny and plump."?
4 Who sang the theme "Since I Fell For You" for the *Moonlighting* TV series?
5 Which album contains the tracks "Hot Stuff" and "Dim All The Lights"?
6 What was Tony Brent's first top ten hit?
7 What is the last word of "Freed From Desire" by Gala?
8 Who had 80s hits with "Every Kinda People" and "Johnny And Mary"?
9 What was Buddy Holly's follow-up to "It Doesn't Matter Anymore"?
10 What is the last word of "You're Not Alone" by Olive?
11 What was Sir Cliff's middle name when he was plain old Harry Webb?
12 Who had an 80s album called *Gatecrashing*?
13 The first No 1 for Gary Barlow was released on which record label?
14 Which album contains the tracks "Bluebird" and "Let Me Roll It"?
15 What was Chicago's second UK top ten hit?
16 What was the first Freddie And The Dreamers song to hit No. 1 in the US but fail to do so in the UK?
17 Where was The Move's final album a Message From?
18 What is the last word of "Everybody" by The Backstreet Boys?
19 What was the first top ten hit for Buggles?
20 How old was Lulu when she achieved her first No. 1?

1 What was Rod's first solo album?
2 What is his birth sign?
3 Which 60s group members were in Rod's class at school?
4 Which football club did he sign with as an apprentice?
5 Why was Rod deported from Spain when he was in his teens?
6 With which group did he make his TV debut?
7 Who was the female vocalist with his Steampacket group?
8 What was the 30-minute documentary about him in 1965 called?
9 Why did his plane have to make a forced landing in 1995?
10 Who is the mother of his daughter who appeared in his "Forever Young" video?
11 Who did he dedicate his album *Vagabond Heart* to?
12 In 1991 it was reported that Rod had been accepted into the Highgate branch of what?
13 Who did he duet with on "Angel" on the Scottish Football Squad's *Easy Easy* album?
14 Which song did he record in 1982 for the Michael Keaton film *Night Shift*?
15 Who played solo guitar on "Infatuation"?
16 Which song was "Do Ya Think I'm Sexy?" said to be "borrowed" from?
17 Who did Rod donate the royalties from the song to?
18 Which album did "Baby Jane" come from?
19 Which single did he release with Sting and Bryan Adams in 1994?
20 Where did he travel on the tour called *Worth Leaving Home For*?

1   Who had 90s hits with "Brain Stew" and "Geek Stink Breath"?
2   Manic Street Preachers first crept in the top 70 in 1991 on which label?
3   What is the last word of "Naked" by Louise?
4   Which Bill and Jimmy were behind KLF?
5   How many copies did "Candle In The Wind 1997" sell worldwide?
6   What is the name of the most sucessful charity hit to make it to No. 1?
7   Charting in the 90s what year was the previous top ten hit for Olivia Newton John?
8   Who had a 90s hit with "Sweet Thing"?
9   What is the first word of Hepburn's first top ten hit?
10   What award did Rod Stewart recieve in 1989?
11   Charting in the 90s what year was the previous top ten hit for 10c.c.?
12   Justin Currie is the main writer with which band?
13   What is the last word of "Bodyshakin'" by 911?
14   Which label do Inspiral Carpets record on?
15   Which song has the line, "Ciga ciga right from Cuba Cuba"?
16   Which outfit did Niki Harris join after eight years recording and touring with Madonna?
17   What label did Tricky record his first top ten entry on?
18   What was the nationality of the duo whose last 90s hit was "Wanna Get Up"?
19   What label did the artist who had a 90s hit with "California Love" record on at that time?
20   Who had a 90s hit with "Blue"?

LEVEL 3

1   In what country are the Beatles skiing in *Help!*?
2   Who drew the cartoons on the back cover of "Between The Buttons"?
3   Which singer celebrated his Bar Mitzvah in Minnesota in May 1954?
4   Who was Torn Between Two Lovers in 1977?
5   Who was the first country singer to tour Britain and appear at the London Palladium?
6   What was a hit for The Ronettes, Dave Edmunds and The Ramones?
7   Who was voted Capital Radio's Best Female Singer from 1978–80?
8   Who wrote "Where Are You Now (My Love)"?
9   Who composed the theme song for *Ghostbusters*?
10 Which ELO album won the British Rock and Pop Best Album award in 1978?
11 What was Def Leppard's best-selling album of the 80s?
12 Which British singer had chart success with "Magic Moments"?
13 Who recorded "I'll Never Fall In Love Again" on an EP in 1990?
14 What was the name of the song from *On Her Majesty's Secret Service*?
15 Who had a 90s hit with "Dedicated To The One I Love"?
16 What was the first Manchester United hit not to have United in the title?
17 Which film did Elvis's "Hard Headed Woman" come from?
18 Who had a hit cover version of the Beatles' "We Can Work It Out"?
19 What is Spice Girl Emma's middle name?
20 Which singer is Whitney Houston's godmother?

1   Who had a 90s album called *Zingalamduni*?
2   What was Frank Ifield's follow-up single to "Confessin'"?
3   What is the last word of "What Can I Do" by The Corrs?
4   Which album contains the tracks "Candidate" and "Sweet Thing"?
5   What instrument did Sandy Nelson play?
6   Prior to charting in the 90s, what year was the previous top ten hit for Yazz?
7   What was the name of Joe Cocker's first band – Vance Arnold and The what?
8   What was The Jimi Hendrix Experience's follow-up to "Voodoo Chile"?
9   The first No. 1 for Coolio was released on which record label?
10 Which song was at No. 1 at the time of the 1983 general election?'
11 Who had 80s hits with "Chances" and "I Gave You My Heart"?
12 Who had the first No. 1 with The Beatles' "Michelle"?
13 Which 50s song was a hit for Al Hibbler, Les Baxter, Liberace and Jimmy Young?
14 What is the last word of "Mi Chico Latino" by Geri Halliwell?
15 What did "Ain't Nobody" replace at the top of the charts?
16 What was Engelbert Humperdinck's last top ten hit of the 60s?
17 Which Eurovison Song Contest winners had a 1974 hit with "I See A Star"?
18 How many members were there in the group that had 80s hits with "Sweetest Girl" and "I Pronounce You"?
19 What was Anthony Newley's first top ten hit?
20 In which year did Dawn first have a No. 1 single?

1 What was on the other side of "Come Outside" in 1975?
2 Who did a cover of Slade's "Merry Xmas Everybody" in 1990?
3 Who said Merry Christmas Darling in 1972 and again in 1990?
4 Who sang "Frosty The Snowman" on the compilation album *A Christmas Gift For You* in 1963?
5 Which Christmas hit was subtitled "Soleado"?
6 What are the Two Little Boys called in Rolf Harris's 1969 Christmas No. 1?
7 Which duo had a hit with "White Christmas" in 1985?
8 Which trio spent Christmas in Vienna in 1993?
9 Who had a *Merry Merry Christmas* album in 1990?
10 For how many consecutive Christmases was Bing Crosby's "White Christmas" in the US charts?
11 Which duo made a *Christmas Collection* in 1990?
12 Who is credited on the label of "Happy Christmas (War is Over)"?
13 Which Christmas No. 1 was from the musical *The Little Match Girl*?
14 Which female was on the *Christmas in Vienna II* album in 1994?
15 What was the Slade Christmas party album called?
16 Who made *The Christmas Album* in 1992?
17 What was on the other side of "My Hometown" in 1985?
18 Which instrumentalist had a 1984 *Christmas* album?
19 Who was in a "Winter Wonderland" in 1958?
20 What was on the other side of "Bluebottle Blues" in 1956?

1   Which No. 1 was co-written by James Honeyman-Scott?
2   Who were the first No. 1 act for producers Stock, Aitken And Waterman?
3   Who had a 1987 Number 1 with "Alone"?
4   Who co-wrote and produced Blondie's "Call Me"?
5   Who were Tony Reynolds and Louise and Lillian Lopez?
6   Which label did Jive Bunny record on?
7   The group that started life in the mid-50s as the Dominocos had an early 80s No. 1 under which name?
8   Which country did Aneka, the singer of "Japanese Boy", come from?
9   What was the first single to be at No. 1 in the 80s?
10 What is the last name of No. 1 artist Sonia?
11 In which year did U2 first make it to No. 1?
12 Which company broke off commercial deals with Madonna following her "Like A Prayer" video?
23 Which song was at No 1 on Prince Charles and Princess Diana's wedding day?
14 Who produced "We Are The World" by USA For Africa?
15 The Police's "Don't Stand So Close To Me" was from which album?
16 Sandy Lizner co-wrote "Working My Way Back To You" and which other 80s No. 1?
17 The New Jersey Mass Choir appear on which 80s No. 1?
18 Which 70s star had material reworked in "Doctorin' The Tardis"?
19 What was the first No. 1 from Abba's *Super Trouper* album?
20 Who followed up a No. 1 with the unlikely-sounding – and unsuccessful – "Reggae Matilda"?

1 Whose debut album was *Green River*?
2 What follows "Volare… oh, oh!"?
3 What was Sly and The Family Stone's debut single?
4 Which Beatle looks directly at the camera on the *Rubber Soul* cover?
5 Whose final 70s No. 1 in the UK was "Give A Little Love"?
6 Who wrote "Johnny Reggae"?
7 Which song title links Jason Donovan and Dooley Wilson?
8 What was the title of Paul Young's 1983 million–selling album?
9 Which problem did Cyndi Lauper have in 1983?
10 What is George Harrison wearing on the *Revolver* album cover?
11 Who sang the theme song from *Licence To Kill* in 1989?
12 In which film did Elvis sing "Teddy Bear"?
13 Which musical instrument did Herbie Hancock play?
14 Who joined Brian May on the 1992 "We Are The Champions"?
15 Which one-man band went into the charts in 1968?
16 Who was Heavy D's backing band?
17 Which female vocalist made an album of Queen songs?
18 What was Françoise Hardy's first hit in English?
19 Which song won an Oscar in *An Officer And A Gentleman*?
20 Who wrote Rod Stewart's "Sailing"?

1 What is the last word of "Coffee And TV" by Blur?
2 The first No. 1 for Charles and Eddie was released on which record label?
3 Which Rolling Stones album did "Tumbling Dice" first appear on?
4 What was Elton John's follow-up single to "Goodbye Yellow Brick Road"?
5 What did "Pump Up The Volume" replace at No. 1?
6 Simon And Garfunkel were in the singles charts in 1991, when were they last in before that?
7 Which album title links Carole King and Don McLean?
8 What is the last word of "Honey To The Bee" by Billie?
9 Who had an early 70s album called *Sunflower*?
10 What was Buddy Holly's first posthumous hit?
11 What is the last word of "Big Big World" by Emilia?
12 Prior to charting in the 90s at No. 6, what year was the previous hit for Joni Mitchell?
13 What was Bert Weedon's first top ten hit?
14 What is the first word in the Shakin' Stevens hit "Green Door"?
15 What was Tom Jones" follow up to "It's Not Unusual"?
16 Jackie Wilson's first top ten hit was called what?
17 The Who failed an audition with which record company and had 15 Top 10 hits?
18 What was the first Phil Collins song to hit No. 1 in the US but fail to do so in the UK?
19 What is the last word of "Lovestruck" by Madness?
20 In which year did George Michael have his first solo No. 1 single?

1 Whose debut UK album was called *Both Sides?*
2 Who made a TV movie called *Buffalo Girls?*
3 Which group did Kenny Rogers join in 1966?
4 How is Sam Hutt better known?
5 How is Nudie important to country stars?
6 Who was Merle Haggard's album *Same Train, A Different Time* a tribute to?
7 Who were reunited for the *Historic Reunion* album in the late 60s?
8 Which country singer starred in the US soap *Washington?*
9 Who had the 80s country hit "If Drinking Don't Kill Me (Her Memory Will!)"?
10 Who wrote "Crazy", a huge hit for Patsy Cline?
11 Who produced Waylon Jennings' first single?
12 Who made the album *King's Record Shop* in 1987?
13 Who is Johnny Cash's country-singer step-daughter?
14 Which cause did Johnny Cash champion in "Bitter Tears"?
15 What was Dolly Parton's first US country No. 1?
16 What was Alabama's best-selling US 80s album?
17 In which prison did Johnny Cash record live in 1968?
18 Who wrote the Johnny Cash hit "Busted"?
19 What was Willie Nelson's film debut with Jane Fonda and Robert Redford?
20 Whose debut album was *Elite Hotel?*

Answers

Christmas Records (Quiz 123)
1 "Christmas In Dreadland". 2 Metal Gurus. 3 The Carpenters.
4 The Ronettes. 5 "When A Child Is Born". 6 Joe, Jack.
7 Keith Harris and Orville. 8 Placido Domingo, Jose Carreras and Diana Ross.
9 New Kids On The Block. 10 Ten. 11 Foster And Allen.
12 John And Yoko And The Plastic Ono Band With The Harlem Community Choir.
13 "Mistletoe And Wine". 14 Dionne Warwick. 15 Crackers. 16 Neil Diamond.
17 "Santa Claus Is Comin' To Town". 18 Richard Clayderman.
19 Johnny Mathis. 20 "I'm Walking Backwards For Christmas".

1   Dave Ball was part of which hit-making combination?
2   Who had 80s hits with "It's Different For Girls" and "Steppin' Out"?
3   Which label did Culture Club record on?
4   Patrick Leonard co-wrote and produced No. 1 hits for which artist?
5   Which group met at school at Roxbury, Massachusetts?
6   Which song contains the line "Who's gonna drive you home tonight?"?
7   "Roll With It" and "Higher Love" were US No. 1s for which British artist?
8   What was the first top ten hit for Bruce Willis?
9   What was the name of the Irene Cara character in Alan Parker's *Fame*?
10 What instrument did Brian Travers play with UB40?
11 What gave Dusty Springfield a solo top 20 hit after a 20-year gap?
12 Who went on a *Serious Moonlight* tour?
13 Which label had three consecutive No. 1s in the 80s?
14 What was the first top ten hit for Tears For Fears?
15 Andy McCluskey provided vocals and synthesizer for which outfit?
16 Whose only top ten hit was "C'est La Vie"?
17 Which singer spent most weeks on the chart in 1989?
18 Who wrote and produced Berlin's "Take My Breath Away"?
19 What next took the Spitting Image team into the charts after "The Chicken Song"?
20 Warren Cann and Chris Cross were part of which group?

1 Who was the promoter of Live Aid?
2 Which group has included Alan Paul, Tim Hauser, Janis Siegel and Cheryl Bentyne among its members?
3 What was the No. 1 produced by Fluck and Law creations in 1986?
4 What is being modelled on the back cover of the Stones' "Some Girls"?
5 Which group with a 1964 No. 1 hit had a girl drummer?
6 Who was lead singer on Python Lee Jackson's "In A Broken Dream"?
7 What was unique about the US top five singles of April 4, 1964?
8 Who was the first female singer to top the UK charts?
9 Whose debut album was *Kimono My House* in 1974?
10 What colour is Paul McCartney wearing on the inside cover of the *Sgt Pepper* album?
11 What was the name of Anthony Hopkins' first – minor – chart venture?
12 Which FA Cup squad featured Tippa Irie and Peter Hunnigale in 1993?
13 How was the Joan Collins Fan Club better known?
14 Who did David Essex duet with on "True Love Ways" in 1986?
15 In which film did Elvis first sing "Return To Sender"?
16 What was the daytime profession of several of the Honeycombs?
17 Who sang the theme for *For Your Eyes Only*?
18 Who formed his own Dark Horse record label in 1974?
19 What was the subtitle of "Arthur's Theme" from the 1982 film?
20 From what was Don Johnson/Barbra Streisand's "Till I Loved You" the love theme?

1 Who had a 90s album called *Homegrown*?
2 What is the last word of "Drop Dead Gorgeous" by Republica?
3 What was Kim Deal known as in The Pixies?
4 What was Jim Dale's first top ten hit?
5 What was The Kinks' follow-up to "Tired Of Waiting For You"?
6 What replaced "Atomic" at the top of the charts?
7 Who had a late 70s album called *Rise*?
8 What was the group Tears For Fears previous name?
9 Where were Chumbawamba scheduled to perform in 1998 but did not appear?
10 In which year did Simply Red first have a No. 1 single?
11 Who had 80s hits with "Flashback" and "In And Out Of Love"?
12 What is the last word of "Ti Amo" by Gina G?
13 The first No. 1 for Billie was released on which record label?
14 What was Roger Daltry's first solo top ten hit?
15 "Chiquitita" first appeared on which Abba album?
16 Who had 80s hits with "Hide And Seek" and "Life In One Day"?
17 What is the last word of "Goodbye" by The Spice Girls?
18 Johnny Otis was known as the what of rhythm and blues?
19 The first 90s No. 1 for Cher was released on which record label?
20 What was Frankie Laine's follow-up to "A Woman In Love"?

1　Which song from *Sweet Charity* did Shirley Bassey chart with in 1967?
2　Who duetted with Patti Labelle on the 1986 "On My Own"?
3　What was David Essex's only chart hit from *Evita*?
4　Who took "Memory" into the Top 50 in 1985?
5　Who made the album *Stage Heroes*?
6　Which song from *A Little Night Music* did Judy Collins take into the charts?
7　Which musical flop contained the songs "If You Want to See Palermo Again" and "They're Naked And They Move"?
8　Which musical play did "Hymne A l'Amour" come from?
9　Who took "The Perfect Year" into the charts?
10　Which show has the song "People"?
11　Who sang Peron on the original recording of *Evita*?
12　Who wrote "Wandrin' Star"?
13　What was the Song part of *Song And Dance* in the West End?
14　Who was the main lyricist on the songs from *Phantom Of The Opera*?
15　Which show had the song "We're The UFO"?
16　What was on the A side of Shirley Bassey's "Reach For The Stars"?
17　Which *Follies* song did Liza Minelli chart with in 1989?
18　"Ain't Nobody Here But Us Chickens" is in which show?
19　Which *Jesus Christ Superstar* song did Petula Clark release as a single in 1972?
20　Who co-wrote the musical *Tallulah Who?* with Willy Russell?

Quiz 132 70s Number 1s

Answers – see page 542

1 On which label were the 70s Abba hits released?
2 What was the first No. 1 of the 70s to enter the charts at No. 1?
3 Which No. 1 included the line, "Rat tat tat tat tat"?
4 Which David Essex song was his last No. 1 of the 70s?
5 What was on the other side of Rod Stewart's "I Don't Want To Talk About It"?
6 "Combine Harvester" involved new words to a song by which writer?
7 Who wrote The Jacksons' "Show You The Way To Go"?
8 Chuck Berry's "Ding-A-Ling" went out on which label?
9 Who wrote "One Day At A Time", a No. 1 for Lena Martell?
10 The sound of an air raid siren started which No. 1?
11 Who was Mike Chapman's partner as a writer and producer?
12 Which No. 1 was recorded live at the International Hotel, Las Vegas?
13 What was the last instrumental No. 1 of the 70s?
14 Who wrote the hits with Gary Glitter?
15 "Kung Fu Fighting" resurfaced in which later movie?
16 A February 12, 1973, TV appearance on *Opportunity Knocks* led to a No. 1 for which act?
17 Mud and Suzi Quatro had No. 1s on which label?
18 How many times is Annie mentioned in "Annie's Song"?
19 Who wrote "Another Brick In The Wall"?
20 The single "You Wear It Well" came from which album?

1 Who won British Rock and Pop Best Band in 1979 and 1980?
2 Who wrote "Eloise"?
3 Which family was Terry Jacks a former member of?
4 Which record label uses the reference number prefix "CAS"?
5 Whose debut album was *Look At Us*?
6 What follows "We don't have to take our clothes off" in Jermaine Stewart's 1986 hit?
7 Which group's career is profiled in *The Great Rock 'N' Roll Swindle*?
8 Who wrote "Jealous Guy"?
9 Which Hungarian had her only chart entry with "Pickin' A Chicken"?
10 Who had the highest chart position with "Hello Dolly"?
11 What relation were Hank and Eddie Cochran, known as the Cochran Brothers?
12 Which school did the teenage Peter Gabriel go to?
13 Who had a one-man show in 1995 called *To The Bone*?
14 What did Chris Rea's "You Can Go Your Own Way" advertise?
15 Who was the Red Hot Chili Peppers' *Working Class Hero* album dedicated to?
16 Who had the original US country hit "Love Can Build A Bridge"?
17 Who has a Gothic mail-order catalogue called *Sanctuary*?
18 Who duetted with Michael Hutchence on "Please (You Got That ...)" on the INXS album?
19 Who replaced Cliff Richard in *Time* in the West End?
20 Who were once known as the BB5?

Quiz 134 Pot Luck 68

Answers – see page 536

LEVEL 3

1 "Mr Wonderful" was the first top ten hit for which singer?
2 Who provided the music for the TV show *Take Me Home*?
3 What was Lulu's follow up to "Boom Bang-A-Bang"?
4 Who played the guitar in the band which had 80s hits with "Communication" and "She Loved Like Diamond"?
5 What was the name of Soft Cell's own record label?
6 Who had an 80s album called *Love Me Tender*?
7 Which piano man on Bobby Darin's "Dream Lover" went on to chart on his own?
8 What is the last word of "I Don't Want To" by Toni Braxton?
9 Who won a 1973 Grammy for Album of the Year with *Innervisions*?
10 What was the first top ten hit for The Lemon Pipers?
11 The first No. 1 for Enigma was released on which record label?
12 From which country does the artist who had a 90s hit with *Fable* come from?
13 The first No. 1 for Erasure was released on which record label?
14 Which fellow-pop star produced the No. 1 "Distant Drums" for Jim Reeves?
15 Which music star wrote the book *I, Me, Mine*?
16 What was Manfred Mann's follow-up single to "Pretty Flamingo"?
17 What is the last word of "Spice Up Your Life" by The Spice Girls?
18 Which singer had an 80s album called *Strange Weather*?
19 Which Jackie Wilson hit was written by Van McCoy?
20 Who had 90s hits with "Bozos" and "Dog Train"?

Answers

LEVEL 3

1   What was Bob Dylan's middle name when he was born?
2   Where did he run away to when he was ten?
3   Where was his first live performance in New York ?
4   Which album was "A Hard Rain's Gonna Fall" first featured on?
5   Where in England did the 1965 *Don't Look Back* Tour start?
6   Which was the first Dylan composition to top the charts?
7   Which Dylan composition was a 1965 chart hit for Manfred Mann?
8   What was Dylan's only live concert in 1971?
9   Which role did he play in *Pat Garrett And Billy The Kid*?
10   Which record label did he launch in 1979?
11   Who painted the "Saved" sleeve?
12   Who produced his *Knocked Out Loaded* album?
13   What was Dylan's name in the Travelling Wilburys?
14   What was the first Dylan song used in a commercial?
15   What type of building did Dylan buy in 1994?
16   Who did he record *The Basement Tapes* with?
17   By 1970 how many No. 1 albums did Dylan have?
18   Which was the first album made with a credited band?
19   Who did he collaborate with on "Steel Bars"?
20   What stopped his live performances in 1966 for many months?

1 What was T-Rex's last top ten hit of the 70s?
2 Who had 70s hits with "Too Hot To Trot" and "Sweet Love/Brick House"?
3 What was the first US No. 1 for disco group Chic?
4 Whose first single was "In The City"?
5 What was the Dave and Ansil Collins follow-up to their No. 1 "Double Barrel"?
6 Who clocked up most weeks on the chart in a year in three different 70s years?
7 Who had a single "S-S-S-Single Bed"?
8 Who had 70s hits with "Good Grief Christina" and "What's Your Name"?
9 Den Haggerty, Griff Fender, Rita Ray and Bob Fish have all been in which group?
10 Who had a minor hit with "The Theme From *The Godfather*"?
11 What was Bryan Ferry's first top ten hit?
12 Who had 70s hits with "Are You Ready To Rock" and "The Story Of My Love"?
13 Under what name did David Cook visit the charts?
14 Whose hits included "Rising Sun" and "Slip And Slide"?
15 Whose first top ten hit was "Lay Your Love On Me"?
16 How many singles did Pink Floyd release in the 70s?
17 Who had 70s hits with "24 Sycamore" and "Maria Elena"?
18 In 1978, what is the name of the voice that speaks in the "Telephone Answering Message Song"?
19 The Blondie hits were on which label?
20 What did one-hit wonders Quantum Jump leap into the charts with in 1979?

1   What is in the centre of the Eagles's *Greatest Hits* album cover?
2   Who had a hit with "Where Will The Baby's Dimple Be?"?
3   Which group had a hit in 1986 with "Rage Hard"?
4   Which British rocker had a rabies jab after biting a rat on stage?
5   Which soap did Sue Nicholls's "Where Will You Be?" come from?
6   What was John Lennon holding in his right hand on the cover of his book *A Spaniard In The Works*?
7   Who released a live recordings album titled *Arena*?
8   Which building has been "the ruin of many a poor boy"?
9   What did Yazoo change their name to for their releases in the US?
10 Which pianist had the album *I'm Mighty Glad*?
11 Where were The Easybeats formed?
12 Who released the album *In The Hot Seat* in 1994?
13 Who released a single of "The Man I Love" in 1994 with Larry Adler on harmonica?
14 Which product did Desmond Dekker's "Israelites" advertise in 1990?
15 Who named themselves after a favourite song of one of their grannies?
16 What was Levi Stubbs's voice used for in the film *The Little Shop Of Horrors*?
17 Who was voted the Face of 1968?
18 What was the first record on the Zang Tumb Tumm label?
19 Which book does the name Heaven 17 come from?
20 Who wrote the children's fantasy *The Point*?

1   What was Frankie Valli's first top ten hit?
2   Which singer named her daughter Tyson after Mike Tyson?
3   What was Marmalade's follow up to "Lovin' Things"?
4   Who had an 80s album called *Vive Le Rock*?
5   Which No. 1 record links Donny Osmond to Tab Hunter?
6   What is the last word of "Fly Away" by Lenny Kravitz?
7   Which 70s group singer passed away on 10 February, 1997?
8   What did "Too Many Broken Hearts" replace at No. 1?
9   The first No. 1 for D:Ream was released on which record label?
10 Who had a UK top ten hit in 1979 with "Who Killed Bambi"?
11 Which No. 1 was written about babysitting for the singer's manager?
12 Which magazine did Chrissie Hynde work on?
13 What was Frankie Vaughan's first top ten hit?
14 The first No. 1 for Meatloaf was released on which record label?
15 What letter does Mel C appear in on the cover of Spice World?
16 What is the last word of "Where's The Love" by Hanson?
17 What is the background colour of Abba's *Gold* album?
18 In which year did Soft Cell first make the charts with "Tainted Love"?
19 What was Dean Martin's follow-up to "Memories Are Made Of This"?
20 Who released an album in 1992 called Back To Front?

1   Which ballad was at No. 1 when Queen Elizabeth II was crowned?
2   Which Tony Bennett hit was based on a tune by Borodin?
3   Which ballad gave the first 1964 No. 1 for a female soloist?
4   Who wrote "Make It Easy On Yourself", a hit for the Walker Brothers?
5   Which single held the record for longest time in the Top 50 in 1967?
6   Which Frank Sinatra song won the Oscar for Best Song in 1954?
7   Which album was "Without You" on in June 1971?
8   Which TV series was "She" the theme song for?
9   Which song was nearly called "It's Only Your Lover Returning"?
10   Which ballad by two different singers had the No. 1 spot in 1953?
11   What is the name of the character which Elaine Paige sings in "I Know Him So Well"?
12   Which ballad was a No. 1 for Dave Lee Travis, Bruce Forsyth and Keith Chegwin among others?
13   Who was the woman to take "The Power Of Love" to No. 1 in the US?
14   Which 80s Whitney Houston hit was a US No. 1 and a UK No. 8?
15   What was the first single by a woman to enter the charts at No. 1?
16   In which year did "He Ain't Heavy, He's My Brother" first get to No. 1?
17   Which ballad was the best-selling song of Les Reed and Barry Mason?
18   Which film did "Secret Love" come from?
19   In which decade was "Who's Sorry Now" written?
20   Which musical was "No Other Love" from?

1   With which record did the original 60s Nirvana make the charts?
2   How many No. 1s did Cliff have in the 60s?
3   Who had hits with "Dear Delilah" and "C'mon Marianne"?
4   Which hit contains the line, "Cross your heart with your living bra"?
5   First released in 1967, when did "Light My Fire" by The Doors reach the top ten?
6   Who had 60s hits with "Lightnin' Strikes" and "I'm Gonna Make You Mine"?
7   Norrie Paramor was the producer for major artists on which label?
8   Which Elvis hit spent most weeks at No. 1?
9   How old was Eddie Cochran at the time of his death?
10 What colour is the jacket worn by John Lennon on the *Sgt Pepper* cover?
11 Who wrote "Do You Love Me?", a big No. 1 for Brian Poole?
12 Who had 60s hits with "Romeo" and "My Friend The Sea"?
13 What was the only No. 1 that legendary Cream bass player Jack Bruce was involved with?
14 Frederick Heath became known as which 60s star?
15 Alan Jones and Mike Smith were on saxophones while Blue Weaver played keyboards in which band?
16 From 1963 to 1970 how many consecutive top 20 hits did The Hollies have?
17 What was Lesley Gore's next top 20 hit after "It's My Party"?
18 Who charted with "Cupid" and "You Got Soul"?
19 Which No. 1 was replaced by "Do You Love Me?" and then "You'll Never Walk Alone" before returning to No. 1?
20 Who was born in Stepney in 1932, became a Butlin's Redcoat then had a No. 1?

Answers

1950s (Quiz 144)
1 Guy Mitchell.   2 Al Martino.   3 The Stargazers.   4 "Mack The Knife".
5 *Moulin Rouge*.   6 Kalin Twins.   7 First sub-four-minute mile.
8 George Clooney (nephew of Rosemary Clooney).   9 Winifred Atwell.
10 "Cherry Pink And Apple Blossom White".   11 "Rose Marie".
12 Jimmy Young.   13 1890s.   14 Dean Martin.
15 "Singing The Blues" by Tommy Steele.   16 "All Shook Up".
17 "That'll Be The Day".   18 The Crickets.   19 "We Are The World".
20 Bacharach and David.

1 Who had hits with "Scarlett O'Hara" and "Applejack"?
2 Whose first album was called *Everybody Loves A Nut*?
3 Whose 1978 album was called *Captain Paralytic And The Brown Ale Cowboy*?
4 Which band became the first to receive royalties from the USSR?
5 Who won the 1979 British Rock and Pop Best Male Singer award?
6 To whom was Marino Marini saying "Ciao, Ciao" in 1959?
7 Who wrote "Spirit In The Sky"?
8 Whose second album was *Rage In Eden*?
9 Which group had "Groovy Train" in the charts in 1990?
10 What , according to Paul Simon, was "only a motion away"?
11 In which decade did *Grease* open on Broadway?
12 How is William Levise better known?
13 Which solo Madonna song from *Evita* was especially written for the soundtrack?
14 Which country does Shabba Ranks come from?
15 Who sang "I'm Your Puppet" in 1976?
16 Who was Zoot Money's backing group?
17 Which musical instrument does Bonnie Raitt play?
18 Who played the piano on Bobby Darin's "Dream Lover"?
19 Why was The Shamen's 1995 concert from Kentish Town Forum unusual?
20 Who was the lead singer with the Sweet Sensations from 1967 to 1970?

1   What was Cerrone's first top ten hit?
2   What is the last word of "Everybody's Free (To Wear Sunscreen)" by Baz Luhrmann?
3   What was Johnny Mathis' follow-up to "Too Much Too Little Too Late"?
4   Who had an early 70s album called *Cucumber Castle*?
5   What replaced "You Got It (The Right Stuff)" at the top of the charts?
6   Who shot the photo for the first solo album cover for Paul McCartney?
7   Which band started life as The High Numbers?
8   What did Doop replace at the top of the charts?
9   What is the last word of "Turn Back Time" by Aqua?
10   Who had a late 80s album called *Hot August Night 2*?
11   Which single followed "Silence Is Golden" for The Tremeloes?
12   In which year did Elton John first have his first solo No. 1 single?
13   The first No. 1 for Doop was released on which record label?
14   What is the last word of "Nothing Really Matters" by Madonna?
15   Flugelhorn player Dick Cuthell and trombonist Rico Rodriguez made No. 1 with which group?
16   What was the first single to get The Lightning Seeds into the top 20?
17   2 Tone was a subsidiary label owned by which major company?
18   Which Paul Simon song has the phrase, "Sail on, 'silver girl'"?
19   What was the first top ten hit for CCS?
20   What is the last word of "Heartbeat" by Steps?

Answers

Pot Luck 70   (Quiz 148)
1 "My Eyes Adored You".   2 Neneh Cherry.   3 "Wait For Me Marianne".
4 Adam Ant.   5 "Young Love".   6 Yeah.   7 Brian Connolly of Sweet.
8 "Belfast Child" by Simple Minds.   9 Magnet.   10 Sex Pistols.   11 Clair.
12 New Musical Express.   13 "Green Door".   14 Virgin.   15 I.   16 Love.
17 Black.   18 1981.   19 "Young And Foolish".   20 Lionel Richie.

1 Who had a 1960s hit with "It's Good News Week"?
2 Who had a hit about artist L. S. Lowry?
3 Which Ms Duncan, née d'Angelo, had her only hit in 1982?
4 Whose only hit had Clint Eastwood's "I Talk To The Trees" on the other side?
5 Who did Terry Waite duet with on his only chart venture?
6 Which one-hit wonder was seen as the forerunner of Alice Cooper?
7 Who were the first group to take a Beatles cover version to No. 1?
8 Which three 50s one-hit wonders had names beginning with K?
9 Who is Laura's boyfriend in "Tell Laura I Love Her"?
10 Which hit was written by Pyotr Ilyich Tchaikovsky and subsequently arranged by Kim Fowley?
11 Which hit group had an Aquarian, a Libran, a Leo and a Cancerian?
12 Who sang "Ring My Bell" in 1979?
13 Whose only UK hit was "Let Me Try Again"?
14 What was Lena Martell's failed follow-up to "One Day At A Time"?
15 Which one-hit wonder was also known as Corporal Jones?
16 Whose hit was used for an ad for Soft and Gentle anti-perspirant?
17 Which country was Robin Beck from?
18 Who wrote their film-track one-hit wonder in less than three days without seeing the film concerned?
19 What was the only UK hit for The Marvelettes?
20 Which Jones had a 1986 hit with "The Rain"?

Quiz 144 1950s
Answers – see page 546

1 Which 50s chart-topper was born Al Cernik?
2 Which 50s chart-topper played the Mafia-owned night club singer in the original *Godfather* movie ?
3 Who were the first British group to top the UK charts?
4 Which 50s chart-topper has the most prestigious of writing credits – Bertolt Brecht and Kurt Weill?
5 The first instrumental to top the UK charts came from which movie?
6 Which brothers knocked the Everly Brothers off the No. 1 spot in 1958?
7 Johnnie Ray's "Such A Night" was at No. 1 in 1954 when which amazing feat took place?
8 The aunt of which 90s hunk topped the UK charts in 1954?
9 Who was the first black person to have a UK No. 1?
10 Which No. 1 was originally called "Cerisiers Rouges Et Pommiers Blancs"?
11 Which song of a girl's name was at No. 1 when James Dean died?
12 Which chart-topper was described by *Record Mirror* as Mr Comeback – aged 32 – in 1955?
13 Max Freedman who co-wrote "Rock Around The Clock" was born in which decade?
14 Which chart-topper from the 50s, who enjoyed a 90s revival used to box under the name Kid Crochet?
15 Which song replaced Guy Mitchell's "Singing The Blues" at No. 1 in 1957?
16 What was Elvis's only No. 1 on the HMV label – his first No. 1 in the UK?
17 Which 1957 No. 1 took its title from a line by John Wayne in *The Searchers*?
18 Who were Messrs Allison, Wellborn and Sullivan who backed a 50s superstar?
19 Harry Belafonte hit the top spot in 1957, but which song took him to No. 1 30 years later?
20 Which songwriting team were the first to write consecutive different No. 1s?

1 Who won Grammy Record of the Year for "Another Day in Paradise"?
2 How was Benjamin Peay better known?
3 Who was 47 when his fourth child Renée was born?
4 Which Frenchman designed the Beatles' early collarless jackets?
5 Which songwriter's last hit show of the 50s was *Silk Stockings*?
6 Who had an album called *Acid Queen*?
7 Who played bass with the Ronnie Pierson Trio on cruise liners before having chart success?
8 Whose first chart entry was "Hold Me", in the 60s?
9 Who produced the banned Frankie Goes to Hollywood hit "Relax"?
10 How many joint Eurovision winners were there in the only ever tie?
11 Who sang the theme for *The Living Daylights*?
12 Where was Robert Palmer born?
13 Which professional sporting career did M.C. Hammer follow?
14 In which film did Elvis Presley play the role of Chad Gates?
15 Which singer wrote under the name of Frere Manston?
16 Who sang "A Whole New World" from Disney's *Aladdin*?
17 Which country were Rednex from?
18 Which drink did "We Have All The Time In The World" advertise?
19 How is John Henry Deighton better known?
20 Whose first album was *Rabbits On And On*?

1   What is the last word in Robbie Williams' "Millennium"?
2   What was Nina and Frederick's first top ten hit?
3   How old was Marc Bolan when he died?
4   What did "Eye Of The Tiger" replace at No. 1?
5   Who had a top 30 hit with a cover of "Alive And Kicking" by Simple Minds?
6   What is the last word of "Unbreak My Heart" by Toni Braxton?
7   Where is Rod Stewart sitting on the album cover Never A Dull Moment?
8   The first No. 1 for Celine Dion was released on which record label?
9   Who had hits with "Rock-a-Billy", "Dime And A Dollar" and "Sippin' Soda"?
10   What was Del Shannon's real name?
11   In which year was Craig Douglas's only No 1 single?
12   Which band were originally called The Spectres prior to 1968?
13   Who in addition to Marmalade had a top 20 hit with The Beatles' "Ob-La-Di-Ob-La-Da" in 1968?
14   Frank Ifield was in the charts in 1991; when was he last in before that?
15   Which animal home was a nickname of a member of The Grateful Dead?
16   Two members of which band started out as The Hootenanny Singers?
17   Which 70s chart-topper was born on the same day that Lenin died?
18   What was The Moody Blues' follow-up to "Go Now"?
19   What was the first top ten hit for Oliver?
20   What is the last word of "Underwater Love" by Smoke City?

1   Who is the mother of Kurt Cobain's daughter Frances Bean?
2   Which serious injury did Def Leppard's Rick Allen suffer in 1984?
3   Where was he racing at the time?
4   Keith Moon's death was from an overdose from a drug used to combat what?
5   Who had died in the same flat four years previously?
6   Who had the original hit with "Born To Be Wild"?
7   Which film did it come from?
8   Why did Pete Townshend break his first guitar?
9   Who fell off the stage and broke six ribs during his *Welcome to My Nightmare* tour?
10 How did Marc Bolan's first T. Rex partner die in 1980?
11 Which other one-time T. Rex member died the following year?
12 Who walked off the *Top of the Pops* stage in 1983 after turning up two hours late and being criticized by the producer?
13 Where in his apartment was Jim Morrison found dead?
14 Who left his last message "I need help bad, man" on his manager's answering machine?
15 Whose solo debut album was *Back Street Crawler*?
16 Who said about a record, when a panellist on "Juke Box Jury", "I'd like it at a party if I was stoned"?
17 Who had a Chelsea shop called Too Fast To Live, Too Young To Die?
18 Who broke his foot during a Swedish tour by jumping off the top of a moving bus?
19 Which band did Ace Frehley leave after a car accident?
20 Whose real name is James Jewel Osterberg?

1   Who was the first Liverpudlian to have two No. 1 hits?
2   Joe Cocker's version of "With A Little Help From My Friends" was released on which label?
3   Which was the No. 1 with the shortest title before Terry Savalas's "If" came along?
4   Which 60s chart-topper was back in the 90s album charts with *Midnight Postcards*?
5   What is the name of the young squaw who was in love with Running Bear in the 1960 No. 1 by Johnny Preston?
6   What was Elvis's last No. 1 of the 60s ?
7   What was at No. 1 when Princess Margaret married Anthony Armstrong-Jones?
8   Which 1961 hit was the first No. 1 for producer George Martin?
9   Who wrote Scott Mackenzie's No. 1 "San Francisco"?
10 Who was at No. 1 in 1961 when the Germans started building a wall across Berlin?
11 Which 60s chart-topper starred in *The Great Escape* with Steve McQueen and Charles Bronson?
12 Danny Williams' 1977 song "Dancing Easy" started life as an advertising jingle for what drink?
13 Which Oscar-winning film did Danny Williams' 1961 No. 1 song come from?
14 Which Elvis No. 1 was based on the French song "Plaisir D'Amour"?
15 Who replaced Jet Harris in The Shadows?
16 "It's Not Unusual" went to Tom Jones after which singer rejected it?
17 Which No. 1 did Carole King write for Herman's Hermits?
18 What was on the other side of Cliff's single "Bachelor Boy"?
19 Which No. 1 starts with the words, "On our block..."?
20 What was at No. 1 when the very first Beatles single entered the UK charts?

1 Who were the first act to take "Something In The Air" to No. 1?
2 How many years did Stevie Wonder wait between his first UK chart entry and his first solo No. 1?
3 Which film uses Huey Lewis's hit "Power Of Love"?
4 What word links song titles by Cliff Richard, Madonna and The Human League?
5 Who released a 60s album called *Hard Nose The Highway*?
6 Who launched a record label called UK?
7 Which Beach Boys hit refers to "My grandpappy and me"?
8 In the Lonnie Donegan song, what was the Stewball?
9 What was the theme tune for *Juke Box Jury* called?
10 What was McGuinness Flint's most successful single?
11 What is the home country of Martha And The Muffins?
12 What is the name of the theme song from *The Spy Who Loved Me*?
13 Mireille Mathieu's only UK hit was a cover of which UK No. 1?
14 Whose 1975 album was *Cop Yer Whack Of This*?
15 Who wrote the lyric for the Oscar-winning "Born Free"?
16 Who wanted to be "Bobby's Girl" in 1962?
17 What was Jon Pertwee's only UK hit?
18 Who said "I intend to delve deeply into the numerous stains I've left on the tapestry of life" when talking about his autobiography?
19 How is Barry Authors better known?
20 Which product did "Move Over Darling" advertise in 1987?

1 Who had an early 70s album cheerfully titled *Death Walks Behind You*?
2 What is the last word of "Perfect 10" by The Beautiful South?
3 Which awards are organised by the National Academy of Recording Arts and Sciences?
4 Who founded his own Anxious record label?
5 What was Johnny Nash's follow-up to "Tears On My Pillow"?
6 What replaced "Relax" at the top of the charts?
7 The first No. 1 for Chaka Demus and Pliers was released on which record label?
8 Whose debut album was called *Cooleyhighharmony*?
9 What is the last word of "Tubthumping" by Chumbawamba?
10 Who wrote "Orville's Song"?
11 Who argued on stage with The Beastie Boys at Reading?
12 Which country is Eurovision Song Contest specialist Johnny Logan from originally?
13 Whose debut album was called *Not Satisfied*?
14 In which year did Mariah Carey first have a No. 1 single?
15 Which Beatles song did Tony Blair choose on *Desert Island Discs*?
16 Who had 90s hits with "Don't Walk Away" and "I Wanna Love You"?
17 Who wrote the Jimi Hendrix hit "All Along The Watchtower"?
18 Which day gave Motorhead a UK No. 5 in 1981?
19 What was The Move's follow-up single to "Blackberry Way"?
20 Who had a minor hit with a cover of "Another Star" by Stevie Wonder?

1 What did Spike Milligan buy 52-year-old Bill Wyman as a wedding present when he married 19-year-old Mandy Smith?

2 Which Stone recorded "Gimme Some Neck" as a solo?

3 What is Bill Wyman's Kensington restaurant called?

4 Who did Keith Richard work for before he became a rock star?

5 Who was known as the sixth Stone?

6 What did the Stones sing on the first *Top of the Pops*?

7 Why was the Stones' appearance on *Jukebox Jury* a first?

8 Who won a Jagger lookalike contest in 1964 under the alias Laurie Yarham?

9 Who said "It took me 17 years to build this show and I'm not going to have it destroyed in a matter of weeks" after Stones fans rioted in the audience?

10 In 1994 Mick Jagger beat Mother Teresa and Carlos the Jackal in a poll to become what?

11 What was the Stones' first No. 1 album on the Virgin label?

12 Who replaced Bill Wyman on bass guitar after he left the group in 1993?

13 What was the first album composed entirely of Jagger/Richard songs?

14 Which husband-and-wife act joined The Stones on their *Rolling Stones '66* tour?

15 What was the name of the daughter of Keith Richard and Anita Pallenberg, born in 1972?

16 Who did The Stones sue in 1970 for "mismanagement of funds"?

17 Who designed the *Sticky Fingers* record sleeve with a real jeans zip fastener on the front?

18 Which Stones video was the first in the UK to have an 18 certificate?

19 What was the meaning of the AIMS acronym for Bill Wyman in 1987?

20 Why was a live Rolling Stones concert in 1994 a famous first?

1 Which January 1990 chart-toppers had five albums in the US album charts at Christmas the same year?
2 What is the last track on *Urban Hymns*?
3 Who is the lead singer of The Charlatans?
4 From whose album does the track "Claustrophobic Sting" come?
5 How many tracks are there on Madonna's *Ray Of Light* album?
6 What is the background colour of The Manic Street Preachers' first album as a trio?
7 Who provided the backing vocals on Massive Attack's *Blue Lines* album?
8 Dr Dre's 90s hit entitled "Nothin' But A "G' Thang" featuring Snoop Doggy Dogg was based on a song by who?
9 From whose album does the track "Bound By A Nutshell" come?
10 What was the name of the guest guitarist on Michael Jackson's *Dangerous* album?
11 From whose album does the track "F.E.E.L.I.N.G.C.A.L.L.E.D.L.O.V.E." come from?
12 Who was the piccolo player on Tori Amos' *Little Earthquake* album?
13 Which album was originally going to be called *I Hate Myself And Want To Die*?
14 From whose album did the track "Farmer" come?
15 How many people appear on The Verve's album *A Northern Soul*?
16 On Celine Dion's *Let's Talk About Love* album what is the only track with a foreign title?
17 From which album does the track "Sissyneck" come?
18 Who was the harp player on Bjork's *Post* album?
19 From whose album did the track "Shake Well Before Opening" come?
20 Who produced the album *Jagged Little Pill*?

1 What is the theme music for *Dr No* called?
2 How is Eunice Waymon better known?
3 Who had a hit in 1961 with "A Hundred Pounds Of Clay"?
4 What word precedes song titles which end Bird, Safari and USA?
5 Who painted the artwork for the cover of *Teaser And The Firecat*?
6 Who wrote "Running Bear"?
7 What was Charlie Rich's biggest hit?
8 Who were Jonathan Richman's backing group?
9 What links "Two Tribes" and "Do They Know It's Christmas"?
10 What did Sammy Davis Jr lose in a 1954 car crash?
11 Which band was Gerry Rafferty in with Billy Connolly?
12 What was the name of the record label established by Queen Latifah?
13 Where is Toyah's home town?
14 Whose first album was *16 Hits From Stars And Garters*?
15 Which is the most southerly point of the US to have a song written about it?
16 Which Tom Waits railroad song did Rod Stewart record?
17 Which song has the lines "When we called out for another drink, The waiter brought a tray"?
18 Who sang the theme from *Moonraker*?
19 Who was Phil Lynott's father-in-law?
20 How is McKinley Morganfield better known?

1 Which 90s album contains the track "Diesel Power"?
2 What was Roy Orbison's follow-up to "Only The Lonely"?
3 Which celebrity chef is the uncle of Radio 1 DJ Judge Jules?
4 What is the last word of "Angel Of Mine" by Eternal?
5 What was The Kingston Trio's first top ten hit?
6 Who had an early 90s album called *Pop Life*?
7 Which Dawn hit preceded their UK No. 1 "Knock Three Times"?
8 Who recorded "Always Look On The Bright Side Of Life" after Monty Python?
9 What waltz was Winifred Atwell dancing in 1953?
10 Who had an early 80s album called *The Way To The Sky*?
11 What is the last word of "No Regrets" by Robbie Williams?
12 Which Paul Simon song did Rowan Atkinson choose on *Desert Island Discs*?
13 Who had 90s hits with "Easy To Smile" and "Hold It Down"?
14 Who won the 1985 Best New Artist Grammy?
15 What was the first Donovan song to hit No. 1 in the US but fail to do so in the UK?
16 What is the last word of "As Long As You Love Me" by Backstreet Boys?
17 What is the last word of "Better Best Forgotten" by Steps?
18 What was the first top ten hit for Kathy Kirby?
19 What was The Osmonds' follow-up to "Love Me For A Reason"?
20 Who had a late 70s album called As It Happens?

1 Which former chart-topper produced Cher's "Shoop Shoop Song"?
2 How were the producers Matt Black and Jonathan Moore known?
3 Who was Norrie Paramor's production assistant on "Lily The Pink"?
4 Which Norrie Paramor production was used as the theme music for *Sounds of the Sixties*?
5 Who gave George Martin his first No. 1 hit single?
6 What is Quincy Jones's middle name?
7 Which performers did Quincy Jones tell to "check your egos at the door" before a 1985 recording?
8 Who called his work "little symphonies for the kids"?
9 Who were Mickie Most's first signing as an independent producer?
10 Whose early claim to fame was St Cecilia's "Leap Up and Down (Wave Your Knickers In The Air)"?
11 Where outside the UK did George Martin open his own studio as an independent producer?
12 What is producer R.J. Lange's nickname?
13 Who was the first UK producer to have No. 1 hits for CBS?
14 Which pop writer went on to produce Blondie and Pat Benatar?
15 Who started out as a DJ in a Coventry ballroom in the early 70s?
16 What was the first label Gamble and Huff formed?
17 Whose real name was Anthony Instone?
18 Which Beatles album did Phil Spector work on?
19 Who produced "Isn't She Lovely?" for Stevie Wonder?
20 Who co-produced "Ashes to Ashes" with David Bowie?

Answers

Beyond the Grave (Quiz 159)
1 "I Won't Forget You". 2 Phil Spector. 3 "All Along The Watchtower".
4 "Raining In My Heart". 5 Jackie Wilson. 6 16 before, one after.
7 *Double Fantasy*. 8 k.d. lang. 9 1977. 10 "Let's Face The Music And Dance".
11 "The Great Pretender". 12 Eddie Cochran. 13 "Buffalo Soldier".
14 "20th Century Boy". 15 10. 16 "My Way".
17 "We Have All the Time In The World". 18 "You Got It". 19 Three.
20 None.

Quiz 156 Forgotten

Answers – see page 566

LEVEL 3

1 Which lead singer with The Undertones became an A&R man with Polydor in 1993?
2 Which group who toured with The Beatles featured Veronica and Estelle Bennett?
3 Which 60s chart-topper was European Fly-Fishing champion in 1987?
4 Which singer-songwriter featured in Tracey Ullman's video *They Don't Know*?
5 Where was Demis Roussos born?
6 Which Spencer Davis Group member became a major Sony executive?
7 Which former UK Eurovision entrant starred as Mrs Johnstone in *Blood Brothers* in 1997?
8 Which film with Ernest Borgnine provided Reginald Leonard Smith with his pop star first name?
9 Which former member of The Moody Blues opened Manchester club Rhythm Station in 1996?
10 Which band had very strange haircuts and were named after birds?
11 How was Evangelos Papathanassiou better known on a record label?
12 Which pair once had an act under the name of Frabjoy and Runcible?
13 Who were called The Invaders before they earned chart success – firstly with 'The Prince"?
14 Which 80s chart-topper also charted with Streetband's "Toast"?
15 Jonathan King left the pop charts as a performer but which record label did he go on to found?
16 Which 80s band were named after characters in a famous European cartoon series?
17 1998 saw the release of *The Hollies At Abbey Road* between which years?
18 Whose last top ten hit was in 1962 but returned to star in *Phantom Of The Opera* in the West End in 1995?
19 Which Page Three Girl moved to the charts in the 80s with hits including "I Only Wanna Be With You"?
20 Stuart Copeland wrote the score for which Michael Douglas movie?

1 What follows in brackets in the Phil Collins hit "Against All Odds"?
2 What group were asking "Don't Bring Me Down" in 1964?
3 Who sang the theme from *The Man With The Golden Gun*?
4 What time is the Rocket Man's zero hour?
5 "Poetry In Motion" was a great success for whom in 1960?
6 Who played bass synthesizer on Whitney Houston's "I Wanna Dance With Somebody (Who Loves Me)"?
7 Which 80s No. 1 has a Spanish title meaning "The Goat"?
8 Which Beach Boy died in 1984?
9 Which film had John Paul Young's "Love Is In The Air" as its theme?
10 Who wrote the Kenny Rogers/Dolly Parton hit "Islands In The Stream"?
11 Who sang "Something Tells Me" as a TV show theme?
12 Which Beatles album was the best-selling album of 1969?
13 In which city was Jason Donovan born?
14 Which character did Elvis Presley play in *Viva Las Vegas*?
15 Whose nickname was Captain Fantastic?
16 What were "made of ticky-tacky" in the 60s hit?
17 Who was "raised by a toothless bearded hag"?
18 Who played Ray Davies' daughter in *Absolute Beginners*?
19 Who wrote a book of poetry called *The Warlock Of Love*?
20 Who was the male half of Vinegar Joe?

1 What replaced "Land Of Make Believe" at No. 1?
2 What was the last of Mud's No. 1s?
3 What was Pink Floyd's follow-up single to "Another Brick In The Wall"?
4 What was Don Partridge's first top ten hit?
5 Prior to charting in the 90s, what year was the previous top ten hit for The Specials?
6 Who titled their first 80s album *All Over The Place*?
7 Who hit the top 20 with a cover of "All You Need Is Love" by The Beatles?
8 Which Rolling Stones album contains the track "You Can't Always Get What You Want"?
9 What replaced "The Lady In Red" at No. 1?
10 Who won the 1979 Grammy Record Of The Year with "What A Fool Believes"?
11 The 2 Tone label was set up in which city?
12 Who made a 70s record called "Desperate Dan"?
13 The first No. 1 for Mr Blobby was released on which record label?
14 From which city do the band with the biggest-selling 12-inch single originate from?
15 From which country do the group who had 90s hits with "Baby It's You" and "Tuff Act To Follow" come from?
16 The first No. 1 for Eternal was released on which record label?
17 Which disc took veteran crooner Donald Peers into the top ten for the first time?
18 What is the last word of "Road Rage" by Catatonia?
19 What was Gilbert O'Sullivan's follow-up to 'Get Down'?
20 In which year did Queen first have a No. 1 single?

1　What was Jim Reeves's first hit after his death?
2　Who produced "Imagine" with John and Yoko, which hit No. 1 in '81?
3　Which 1968 Hendrix hit was re-released 20 years after his death?
4　What was on the flip-side of Buddy Holly's first posthumous No. 1 "It Doesn't Matter Anymore"?
5　Who was shot on stage in 1961, died in 1984 and had a No. 1 hit two years after that?
6　How many No. 1 hits did Elvis have before, then after, his death?
7　Which album was "Woman" on?
8　Who duetted with Roy Orbison on the 1992 "Crying"?
9　When did Bing Crosby's "White Christmas" first chart in the UK?
10　Which 90s top 30 hit for Nat King Cole came back to fame as Torvill and Dean dance music?
11　Which 1987 hit for Freddie Mercury was re-released in 1993?
12　Who was the second artist to reach No. 1 posthumously?
13　What was the second record by Bob Marley to chart after his death?
14　What was the first Marc Bolan and T. Rex single re-released in the 90s?
15　How many albums did Queen have in the top 100 in December 1991?
16　Which Elvis single was released just before Christmas 1977?
17　Which Louis Armstrong hit was re-released in 1994?
18　What was Roy Orbison's first chart hit after his death?
19　How many singles did John Lennon have in the UK top five in the week beginning January 10, 1981?
20　How many No. 1 hits has Marvin Gaye had since his death?

LEVEL 3

1 Which label had the million-selling soundtrack albums of *Evita*, *Batman* and *Space Jam*?
2 What was Aristocrat renamed?
3 In which country was the Parlophone label founded?
4 Which Brothers were Warner Bros first major record success?
5 What was A&M's first international hit?
6 What did R stand for on the techno label WARP?
7 What was Apple Records' electronic division called?
8 Which star's record label did Cleopatra sign to?
9 Which label was founded by Alan McGee in 1983?
10 Which label started life as a phonograph company back in the 19th century?
11 What was the second label launched by Richard Branson?
12 Which label replaced Satellite Records and had a huge hit with Otis Redding's "The Dock Of The Bay"?
13 Whose early 90s financial difficulties were overcome when they signed a band called Oasis?
14 Which label did Chris Blackwell found in 1957?
15 Who was the first white star to record on Atlantic, through its sister label Atco?
16 Which label released Atlantic records in the UK in the 50s?
17 Who charted with "California Love" and founded the Death Row label with Marion "Suge' Knight?
18 Which studio famous for Elvis recordings did U2 visit to record "Angel Of Harlem" for their album *Rattle And Hum*?
19 Which act gave the first No. 1 to the Beggars' Banquet record label?
20 What was Decca renamed after the death of its founder and its purchase by PolyGram?

1 What was the second UK hit to be sung in Italian?
2 What is Dean Martin's only UK No. 1 hit in his lifetime?
3 Who beat the Beatles for the most gold singles and albums in a year from 1971–72?
4 Which song was turned down by 30 acts before being a hit for The Everlys?
5 Which musical instrument were the Lemon Pipers singing about?
6 Which country is Frances Ruffelle from?
7 How many members of Love Affair performed on "Everlasting Love"?
8 Who was killed in a plane crash in 1986 with five band members?
9 Which album has the tracks "Human Nature" and "Lady In My Life"?
10 What was Humble Pie's first album?
11 In which film did Elvis play the role of Ross Carpenter?
12 Who is known as Soul Brother No. 1?
13 Which folk singer has the middle name Chawdos?
14 What was Charlie Chaplin's best-selling composition of the 60s?
15 Who was manager of Tom Jones and Gilbert O'Sullivan?
16 What did Cliff Adams's "Lonely Man Theme" advertise in 1960?
17 Who produced "Telegram Sam" for T. Rex?
18 Who wrote under the pseudonym Mark Anthony?
19 What was at No. 1 when "Reet Petite" first entered the UK charts?
20 Who had the best-selling album of 1975?

1   What is the last word of "I Know Where It's At" by All Saints?
2   Who had a 90s album called *Parcel Of Rogues*?
3   What was Brian Poole and The Tremeloes' follow-up to "Do You Love Me"?
4   Which song was at No. 1 at the time of the 1987 general election?
5   What was Twinkle's first top ten hit?
6   Which album cover shows Cliff Richard wearing boxing gloves?
7   Who had an early 80s album called *Happy Birthday*?
8   Which state was Buddy Holly heading for when his plane crashed?
9   What replaced "I Know Him So Well" at the top of the charts?
10   Which No. 1 mentions Lois Lane in the lyrics?
11   Which US male vocalist was imprisoned in 1960 for stealing car tyres?
12   In which year did Lulu first appear on a No. 1 single?
13   Who had 90s hits with "Right Here Right Now" and "Who Where Why"?
14   Who had a late-70s album called *Private Practice*?
15   What is the last word of "Dance The Night Away" by The Mavericks?
16   Other than America, in which country was Joan Baez brought up?
17   The first No. 1 for DJ Jazzy Jeff and The Fresh Prince was released on which record label?
18   Which singer who first charted in the 70s wrote the children's book *Amy The Dancing Bear*?
19   Who starred in the film when Tom Jones sang "What's New Pussycat"?
20   Which Roxy Music album first contained the track "More Than This"?

1 Where was Diana Ross born?
2 Who produced her first solo album?
3 Who did Diana Ross introduce as her replacement at her final concert with
   The Supremes?
4 What was her second film?
5 Which album was "Chain Reaction" from?
6 Who told Tamla he'd make "I'm Still Waiting" his record of the week if they'd release it
   as a single?
7 Which single had a pseudo-60s video in black and white?
8 What was her first solo No. 1 album?
9 Who was her single "Missing You" dedicated to?
10 Which hit was intended to ask parents of drug addicts to be understanding about their
   children ?
11 Where did she broadcast a 1992 Christmas concert from?
12 Who did she duet with on "All Of You"?
13 Which record label did she move to after leaving Motown?
14 In which year did she make her first solo British tour?
15 Who was the album *Pops We Love You* dedicated to?
16 What is her fourth child called?
17 What did she open in January 1992?
18 Which Radio 1 DJ did she deputize for in July 1992?
19 Who directed her in *Mahogany*?
20 Which album was "Muscles" on?

1 The first No. 1 for Sinéad O'Connor was released on which record label?
2 Who was the first British female to win a Grammy Award?
3 In which year did Belinda Carlisle first have a No. 1 UK single?
4 How many US No. 1s did The Bangles have?
5 Cindy Walker was the first female solo writer to compose a No. 1 – what was its title?
6 The first No. 1 for Lulu was released on which record label?
7 What is the last word of "2 Become 1" by The Spice Girls?
8 Whose debut album released in 1970 was called *First Take*?
9 What was Madonna's first No. 1 on her Maverick label?
10 Under which name did American Ms Darwisch make No. 1?
11 In which year did female soloists first have three consecutive No. 1 hits?
12 Who had the longest-running No. 1 single of 1998?
13 What was Mary .J Blige's first album to top the US charts?
14 Stockholm-born Emilia's mother was Swedish but what was the nationality of her father?
15 Which Roxy Music cover launched a Mancunian's music career in January 1999?
16 What was Toni Braxton's follow-up US No. 1 to "You're Making Me High" which stopped at No. 2 in the UK?
17 What was Neneh Cherry's follow-up to her first No. 1?
18 Sheryl Crow left the University of Missouri with a degree in what?
19 What was Björk's first solo hit which just edged into the UK top ten?
20 Whose rendition of "Kissing You" is on the soundtrack of *Romeo + Juliet* when the lovers first meet in the 1997 movie?

1 Which film was "Living Doll" written for?
2 What was the Kinks' *Greatest Hits* album subtitled?
3 Which of Elizabeth Taylor's husbands had two chart hits in 1953?
4 Which Brotherhood of Man No. 1 title has an operatic title?
5 Who recorded the theme song for *Live And Let Die*?
6 Who had *Presence* at No. 1 in the album charts in 1976?
7 What maritally links Jerry Lee Lewis and Sebastian Bach?
8 Where was Allan Sherman in "Hello Muddah Hello Faddah"?
9 In which film did Elvis play the role of Mike Windgren?
10 Who was Rocky Sharpe's backing group?
11 Who co-wrote "From Russia With Love" with John Barry?
12 Who were top of both the single and album charts in December 1995?
13 What replaced *Please Please Me* at the top of the album charts?
14 What was the first of Boney M's trio of No. 1 albums between 1978 and 1980?
15 Which event of 1981 produced a No. 1 album?
16 Who spent 36 consecutive weeks in the charts with "I Pretend"?
17 Who were in Blind Faith with Rick Grech and Ginger Baker?
18 Which was the first-ever album to go straight to No. 1?
19 What was Georgie Fame's "Get Away" first used to advertise?
20 Which language was Kaoma's "Lambada" sung in?

1 What is the last word of "You Have Been Loved" by George Michael?
2 What did "Orinoco Flow" replace at the top of the charts?
3 In "Tell Laura I Love Her" what is Laura's lover doing when he dies?
4 In the No. 1 "Perfect" what rhymes with Perfect?
5 Who had an early 90s album called *Enchanted*?
6 In which year did the Pet Shop Boys first have a No. 1 single?
7 Who replaced Tony Meehan in the Shadows in 1961?
8 Which veteran band cancelled their UK tour in 1998?
9 What was Freddie Mercury's first posthumous solo hit that was not a re-entry?
10 What was Jim Reeves' follow-up to "Distant Drums"?
11 Which Elton John record was dedicated to a motor cycle messenger boy killed in an accident?
12 Which band includes members Al "Blind Owl' Wilson and Bob "The Bear" Hite?
13 Who had a 80s album called *Centre Stage*?
14 Who had a 70s hit with The Beatles' "Got To Get You Into My Life"?
15 Which No. 1 has the words, "So Mary marry me, Let's not wait"?
16 What is the last word of "All That I Need" by Boyzone?
17 What were The Temptations originally known as?
18 It seems to chart every year, but when was Slade's "Merry Xmas Everybody" first released?
19 What was the first top ten hit for The Platters?
20 The first No 1 for Jamiroquai was released on which record label?

LEVEL 3

1 Which country won the very first Contest?
2 Who compered the show in the UK the year Sandie Shaw won?
3 Which Swiss representative has had the most UK No. 1 hits?
4 Who was the UK's first-ever Eurovision entrant?
5 Until 1996 who won the Contest by the biggest margin?
6 Who tied with the UK when there were four winners?
7 Who was the first Irish winner?
8 Who was the first artist to win the Contest twice?
9 What did Cliff Richard sing the second time he sang for the UK?
10 Who has done the Radio 2 commentary in the UK in the mid-90s?
11 Under which title did "Après Toi" reach No. 2 in the UK charts?
12 Who were the first Israeli winners?
13 Who performed the UK's first rap entry?
14 How did "Ein Bißchen Frieden" translate at the top of the UK charts?
15 Where did Bucks Fizz have their 1982 win?
16 Who represented the UK the year Abba won?
17 Who were the first duo to represent the UK?
18 Which country broke the Irish run of wins from 1992–96?
19 Which male singer represented the UK without wearing any trousers?
20 Who represented the UK with "Rock Bottom"?

1 Which No. 1 was written by Francis Rossi, Andy Bown and John Edwards?
2 Who were Doc and Mort?
3 What is the last word of "The National Express" by The Divine Comedy?
4 Which Elton John hit has the line, "Some things look better, baby, just passin' through"?
5 Who is credited as co-writing George Michael's first solo No. 1, "Careless Whisper"?
6 Which song finishes with, "It might be my old dad."?
7 In a 90s film theme song what follows, "Far across the distance"?
8 Who wrote the English lyrics to 70s No. 1 "Seasons In The Sun"?
9 What is the last word of "Perfect Moment" by Martine McCutcheon?
10 What precedes "And would not let her be," in "A Whiter Shade Of Pale"?
11 What was Neil Diamond's next No. 1 as a writer after "I'm A Believer"?
12 Which song was penned for a babysitter called Diana Ayoub?
13 Who wrote "Both Sides Now", a hit for Judy Collins?
14 In 1991 Celine Dion recorded a whole album of songs by which writer?
15 What is the last word of "Say What You Want" by Texas?
16 Which song has the lines, "Singing in the sighing of the wind, blowing in the treetops"?
17 What is the last word of "Always Have Always Will" by Ace Of Base?
18 Which 80s No. 1 did Mungo Jerry's Ray Dorset write?
19 What was Neil Diamond's top 20 single from *The Jazz Singer*?
20 What is the last word that Robbie Williams sings in "Strong"?

1 Who co-wrote and produced "Let The Heartaches Begin"?
2 Whose show won Radio Programme of the Year in 1978?
3 Which album won a Grammy in 1973 for Neil Diamond?
4 Who was found dead at Hollywood's Landmark Hotel on October 4, 1970?
5 Who wrote "The Last Waltz"?
6 Which Donovan hit is sung partly in French?
7 Out of Dave Dee's group who were Trevor Davies and John Dymond?
8 Who won *Melody Maker*'s Instrumentalist of the Year award in 1961?
9 What is on the other side of the Everlys' "Claudette"?
10 Who had a No. 1 with "You Belong To Me" in 1952?
11 Who had most weeks in the UK charts in 1994?
12 Who has had a hit with Delaney and Bonnie and Friends, Tina Turner and Elton John?
13 Who did Annie Lennox duet with on "Why"?
14 What was Julie Covington's second 70s hit?
15 Who had the one-hit-wonder album *Blast* in 1989?
16 What was the Oscar-winning song from *Dick Tracy*?
17 In which film did Elvis Presley play the role of Josh Morgan?
18 How is Angus McKenzie better known?
19 Which album knocked *A Hard Day's Night* off the top of the charts?
20 Which songwriters used the pseudonym Elmo Glick?

1 What was The Rolling Stones' follow-up to the single "Brown Sugar"?
2 Who had an early 90s album called *East Of The Sun West Of The Moon*?
3 What is the last word of "Insane" by Texas?
4 Who wrote The Everly Brothers' 1980s comeback hit "On The Wings Of A Nightingale"?
5 What was Bruce Channel's first top ten hit?
6 What did "What Becomes Of The Broken Hearted" replace at No. 1?
7 In which year did Status Quo first have a No. 1 single?
8 Which artist was the first to have a digitally-recorded rock album?
9 In which decade was Julio Iglesias first solo hit "Begin The Beguine" written?
10 Who described Pink Floyd as a con while on *Juke Box Jury*?
11 The first No. 1 for The Fugees was released on which record label?
12 Who had 90s hits with "I'll Be There" and "Natural Thing"?
13 Who won the 1985 Ivor Novello award for Songwriter of the Year?
14 Who had a 90s hit with "The Majesty Of Rock"?
15 What was The Searchers' follow-up to "Sweets For My Sweet"?
16 Whose backing group were The Melody Makers?
17 Prior to charting in the 90s, what year was the previous top ten hit for Neil Young?
18 What was Phil Lynott's book of poems called?
19 Who co-wrote "Bachelor Boy" with Cliff Richard?
20 What form of transport are Gallagher and Lyle taking on the *Breakaway* album cover?

1   Which Abba hit was rejected as a Eurovision song in 1973?
2   Who co-wrote it with them?
3   What was the orchestra conductor wearing when Abba won the Eurovision Song Contest?
4   Where was *Abba – The Movie* set?
5   Who was Abba's manager and co-writer of many of their hits?
6   What was Abba's only US No. 1?
7   Which city was "Summer Night City" about?
8   What was Abba's publishing company called?
9   To which charity did Abba give all their royalties from "Chiquitita"?
10   What were the surnames of the group members?
11   What was the name of Abba's own studio in Stockholm?
12   Björn and Agnetha were investigated in 1987 about what?
13   Which Stock and Waterman production had a hit with "Dancing Queen" in in 1992?
14   Why were the group barred from touring the USSR in 1982?
15   Who had recorded a solo of "Fernando" before the group recorded it together?
16   A Swedish company also had the name Abba. What did they do?
17   Who produced Frida's solo album *Something's Going On*?
18   Which top Swedish rock 'n' roll band of the 60s was Benny a member of until they folded in 1969?
19   On which label did Abba record all their hits in the 70s and 80s?
20   In which film, set in Australia, did Abba music feature in 1994?

1 Which co-winner of the Best British Hit Single 1952–77 starred in *Evita*?
2 Which musical legend was born on 30 March, 1945 in Surrey?
3 In which year did the Everly Brothers first have a No. 1 single?
4 What was Billy J. Kramer's real name – William Howard what?
5 Whose autobiography was called *Laughter In The Rain*?
6 Which 50s and 60s chart-topper was made deputy Lord Lieutenant of Buckinghamshire in 1993?
7 Who released the album *Mamouna* in 1994?
8 Which 60s pop star wrote "Ice In The Sun" for Status Quo?
9 Who produced Bette Midler's album *The Divine Miss M*?
10 What is the name of Ray Davies's brother in The Kinks?
11 Which performer was commissioned by the BBC to produce the music score for the run up to France 98?
12 Which 70s chart-topper played Gaston in *Beauty And The Beast* in London's West End in 1996?
13 What was the average age of the top four chart position-holders in November 1998 – Cher, Boy George, George Michael and U2?
14 What was the real name of Nelson Wilbury whose first album, *Traveling Wilburys Volume I* was released in 1988?
15 Which 47-year-old re-issued and charted with "Secret Garden" in 1997?
16 Which 50s star still tours backed by The Richochets and released an album of Buddy Holly classics in 1998?
17 How old was the singer of "Maria", when it topped the charts in February 1999?
18 Which 50+-year-old 1990s chart-topper's biography was titled *Totally Uninhibited*?
19 Which solo star made "All You Need Is Love" on the Childline label in 1993?
20 Who had her first No. 1, at age 44, in the same year as an album and single called Independence?

1　Which Led Zeppelin LP won *Melody Maker*'s LP of the Year award in 1970?
2　In which film did Elvis play the role of Guy Lambert?
3　Who produced the album *Out Of The Blue*?
4　Who had his only top ten entry with "Guitar Boogie Shuffle" in 1959?
5　Which DJ was on the panel on the first "Juke Box Jury"?
6　What is the main colour of the *West Side Story* album cover?
7　Which group's first Australian No. 1 was "Spicks And Specks"?
8　Who said, "Paul is really writing for a 14-year-old audience now."?
9　Which label released the first Dire Straits recordings in the UK?
10　Who, according to The McCoys, lives "in a very bad part of town."?
11　Whose debut album was *I Should Coco*?
12　Which was the first French disc in the charts with a wholly French act?
13　Who has had a hit with Visage, Rich Kid and Mick Karn?
14　How did the 60s top ten artist Kyu Sakamoto meet his death?
15　What was the best-selling single of 1975?
16　Who had most weeks in the UK charts in 1993?
17　What was the first of David Bowie's trio of No. 1 albums between 1973 and 1974?
18　What was the first UK single to sell more than 2 million copies?
19　What was the previous record-holder?
20　Which album knocked *Freewheelin' Bob Dylan* off the top of the charts?

1 Who provided the music for the TV action drama *Edge Of Darkness*?
2 Which 90s album contains the track "Small Black Flowers That Grow In The Sky"?
3 What was Gary "US" Bonds' first top ten hit?
4 What was Sandie Shaw's follow-up to "A Puppet On A String"?
5 What is the last word of "The Drugs Don't Work" by The Verve?
6 Under which name did Harold Jenkins make No. 1?
7 What did "Ooh Aah... Just A Little Bit" replace at the top of the charts?
8 In which year did Alvin Stardust first have a No. 1 single?
9 Which first was achieved in the US by the British artist Lonnie Donegan?
10 The first No. 1 for Gabrielle was released on which record label?
11 What appears in brackets in the title of Engelbert Humperdinck's "Release Me"?
12 Who had an 80s album called *Batteries Not Included*?
13 Which female singer had a minor hit with a cover of Roy Orbison's "Blue Bayou"?
14 Which UK top ten hit for The Yardbirds was also a top ten in the US?
15 What is the last word of "Stranded" by Lutricia McNeal?
16 Bill Wyman served for two years in which military organisation?
17 What was Breathe's first top ten hit?
18 What replaced "The Only Way Is Up" at No. 1?
19 Which band had Jim Capaldi as drummer and vocalist?
20 Who was a "Moonlight Gambler" in a 1956 hit?

1 Who plays keyboards with Kula Shaker?
2 Whose debut album was *So Close*?
3 Where are Ocean Colour Scene based?
4 Who won the Brit Award for Best Newcomer in 1994?
5 How did Jarvis Cocker injure a foot during a Norwegian TV show?
6 Which album won the Best Album award at the 1996 Brit Awards?
7 On which album was Eddi Reader's "Town Without Pity"?
8 On whose TV show did Oasis make their US debut?
9 What was Babybird's debut album?
10 Who was the original Kula Shaker?
11 Who won the Brit award for Best Male Singer in 1995 and 1996?
12 Why did Liam Gallagher walk off stage on a US tour in March 1995?
13 Who left Eternal and went Naked?
14 What is the musical accompaniment on "Forever Love"?
15 Who won the Brit Award for Best Group in 1995?
16 Where is Eddi Reader from?
17 To which film did Blur and Damon Albarn contribute a track in 1996?
18 Who won the Brit Award for Best Female Singer in 1992?
19 Where did Mark Morrison grow up?
20 Which actor spoke on Blur's "Parklife"?

1 Mariah Carey's first UK chart duet was with which named artist?
2 What is the last word of "In Too Deep" by Belinda Carlisle?
3 What was Celine Dion's first million-seller in the UK?
4 In what year did Robert Palmer make the top 60?
5 Which song gave Marty Wilde his highest chart placing?
6 Who was the first woman to have a solo album go straight to No. 1 in the US charts?
7 What was Janet Jackson's follow-up US No. 1 to "When I Think Of You"?
8 Who had his own Paisley Park studio built in Minneapolis in the 1980s?
9 Who had a 50s – and his only – No. 1 with "Here Comes Summer"?
10 On which Simply Red album did "Say Love Me" first feature?
11 Which musical instrument does Oleta Adams play?
12 What was Peter Andre's follow-up to his second UK No. 1?
13 What was Frankie Avalon's second US No. 1?
14 How is Andre Young better known in the charts?
15 Who took a cover version of Percy Sledge's biggest hit to the top of the US chart in 1991?
16 Which *EastEnders* star recorded "Subterranean Homesick Blues"?
17 What is Tori Amos's real first name?
18 R Kelly's first minor chart hit, "She's Got That Vibe", was with whom?
19 As the 1990s began who held the record as the youngest woman to have topped the album charts?
20 A remix of which Phil Collins single was used in a Mercury Communication ad?

Answers

Oldies And Goldies (Quiz 172)
1 Gary Brooker.   2 Eric Clapton.   3 1958.   4 Ashton.   5 Neil Sedaka.
6 Frankie Vaughan.   7 Brian Ferry.   8 Marty Wilde.   9 Barry Manilow.
10 Dave.   11 Rick Wakeman.   12 Alvin Stardust.   13 40.
14 George Harrison.   15 Bruce Springsteen.   16 Bobby Vee.   17 53.
18 Cher.   19 Tom Jones.   20 Lulu.

1 Which band was Eddi Reader in in the late 80s?
2 What was the first of Dire Straits' trio of No. 1 albums between 1985 and 1991?
3 Which two rock rebels died on the same day two years apart in 1969 and 1971?
4 Which cellist is credited on the *Variations* album?
5 What was Petula Clark's first No. 1 in 1961?
6 Who did Clyde McPhatter join after leaving The Dominoes in 1953?
7 Who won five Grammys in 1980 including Best Single?
8 What was Boyzone's first No. 1 single?
9 Who had a 60s hit with "Les Bicyclettes De Belsize"?
10 Which song says "Don't hang around 'cause two's a crowd"?
11 What was Elvis Presley's first million-selling record?
12 Who played percussion on the Bee Gees' "You Should Be Dancing"?
13 Who wrote the soundtrack for the film *La Passione*?
14 Who produced Alisha's Attic's album *Alisha Rules the World*?
15 Who had the one-hit wonder album *Turn Back The Clock* in 1988?
16 Who had most weeks in the UK charts in 1989?
17 What was the best-selling single of 1972?
18 Who has had a hit with Fun Boy Three, Vegas and The Specials?
19 What did Gene Pitney's "Town Without Pity" advertise?
20 What was the Oscar-winning song from *Pocahontas*?

Answers

Pot Luck 91 (Quiz 181)
1 Red. 2 *Not The Nine O'Clock News* cast. 3 Jermaine. 4 The Gibb brothers.
5 Six. 6 New Kids On The Block. 7 *Touch*. 8 *Abracadabra*. 9 Dressing gown.
10 Seal. 11 *Mercury Falling*. 12 Brian Poole. 13 Tina Turner. 14 *Life*.
15 Richey James. 16 *Genesis*. 17 David Sylvian.
18 "Can You Feel the Love Tonight". 19 "We're In This Together".
20 "I Remember You".

1 Which 90s album contains the tracks "Life Is Sweet" and "In Dust We Trust"?
2 What was The John Barry Orchestra's first top ten hit?
3 Which singer named his son Otis after Otis Redding?
4 What according to the Crash Test Dummies debut album did God Shuffle?
5 Who played in the group Aphrodite's Child with Vangelis?
6 What is the last word of "Doo Dah" by The Cartoons?
7 What Deep was Tommy Steele's follow-up to "Singing The Blues"?
8 Who had a 90s album called *Titanic Days*?
9 Who recorded "All The Way From Memphis" after Mott The Hoople?
10 What was Helen Shapiro's debut album called?
11 In which year did Madness first have a No. 1 single?
12 The first No. 1 for Iron Maiden was released on which record label?
13 What was The Supremes' follow-up to "Baby Love"?
14 Who had an 80s album called *Live And Direct*?
15 Who had 90s hits with "Dagenham Dave" and "Roy's Keen"?
16 Pettigrew and Chacon made No. 1 in the 90s under which name?
17 What is the last word of "Doctor Jones" by Aqua?
18 What was William Bell's first top ten hit?
19 What was John Lennon's first No. 1 after the split from The Beatles?
20 At which stadium did the US part of the Live Aid concert take place?

LEVEL 3

1 Who awarded Mark Knopfler an honorary music doctorate in 1993?
2 Which heavy-metal guitarist said, "If it's too loud you're too old"?
3 Who inspired Eric Clapton to write "Layla"?
4 What was Eric Clapton's No. 1 album of 1994?
5 Which guitarist's first two names were Brian Robson?
6 Which album did Mark Knopfler release with Chet Atkins in 1990?
7 Who was guest vocalist on Ted Nugent's *Free For All album*?
8 Who duetted on "Wonderful Land" on the 1993 *Heartbeat* album?
9 Which film soundtrack did Mark Knopfler work on after *Local Hero*?
10 Who asked Hank Marvin to join which band in 1970?
11 Which group has included the guitarists John Williams and Kevin Peek?
12 What did Brian May reputedly make his first guitar from?
13 What type of guitar did Jimi Hendrix use on the *Are You Experienced*? album?
14 Which two acts took "Cavatina", the theme from *The Deer Hunter* into the top ten?
15 Where did Jimi Hendrix take part in a fund-raising "Guitar-In" in 1967?
16 Whose career history album was called *Crossroads*?
17 What did Brian May play at the end of the *Concert For Life* at Wembley in 1992?
18 What was Jeff Beck's debut solo album called?
19 What honour did Eric Clapton receive in January 1995?
20 What was the debut album by the Brian May Band?

1   The first No. 1 for Manic Street Preachers was released on which record label?
2   Who are Robert Smith, Lol Tollhurst, Simon Gallup, Porl Thompson and Boris Williams?
3   Deacon Blue are named after a song by which band?
4   How many US No. 1's did Queen have?
5   Which album did 2 Unlimited's "Workaholic" first appear on?
6   Which single was Erasure's follow-up to their first No. 1?
7   Who created the characters that the Thompson Twins are named after?
8   What is the last word of "The Sweetest Thing" by U2?
9   Which record label released the first No. 1 for Livin' Joy?
10 Who had a 90s album called *Thrak*?
11 The group Clannad consisted of the Duggans and which other family?
12 "Fire And Skill" was the motto written on the bass amp of which band?
13 What was Culture Club's last top ten hit before "I Just Wanna Be Loved"?
14 What was The Housemartins' second album called?
15 Which album did Wet Wet Wet's "Julia Says" first feature on?
16 Whose backing group were The Bruisers?
17 Which single immediately followed The Pet Shop Boys' two consecutive 1987/1988 No. 1s?
18 How is Snap's Michael Munzing better known?
19 Which album won M People the Mercury Music Prize in 1994?
20 What was the group Marmalade originally called?

1 What is the predominant colour of the *Making Movies* album cover?
2 Who made a comedy album called *Hedgehog Sandwich*?
3 Which Jackson brother suggested "Let's Get Serious"?
4 Which brothers starred in a weekly TV series in Australia in the 60s?
5 How old is Marie in the Chuck Berry hit "Memphis Tennessee"?
6 Who had most weeks in the UK charts in 1990?
7 On which Eurythmics album cover is Annie Lennox in a black mask?
8 What album and single gave the Steve Miller Band chart success in 1982?
9 What is Nilsson wearing on the album cover of *Nilsson Schmilsson*?
10 Who won the Brit Award for Best Male Singer in 1992?
11 On which album was Sting's "Let Your Soul Be Your Pilot"?
12 Who is the father of Alisha's Attic sisters Karen and Shellie?
13 Who was made a Chevalier des Ordres des Arts et Lettres in February 1996?
14 Which Simply Red album is "Fairground" on?
15 Which founder member of Manic Street Preachers left the group in 1995?
16 What was the first of Genesis's trio of No. 1 albums between 1983 and 1991?
17 Who has had a hit with Robert Fripp and Mick Karn?
18 What was the Oscar-winning song from *The Lion King*?
19 What was Simply Red's song for Euro 96?
20 What was the best-selling single of 1962?

1 Who had a 90s album called *You Gotta Sin To Get Saved*?
2 What is the last word of "Lazy Days" by Robbie Williams?
3 What did "Feel It" replace at No. 1?
4 At which Polytechnic did Marc Almond study music?
5 Which band started life as The Makers?
6 What was The Avons' first top ten hit?
7 Who had a 90s album called *Choba B CCCP*?
8 What was the name of the last top ten hit that the group led by Dave Bartram on vocals achieved?
9 Which group included Larry Cunningham as lead vocalist?
10 In which year did Manchester United Football Club have a top ten single?
11 Who had a 80s album called *Alphabet City*?
12 How did James Taylor break both his hands in 1969?
13 Who became the most successful group from Sheerwater in Surrey?
14 Who had an early 90s hit with "Roobarb And Custard"?
15 Who made a recording of "Together We Are Beautiful" before Fern Kinney's No. 1?
16 In 1962 who made the album *Pot Luck*?
17 Who had a 90s album called *Independence*?
18 The first No. 1 for Lightning Seeds was released on which record label?
19 Which solo singer did The Tornados originally back?
20 What is the last word of "A Life Less Ordinary" by Ash?

1 What was Elton's original middle name?
2 Which record label did he launch in 1972?
3 Which soul band did Elton play with when he worked for a music publisher ?
4 Which album reflected Bernie Taupin's influence by the Wild West?
5 Who did Elton John marry in 1984?
6 In what year was he knighted?
7 Who sang a prospective Eurovision song by John and Taupin in 1969, but it came last in the viewers' poll?
8 Who duetted with Elton on "Don't Go Breaking My Heart" in 1994?
9 Why did Elton cut short an encore in Australia in February 1993?
10 What was the publishing company founded by Elton in 1974?
11 Who did Elton write "Philadelphia Freedom" for?
12 Elton became godfather to which pop star's child in 1975?
13 Who was the album *Sleeping With The Past* dedicated to?
14 Who became Elton's personal manager in 1971?
15 What was the name of Elton's dog which he chose in Battersea Dog's Home because it looked the saddest?
16 On which part of him did he undergo surgery in Australia in 1987?
17 Why did he fly out of Tel Aviv airport just after arriving in 1993?
18 Who sings "Crocodile Rock" on the tribute album *Two Rooms*?
19 Who was Elton dressed like when he appeared in Rod Stewart's Wembley concert in 1991?
20 On whose *Without Walls* album did Elton duet with on "What A Woman Needs"??

1   What was Roxette's follow-up to US No. 1 "The Look"?
2   What was Aqua's UK follow-up to their second No. 1?
3   What nationality of label did Ace Of Base sign to in the early 90s?
4   Incognito of "Always There" fame were based in the UK and which other European country?
5   In which city were Berlin formed?
6   What nationality were Pussycat?
7   The Wannadies first entered the UK top 20 with which single?
8   Which Whale single entered the top 20 at the second attempt and became their first top 20 hit?
9   Who recorded the album *Moon Safari*?
10 What was the first album on which Björk collaborated with Mark Bell?
11 Europe come from which country?
12 Whose "Alabama Blues (Revisited)" edged into the lower charts in the summer of 1996?
13 On which label did Swedish band The Cardigans have their first top ten hit?
14 Which country did Nicole come from?
15 Who, with Nicolas Godin, was part of Air?
16 In which band does Per Gessle share vocals?
17 What was Whigfield's follow-up to "Another Day"?
18 Who took Crispy Bacon into the lower reaches of the charts?
19 On which label did The Sugarcubes record their first five releases in the UK?
20 Magna Furuholmen played keyboards for which band who were the biggest-selling group in their home country?

1   Who was the first solo male pianist to reach No. 1 twice?
2   Who first took a cover version of Little Richard's "Good Golly Miss Molly" into the top ten?
3   Who plays sitar on "Paint It Black"?
4   What was the first of Prince's three No. 1 albums between 1988 and 1991?
5   Who made his chart debut in 1957 with "School Day"?
6   Which Kraftwerk hit lasted 22.5 minutes in its album version?
7   Who had most weeks in the UK charts in 1991?
8   On which label did Human League record "Don't You Want Me?"?
9   What was the first top ten hit for Champs?
10 Whose first album was called *Have Twangy Guitar Will Travel*?
11 Who said "Elvis taught white America to get down"?
12 What is Robert Miles's home country?
13 What was U2's first No. 1 album?
14 What is Beck's surname?
15 Who had the one-hit wonder album *Spartacus* in 1991?
16 What was the best-selling single of 1959?
17 How much did the original collarless Beatles suits cost?
18 Who produced Dire Straits' first album?
19 Who joined Ozzy Osbourne on "The Urpney Song" from the TV series *The Dreamstone*?
20 Which TV drama featured the fictional Little Ladies and starred Julie Covington and Rula Lenska?

1 Who had a 90s album called *The Bridge*?
2 What is the last word of "Black Eyed Boy" by Texas?
3 Which football team does Robbie Williams support?
4 What was the first top ten hit for Atomic Rooster?
5 Who is the "E" on the cover of *Spice World*?
6 Who is wearing a donkey jacket on the album cover of *After The Goldrush*?
7 What was Sheryl Crow's first hit?
8 Who released a debut album called *Child Is The Father Of The Man*?
9 Whose backing group was The Mighty Avons?
10 What was Marty Wilde's first hit?
11 Who had a 90s album called *The Good The Bad And The Live*?
12 What is the last word of "Fresh" by Gina G?
13 Lisa Stansfield first sang in which group formed in Rochdale?
14 Who had a 70s hit with The Beatles' "Here, There And Everywhere"?
15 What was the first Rick Astley song to hit No. 1 in the US but fail to do so in the UK?
16 Who, in the Eurythmics song of the same name, has organge hair and green eyes and is underneath the ocean?
17 What was the first top ten hit for The Average White Band?
18 Who had an 80s album called *Swing Street*?
19 Who had 90s hits with "So Close" and "This Time"?
20 Which rock star died on exactly the same day as Maria Callas?

1 What was the best-selling single of 1960?
2 Which song has the lines "Sunshine, yellow orange blossom, laughing faces ev'rywhere"?
3 Who won the Grammy Record of the Year in 1964 for "The Girl From Ipanema"?
4 Who had the album *On The Threshold Of A Dream*?
5 Which band did John Fogerty sing with, write for and produce?
6 What was the first Stones No. 1 after Brian Jones left?
7 Who played keyboards with Amen Corner?
8 What was the top-selling album of 1960?
9 On which album did "While My Guitar Gently Weeps" feature?
10 In Des O'Connor's "1-2-3- O'Leary" what does "O Leary" rhyme with?
11 Which band had twins Derv and Lincoln Gordon?
12 Which was the only other album to top the 1966 album charts, apart from *Revolver* and *Aftermath*?
13 Which song beat Cliff's "Congratulations" into second place in the Eurovision Song Contest?
14 Whose version of "This Is My Song" reached No. 2?
15 What was the Beach Boys' first top ten hit?
16 Which record got to No. 1 on Glenn Hoddle's ninth birthday?
17 Who had the album *Stand Up*?
18 Which Beatles song features the tune of "Greensleeves"?
19 What replaced "Yellow Submarine"/"Eleanor Rigby" at No. 1?
20 Which album did Dusty Springfield's "Son Of A Preacher Man" come from?

1 What date is her birthday and her first wedding?
2 What was her first US No. 1 which was not a No. 1 in the UK?
3 At which US university did Madonna get a dance scholarship?
4 What was her first hit on her own label?
5 Who co-produced and co-wrote her first hit of the 90s with her?
6 In which band did she play drums?
7 What was her third hit from *Evita*?
8 Which song came from husband Sean Penn's film *At Close Range*?
9 Her 1983 album *Madonna* was later re-released under what title?
10 Which pop star's production company made the film Madonna starred in with her first husband?
11 Whose record as the female writer of three No. 1 hits did Madonna overtake with her fourth No. 1, "La Isla Bonita"?
12 Where is Madonna on the video of "Like A Virgin"?
13 Which knight appeared in Madonna's movie *Who's That Girl*?
14 In which Woody Allen movie did she play a trapeze artist?
15 In which David Mamet play did Madonna appear on Broadway?
16 Which hit came from the movie *Vision Quest*?
17 What was her first No. 1 on both sides of the Atlantic?
18 In what year did she first appear on *Top Of The Pops*?
19 Who carried her off stage on the last night of her *Virgin* tour?
20 What was her first US chart hit after her wedding?

1 Which 60s No. 1 was originally called "Io Che No Vivo Senza Te"?
2 Who recorded the album *Tonic For The Troops*?
3 Which record was at No. 1 as Margaret Thatcher was celebrating her 44th birthday?
4 What was the first of Queen's three No. 1 albums between '89 and '91?
5 Whose blue suede shoes were bought by Dan Ackroyd in 1984?
6 Who won the Brit Award for Best International Group in 1994?
7 Which album does Billy Joel's "Just The Way You Are" come from?
8 Who, according to Stevie Wonder, is "as distant as the Milky Way"?
9 Which Van Halen hit says "I get up and nothin' gets me down."?
10 Whose 1980 album *Empty Glass* included the track "Rough Boys"?
11 Which James Bond shares his birthday with Cliff Richard?
12 Which two European countries do Enigma come from?
13 Who said they could not spell the title of their first No. 1 hit?
14 What was the best-selling single of 1981?
15 Who had most weeks in the UK charts in 1992?
16 Which song has the line "Like a river flows surely to the sea."?
17 Which 1988 film featured the 1968 song "What A Wonderful World"?
18 Which country star married the singer Jim Stafford in 1978?
19 Which future No. 1 was on the other side of the Four Seasons' "Rag Doll"?
20 Which country star was a DJ on Texan KGRI in the early 1950s?

1 Who released the album *Imperial Bedroom*?
2 What was Eddy Arnold's first top ten hit?
3 Who had an 80s album called *You Want It, You Got It*?
4 What is the last word of "Looking For Love" by Karen Ramirez?
5 Which fellow-pop star produced the No. 1 "We Don't Talk Anymore" for Cliff Richard?
6 Which blonde actress appeared in Adam And The Ants' video "Prince Charming"?
7 What was Rod Stewart's only UK top ten hit in 1994?
8 What was the title of Marianne Faithfull's 1979 comeback album?
9 Who was England boss when "Three Lions" first made No. 1?
10 What was Ashford and Simpson's first top ten hit?
11 Which comic artist recorded tracks called "Grutz" and "Making A Friend"?
12 The first No. 1 for KWS was released on which record label?
13 Which Elton John song did Billy Connolly choose on *Desert Island Discs*?
14 Whose first two albums were *Children Of The Future* and *Sailor*?
15 Whose biography by Mark Ribowsky was called *He's A Rebel*?
16 Who had 90s hits with "Don't Talk About Love" and "Walking On Air"?
17 In which year did Madonna first have a No. 1 single?
18 Which Spice Girls No. 1 did "Block Rockin' Beats" replace at the top of the charts?
19 What colour is the cover of Garbage's *Version 2.0* album?
20 For which party did Jonathan King unsuccessfully stand for Parliament?

1 What was the best-selling single of 1971?.
2 Who got to No. 1 in 1979 with a hit from a West End show – although he was actually starring in a different one?
3 What was the best single of 1979 in the British Rock and Pop Awards?
4 Which song won Larry Henley and Jeff Silbar the songwriter Grammy Song of the Year?
5 Who wrote and produced "Bright Eyes" for Art Garfunkel?
6 Who had a 70s hit about a Russian priest?
7 Which 70s film was most successful in terms of spin-off chart singles?
8 Which Shadow wrote "You're The One That I Want"?
9 Who had two No. 1s in succession ending in "O"?
10 What sort of outfits did Slim wear?
11 Which album featured Deniece Williams's No. 1 "Free"?
12 Whose album titles usually consisted of their name plus a Roman numeral?
13 Who was the first Continental act to have a No. 1 in 1976?
14 Which police officer was Going In With his Eyes Open?
15 Who werethe members of Wings when "Mull Of Kintyre" was recorded?
16 What was Brotherhood Of Man's first hit?
17 What is the cause of "D.I.V.O.R.C.E." in Billy Connolly's version?
18 Which song kept repeating "Rat-tat-tat-tat-tat"?
19 Who were a combination of The Percussions and The Monarchs?
20 What were the combined ages of Althia and Donna when they made "Uptown Top Ranking"?

1 Their first single failed to chart – what was it called?
2 Prior to joining Queen, Brian May had been studying for a PhD in what?
3 What was their first UK No. 1?
4 Who was producer on "Bohemian Rhapsody"?
5 What did "Under Pressure" replace at the top of the charts?
6 What was *A Night At The Opera*'s highest US chart position during Freddie's lifetime?
7 What was *Greatest Hits II* called when it was revamped for the US market?
8 Which then major band did they support on a US tour in 1973?
9 Freddie Mercury's funeral followed the rites of which religion?
10 What colour is Freddie Mercury's jacket on the cover of *A Kind Of Magic*?
11 What was the final track on *Made In Heaven*?
12 What was the title of the single put out by May and Taylor while they were at college?
13 What was the band's name before Freddie changed it to Queen?
14 On which album did "Princess Of The Universe" appear?
15 Which song has the line, "It seems like there's no way out of this for me."?
16 According to Roger Taylor, "When Queen do something we do it..." what?
17 Which album had the song "No One But You (Only The Good Die Young')"?
18 What was their first single to go straight to No. 1?
19 On which label was *A Kind Of Magic* released in the US?
20 Who had a solo project called *Fun In Space*?

1 Who went to No. 1 with their debut album in November 1995?
2 What was on the A side of Yoko Ono's "Who Has Seen the Wind"?
3 Who did Stephen Stills unsuccessfully audition for in the 60s?
4 Which *Carry On* actor had a No. 2 with "Be My Girl" in 1957?
5 Who was nicknamed the Prince of Wails?
6 Who won the 1990 Grammy for Best Female Vocal Performance with "Vision Of Love"?
7 Which 50s pianist was a qualified chemist?
8 Who worked with Paul McCartney on his *Liverpool Oratorio* and conducted the orchestra that performed it on the album?
9 Which newscaster's offering won Capital Radio's World's Worst Record in 1980?
10 Which American had a 1962 hit with "A Little Bitty Tear"?
11 Who were the first pair of brothers to have separate solo No. 1 hits?
12 Who did Jeff Lynne replace in The Move?
13 Which then current No. 1 might the passengers on the QEII's maiden voyage have danced to?
14 What was the real first name of the Tremelo "Chip" Hawkes?
15 Who had Jimmy McCulloch topped the charts with in 1969 before he joined Wings?
16 Who had most weeks in the UK charts in 1985 and 1986?
17 What was the best-selling single of 1983?
18 Who had the one-hit wonder album *Tease Me* in 1994?
19 Who was Brian Jones's immediate replacement in the Rolling Stones?
20 What was the first of R.E.M.'s three No. 1 albums between 1991 and 1994?

1 What was Elton John's first hit from his *Sleeping With the Past album*?
2 Which Roxy Music album contained a version of the soul classic "The Midnight Hour"?
3 Who had an early 90s album called *Homebrew*?
4 Who is in the C on the cover of *Spice World*?
5 What is the Björk-like figure wearing on the cover of *Homogenic*?
6 In *The Best Of Suzanne Vega*, what colour is the lettering on the cover?
7 Who had a 60s album called *Hello Dolly*?
8 Who had the best-selling album of the 70s?
9 Who had a 70s album called *The Higher They Climb*?
10 Which Queen album included the track "I'm Going Slightly Mad"?
11 Which animal is on the cover of Bryan Adams' *On A Day Like Today*?
12 Whose second album was *Cross Of Changes* in 1994?
13 Where is Jon Bon Jovi sitting on the cover of *Destination Anywhere*?
14 Who had an 80s album called *Well Pleased*?
15 In which year did Kylie Minogue have the best-selling UK album?
16 What is Bette Midler playing on the cover of *Bathhouse Betty*?
17 What is on the cover of George Martin And Friends' *In My Life*?
18 What is on the cover of Deacon Blue's *Our Town*?
19 Who released the gold album *Brain Salad Surgery*?
20 Who had a late 70s album called *Itchy Feet*?

1   What was the best-selling single of 1988?
2   Which song was based on "She Moved Through The Fair"?
3   Which instrument did Enya play on "Orinoco Flow"?
4   Which film won the Brit Award for best soundtrack in 1988?
5   Yazz's Plastic Population were initially DJs on which radio station?
6   Whose debut album was *Push*?
7   Who was the only Scot in Fairground Attraction?
8   Who followed up a No. 1 with "Superfly Guy"?
9   Where was Tiffany's first live UK performance?
10 Which album did "I Just Can't Stop Loving You" come from?
11 Which song had the line "Life, Jim, but not as we know it"?
12 What was Mel and Kim's surname?
13 How was Johann Holzel better known?
14 Which quotation attributed to Joseph Kennedy – father of the assassinated president – provided the title of a 1986 hit?
15 Who won the Eurovision Song Contest for Norway the year their countrymen A-Ha had their first UK No. 1?
16 Who wrote "Saving All My Love For You" with Michael Masser?
17 Where was Feargal Sharkey singing "A Good Heart" live on British TV for the first time?
18 What was the 80s best-selling single by a woman?
19 Who joined the Communards on "Don't Leave Me This Way"?
20 Who produced Ultravox's "Quartet" and where?

1 How many Transatlantic No. 1s did Elvis Presley have?
2 How many Transatlantic No. 1s did The Beatles have in total?
3 After Elvis Presley and The Beatles, who has spent most time at the top of the US charts?
4 Louis Armstrong's "What A Wonderful World" was a UK hit in 1968; when did it make the US top 40?
5 How many US No. 1s has Lionel Richie had?
6 What was Manfred Mann's only Transatlantic No. 1?
7 Who was the first artist to enter the US album chart at No. 1?
8 Who penned Kenny Rogers' US No. 1 "Lady"?
9 What was Dawn's first Transatlantic No. 1?
10 Which Beatles track spent nine weeks at No. 1 in the US?
11 How many weeks did Foreigner's "Waiting For A Girl Like You" stay at No. 2?
12 Which A-Ha song went to No. 1 in the US but not the UK?
13 After "Diana" how many more US No. 1s did Paul Anka have?
14 What was Blondie's most successful US hit?
15 What was the first Lulu song to hit No. 1 in the US but fail to do so in the UK?
16 What was The Beatles' second Transatlantic No. 1?
17 Bad English were unsuccessful in the UK but topped the US chart with which song?
18 Which US No. 1 was voted best instrumental for 1962?
19 What was Ray Charles' only Transatlantic No. 1?
20 How many US No 1s did Paula Abdul have in the period 1990–91?

1   Who was the first Monkee to leave the group?
2   Who had a No. 1 hit in 1954 with "Cara Mia"?
3   What completes the title of the 1984 Wham hit "Young Guns"?
4   Which film featured the music "Foggy Mountain Breakdown"?
5   What country were America formed in?
6   What was Neil Diamond's second UK No. 1 as a writer?
7   What did Phil Collins win the Grammy for Record of the Year for in 1990?
8   Which Temperance Seven hit began "Oh you railway station, oh you Pullman train."?
9   What was the first of Simple Minds' four No. 1 albums between 1984 and 1989?
10 Who took "Blinded By The Light" to No. 1 in the US and No. 6 in the UK?
11 In which film did the Four Tops sing "Loco In Acapulco"?
12 How did Steve Marriott die in 1991?
13 What is Reg Presley's real surname?
14 Who revived Tommy James and The Shondells' "Mony Mony" in 1987?
15 Who had most weeks in the UK charts in 1975?
16 What was the best-selling single of 1964?
17 Who described Elvis's music as "a rancid-smelling aphrodisiac"?
18 Which 1969 hit was about a Mississippi paddle steamer?
19 Who replaced Eric Clapton in John Mayall's Bluesbreakers?
20 What was the first of Simply Red's trio of No. 1 albums between 1989 and 1995?

1 What is the last word of "Return Of The Mack" by Mark Morrison?
2 Bell Biv Devoe first made the top ten guesting on which song?
3 Eugene Record was the leader of which 70s vocal group?
4 Rose Windross and Do'reen have sung with which outfit?
5 What was the last Ray Charles hit to make the UK top ten?
6 What did "You Are Not Alone" replace at the top of the charts?
7 Who had 80s hits with *Everlasting* and *Jump Start*?
8 In what year did Sam Cooke first make the UK top three?
9 Who makes up the Pointer Sisters with Kathy, Debra and Kim?
10 Milan Williams and Walter Orange were in which group?
11 What is the last word of "Escaping" by Dina Carroll?
12 What was the last of the 70s top ten hits for the Chi-Lites?
13 What was Soul II Soul's follow-up to their first UK No. 1?
14 Who was the first UK act to have three US R & B No. 1 hits?
15 Which hit, along with "Share Your Love", did Lionel Richie produce for Kenny Rogers before embarking on a solo career?
16 In which country did Donna Summer's career begin?
17 What was The Supremes final top ten hit before the death of Florence Ballard?
18 What was MN8's follow up to "I've Got A Little Something For You"?
19 Which single by SWV reached No. 1 in the US before its UK follow-up "Right Here" stopped at No. 3?
20 How is Charles Hatcher better known?

1　Which-country boy recorded "The Red Strokes"?
2　Shania Twain featured on the soundtrack of which 1999 film with Hugh Grant?
3　What type of bedcover did Billie Jo Spears put On the Ground in the 70s?
4　As well as playing the guitar Bob Dylan blows into which musical instrument?
5　What kind of family name goes after Bellamy?
6　What colour is Kenny Roger's beard?
7　To which lady did Dolly Parton plead, "I'm beggin' of you please don't take my man."?
8　What language was Steeleye Span's hit "Gaudete" sung in?
9　Which huge Tammy Wynette hit was inspired by her split from husband, George Jones?
10　Willie Nelson wrote "Always On My Mind" for which pop legend?
11　Johnny Cash recorded a number of live albums at what unusual institutions?
12　Which country song did Hillary Clinton famously refer to?
13　Shania Twain's first UK hit was You're Still The what?
14　According to his name, which state did Ernie Ford come from?
15　Who was dubbed "Gentleman Jim"?
16　In which decade of the 20th century were most of Joan Baez's hits?
17　Crystal Gayle's Eyes were made what colour in the title of her hit song?
18　What did Loretta Webb change her surname to?
19　Ralph McTell's classic song tells of the Streets of which city?
20　Which Reba McEntire song shares its name with the Little capital of Arkansas?

1   How was Brooklyn rapper Christopher Wallace better known?
2   Who formed The Wink Westerners in his teens – the name coming from his home town?
3   Whose death prompted a remaining band member, Dave Grohl, to found The Foo Fighters?
4   Pete Farndon was a founder member of which band?
5   How was Benjamin Peay who charted with Kiddio in the 60s better known?
6   What was the name of Aretha Franklin's sister who penned her hits "Ain't No Way" and "Angel"?
7   Whose involvement with the film *Go Johnny Go* meant he avoided the fateful Buddy Holly flight, only to die in a car accident a year later?
8   Which Motown star was married to Berry Gordy's sister Anna before having 28 chart hits on Gordy's Motown label?
9   What was the name of Janis Joplin's first posthumous big selling album?
10 Who had a 90s album called *The Lost Recordings*?
11 Who recorded "Where Is The Love" with the singer most famous for "Killing Me Softly"?
12 The late Ral Donner played which major part in the movie *This Is Elvis*?
13 What was Michael Hutchence's first single to enter the UK top twenty?
14 How is the artist who first called himself Toby Tyler now remembered?
15 In which band did Peter De Freitas find fame before his death in 1989?
16 Which Bob Marley album went to No. 1 three years after he died?
17 The lead singer of The Small Faces and Humble Pie died in what circumstances?
18 Which chart-topper became mayor of Palm Springs?
19 Who produced Nilsson's album *Pussy Cats*?
20 Andreas Cornelis Van Kuisk had an enormous influence on rock music through which man he managed?

LEVEL 3

1 Who recorded "Something's Gotten Hold Of My Heart" with its originator Gene Pitney more than 20 years after the original?
2 Who was famous for his Ding-A-Ling?
3 Whose autobiography was called Rhinestone Cowboy?
4 Who made a dance remake of "Quando Quando Quando" in the late 90s?
5 Ray Charles came from which state, which was also the title of one of his greatest hits?
6 Carnie and Wendy Wilson of Wilson Phillips were daughters of members of which legendary band?
7 Who were the first Liverpool band to top the UK charts?
8 Which female singer has had over 30 singles and 33 albums in the charts in 40 years?
9 Which Bob Dylan hit from the 70s was used as a 90s charity record?
10 Which band did Ron Wood join after leaving The Faces?
11 Who billed himself as Professor Yaffle Chucklebutty, Operatic Tenor and Sausage-Knotter?
12 Which ABC song was about oldie but goldie Smokey Robinson?
13 Which Frank Sinatra classic was written by 50s chart star Paul Anka?
14 60s singer Adam Faith has made a name for himself in the 80s and 90s as an adviser on what?
15 Who was Cilla Black's first manager's during The Beatles era?
16 Which Roberta Flack song was revived by The Fugees in 1996?
17 Which ex-member of Take That duetted with Tom Jones at the 1998 Brit Awards ceremony?
18 Drummer Peter Baker was known by what name?
19 Who still tours in the 90s and had their first US chart-topper, "Wake Up Little Susie", in 1957?
20 Who duetted with Damon Albarn on TV's The White Room singing "Waterloo Sunset"?

1 Who was nicknamed the Tycoon of Teen?
2 Who had most weeks in the UK charts in 1970 and 1971?
3 In which film did Elvis play the role of Walter Gulick?
4 How is Patricia Louise Holt-Edwards better known?
5 What was the sixth of Rod Stewart's six No. 1 albums between 1971 and 1976?
6 Which song begins "Almost heaven West Virginia"?
7 What was the best-selling single of 1980?
8 Whose first UK single was "Halfway Down the Stairs"?
9 In which musical will you find Grizabella and Rumpleteazer?
10 Who won the 1965 Grammy for Record of the Year for "A Taste Of Honey"?
11 Who sang Norway's 1995 Eurovision winner "Nocturne"?
12 What was the first of Tom Jones's three No. 2 hits between '67 and '68?
13 Which David Bowie Top Thirty hit has only two letters?
14 Which Desmond Dekker hit has a number as its title?
15 Which soccer team had a hit called "We Can Do It"?
16 What was the first of Slade's trio of No. 1 albums between 1973 and 1974?
17 How did the Beach Boy Dennis Wilson meet his death?
18 Who starred as Pink in Alan Parker's 1982 film *The Wall*?
19 Why did the Police dye their hair blond?
20 Which lady provided Kenny Rogers and Little Richard with hit records?

1   How is Norma Eggstrom better known?
2   What was the first of Sweet's three No. 2 hits between 1973 and 1974?
3   Which Who hit has a number as its title?
4   Which song was subtitled "Spurs Are On Their Way to Wembley"?
5   Which song begins "Music is a world within itself with a language we all understand"?
6   Which was Cliff Richard's first hit to go straight to No. 1?
7   Which Scott Fitzgerald hit has only two letters?
8   Who had most weeks at No. 1 in 1958?
9   Which two instrumentalists had 22 weeks at No. 1 before their 20th birthdays?
10 Who was the first woman aged over 50 to have three top ten hits?
11 What was the first of the Rolling Stones' five No. 1 albums between 1969 and 1973?
12 What was the best-selling single of 1982?
13 Which 70s band was Stewart Copeland in before joining the Police?
14 Who was the first British woman to have a solo No. 1 album?
15 Who was nicknamed Sassy?
16 What was the first of Abba's eight No. 1 albums between '76 and '82?
17 Who had most weeks in the UK charts in 1966?
18 Who attempted a 1980s revival medley called "Golden Shreds"?
19 Which 70s hit do Wayne and Garth mime to in a gay disco in the 1994 film *Wayne's World 2*?
20 In which film did Elvis play the role of Rusty Wells?

1   What does KLF stand for in the context of the 1991 chart-toppers?
2   Which female singer starred in the TV series *Your Cheatin' Heart* about the Scottish country music scene?
3   Who was nicknamed the Cappuccino Kid?
4   In which film did Elvis play the role of Walter Hale?
5   Who had most weeks in the UK charts in 1964?
6   How is Defosca Ervin better known?
7   What was the first of Darts' three No. 2 hits in 1978?
8   Which No. 1 hit has the shortest title?
9   Which Prince hit has one digit as its title?
10 Which soccer team sang "Blue Is The Colour" in 1972?
11 What was the first of T. Rex's trio of No. 1 albums between 1971 and 1972?
12 Which was Slade's first No. 1 to go straight to No. 1?
13 Who had most weeks at No. 1 in 1991?
14 His playing of which instrument brought Cozy Powell fame?
15 What was the first of Erasure's five No. 1 albums between 1988 and 1994?
16 What was the best-selling single of 1989?
17 Who were the second pair of brothers to have separate solo No. 1 hits?
18 Which song had the line "Teacher, leave those kids alone."?
19 Who was the first woman credited an artist on a UK No. 1 album?
20 Who duetted with Bobby Brown on "She Ain't Worth It"?

1   Who has a production company called Handmade Films?
2   Which country won the Eurovision Song Contest with "Rock Me" sung by Riva?
3   Who was nicknamed Mr Excitement?
4   In which film did Elvis play the role of Dr John Carpenter?
5   How is Glyn Ellis better known?
6   Which Gloria Estefan hit has a number as its title?
7   Which soccer team recorded "Glad All Over" in 1990?
8   Who was "dynamite with a laser beam"?
9   What was U2's first No. 1 to go straight to No. 1?
10 Who had most weeks at No. 1 in 1978?
11 What was the eighth of Led Zeppelin's eight No. 1 albums between 1970 and 1979?
12 Who used the code name John Burrows for telephone messages?
13 Which band did the two member of Buggles join in the early 80s?
14 Who was nicknamed the Rockville Rocket?
15 Who named themselves after a US spy plane?
16 What was the first of Bon Jovi's four No. 1 albums between 1988 and 1995?
17 What was the best-selling single of 1977?
18 Who were the first Spanish group to have a No. 1 hit in the UK?
19 Who had most weeks in the UK charts in 1953 and 1954?
20 What is Yazz said to have wanted to be rather than a singer?

Running your own quiz night

There is a theory that organising and running your own quiz night is a highly technical and difficult operation. Well, if drinking, having a good time and seeing other people enjoying themselves – even if it is in a tortured way – is complicated, then I suppose it may be. A quiz night is F–U–N. I thought it might help to spell it out just in case some of you want to be miserable.

A well-organised quiz, whether in a pub/bar, office, local hall, place of worship, wherever, is not a deadly serious event and if the proceeds are going to charity, then they can be very lucrative.

It is, however, most important that you are well prepared before the quiz starts. Here is what you will need:

Paper and pens: Lots of both, too, because people have a strange tendency to forget to bring either with them. If it is a charity night, you might want to contact some local businesses and ask if they would be interested sponsoring the pens. For the answer sheets, it looks better if the teams can see where they can write the team name and round number, so it might be an idea to copy sheets with "Team Name" and "Round No." already printed.

Scoreboard: No, you don't need a giant screen, just a large board upon which you can place the running totals for the various teams after every round.

Sound system: If the quiz is going to be for hundreds, as opposed to dozens, of people, you may want to consider a sound system. It will help your and the quiz-master's vocal chords if shouting is kept to a minimum. Most venues have a system that can be hired.

Runners: It is always useful to have a few helpers around. They can help to collect the answer sheets at the end of each round, hand out paper and pens, etc. This might be a good way of getting some of the younger generation involved, provided, of course, it doesn't interfere with schooling or if the quiz is held at a venue where children aren't welcome!

Markers/scrutineers: To ensure any sort of written quiz goes well, it is a good idea to have two or three people who can quickly check the contestants' answers and award the scores. If you are running the quiz yourself, you cannot mark answers at the same time as reading out the questions, even with double vision! Having independent markers also reduces the possibility of claims of partiality.

Power: If you are going to bring in your own sound system or include a video or audio round, make sure that there is somewhere to plug it in close at hand. It would be a shame if you spent hours cutting audio and video tapes only to find you can't use them. Also if you are hiring equipment from the venue, make sure you know how to operate them and the remotes, etc., are in good working order before the quiz starts.

A watch: Some places have strict curfews, so you want to be sure that the quiz will finish in time. Being aware of the time is also very important, because some of the more relaxed teams may start to get bored if things drag on too long.

Prizes: Not everybody is going to win a prize, but there should be enough for the winners, maybe the runners-up and also the last-placed team. For the wooden-spoonists, the prize should be something funny, but not too offensive because they may have been trying really hard and just weren't very good. You might want to consider token prizes for the winners of each round, but make sure that one team doesn't win everything! Nobody likes a smartypants!! Again, if it is a charity night, you may be able to persuade a sponsor to pay for them.

Answers

Part One

1 _____

2 _____

3 _____

4 _____

5 _____

6 _____

7 _____

8 _____

9 _____

10 _____

11 _____

12 _____

13 _____

14 _____

15 _____

16 _____

17 _____

18 _____

19 _____

20 _____

Answers

Part Two

1 _____

11 _____

2 _____

12 _____

3 _____

13 _____

4 _____

14 _____

5 _____

15 _____

6 _____

16 _____

7 _____

17 _____

8 _____

18 _____

9 _____

19 _____

10 _____

20 _____

Answers

Part Three

1 _____

2 _____

3 _____

4 _____

5 _____

6 _____

7 _____

8 _____

9 _____

10 _____

11 _____

12 _____

13 _____

14 _____

15 _____

16 _____

17 _____

18 _____

19 _____

20 _____

Answers   Part One

1 _____   **11** _____

2 _____   **12** _____

3 _____   **13** _____

4 _____   **14** _____

5 _____   **15** _____

6 _____   **16** _____

7 _____   **17** _____

8 _____   **18** _____

9 _____   **19** _____

10 _____   **20** _____

Answers

Part Two

1 _____

2 _____

3 _____

4 _____

5 _____

6 _____

7 _____

8 _____

9 _____

10 _____

11 _____

12 _____

13 _____

14 _____

15 _____

16 _____

17 _____

18 _____

19 _____

20 _____

Answers

Part Three

1 _____

2 _____

3 _____

4 _____

5 _____

6 _____

7 _____

8 _____

9 _____

10 _____

11 _____

12 _____

13 _____

14 _____

15 _____

16 _____

17 _____

18 _____

19 _____

20 _____

Answers

1

2

3

4

5

6

7

8

9

10

11

12

13

14

15

16

17

18

19

20

Useful notes

Inevitably with any quiz you will get disputes over the answers. There is always someone who just has to know better. The trouble is, sometimes they actually do know better and you end up looking a complete Charlie. So use these pages to keep a note of any extra facts and figures that you pick up as you go along. With luck, when you have run the quiz a few times, you will be completely fireproof.

Useful notes

Useful notes

Useful notes